The Women, Gender and Development Reader

ABOUT THE EDITORS

Nalini Visvanathan is active in the international women's health movement, a member of the Committee on Women, Population and the Environment and a contributing author to the 1998 edition of *Our Bodies, Ourselves*. A native of India, she teaches courses on women, health and development at the School for International Training, Vermont, USA.

Lynn Duggan is an economist who has written articles on free trade and social policy, family policy in East and West Germany, and reproductive rights in the Philippines. She has taught at Fitchburg State College and Michigan State University, USA, and is currently consulting for unions and teaching Labor Studies at Indiana University Northwest.

Laurie Nisonoff, Professor of Economics, has taught economics, economic history and women's studies at Hampshire College in Amherst, Massachusetts, USA, since 1974. She is an editor of the *Review of Radical Political Economics*, and served as the co-ordinator of the RRPE 6th Special Issue on Women, 'Women in the International Economy'. She has published alone and with Marlyn Dalsimer on women in China, and on the labour process.

Nan Wiegersma is Professor of Economics at Fitchburg State College, Fitchburg, Massachusetts. She worked for the US Department of Agriculture Economic Research Service in 1969–73 on the Southeast Asia Desk, and she was UN representative on a World Food Programme mission to Vietnam in 1987. She has published numerous articles about land tenure, gender and development in journals, and a book, *Vietnam: Peasant Land, Peasant Revolution* (Macmillan Press and St. Martin's, 1988). She was a Fulbright Fellow in Nicaragua in 1991, studying women's work in export processing zones.

The Women, Gender and Development Reader

Edited by

Nalini Visvanathan (co-ordinator)
Lynn Duggan
Laurie Nisonoff
Nan Wiegersma

ZED BOOKS LTD
London and New Jersey

UNIVERSITY PRESS LTD
Dhaka

WHITE LOTUS CO. LTD
Bangkok

FERNWOOD PUBLISHING LTD
Halifax, Nova Scotia

DAVID PHILIP
Cape Town

The Women, Gender and Development Reader was first published in 1997 by:

In Bangladesh: The University Press Ltd, Red Crescent Building,
114 Motijheel C/A, PO Box 2611, Dhaka 1000.

In Burma, Cambodia, Laos, Thailand and Vietnam:
White Lotus Co. Ltd, GPO Box 1141, Bangkok 10501, Thailand.

In Canada: Fernwood Pubishing Ltd, PO Box 9409, Station A,
Halifax, Nova Scotia, Canada B3K 5S3.

In Southern Africa: David Philip Publishers (Pty Ltd),
208 Werdmuller Centre, Claremont 7735, South Africa.

In the rest of the world:
Zed Books Ltd, 7 Cynthia Street, London N1 9JF, UK, and
165 First Avenue, Atlantic Highlands, New Jersey 07716, USA.

Editorial copyright © Nalini Visvanathan, Lynn Duggan,
Laurie Nisonoff, Nan Wiegersma, 1997
Individual chapters copyright © individual authors, 1997.
The sources given on pages xi–xiii constitute an extension
of this copyright page.

Cover designed by Andrew Corbett
Typeset by Action Typesetting Ltd, Gloucester.
Printed and bound in the United Kingdom by Biddles Ltd, Guildford & King's Lynn

Library of Congress Cataloging-in-Publication Data

The women, gender, and development reader / edited by Nalini Visvanathan (co-ordinator) ;
Lynn Duggan, Laurie Nisonoff, and Nan Wiegersma.
    p.   cm.
    Includes bibliographical references and index.
    ISBN 1-85649-141-2. — ISBN 1-85649-142-0 (pbk.)
    1. Women in development. 2. Women—Social conditions. 3. Women—
Economic conditions.4. Women—Developing countries.
    I. Visvanathan, Nalini, 1945– . II.Duggan, Lynn, 1956– .
III. Nisonoff, Laurie, 1949– . IV. Wiegersma, Nancy.
HQ1240.W6568   1996
305.4—dc21   96-47238
                                            CIP

Canadian Cataloguing in Publication Data

The women, gender, and development reader.
    Includes bibliographical references and index.
    ISBN 1-895686-86-5
    1. Women in development. 2. Women—Social conditions. 3. Women—
Economic conditions.4. Women—Developing countries.
    I. Visvanathan, Nalini, 1945– . II.Duggan, Lynn, 1956– .
III. Nisonoff, Laurie, 1949– . IV.Wyss, Brenda.
HQ1240.W6568   1997   305.4 C97-950136-9

A catalogue record for this book is available from the British Library

Bangladesh: ISBN 984 051399 X Pb
Canada: ISBN 1 895686 86 5 Pb
Southern Africa: ISBN 0 86486 342 X Pb
Rest of the World: ISBN 1 85649 141 2 Hb; 1 85649 142 0 Pb

CONTENTS

PART 2: Households and Families

PART 3: Women in the Global Economy

PART 4: International Women in Social Transformation

PART 5: Women Organizing Themselves for Change

TABLES

FIGURES

PREFACE

In 1978, Lourdes Benería, Hamideh Sedghi and Grace Horowitz organized the initial Women and Development Discussion Group composed of women students or teachers then residing on the East Coast, USA. Involved in empirical and theoretical research about women's roles in development and/or history, group members gathered monthly on Saturdays in New York City to discuss their work-in-progress. They shared an understanding of the centrality of women's roles in political-economic development and a sense of the importance of class differences. The group self-consciously called its topic Women and Development, rather than Women in Development to underline the importance of class distinctions in determining the impact of the development process on women. Participants in these meetings whose work is included in this reader are: Lourdes Benería, Carmen Diana Deere, Jeanne Koopman (Henn) and Gita Sen.

In 1984, Laurie Nisonoff and Nan Wiegersma noted that an increasing number of women who were living or teaching in the New England region were also involved in similar research. They called these women together and the New England Women and Development Discussion Group began meeting. Three of the participants, Carmen Diana Deere, Jeanne Koopman (Henn) and Nan Wiegersma, had been members of the New York group and they shared this experience with their New England colleagues. Work by Carmen Diana Deere and Jeanne Koopman is included here, together with that of Betsy Hartmann, Mieke Meurs and Laurie Nisonoff, other New England-group members.

Zed Books approached Betsy Hartmann originally, in 1991, with the ideas of a reader that would feature landmark articles and essays on the impact of development on women's lives. Betsy was too busy to work on this project, but Nalini Visvanathan, Brenda Wyss, Lynn Duggan and Laurie began to outline the book that summer. Nan joined the project in 1992 when Brenda had to withdraw because of other commitments.

We would like to thank the multiple incarnations of the Women and Development Discussion Group for providing us with the inspiration and insights we needed to sustain us through the many trials we have encountered over the past five years. In addition to the discussion-group members noted above, others from the original group or its next generation have provided advice and support, including S. Charusheela, Nancy Folbre, Lynn Morgan, Eva Paus, Jeanne L. Pyle and Nola Reinhardt. We also want to thank Asoka Bandarage, Amrita Basu, Christine Bose, Lourdes Benería, Rita Gallin, Aiwha Ong, Carlos Salas and Gita Sen.

We would like to record our gratitude to the authors and editors whose works appear in this reader and thank all of them. The book would not have been completed without the cooperation and support we received from the authors and editors in abridging their works. We would especially like to thank Irene Tinker for adding a postscript on the Beijing conference to update her 1990 essay. We would also like to thank the authors of original articles in Part 4: Delia Aguilar; Marlyn Dalsimer and Laurie Nisonoff; Betsy Hartmann; and Mieke Meurs. Both authors and editors have contributed in various ways to this project. Some of the authors waived their copyrights and relinquished their royalties in order that we could stay within a strictly defined budget. We appreciate their generosity and their commitment to making their writings available to a larger circle of readers.

Many students and librarians helped us with this project, including research assistants Molly Bailey-Dillon, Gladys McCormick and Liz Miller. We tried out the proposed readings and draft essays on our students, whose feedback was invaluable. We would like to thank World Issues Program students in Nalini's 1994 Women, Health, and Development course for evaluating many of the readings; Pernille Dyg for her comments on the draft essay; and the School for International Training librarian Shirley Capron for her support.

We want to thank especially Betsy Hartmann and Brenda Wyss for their roles in initiating the project and their support throughout its gestation. We are grateful also to our colleagues and the administrations at Fitchburg State College, Hampshire College, Michigan State University (particularly the Women and International Development Program), Jawaharlal Nehru University's Centre of Social Medicine and Community Health and the Five College Women's Studies Research Center.

Finally, we appreciated the feedback we received from Association for Women In Development (AWID) President Norge Jerome and her colleagues in the early stage of this reader.

There are many women and development anthologies and readers available for use by experts in the field. This reader is intended to be accessible to students and practitioners and we have chosen and excerpted articles, and prepared the introductions with this in mind. Our selections have been made in order to represent the lives of women of many different regions. We hope that the reader will reach women worldwide and help expand the set of tools, concepts and frameworks available to share their experiences of development within our global community.

Lynn Duggan   Amherst, Massachusetts
Laurie Nisonoff
Nalini Visvanathan
Nan Wiegersma

SOURCES

The Editors and Zed Books Ltd are grateful to the following publishers for their permission to reproduce excerpts from previously published material as abridged versions in this reader. Any omission is unintentional, and the publisher would be glad, if notified, to make due acknowledgement in any future edition.

Chapter 1: 'Development as History and Process', in S.E.M. Charlton, *Women in Third World Development*, Boulder, CO, Westview Press, 1984.

Part 1

Chapter 2: 'The Making of a Field: Advocates, Practitioners and Scholars', in I. Tinker (ed.), *Persistent Inequalities: Women and Development*, Oxford, Oxford University Press, 1990.

Chapter 3: 'Accumulation, Reproduction and Women's Role in Development: Boserup Revisited', *Signs*, Vol. VIII, No. 2, Winter, 1981.

Chapter 4: 'Gender and Development', in K. Young (ed.), *Gender and Development Reader*, Ottawa, Canadian Council for International Cooperation, 1992.

Chapter 5: 'Women, the Environment and Sustainable Development', in R. Braidotti, E. Charkiewicz, S. Häusler and S. Wieringa, *Women, the Environment and Sustainable Development: Towards a Theoretical Synthesis*, London, Zed Books, 1994.

Chapter 6: 'Women in Nature', *Staying Alive*, London, Zed Books, 1989.

Chapter 7: 'The Gender and Environment Debate: Lessons from India', *Feminist Studies*, Vol. 18. No. 1, 1992.

Chapter 8: 'The African Context: Women in the Political Economy', in M. Snyder and M. Tadesse, *African Women and Development*, London, Zed Books, 1995.

Chapter 9: 'Under Western Eyes: Feminist Scholarship and Colonial Discourses', in C. Mohanty, A. Russo and L. Torres, *Third World Women and the Politics of Feminism*, Bloomington, Indiana University Press, 1991.

Chapter 10: 'Bargaining with Patriarchy', *Gender and Society*, Vol. II, No. 3, September 1988.

Part 2

Chapter 11: 'Accounting for Women's Work: The Progress of Two Decades', *World Development*, Vol. 30, No. 11, 1992.

Chapter 12: 'Daughters, Decisions and Domination: An Empirical and Conceptual Critique of Household Strategies', *Development and Change*, Vol. 21, 1990.

Chapter 13: 'The Hidden Roots of the African Food Problem: Looking within the Rural Household', (in N. Folbre, B. Bergmann, B. Agarwal and M. Floro (eds), *Women's Work in the World Economics*, New York, New York University Press, 1992.

Chapter 14: 'Subordination and Sexual Control: A Comparative View of the Control of Women', *Radical Review of Political Economics*, Vol. 16, No. 1, 1984.

Chapter 15: 'Wife Abuse in the Context of Development and Change: A Chinese (Taiwanese) Case', in D.A. Counts, J.K. Brown and J.C. Campbell (eds), *Sanctions and Sanctuary: Cultural Perspectives on the Beating of Wives*, Boulder, CO, Westview Press, 1992.

Chapter 16: 'Single-parent Families: Choice or Constraint? The Formation of

Female-headed Households in Mexican Shanty Towns', *Development and Change*, Vol. 16, 1985.

Part 3
Chapter 17: 'The Subordination of Women and the Internationalization of Factory Production', in K. Young, C. Wolkowitz and R. McCullagh (eds), *Of Marriage and the Market*, London, CSE Books, 1981.

Chapter 18: *'Maquiladoras*: The View from the Inside', in K.B. Sacks and D. Remy (eds), *My Troubles Are Going to Have Trouble with Me*, New Brunswick, Rutgers University Press, 1984.

Chapter 19: 'Capitalism, Imperialism and Patriarchy: The Dilemma of Third World Women Workers in Multinational Factories', in J. Nash and M.P. Fernández-Kelly (eds), *Women, Men and the International Division of Labour*, Albany, SUNY Press, 1983.

Chapter 20: 'Women in the Informal-labour Sector: The Case of Mexico City', *Signs*, Vol. 3, No. 1, 1977.

Chapter 21: 'Deindustrialization and the Growth of Women's Economic Associations and Networks in Urban Tanzania', in S. Rowbotham and S. Mitter, *Dignity and Daily Bread*, London, Routledge, 1994.

Part 4
Chapter 22: 'Impact of the Economic Crisis on Poor Women and their Households', *In the Shadows of the Sun: Caribbean Development Alternatives and US Policy*, Boulder, CO, Westview Press, 1990, published with permission of the coordinating editor.

Chapter 23: 'Ghana: Women in the Public and Informal Sectors under the Economic Recovery Programme', in P. Sparr (ed.), *Mortgaging Women's Lives*, London and New York, Zed Books, 1994.

Chapter 25: 'Women, Population and the Environment: Whose Consensus, Whose Empowerment?' is published concurrently by Routledge, London.

Chapter 26: 'Aids: Women Are Not Just Transmitters', in T. Wallace and C. March (eds), *Changing Perceptions*, Oxford, Oxfam, 1991.

Chapter 28: 'Women, Marriage and the State in Iran', in H. Afshar (ed.) *Women, State and Ideology*, New York, SUNY Press, 1987.

Chapter 29: 'Return to the Veil: Personal Strategy and Public Participation in Egypt', in N. Redclift and M. T. Sinclair (eds), *Working Women: International Perspectives on Labour and Gender Ideology*, London, Routledge, 1991.

Chapter 30: 'Capitalism and Socialism: Some Feminist Questions', in R. Rapp and M.B. Young (eds), *Promissory Notes: Women in the Transition to Socialism*, New York, Monthly Review Press, 1989.

Chapter 31: 'Downwardly Mobile: Women in the Decollectivization of East European Agriculture', Working paper No. 247, Women in International Development Series, Michigan State University.

Part 5
Chapter 32: 'Planning from a Gender Perspective', *Planning Development with Women*, New York, St Martin's Press, 1993, published with permission of the author.

Chapter 33: 'Women as Political Actors in Puerto Rico: Continuity and Change', in F.A. Rothstein and M.L. Blim (eds), *Anthropology and the Global Factory*, New York, Bergin and Garvey, 1992.

Chapter 34: 'Women and the Labor Movement in South Korea', *Anthropology*

and the Global Factory, New York, Bergin and Garvey, 1992.
Chapter 35: 'SEWA: Women in Movement', *Where Women Are Leaders: The SEWA Movement in India*, London, Zed Press, 1992.

RESOURCES AND ORGANIZATIONS

The *Third World Resource Directory* 1997–99 (800pp) is a guide to educational services, curriculum materials, reference books, directories, and audio-visual, periodical and organizational resources on Africa, Asia and the Pacific, Latin America and the Caribbean, and the Middle East, to be published in summer 1997 by Orbis Books. Yearly regional resource guides include up-to-date information related to the region. These are published on a rotating schedule by:

> Worldviews, c/o DataCenter
> 464 19th St, Oakland, CA 94612-2297
> (510) 835-4692 (tel.), 835-3017 (fax)
> worldviews@igc.apc.org (email)

Worldviews Africa is compiling an annotated guide to print and audio-visual resources from and about Africa, the *Africa World Press Guide* (180pp), to be published in summer 1997 by Africa World Press, Lawrenceville, New Jersey.

GENERAL INTRODUCTION

Nalini Visvanathan

As members of the New England Women and Development Discussion group (see Preface), we have collaborated in creating this anthology, which we have divided into five parts: Theories of Women, Gender and Development; Households and Families; Women in the Global Economy; International Women in Social Transformation; and Women Organizing Themselves for Change. Within each part important essays and significant studies outline and challenge established theories in the field and document their progression over time. These are presented as chapters. An introduction to each part highlights the thematic issues and the conceptual frameworks for viewing the chapters and discusses relevant research. These introductions are themselves subdivided, with readings grouped and discussed at the end of each section.

Our selection of readings (whose sources are listed), constrained as with all such selections by space (word) limits, has inevitably had to exclude some important contributions to the literature. We refer to these works in our introductions and further reading. Others are cited in the excerpts, which should lead the users to the full text and more extended bibliographies. We recognize and regret these limitations.

The study of women and development processes is located at the intersection of development studies and women's studies. Each of these fields has evolved from study and research, which draw from one or more of the social sciences for knowledge of historical events and academically grounded theories. Like development studies, the field of women's studies is a complex of disciplines; it is, however, distinguished by its links to the radical social movements of this century, which have shaped its formative years and continue to alter its trajectory.

Imbued with an activist spirit rarely found in the academy, women's studies has been regarded as a movement directed at changing women's status. During its brief existence, it has re-evaluated dominant paradigms and redefined the boundaries of knowledge, and it has recast the canons that govern social research by embracing eclectic methods of inquiry. Through activism in public arenas and academic forums, women's studies' scholars and students have initiated societal changes. Endowed with this rich and remarkable inheritance, the field of women and development processes is propelled by public policies and popular movements as much as it is moulded by scholarly works.

HISTORICAL BACKGROUND

International development as an area of intellectual inquiry can be traced to the 1950s and the post-World War II period of reconstruction. The revival of subdued nations in Europe through recovery programmes like the United States Marshall Plan convinced western and western-trained economic planners that aid-based strategic planning would enable developing countries to bridge the gap that separated them from the industrialized world. (The terms 'developing countries', 'lesser developed countries' [LDCs] and 'Third World' are used interchangeably. North and South refer to global regions of industrialized and non-industrialized nations.) Consequently, the birth of the 'development project' in the 1950s was a global phenomenon that swept across political and ideological differences. (Eds: We recognize that 'development' is a problematic construct and use it reluctantly for lack of a better alternative.) High-income nations committed themselves to monetary and technical aid channelled through United Nations (UN) agencies, based on the theory that this aid would foster economic growth that would trickle down to the masses. Most aid was, however, in the form of loans in US dollars tied to the purchase of technology from the West. Neoclassical economic theorists and planners argued that this strategy would ultimately benefit the poor and transform the economies of developing countries. Instead of the income from new technology trickling down, however, the gap between the rich (haves) and poor (have-nots) in the Third World has widened. This trickle-down approach to economic planning contributed to the failure of development work in the first UN Development Decade (1961–70).

As development projects were initiated during the Cold War era, industrial countries' aid and technical assistance were structured by the struggle between capitalist (First World) and communist (Second World) blocs of nations for dominance over the former colonial countries, which later came to be called the Third World. Spurred on by political and economic interests, the First and Second worlds engaged in bilateral aid and established bureaucratic agencies in their capitals to administer these programmes. These industrial nations determined their aid priorities on the basis of both political exigencies and trading interests. By the end of the First Development Decade, the failure of these programmes to reduce the increasing economic disparities between the North and South spawned a growing reaction against the 'development establishment', its philosophical premises and its mode of operation (Nerfin, 1977). Former colonial nations called for a New International Economic Order that would bring about greater equity in the distribution of capital and of the world's resources.

It was during this period of ferment, when the fundamentals of economic development were being challenged, that the situation of women gained urgency. In the early 1970s, at the start of the second development decade, Danish economist Ester Boserup analysed economic data from three continents. Boserup's (1970) pioneering work showed that women's agricultural production was critical in sustaining local and national economies; it also documented the negative impact of colonialism and modernization in these

societies, especially in sub-Saharan Africa. She noted that European administrators had imposed western values through their governance; in particular,
they redefined the concept of 'work' in African societies to exclude women's
labour, undermining the status of rural women. They elevated the value of
men's work by giving males greater land rights and sole access to farm technology. Significantly, Boserup provided documentary evidence of Third World
women's marginalization and lack of access to technology and resources
after a decade of developing programming. Women development professionals in the US capital used the book to pressure their government to
effect policy changes that would advance women's interests (see Part 1,
Chapter 2). Aid agencies and non-governmental organizations in the North
made visible efforts to integrate women into sectoral planning and create
programmes for improving women's livelihoods.

The international women's movement also had a formative impact on the
field. It provided the impetus for the UN International Women's Decade
(1976–85), which led to three UN conferences, in Mexico City (1975),
Copenhagen (1980) and Nairobi (1985). These conferences in turn invigo-
rated and expanded the movement and elevated the role of feminist organizing and the legitimacy of feminist concerns in international politics.

During the last ten years, women have organized in opposition to the role
of western banks and multilateral financial institutions like the International
Monetary Fund (IMF) in defining the form and character of economic development in their countries. After the 1973 oil crisis, when world oil prices rose
steeply, vast sums of petro-dollars were deposited in northern banks, which
in turn began to loan huge amounts of hard currency to the governments of
southern countries. Since the 1980s, a number of oil-importing countries, as
well as some oil-exporting nations such as Mexico, have become heavily
indebted to northern bankers. In order to allow these countries to reschedule
their often-crippling debts, the IMF has forced them to expand export sectors
and scale down public programmes (see Part 4). These events have served
to mobilize and unite southern activists, who have seen the crushing impact
of macro-economic policies on the poor.

Meanwhile, over the 1980s and 1990s non-governmental organizations
and groups have gained prominence in official forums. Many of them are led
by feminist activists who have slowly built coalitions across regional and
political differences to strengthen their advocacy efforts and have gained
widespread acceptance for their feminist agenda. The emergence of the
international women's movement as a powerful political force has also been
highly evident at decisive UN conferences in the 1990s, especially the
Environmental Summit (1992), the Human Rights Conference (1993), the
International Conference on Population and Development (1994) and the
Social Summit (1995).

At the Fourth World Women's Conference in Beijing (1995) women's
groups consolidated the ground they had gained in previous meetings and
strengthened their articulation of women's rights, including equality in decision-making, balance in gender representation, sexual and reproductive
rights, and freedom from violence. They exacted commitments from partici-

pating governments in such areas as the rights of the girl child, education of women and institutional mechanisms to implement recommendations from the Beijing platform.

Reading

Chapter 1 is an excerpt from Sue Ellen Charlton's *Women in Third World Development*, a popular text for women and development courses during the 1980s. Charlton introduces development by examining the value systems, ethical issues and gender biases that affect this critical concept, and comparing the history of western development to the colonial and contemporary experiences of Third World countries. Her sweeping introduction describes the political movements after World War II, which instigated the 'development project' by the North and created the powerful multilateral institutions and agencies that guide the progress and path of this continuing project.

SIGNIFICANT IDEOLOGIES AND THEORIES

In the Cold War period ideological differences sharply divided economic development scholars, planners and policymakers. The two paradigms that have dominated and divided the field, however – capitalism and socialism – do not constitute a simple dichotomy either in theory or in the actual Third World economies. Within these polarized ideological tracks variations of the dominant paradigm have emerged and extended the theoretical discourse. Their overemphasis in development theory makes it necessary to examine the ways in which these ideologies have influenced the field of women and development (see Isbister [1995] for a critical review of development concepts and theories).

In their lucid overview of competing development paradigms, James H. Weaver *et al.* (1989) categorize most economic theories as falling within the capitalist paradigm or the radical-political economy framework. Within the former, they find three variations: the free-market model, which advocates a reduced role for government in favour of private capital and market forces; the Malthusian approach, which addresses resource scarcity by controlling population growth; and an interventionist model, which advocates government intervention through regulatory and technocratic mechanisms to redistribute income and provide public goods. Implementation of this last approach was reflected in the creation at Bretton Woods in 1944 of the three agencies that regulate today's global economy: the IMF; the World Bank; and the General Agreement on Trade and Tariff (GATT; now the World Trade Organization [WTO]). Contrary to the intent of the interventionist model, these organizations have pursued an increasingly neoliberal agenda that concentrates wealth and reduces public goods. All theories within the capitalist paradigm use individuals as the unit of analysis; they assume that individuals are 'economically' rational and attempt to increase their individual consumption without regard for an equitable distribution of income. Similarly, within this framework development is equated with economic growth, and nations are seen to strive for the highest rate of economic growth, as measured by the gross domestic product (GDP).

By contrast, the radical political-economy paradigm assumes that people are social beings who act together rather than in isolation. Undergirding this approach is a belief in the equality of all peoples and in their right to an equitable share of material goods. Within this perspective, two schools of thought can be distinguished – dependency analysis and Marxism. Dependency analysts believe that economic growth and industrialization of the western world came at the expense of those nations that were subjugated and exploited under colonial rule. The First World is seen as the 'centre' or the 'core', and the Third World as the 'periphery' through which the centre has been continually sustained. The dependency model extends to include élites in the Third World who replicate core–periphery dynamics within their countries by siphoning wealth from the poor to enhance their lifestyles and expand their foreign bank accounts. Dependency theorists conclude that the periphery will develop only when it is freed from its link with the centre.

While the dependency framework centres on 'relations of exchange', Marxist approaches focus on 'relations of production' to explain the exploitation of the colonies by foreign capitalists and their domestic partners. Their emphasis on production efficiency influences the Marxian approach to economic development; in their view, the more dynamic capitalist relations overpower feudal relations, which restrict economic growth. Marxists examine internal causes of countries' underdevelopment and place little stress on the legacy of colonial exploitation. Marxian development approaches have tended to advocate dismantling feudal structures and incorporating the peasantry into wage labour. According to Weaver *et al.* (1989), Marxian strategies for social and economic development include much diversity, from union organizing and grassroots movements to centralized planning and land redistribution.

Not only economists, but also other social theorists have approached development through oppositional world-views that reflect the Cold War bifurcation in development economics. Patricia Maguire (1984) characterizes these approaches as the dominant equilibrium model and the alternative critical approach. The former is rooted in neoclassical economic theory (the capitalist paradigm), with its emphasis on supply and demand in markets as a source of balance within systems, on individuals as rational decision-makers, and on efficiency as the ultimate standard for all interventions and reforms, whether these are directed at individuals or systems.

The alternative critical approach defined by Maguire posits that society is in a state of conflict brought about by struggles between unequal groups to gain power and control over resources. Emphasis is placed on analysing structural factors that have given rise historically to inequitable distributions of power and wealth. Interventions are aimed at structural reform to redress current inequities through redistribution of political and economic resources.

A widely prevalent body of theory that is closely related to the neoclassical economic approach is modernization theory. This world-view guided the development establishment in the 1950s and 1960s and was influenced by the works of sociologists, political scientists and psychologists (Inkeles, 1974; Lerner, 1958; McClelland, 1961). Although many disciplines have explicated the concept of modernization, the intellectual roots of this approach are grounded in the capitalist paradigm, discussed above. According to modernization theory, development takes place as societies move on a linear path from agrarian systems and subsistence farming to industrialized economies and market production. Originating in the West, this dominant paradigm locates the causes of Third World poverty as internal to each country. Using western industrial nations as the norm, modernization thinkers perceive grave deficiencies in Third World societies that stem from long-standing traditions and customs that inhibit both individual and the society's entry into the modern world. Consequently, this ethnocentric model promotes changes through motivating individuals to take entrepreneurial risks, to alter their values and attitudes, to adopt new technologies and to participate in political and civil life.

In today's international economy, where the capitalist paradigm is dominant and southern nations' economies are being restructured through the IMF and the World Bank, the influence of modernization theory is pervasive. Working against this influence, women's movements at the national and international levels are challenging the increasingly market-based global capitalist model and are calling for alternative forms of development. These include monitoring institutions to govern and regulate the actions of transnational firms and banks, and to protect poor communities around the world from the harmful pursuit of profit by wealthy international actors.

FURTHER READING

Boserup, E. (1970) *Women's Role in Economic Development*, New York: St Martin's Press.

Inkeles, A. (1974) *Becoming Modern: Individual Change in Six Developing Countries*, Cambridge, MA: Harvard University Press.

Isbister, J. (1995) *Promises Not Kept*, Hartford: Kumarian Press.

Lerner, D. (1958) *The Passing of Traditional Society: Modernizing the Middle East*, Glencoe, IL: Free Press.

McClelland, D. (1961) *The Achieving Society*, Princeton, NJ: Van Nostrand.

Nerfin, M. (ed.) (1977) *Another Development*, Uppsala: Dag Hammarskjöld Foundation.

Weaver, James H., S.H. Arnold, P. Cruz and K. Kusterer (1989) 'Competing Paradigms of Development', *Social Education*, April/May.

History

Looks at pre-colonial, colonial and neocolonial periods as well as debates over theories of underdevelopment.

1. DEVELOPMENT AS HISTORY AND PROCESS
SUE ELLEN CHARLTON

CONCEPTUALIZING DEVELOPMENT

Analysing the various definitions and interpretation of the word 'development' in order to understand the issues facing women, one must be aware of some of the problems debated by scholars and practitioners. For both intellectual and practical reasons, conceptualizations of development reflect historical experience and individual values.

The very use of the term 'development' implies a notion of historical change derived from western European secular and scientific thought. We assume that change is more linear than cyclical. Development is, by definition, an historical process, so one presumes direction in this process. In the words of one political scientist, Samuel Beer, 'The concept of development recognizes the importance of the time dimension'.[1] The notion of development assumes the human ability to influence and control the natural and social environment. Static, agrarian societies may seek to live in harmony with the environment, but virtually every non-static society attempts to influence it, whether by tools, laws, religion, or even magic. What is distinctive about our modern times is the rationality that is associated with scientific knowledge in societies' efforts to influence and control.[2]

The difficulty with this characterization of modernity is that both rationality and scientific knowledge have varied through history and across cultural systems. One of the political realities of development in the late twentieth century, however, is that policymakers typically define the developmental process in terms of western rationality and scientific knowledge. Thus, the environmental control that is inherent in the concept of development is an example of the western influence.

There are four clusters of issues surrounding the definitions of development that are especially important for women, and they need to be examined briefly:

1   the role of ethical and moral choice in development;
2   the structure of the international system in the late twentieth century;
3   the influence and, in some instances, domination of western norms and institutions in development concepts and policies; and
4   the political control of development.

ETHICAL CHOICE

All people concerned with development must recognize that there are different value systems throughout the world, and it is precisely this diversity that makes the concern for moral and ethical questions so pressing. For most people, the ideal development process harmonizes with the traditional values of a particular society. Changes originate both inside and outside a society. They may result from broad historical movements (such as nationalism), from government planning or from contact with individuals.

THE INTERNATIONAL SYSTEM

There are some basic features of this international system that need to be recognized in any discussions of development, and perhaps the most important is the role of the nation-state, the system's primary unit. Although many forces have combined to weaken nation-states and to make them more 'permeable', they are still the most widespread international units, and are reinforced by the ideology of nationalism and the political–legal concept of sovereignty. In theory, nation-states are equally sovereign; in practice, there are enormous differences in their size and strength.

Hierarchy of nation-states

There is an international hierarchy of nations. The hierarchy may not be clear, but few deny its existence. Power and influence are widely-used criteria in any ranking of states, and these criteria, in turn, incorporate subsidiary measures such as size of population, military strength and level of industrialization.

Third world

Originally, the term 'Third World' characterized those countries that eschewed alignment with either the First World of the West or the Second World of the East. Although the term now has an economic meaning as well, the idea of the Third World is still most accurately described as a political concept.[3]

These are the countries that are the focus of development projects and whose populations are usually described by planners as the 'targets' of development efforts. The countries may be both proud and jealous of their sovereign status, just as they may be too weak to resist the influence, if not the control, of countries like the United States. Nonetheless, however weak the government of a Third-World state may be in some spheres, [it] is still most often the key factor in determining whether development occurs, how it occurs, and who benefits from it.

New international units

Another characteristic of the international system should be mentioned here—the rise of a wide variety of participants in international relations in addition to nation-states. Sometimes these groups conflict with national governments; sometimes they reinforce or complement them. [They] encompass both private and public international organizations, including dozens that are important to women in developing countries: international public organizations, such as the UN and its affiliates (e.g., the Food and Agricultural Organization); international private organizations, such as churches; and multinational corporations. Although women generally are not well-represented in these organizations, as they are not well-represented in the governments of their respective nation-states, they are affected by the decisions of both.

WESTERN INFLUENCE

The pervasiveness of the West in the conceptualization and implementation of development projects is only one part of western influence. This influence ranges from the most common definitions of development, which rely heavily on western scientific thought and reflect western cultural and religious norms (such as equality), to the effects of the historical experience of industrialization in western Europe and North America. The western heritage of colonialism throughout most of the Third World is important both directly and indirectly. The direct importance lies in the history of colonial control over the structures of government in the colonies or territories and colonial influence in determining the boundaries of governmental jurisdiction. Indirectly, formal education, insofar as colonial regimes permitted or encouraged its development, reflected British, French, Spanish, Portuguese, Dutch or US ideas about the proper subjects to teach and the students to be taught.

The socio-economic impact of colonialism was also both direct and indirect. Slaves were taken, plantations were organized, and markets and trade routes were created. Although colonial regimes generally assumed that the people directly affected by these and other such policies would be men, the indirect effects on women included the opportunities and disadvantages presented by urbanization, the shift in female labour caused by the introduction of cash crops, the introduction of western diseases as well as of western cures, along with innumerable other changes in the traditional ways of life.

Western influence and domination did not terminate with decolonization. The leaders of nationalist movements had often been educated in western schools, either in Europe or North America or in schools established in the colonies, so their educational experience had been filled with western values, ideologies (whether liberal-democratic, socialist or communist) and organizational habits. A more direct source of continuing western influence was the willingness of many new states to maintain close cultural, military, and/or economic ties with the countries that had colonized them.

Colonialism, imperialism, dependency

As noted above, the impact of colonialism was explicit and political. Regardless of the pre-colonial status of women in a particular society, the immediate impact of colonial control was either to remove the primary locus of decision-making from the local level to the regional colonial capital or to superimpose colonial decision-making mechanisms on the traditional ones. In either case, the decisionmakers were male, as was the colonial administration. Furthermore, the men in the colonial administration had been raised to believe in the traditional western values regarding the 'proper' roles of men and women. In the British Empire of the nineteenth and early twentieth centuries, these dominant values were those associated with the Victorian era in England.

The impact of colonial educational, legal and economic policies was equally important. For instance, education was emphasized by the Catholic missionaries in the French colonies, and although the missionaries were interested in educating girls as well as boys, female instruction was largely religious and oriented toward helping the girls become better mothers and housewives (in the European sense). Technical or agricultural training, even in sub-Saharan Africa where the women had major responsibilities in farming, favoured boys heavily.

The colonial emphasis on regularizing laws on land tenure, on making the colonized peoples more sedentary, and on shifting agriculture toward the production of crops for export worked to the detriment of women in a number of societies.[4]

Many supporters of the New International Economic Order, for example, have claimed that the relationship that exists between most northern (industrialized) and southern (developing) states is one of imperialism or neo-imperialism. One country may not directly control or govern another, but its influence can be so strong that it undermines the sovereignty of the weaker nation-state. US influence in Latin America and French influence in that country's former African colonies are frequently-cited examples of this kind of relationship, a relationship that includes cultural, economic and financial ties.

Since the 1960s, people studying neo-imperialist influences have looked closely at multinational, or transnational, corporations. Since most multinational corporations are based in western industrialized countries (and Japan), the attack on the corporations fuses with the broader concern about western influence on economic and development issues as a whole.

Imperialism and neo-imperialism are significant not only for their political and historical roles, but also for their contributions to the contemporary dependency scholars. Marxist analyses of imperialism foreshadowed the emergence in the 1970s of a movement of social-science scholars, led by Latin Americans, who distinguish between a great deal of the Third World development and the development that had occurred in western Europe and North America.[5] The essential difference, they argue, lies in an inter-relationship of dependency between two states, or a state and the dominant international system. In this relationship, the economic development of one state is subjected to the economic development and expansion of the other. According to this analysis, the dependent position of Latin American states *vis-à-vis* European and North American states has created a pattern of industrialization in the first area that is very different from that experienced in the last two groups of countries.

Westernized organizations

Barbara Rogers has attacked the western male bias in development planning in her book, *The Domestication of Women*, and she points out that international organizations are not exempt from this male bias.[6]

The staffs of most international organizations have been dominated since World War II by men with a western educational background [which] has limited the diversity of perspectives in development planning. More important, Third World women have very little control at any level.

Western culture and communications

Development occurs in the context of many different cultures, yet it is difficult for westerners and many non-westerners to envisage something called development if it does not resemble both western values and the western historical experience.

Communications link the areas that have just been discussed: ethical choice, the nature of the international system and western influence. People in any society rely on their ability to communicate in order to form collective ideas of what is desirable development for them. It is, in fact, impossible to conceive of development without communications.

The more important the need for communication, the more important it is to recognize disparities in access to or control of the means of communication.

THE POLITICAL DEPENDENCY OF WOMEN

Women are dependent upon men in formal politics at the local, national and international levels. Events at the local level, whether in the private (family/kin group) or public sphere are more and more influenced by the institutions of the nation-state. Moreover, the expansion of multinational organizations means that virtually no country can be considered impermeable to influences that originate outside its border. The choice by a village woman to breast-feed her infant is conditioned in part by forces over which she has no control: the availability of manufactured formulas, advertising and other sources of information (such as health workers), prices and cash income, and government policies regulating the operations of multinational corporations. This example is a reminder that the conditions of a woman's life—even in remote villages—are influenced by institutions and events that are physically far removed from her.

From personal to political dependency, the private and the public spheres

Marxist-feminist scholarship has been instrumental in suggesting the way in which patriarchal control within the family or kin group is linked to the division of labour by gender ... As men become more involved in production for exchange (rather than for immediate consumption), the work the women do is increasingly restricted to the domestic sphere. A number of scholars have argued that the greater the involvement of women in the non-domestic, or public, sphere, the greater their status in their culture and the greater their influence in community matters. This linkage between the non-domestic functions performed by women, cultural norms, and ultimately, status and influence has often been characterized as a private/public dichotomy or paradigm. The linkage relies on two arguments: (1) women's lives have always been defined by dual activities—reproductive and productive—but male activity is productive only, and (2) there is a direct relationship between the ability of women to define themselves by non-reproductive labour and their broader social status and influence.

Part of the decline in women's status may be measured by the creation of male-dominated state bureaucracies at the local, regional and national levels. As public agencies influence or absorb activities that were formerly handled privately, women may lose ground in their ability to control their lives.

In an era when development is the subject of intense government concern, we must recognize that the ultimate impact of modernization policies on women will be determined to a large degree by how much power and influence the women have. Development does not happen in a vacuum; it is subject to innumerable political and administrative influences, from the headman or caste leader of the smallest village to international agencies and multinational corporations.

In summary, the movement of women to organize themselves from the village to the transnational level; the integration of women into political and administrative bodies, both public and private; the equalization of political power at every stage and level of organization; and the formal, legal recognition of women's rights are all 'women-and-development issues' as much as the questions of maternal and child nutrition or credit are for farm women.

NOTES

CHAPTER 1

1. Samuel H. Beer, *Modern Political Development*, New York: Random House, 1974, p. 59.
2. Ibid., pp. 61–2.
3. Wayne M. Clegern, 'What is the Third World?' *Technos* 8, January–December 1980: 9–18. Originally, the term referred to the Third Estate (bourgeoisie) at the time of the French Revolution, when the bourgeoisie was a rising, but under-represented group.
4. Achola Pala Okeyo, 'Daughters of the Lakes and Rivers: Colonization and the Land Rights of Luo Women', in Mona Etienne (ed.) *Women and Colonization: Anthropological Perspectives*, New York: Praeger, 1980, pp. 186–213.
5. For a summary of the extensive literature on dependency, with an analysis of the various approaches, see Ronald H. Chilcote, *Theories of Comparative Politics: The Search for a Paradigm*, Boulder, Colo.: Westview Press, 1981, pp. 296–312. Several authors discuss both dependency and the strategies to overcome it in Heraldo Munoz (ed.), *From Dependency to Development: Strategies to Overcome Underdevelopment and Inequality*, Boulder, Colo.: Westview Press, 1981.
6. Barbara Rogers, *The Domestication of Women: Discrimination in Developing Societies*, New York: St Martin's Press, 1980; London: Kogan Page, 1979.

Part 1
Theories of Women, Gender and Development

INTRODUCTION TO PART 1

NALINI VISVANATHAN

The multidisciplinary nature of the subfield of women and development has generated an array of theoretical perspectives, many of which have evolved through cross-fertilization. Guided by these viewpoints, researchers and practitioners apply experiential knowledge from field settings to recast old theories and give them greater currency. Scholars have mapped the domain to clarify easily distinctions among streams of feminist discourse and debate that converge on many issues. In Part 1, at the risk of oversimplifying these differences, we present the major theories that animate this new field. We follow this with perspectives specifically from Third World women, living in the North as well as the South.

A. SURVEY OF THEORETICAL DEBATES

Eva Rathgeber (1990) outlines the general frameworks that have guided most development researchers and practitioners to date, illustrating how powerfully and pervasively certain theoretical perspectives tend to shape scholarly and practical work. She identifies three distinct theoretical paths in the field: Women in Development (WID), Women and Development (WAD) and Gender and Development (GAD).

In order to understand the elements that distinguish these frameworks, we review several recently published works which elaborate on the basic structures of each of these approaches and offer some conceptual insights as well as some categorical changes.

WOMEN IN DEVELOPMENT (WID)

As the oldest and most dominant perspective, WID has manifestly influenced the course of the field. (WID, which we use here to characterize a school of thought within the field, continues to be a popular term for the field itself.) WID subscribes to the assumptions of modernization theory; its programmes generally stress western values and target individuals as the catalysts for social change. Modernization theory depicts traditional societies as authoritarian and male-dominated and modern ones as democratic and egalitarian; thus it appears to show sensitivity to the oppression faced by women. For the most part, liberal feminists have accepted and endorsed this world-view. In contrast, progressive feminist critiques of modernization theory find it implicitly gendered and its characterization of Third World women distorted and detrimental (Mohanty, 1991; Scott, 1995).

Boserup's (1970) documentation of the regressive impact of development on women's lives and livelihoods signalled the start of liberal feminists'

Table 1: Changing Perspectives on Women, Gender and Development

	Women in Development (WID)	Women and Development (WAD)	Gender and Development (GAD)
Origins	Early 1970s after the publication of Ester Boserup's book *Women's Role in Economic Development*. Term WID articulated by American liberal feminists.	Emerged from a critique of the modernization theory and the WID approach in the second half of the 1970s.	As an alternative to the WID focus this approach developed in the 1980s
Theoretical base	Linked with the modernization theory of the 1950s to 1970s. By the 1970s it was realized that benefits of modernization had somehow not reached women, and in some sectors undermined their existing position.	Draws from the dependency theory.	Influenced by socialist feminist thinking.
Focus	Need to integrate women in economic systems, through necessary legal and administrative changes. Women's productive role emphasized. Strategies to be developed to minimize disadvantages of women in the productive sector.	Women have always been part of development processes—therefore integrating women in development is a myth. Focuses on relationship between women and development processes.	Offers a holistic perspective looking at all aspects of women's lives. It questions the basis of assigning specific gender roles to different sexes.
Contribution	Women's questions became visible in the arena of development theory and practice.	Accepts women as important economic actors in their societies. Women's work in the public and private domain is central to the maintenance of their societal structures. Looks at the nature of integration of	Does not exclusively emphasize female solidarity—welcomes contributions of sensitive men. Recognizes women's contribution inside and outside the household, including non-commodity production.

	WID	WAD	GAD
Contribution (cont.)		women in development which sustains existing international structures of inequality.	GAD rejects the public/private dichotomy. It gives special attention to oppression of women in the family by entering the so called 'private sphere'. It emphasizes the state's duty to provide social services in promoting women's emancipation. Women seen as agents of change rather than as passive recipients of development assistance.
Features	WID was solidly grounded in traditional modernization theory which assumed wrongly that women were not integrated in the process of development. It accepted existing social structures—it did not question the sources of women's subordination and oppression. Non-confrontational approach. It did not question why women had not benefited from development strategies. It treated women as an undifferentiated category overlooking the influence of class, race and culture. Focused exclusively on productive aspects of women's work, ignoring or minimizing the reproductive side of women's lives.	Fails to analyse the relationship between patriarchy, differing modes of production and women's subordination and oppression. Discourages a strict analytical focus on the problems of women independent of those of men since both sexes are seen to be disadvantaged with oppressive global structure based on class and capital. Singular preoccupation with women's productive role at the expense of the reproductive side of women's work and lives. Assumes that once international structures become more equitable, women's position would improve WAD doesn't question the relations between gender roles.	Stresses the need for women to organize themselves for a more effective political voice. Recognizes that patriarchy operates within and across classes to oppress women. Focuses on strengthening women's legal rights, including the reform of inheritance and land laws. It talks in terms of upsetting the existing power relations in society between men and women.

Source: Adapted by Suneeta Dhar and Aanchal Kapur, *Kriti Newsletter*, 1, 1992–3, from Eva M. Rathgeber (1990).

advocacy of the integration of women into development, as workers and producers. Tiano (1984) notes that some scholars, upon seeing that modernization costs were being shouldered largely by women, advocated changes in this approach. She labels this move to address gaps in modernization theory (but not its basic premises) as 'developmentalism'. Although developmentalists appear to make radical demands for women's inclusion, they do not advocate structural change in the system in which women are to be included; nevertheless, their advocacy efforts have contributed to the shifts in policy that led to new variants of WID described below.

It is important to note that programmes directed at Third World women have a long history. Surveying four decades of development policy Moser (1993) finds five distinct WID approaches that reflect policy evolution. Building on concepts developed by Molyneux (1985), Moser evaluates each approach in terms of its ability to meet those practical needs of women that require urgent attention (such as employment, health services and water supply) and women's more strategic needs, which must be met to change their subordinate status in society (e.g. legal rights, gender-based division of labour and domestic violence).

Moser's first category, the 'welfare approach', predates Boserup's landmark work. It focuses solely on women's reproductive roles and includes programmes to control population growth, which is seen as the primary cause of poverty. It targets practical rather than strategic needs, therefore. The 'equity approach', Moser's second category, dominated the agenda of WID advocates during the UN Decade for Women (1976–85) and represented the initial phase of feminist organizing, which called for gender equality. The UN's backing of women had a lasting impact on social legislation, which enhanced women's civil and political rights in many countries. However, feminists encountered continued resistance to their demand for equality with men; they changed their policy emphasis, therefore, to resonate with the general direction of development in the 1970s, when the goal of meeting people's basic needs was stressed. Consequently, the third approach was 'anti-poverty', and concentrated on enhancing women's productive role through waged work and income-generation, thereby neglecting strategic needs.

In Moser's typology, the fourth approach, 'efficiency', is associated with the IMF structural adjustment programmes of the 1980s and stresses women's reaction and response to the debt crises through their participation in the newly restructured economies. In the climate of the current economic reforms, the urgency of addressing practical problems has overburdened women and stalled their progress towards meeting strategic needs. The fifth WID approach, 'empowerment', represents Third World feminist writing and grass-roots organizing. It addresses women's strategic need to transform laws and structures that oppress them through a bottom-up process of organizing around practical needs.

A major WID policy initiative has been the mainstreaming of gender issues in development agencies (Anderson, 1993). Jahan (1995) notes that WID advocates have promoted this practice through increasing women's visibility, reporting development data by gender, and setting the agenda for planning.

Her study of four agencies showed significant gains in the first two areas and limited progress in agenda-setting.

Readings

Spread over two decades, WID policy and planning display mixed success with regard to social change. Chapter 2 documents the origin and growth of the WID establishment, the historical events that ran concurrently and the theoretical discourses that extended the field. Like Moser, Tinker highlights the two themes that dominate WID policy and pervade official discourse: gender equality and economic efficiency. She clarifies the WID discourse by categorizing the players—advocates, practitioners and scholars—who have staked the field and helped secure a legitimate place for women's issues on the agenda of the UN and other international agencies.

WOMEN AND DEVELOPMENT (WAD)

Marxist historians, beginning with Frederick Engels (1942), assert that the Agricultural Revolution, through the establishment of stationary communities for growing crops and domesticating animals, led to hierarchical structures in societies presumed to have been previously classless. Engels argued that the institution of private property and consequent exaltation of monogamy contributed to the decline of women's status. Marxist feminists hypothesize that the desire to retain privately held property within blood-lines (a need that did not arise in the period of communal ownership) as well as to control children's labour made men attempt to control their wives' sexuality through monogamous marriage. This gender hierarchy was intensified with the spread of capitalism. Production for direct use, which was a hallmark of more communal societies, was replaced by production for exchange, which was taken over by men and came to be viewed as a 'public' function. The areas of reproduction and consumption associated with the 'private' domain were assigned to women. The historical significance of this public–private cleavage is apparent in the importance attached by feminists of all persuasions to women's paid employment as a source of status and autonomy.

Jaquette (1982) notes that Marxist and liberal feminists share the view that structures of production determine women's inferior status; liberal analysis cites technological change as the causal mechanism, however, without considering its impact on class differentiation as do Marxists. Jaquette stresses the importance of the recognition within Marxist theory that women's unpaid domestic work and reproductive services are critical for capitalist employers, whose profits hinge on paying workers less than the true value of their labour.

Based on her research review, Bandarage (1984) argues that liberal feminists using a WID framework tend to focus narrowly on sexual inequality and ignore the structural and socio-economic factors within which gender inequalities are embedded. By contrast

> [Marxist feminists'] studies show that the changing roles of women in economic production are determined by the confluence of a number of

historical factors: the sexual division of labour in reproduction, local class structure, the articulation of specific regions and sectors of production within national economies and the international economy. The result is a great diversity and complexity in the integration of women into the processes of capitalist development. (Bandarage, 1984: 502)

The theoretical stance of the Marxist and the dependency theorists is exemplified in their focus on the exploitation of women by multinationals. Poor, young non-white women are sought out for their purported pliancy and are paid low wages to staff the factory complexes that amass profits for foreign companies. As they have multiplied around the world, these export-processing zones have provided a microcosm of transnational exploitation of women that has become a laboratory site for innumerable studies by feminists and scholars representing diverse disciplines and ideologies. (See Part 2, Chapter 12; Part 3, Chapters 17–19; and Part 5, Chapter 34.)

Examining structuralist perspectives on women and development, Kabeer (1994) finds, like earlier critics, that the Marxists have given scant attention to the sphere of reproduction and household-level relations between men and women. She notes that their preoccupation with the structures of production for exchange has downplayed men's role in the oppression of women. Kabeer reviews the work of feminists whose views converge with those of Marxists on class analysis but diverge on issues of gender relations, and determines that the issue of sexual inequality divides their perspectives into three groups: 'dependency feminism'; 'global capitalist patriarchy and male violence'; and 'capital accumulation and the social relations of gender'.

The dependency feminists, according to Kabeer, use the traditional Marxist-feminist framework and view the inequalities between women and men as part of the larger picture of the global economy. Similarly, this group sees sexual inequality as just another aspect of the inequity created by capitalist accumulation. Nevertheless, Kabeer recognizes that this analysis vastly extends the WID critique of mainstream development theory, which ignores structural causes and focuses on individual-based change.

Kabeer's second grouping of scholars, those who focus on global capitalist patriarchy and male violence, has been characterized as one of radical feminists. In Kabeer's formulation, the work of this group is dominated by the writings of the German anthropologist Maria Mies, who gives gender precedence over class analysis. She notes that Mies contributed significantly to the extension of the Marxist-feminist critique in identifying the female body as the site of patriarchal violence. However, Kabeer believes that Mies's world-view, with assumptions and generalizations about the static nature of patriarchal history, is flawed: 'All men appear as monsters, their culpability in direct inverse proportion to their location in the global patriarchal hierarchy; all women appear as their victims' (1994: 53).

According to Kabeer, the uncompromising stand taken by Marxist and dependency feminists for radical structural transformations underscores their strong ideological and ethical position. The rigidity of this position has, however, also restricted their involvement in official efforts to address Third World women's immediate needs. (Kabeer's third grouping, 'capital accumulation and the social relations of gender', will be reviewed in Gender and Development below.)

Readings

Bería and Sen (Chapter 3) critically assess Boserup's work and conclude that, while this important liberal economist highlights women's role in economic systems, she fails to challenge the capitalist model of development. They argue that Boserup focuses on women's occupational roles outside the home and ignores those within. Her analysis, lacking a clearly developed theoretical base, leads to findings that are broadly descriptive about gender relations but devoid of insights on class divisions; consequently, she concludes that discrimination against women is rooted in cultural values which can be overcome through access to technology and jobs. (Parts 3 and 4 provide a fuller exposition and evaluation of the theoretical perspectives of Marxist and socialist feminists.)

GENDER AND DEVELOPMENT (GAD)

The third major theoretical track in the field, GAD, emerged in the 1980s and represents the confluence of diverse feminist perspectives. It draws its heritage from feminist activism in the women's movement as well as from a schism in the ranks of Marxist feminists, many of whom challenged the notion that class analysis alone could explain women's oppression. The socialist feminists who dominate this track have incorporated lessons learned from WID failures and WAD limitations. The outcome is an analytical framework that emphasizes gender relations in both the labour force and the reproductive sphere. According to Kate Young (1992), GAD focuses not just on women (as with WID and WAD), but on the social relations between men and women, in the workplace as well as in other settings. GAD uses gender relations rather than 'women' as a category of analysis and views men as potential supporters of women.

The GAD model adopts a holistic approach and treats development as a complex process influenced by political and socio-economic forces. Young emphasizes that GAD expects the state to assume a critical role in providing programmes to support the work of social reproduction, namely the care and nurturance of children. GAD proponents recognize that household conflicts arise both from gender divisions and from generational differences. They acknowledge women's concerns for economic independence, and give weight to political activism advocating strategies such as community organizing, transformative action, public education and coalition-building.

Kabeer's third grouping of feminist structuralists, 'capital accumulation and social relations of gender', is clearly an exposition of the GAD model. In her depiction of this group, she underscores GAD's common base with Marxist and dependency approaches that seek structural reforms. Elaborating on its implications, she points out that GAD goes beyond Marxist analysis and its absorption with production to the area of social reproduction. This approach tends to avoid the sweeping generalizations found among some Marxist (and liberal) feminists who universalize the characteristics of patriarchal oppression. Finally, Kabeer argues that GAD opens up new strategies for feminist intervention. She points out that 'early Marxist feminists' refused to work with official development agencies, which are the principal funding sources for women's projects. She maintains that GAD's multifarious approach distinguishes between capitalism, patriarchy and racism and enables feminists to identify chinks in official policies for strategic interventions to promote their agenda. She views such strategies as transitional and necessary in order for feminists to respond to the needs of desperately poor women.

There is a growing trend within the field to draw on the concept of gender, because its social construction and cultural context provide a rich information base for understanding male–female relations and interactions (Ostegaard, 1992). Development planners and practitioners are taking the lead in creating gender-analysis frameworks for evaluating the distribution of household power, land and resources. Oxfam is foremost in this among the non-governmental organizations (NGOs) that focus on gender relations in designing projects for women. Two Oxfam publications (Wallace and March, 1991; Cleves Mosse, 1993) discuss examples. Practitioners have developed frameworks for gender analysis in such areas as agriculture (Sims Feldstein and Jiggins, 1994), environment and land use (Rocheleau, 1992), and community participation (Parker, 1993). Through these tools the GAD model sharpens and extends our knowledge of women's issues in settings such as farms, households and communities.

In her criticism of the use of gender analysis in development theory, Elizabeth Reid (1995) stresses the problematic aspects of using a dichotomous framework for categorizing social relations: 'Such a gender template is not strategic. It substitutes a static and incomplete description for a dynamic analysis of power and difference' (p. 114).

Reading
In Chapter 4, Kate Young introduces readers to the fundamentals of this approach. Her exposition underscores the critical ways in which GAD differs from WID. By considering development as a complex process rather than a discrete state, GAD goes beyond economic well-being to address the individual's social and mental needs. While GAD emphasizes women's empowerment and male responsibility, it includes a definite role for the state in programmes to bring about equality between the sexes.

WOMEN, ENVIRONMENT AND DEVELOPMENT (WED)
For almost two decades, the important interactions of women with their environment have formed a major theme within development studies. Now, Women, Environment and Development (WED) has joined Rathgeber's WID, WAD and GAD typology as a distinct theoretical path in the field.

Starting in the 1970s, northern feminists had drawn parallels between male control over nature and over women. These ecofeminists, as they became known, exposed the assault by masculinist scientific and industrial systems on the ecological health of the planet. Rosi Braidotti and her co-authors (Chapter 5) see ecofeminism as a theoretical stream within the feminist movement, as well as a progressive social movement that also attracts men. Despite some remarkable successes within the peace movement, however, its impact on mainstream thinking has been limited.

Harcourt (1994) presents feminist models of sustainable development as alternatives to those put forward by development economists. The authors in this anthology find that the traditional cultural heritage of southern communities has been overshadowed by the 'poverty-status' they have acquired in the age of 'development'. At the centre of the problem is the dominance of northern actors and agencies in the process of knowledge-creation for these communities. They recommend fundamental changes in the dominant discourse of development to incorporate women's voices and such contextual considerations as local-knowledge systems, gender relations, cultural specificity and political ecology.

Maria Mies and Vandana Shiva (1993) train their ecofeminist lens on global-market encroachment on forests and farming systems, and contrast this pernicious trend with the traditional practices of indigenous peoples. Feminist political ecology melds several areas of feminist theorizing on the environment with the perspectives of political ecologists concerned about inequities in ownership and control of land and resources (Rocheleau, *et al.*, 1996); although their coverage extends beyond the global South, the authors construct a theoretical framework to give coherence to women's environmental activities in diverse gendered spaces and across geographic regions.

Readings

Chapter 5 describes the different theoretical viewpoints within the WED literature and discusses their relative merits. Radical feminists reject western development thinking and call for alternative approaches grounded in indigenous systems. As Braidotti *et al.* delineate, both Mies and Shiva have traced environmental decline to the dominance of patriarchal and western scientific authority in development planning. The result of the technocratic strategies they describe has been the global spread of capitalism and of a market-based economic system which has destroyed the long-established bonds between communities and their environment. Both Mies and Shiva favour a return to subsistence agriculture, a solution their critics dismiss as romantic. Braidotti also points out that WID developmentalists, who emphasize the pivotal role of women in natural-resource management, are viewing women as an instrument to attain the goal of environmental preservation. By using gender-based analysis in their studies of women's roles in agricultural communities and rural households, some environmental scholars and practitioners have been able effectively to avoid the instrumentalization of women.

Chapter 6, a selection from *Staying Alive*, Shiva's acclaimed ecofeminist treatise on India, depicts an idealized relationship between Indian women and nature. The omission of any analysis of the class hierarchy entrenched in Indian society weakens her powerful indictment of the western model of development.

Bina Agarwal (Chapter 7), whose studies of Indian rural women and their deteriorating forest and field environments span two decades, warns against the essentialist bias found in ecofeminist analyses. She examines closely the distinguishing features of ecofeminism and comments critically on Shiva's generalization about the intrinsic relationship between Indian women and nature. She locates her position within the sphere of feminist environmentalism and advocates transformative approaches in the area of gender relations.

SOUTHERN THEORETICAL PERSPECTIVES

The WID, WAD, GAD and WED approaches represent theoretical viewpoints of mostly northern scholars and practitioners and the southern institutions and individuals who work with them. Other Third World women have proposed alternatives.

In the mid-1980s, at the end of the UN Decade for Women, members of a southern feminist research network, Development Alternatives for a New Era (DAWN), published a landmark critique of development's impact on women. Sen and Grown (1987) analyse the impact of development policies on Third World women from the perspective of poor women, and propose an alternative model. The authors challenge the universality of feminism by underscoring the significance of race, class and nation. Their vision is universal in its compass and feminist in its tone; it calls for a utopian world where 'basic needs become basic rights' and men share equally in the care and nurturance of children. It is to be operationalized through women's organizations that work for the empowerment of women, movements that revolve around specific issues and causes, and networks and coalitions that bridge women's groups.

Sen and Grown's work popularized the concept of empowerment, which has been cited by Moser as a WID policy stance. Economist Diane Elson (n.d.) calls this the 'self-empowerment' approach, which underscores 'the agency of organized women. Political consciousness-raising and popular education are emphasized as much as income-earning opportunities' (p. 14). Locally and globally, empowerment defines both a goal and a preferred route for accomplishing strategic objectives. Widespread use of this concept in mainstream development discourse has, however, distorted its original meaning (changing power relations) and endowed it with unlimited potential. Northern population and development agencies misinterpret the term, often uncritically treating 'education' and 'employment' as empowering instruments that lead to women's fertility reduction. Southern scholars offer different interpretations. For Latin American feminists (Leon, 1993, in Escobar, 1995) 'empowerment' implies greater equality for women in the performance of their 'productive activities'. In the Indian context, the term emphasizes the changing of power relations through individual challenge to patriarchal relations or group resistance to oppressive practices (Batliwala, 1995; Bhatt, 1989).

SOUTHERN WOMEN'S MOVEMENTS AND EMPOWERMENT PROCESSES

Feminist historians disagree about the origins of the women and development field, which some practitioners characterize as a movement. Most northern feminists view Boserup's 1970 publication as marking the birth of the movement and attribute its swift growth to the high profile conferred on the international women's movement by the UN Decade for Women (1976–85). In her account of that decade, academic Irene Tinker (1990) claims that the UN Commission on the Status of Women and the US women's movement played a leading role in the creation of the field. Snyder and Tadesse (1995) challenge Tinker's latter assertion. They argue that in Africa this movement was formed and shaped by pre-colonial traditions of economic and political activism and by the wars of liberation from colonial rule. Chronologically, African liberation movements preceded or coincided with the activities of the UN decade and, in all probability, contributed to the women and development movement even before Boserup's work was published. There are parallels elsewhere, at different historical periods, when anti-colonial and liberation struggles united Third World women who had previously been separated by ethnic, racial, class or linguistic barriers; in some instances, these struggles contributed to the growth of feminist orga-nizing. More recently, in Latin America, their protests against authoritarian regimes unified women's groups engaged in oppositional politics (Jaquette, 1994). It must be noted, however, that liberation struggles were only one of the many catalysts for women's movements (see Part 4).

Saskia Wieringa (1995) stresses the need to dispel myths about women's movements, in particular two myths about the South. The first limits women's political activism to anti-colonial struggles. In fact, historical accounts from Peru, Trinidad, Jamaica and Somalia establish that feminists there had long challenged sexual norms and male-dominated unions, had demanded social and economic rights, and had protested against labour discrimination. The second myth is that southern women are interested in survival issues rather than political analysis and activism. Wieringa refutes this generalization, pointing out that there are more similarities than differ-ences between northern and southern women.

How do women's movements influence the range and direction of the field? Whether they organize locally or transnationally, women's move-ments have been influential in setting the policy agendas and prioritizing women's concerns. Their divergent issues have encompassed food prices, domestic violence, state and military persecution and contraceptive abuse; their targets have been state policies and corporate actions. Using a transnational lens, Amrita Basu (1995) concludes that they resist simple definition. Her anthology of women's organizations and activities in differ-ent countries of the world suggests that the international women's move-ment is not a monolithic entity but a bridge across heterogeneous national and regional groups.

Reading

Chapter 8 illuminates gender divisions, which were based on complementar-ity, in pre-colonial African agriculture and commerce. The invasion by European capitalist economies, followed by colonial governance, created inequalities in gender divisions. Snyder and Tadesse document the growth of small women's collectives into women's movements that led the protest against unjust colonial policies. These uprisings, which were a vital part of the liberation struggles, shaped the nascent indigenous women and development movement.

B. DISCOURSE/LANGUAGE OF WID

In the preceding section we examined southern women's responses to northern theorizing about the conditions affecting poor women. In this section we look briefly at some postmodern critiques of terminology and categories embedded in development literature and of northern feminist presentations of southern women's lives. Postmodern thinking has fostered a growing awareness of the absence of race and class analysis in mainstream feminist thought. As noted previously (Sen and Grown), southern feminists have called for the inclusion of class and race in mainstream analyses and have made an unremitting attack on the concept of modernization.

Aihwa Ong (1988) provides a notable critique of the WID and WAD literature, including one of our selections (Chapter 3). Ong questions the validity of using the gender division of labour as a yardstick to assess women's status in southern countries, a practice followed by both liberal and left-leaning feminists. She notes that these feminists make use of colonial forms of discourse in presenting Third World women through negative stereotypes and implying that western women are superiorly positioned.

Feminist postmodernist scholars have amplified the WID critique initiated by Mohanty et al. (1991) and Ong and scrutinized the literature intensely. Hirschmann (1996) examines Sen and Grown's (1987) articulation of the DAWN manifesto and disputes their claim to an alternative vision. She discerns the influence of Marxist feminist theory burdened by its historical specificity and Eurocentric biases and the implication that western feminist values define and demarcate the terms of women's empowerment. Marchand (1996) argues that by popularizing the dichotomous categories of practical/strategic gender needs and linking them to class-based feminist/feminine movements in Latin America, western feminists have simplified the structure of women's political participation and constrained theory formation. She proposes the use of testimonies as a valid approach to incorporating knowledge from marginalized women into the GAD discourse.

Arturo Escobar's (1995) analysis of WID discourse, which includes a critique of important literature, provides some significant insights. For Escobar, 'women' constitutes a 'client category' analogous to 'peasant' and 'environment' in the mainstream development discourse. This discourse leans heavily on the representation of Third World women's reality by bureaucrats in aid agencies, who distort that reality by converting women's vital experiences into numerical scores.

Geographers Momsen and Kinnaird (1993) emphasize the importance of context (place) in the recording of voices from the field and, therefore, an alternate way of viewing gender relations, in addition to race and class. Feminist researchers are increasingly evaluating their field methods through self-conscious and self-critical approaches in the portrayal of Third World subjects (Wolf, 1996).

Finally, Udayagiri (1996) cogently analyses the limitations of postmodernist theorizing for social change and development practice and calls for greater flexibility. She maintains that academic feminism, which leans on social criticism through scholarly textual analysis, is inaccessible to poor women and removed from feminism that builds on resistances and social movements. Moreover, the political mobilization of women requires the recognition of common problems and shared values among them, reflecting an essentialist bond. Udayagiri concludes that in its current form postmodernist theorizing is not pertinent to projects for social change.

Readings

Chapter 9 analyses the imperial nature of western feminism methodically, including the dominance of western economic rationalism in the WID literature. Citing examples, Mohanty shows how WID scholars have failed to differentiate between women of different classes and ethnic identity, have generalized women's subordination and have assumed that those women were a unified, coherent group. She offers, in contrast, Mies's (1982) multi-layered analysis of Narsapur lace workers, a study which probes carefully the intersection of the women's personal lives with the political world.

In Chapter 10, Deniz Kandiyoti (1988) decries the universalization of patriarchy by western feminists. She documents some of the different types of patriarchy prevalent in southern regions and contends that women negotiate concessions and benefits through actions that range from open resistance to subtle forms of non-cooperation. While the assertiveness of African women is clearly visible, the strategizing of Asian women is not so evident to outsiders. In both cases, Kandiyoti establishes that women are actors and agents directing their own lives.

Southern feminist activists have contributed markedly to theory construction and new research methodology by raising epistemological concerns and validating the experiences and voices of disempowered women. By rethinking 'development' they have questioned the very foundations of the field. In their articulation, development is a transformation of institutions, structures and relations that perpetuate injustice, inequality and inequity—a transformation that can happen only through the exercise of a collective will. The challenge to feminists is to mobilize this collective spirit and channel it towards specific goals. In this way, the close interaction of theory and praxis that distinguishes the field is best exemplified in grassroots-based southern women's movements.

FURTHER READING

Alexander, M.J. and C.T. Mohanty (1997) *Feminist Genealogies, Colonial Legacies, Democratic Futures*, London, Routledge.
Anderson, M. (1993) *Focusing on Women*, New York: UNIFEM.
Bandarage, A. (1984) 'Women in Development: Liberalism, Marxism, and Marxist Feminism', *Development and Change*, Vol. XV: 495–515.

Basu, A. (ed.) (1995) *The Challenge of Local Feminisms*, Boulder, CO: Westview Press.

Batliwala, S. (1995) 'The Meaning of Women's Empowerment', *Women's World*, No. 29: 23–8, 33–4.

Benería, L. (1979) 'Reproduction, Production and the Sexual Division of Labour', *Cambridge Journal of Economics*, Vol. III: 203–25.

Benería, L. and G. Sen, (1982) 'Class and Gender Inequalities and Women's Role in Economic Development', *Feminist Studies*, Vol. I: 157–76, Spring.

Bhatt, E. (1989) 'Toward Empowerment', *World Development*, Vol. XVII, No. 7: 1059–65.

Boserup, E. (1970) *Women's Role in Economic Development*, New York: St Martin's Press.

Bourque, S.C. and K. Warren (1981) *Women of the Andes: Patriarchy and Social Change in Two Peruvian Towns*, Ann Arbor: University of Michigan Press.

—— (1987) 'Technology, Gender and Development', *Daedalus*, Vol. 1, No. 6: 173–97.

Burgos-Debray, E. (ed.) (1984) *I, Rigoberta Menchu: An Indian Woman in Guatemala*, New York: Schocken Books.

Buvinic, M. (1986) 'Projects for Women in the Third World: Explaining Their Misbehavior', *World Development*, Vol. XIV: 653–64, May.

Cleves Mosse, J. (1993) *Half the World, Half a Chance*, Oxford: Oxfam.

Elson, Diane (n.d.) 'Gender Issues in Development Strategies', mimeo, Dept. of Economics, University of Manchester.

Engels, F. (1942) *The Origins of the Family, Private Property and the State*, New York: International Publishers.

Escobar, A. (1995) *Encountering Development: The Making and Unmaking of the Third World*, Princeton: Princeton University Press.

Etienne, M., and E. Leacock (eds) (1988) Introduction, *Women and Colonization*, pp. 8–24.

Fernea, E. and B. Bezirgan (eds) (1984) *Middle Eastern Muslim Women Speak*, Austin: University of Texas Press.

Goetz, A.M. (1988) 'Feminism and the Limits of the Claims to Know: Contradictions in Feminist Approach to Women and Development', *Millenium*, Vol. XVII: 3, Winter.

Grier, B. (1992) 'Pawns, Porters, and Petty Traders: Women in the Transition to Cash Crop Agriculture in Colonial Ghana', *Signs*, Vol. XVII: 304–28.

Harcourt, W. (ed.) (1994) *Feminist Perspectives on Sustainable Development*, London: Zed Books.

Hirschman, M. (1996) 'Women and Development: A Critique', in M. Marchand and J. Parpart (eds), *Feminism, Postmodernism, Development*, New York: Routledge.

Jahan, R. (1995) *The Elusive Agenda*, London: Zed Books.

Jaquette, J. (1982) 'Women and Modernization Theory: A Decade of Feminist Criticism', *World Politics*: 267–84.

—— (1994) *The Women's Movement in Latin America*, Boulder, CO: Westview Press.

Joekes, S. (1987) 'The Position of Women in a Changing World', Chapter 2 in *Women in the World Economy*, Oxford: Oxford University Press.

Kabeer, N. (1994) *Reversed Realities: Gender Hierarchies in Development Thought*, London: Verso.

Kardam, N. (1991) *Bringing Women In*, Boulder, CO: Lynne Rienner Publishers.

Maguire, P. (1984) *Women in Development: An Alternative Analysis*, Amherst, MA: CIE, University of Massachusetts.

Mani, L. (1987) 'The Debate on Sati in Colonial India', *Cultural Critique*, Fall.

Marchand, M. (1996) 'Latin American Women Speak on Development: Are We Listening Yet?', in M. Marchand and J. Parpart (eds), *Feminism, Postmodernism, Development*, London: Routledge.

Mies, M. (1982) *The Lace Makers of Narsapur: Indian Housewives Produce for the World Market*, London: Zed Books.

Mies, M., and V. Shiva (1994) *Ecofeminism*, London: Zed Books.

Mohanty, C., A. Russo and L. Torres (1991) *Third World Women and the Politics of Feminism*, Bloomington, IN: Indiana University Press.

Molyneux, M. (1985) 'Mobilization Without Emancipation? Women's Interests, State and Revolution in Nicaragua', *Feminist Studies*, Vol. XI, No. 2.

Momsen, J.H. and V. Kinnaird (1993) *Different Places, Different Voices*, London: Routledge.

Moser, C.O.N. (1993) *Gender Planning and Development*, New York: Routledge.

Ong, A. (1988) 'Colonialism and Modernity: Feminist Representations of Women in Non-Western Societies', *Inscriptions*, Vols III & IV: 79–93.

Ostergaard, L. (1992) *Gender and Development*, London: Routledge.

Pala, P.O. (1977) 'Definitions of Women and Development: An African Perspective', in I. Tinker and M.B. Bramen, *Women and National Development*, Washington, DC: Overseas Development Council.

Parker, A.R. (1993) *Another Point of View*, New York: UNIFEM.

Radcliffe, S.A. and S. Westwood (1993) *'Viva: Women and Popular Protest in Latin America'*, London: Routledge.

Rathgeben, Eva M. (1990) 'WID, WAD, and GAD: Trends in Research and Practice', *Journal of Developing Areas*, Vol. XXIV, July.

Reid, E. (1995) 'Development as a Moral Concept. Women's Practices as Development', in N. Heyzer (ed.) *A Commitment to the World's Women*, New York: UNIFEM.

Rocheleau, D. (1992) 'Whose Common Future? A Land User Approach to Gendered Rights and Responsibilities in Rural Landscapes', *Gender, Environment and Development. Some Interlinkages*, Stockholm: SIDA.

Rocheleau, D., B. Thomas-Slayter and E. Wangari (1996) *Feminist Political Ecology*, London: Routledge.

Rogers, Barbara (1981) *The Domestication of Women: Discrimination in Developing Societies*, New York: Routledge.

Scott, C.V. (1995) *Gender and Development: Rethinking Modernization and Dependency Theory*, Boulder, CO: Lynne Rienner Publishers.

Sen, G. and C. Grown (1987) *Development, Crises and Alternative Visions: Third World Women's Perspectives*, New York: Monthly Review Press.

Sims Feldstein, H. and J. Jiggins (1994) *Tools for the Field*, W. Hartford: Kumarian Press.

Snyder, M.C. and M. Tadesse (1995) *African Women and Development*, London: Zed Books.

Tiano, S. (1984) 'The Public–Private Dichotomy: Theoretical Perspectives on "Women in Development"', *Social Sciences Journal*, Vol. XXI, No. 4: 11–28.

Tinker, I. (1990) *Persistent Inequalities*, New York: Oxford University Press.

Tinker, I. and J. Jaquette (1987) 'UN Decade for Women: Its Impact and Legacy', *World Development*, Vol. XV, No. 3: 419–27.

Udayagiri, M. (1996) 'Challenging Modernization: Gender and Development,

Postmodern Feminism and Activism', in M. Marchand and J. Parpart (eds) (1996), *Feminism, Postmodernism, Development*, London: Routledge.

Wallace, T. and C. March (eds) (1991) *Changing Perceptions*, Oxford: Oxfam.

Wieringa, S. (1995) *Subversive Women*, London: Zed Books.

Wolf, D. (1996) *Feminist Dilemma in Fieldwork*, Boulder, CO: Westview Press.

Young, K. (1992) *Gender and Development Readings*, Ottawa: Canadian Council for International Cooperation.

A. Survey of Theoretical Debates

Introduces the field of women/gender and development, surveys theoretical debates, evolutionary trends and alternative theoretical perspectives.

2. THE MAKING OF A FIELD: ADVOCATES, PRACTITIONERS AND SCHOLARS

IRENE TINKER

Women in development, like any applied field, not only crosses disciplinary boundaries but establishes goals and priorities consonant with the constraints of those systems within which its practitioners work. Scholars commenting on the field too often confuse this art of the possible with their own more abstract view of the world and so criticize development programmes from an idealistic, if not ideological, perspective rather than from [that of] the realism of the practitioner. This confusion is exacerbated in the case of women in development by the existence of a strong international women's movement which first raised the issue and then continued to monitor its incorporation into development programmes. These advocates have their own agenda: equity between women and men. How this ultimate goal translates into action in particular circumstances is the subject of global debate among the advocates themselves and between the advocates and both practitioners and scholars who share the goals but not the perspectives.

ADVOCATES

The impetus for integrating women into development programmes arose out of two very different conglomerations of women, the UN Commission on the Status of Women[1] and the US women's movement. In the early 1970s, neither the staff and members of the women's commission nor the activists involved in the growing number of new women's organizations in the United States were particularly interested in economic development; rather, they drew on their suffragist heritage in their concern for equality before the law and greater access of women to education. In addition, the US women were increasingly demanding the right to equal employment, which they saw as basic to equal status in a society that measures achievement by income or profession. The objective of both groups of women was to influence governmental policies concerning women.

Women-in-development advocates emerged from these two arenas quite separately and, conditioned by the different environments in which they operated, brought differing interests and priorities to the field. However, it was the conflation of these two groups during the UN Decade for Women that produced the remarkable expansion of the field.

ORIGINS OF WOMEN IN DEVELOPMENT

Development was the more recent issue within the UN system, which had begun to shift toward this emphasis as the number of newly independent countries became the majority of UN member nations during the 1960s. The First Development Decade 1961–70 declaration did not mention women specifically, but in 1962 the General Assembly instructed the women's commission to prepare a report on the role of women in the social and economic development plans of member governments. At that time most governments and non-governmental organizations (NGOs) consulted assumed that economic and social development would bring about any desired changes for women, according to Margaret Bruce, who for many years served as head of the secretariat for the women's commission.

In 1970 the General Assembly included in the International Development Strategy for the Second Development Decade a phrase— later widely copied— which stated the importance of encouraging 'full integration of women in the total development effort'. In 1974 the SID/WID group produced a bibliography, a mere five pages long, and in the process 'discovered' Ester Boserup's *Woman's Role in Economic Development*.[2] Her book was instantly embraced because Boserup's theory legitimized efforts to influence development policy with a combined argument for justice and efficiency. This utilization of scholarly materials to bolster policy arguments was characteristic of the WID effort during its first decade as women advocates sought to influence and work within the development community at both national and international levels.

In the fall of 1973 the Department of State held a briefing on foreign affairs, including the proposed International Women's Conference. During an unprecedented early morning hearing, State Department officials listened to women's organizations present their ideas about the issues of the conference. The testimony of SID/WID was so persuasive that two State Department staff members, Clara Beyer and Mildred Marcy, determined to promote an amendment to the US Foreign

Assistance Act of 1973, then on the floor of the Senate. This amendment required that the US Agency for International Development administer its programmes 'so as to give particular attention to those programs, projects, and activities which tend to integrate women into the national economies of foreign countries, thus improving their status and assisting the total development effort'. This amendment became known as the Percy Amendment after Senator Charles Percy.

THREE WORLD CONFERENCES ON WOMEN

Once the concept of women in development was articulated in economic as opposed to equality terms, it was swiftly incorporated into documents of the General Assembly and the various UN specialized agencies even before the World Conference for the International Women's Year, held in Mexico City in July 1975. Unlike many other issues raised in Mexico and repeated at the two other world conferences that punctuated the UN Decade for Women 1976–85—the explosive Mid-Decade Conference in Copenhagen in 1980 and the colossal Nairobi Conference in 1985—women in development was a popular concept to governments as well as women.[3]

The three official United Nations conferences were extremely important symbolically since such international meetings legitimized women's concerns in the eyes of national leaders and required them to address and then vote on statements that clearly deplored the devaluation of women's productive and reproductive roles and recorded women's continued inequality and growing poverty in most countries of the world.

The necessary documentation for each conference required member governments to submit sex disaggregated data on a multitude of basic indicators, which forced national planners to confront—often for the first time—the implications of their own development policies as they were differentially affecting women. These data have also provided researchers with a surfeit of macro-information useful to test against independent surveys and studies on particular issues such as women's health, education and employment in agriculture, industry and the informal sector.

Perhaps the most far-reaching impact of the conferences was the mobilization of women which they engendered. Although the official conferences provided the impetus and incentive to investigate global concerns of women, participation in UN conferences is necessarily limited.

Thus it was not the official conferences that provided a forum for free-flowing debates on all matter of issues relating to women. Rather it was the parallel non-governmental meetings, open to anyone for a modest registration fee, that engaged women's hearts and minds and provided a venue for global interchange. Part fair, part revival meeting, part open university, these meetings were a market-place for ideas and handicrafts, a showcase for songs and movies and debates, a gigantic international party where women from every country in the world could meet women with similar interests to form friendships, networks and organizations. Attendees went from 6000 in Mexico to 14,000 in Nairobi, in addition to the 3000 women and men accredited to each of the official conferences.

By 1985 women in development had become synonymous with the processes of change that were affecting women in the developing countries. Instead of being seen as a programmatic concept utilized by development agencies to include women in their activities, its meaning had been enlarged to encompass the much broader goals of the advocates.

MEANINGS OF WOMEN IN DEVELOPMENT

From this brief history, it becomes clear that there are many strands of women's rights bound up in the term *women in development*. The new concept of ensuring women a fair stake in *economic development* carried with it the earlier ideas of legal *equality, education, employment* and *empowerment*. During the UN Decade for Women, various of these goals predominated at different times; policies and programmes were not always clear as to the intended objectives when working with women.

Equality before the law, as the focus of much of the effort of the UN Commission on the Status of Women, resulted in the passage in 1951 by the General Assembly of the Convention on the Political Rights of Women. In subsequent years the scope of such conventions increased greatly until, in 1979, the General Assembly adopted the Convention on the Elimination of All Forms of Discrimination Against Women.

Education was understood by women both in the UN Women's Commission and in the US women's movement to be the prerequisite for improvement in women's status. At the United Nations the commission has repeatedly urged governments to increase the access of girls and women to formal education.

Employment of women professionals in the United States and in development agencies is advocated both as a right in itself and as a more effective way of ensuring that development programmes both reach and involve women.

Empowerment is a relatively new term, but the relationship between organization and influence has long been understood. Many international women's organizations were formed during the suffragist period; after World War II they rapidly expanded their membership to the newly independent countries. As NGOs in consultative status to the Economic and Social Council of the United Nations, they worked closely with the Women's Commission and lobbied their own governments to support the International Women's Year. As development issues took on added importance, some of these organizations began to work with grassroots women's groups, funnelling information and funds to them. In contrast, most of the women's organizations actively lobbying the US government were newly formed groups representing the new wave of the women's movement. Consciousness-raising was a key element in this feminist organizing approach; when a few of these organizations turned to development work, they drew on this model for training women to recognize and change cultural stereotypes that limited women's leadership roles. But outright efforts at changing attitudes could not be accomplished within the confines of most international development agencies, since they maintained that foreigners had no business tampering with culture. Thus there arose a distinction between global feminism and women in development.

Economic development was the original primary focus of WID. In both the United Nations and the US Congress, the motivation to integrate women into development programming arose from the gender bias that had characterized previous attempts at economic development and so had ignored or undercut women's economic activities. The growing number of women who headed households were particularly disadvantaged, a trend encapsulated in the phrase 'the feminization of poverty'. National planners may have seen women as an unused labour force, but the thrust of the WID argument was that women were overworked and underproductive in their economic activities. Before being available for alternative work, women needed to be relieved of much of the drudgery characterizing their daily struggle to supply basic necessities to their families.

The documentation and valuation of women's work remained the dominant concern throughout the Decade for Women not only for the advocates but for practitioners and scholars as well.

PRACTITIONERS

Practitioners is the term used to describe those women and men working inside development agencies (or on contract to them) who must, by definition, be constrained by the policies and bureaucratic behaviour of those organizations. Failure to distinguish such constraints from the ambitious policy goals of advocates has led to unrealistic expectations of WID programming and consequent disappointment. For practitioners, the central question was *how* to fulfil the mandate to 'integrate women into the national economies of foreign countries'. The two major approaches used by development agencies in their programming for women since the mid-1970s were *welfare* and *efficiency*. Each approach emphasized only one part of a woman's life: as mother or as worker. Current debates revolve around ways to support women in their dual roles.

PROGRAMMING FOR WOMEN'S WELFARE

Early development programming had ignored women as economic actors and dealt with women only in their reproductive role, and then only as mothers, not as women. Health programmes, although called Maternal Child Health (MCH), in reality were child focused; no consideration was given to the fact that a healthy mother is the most important indicator for having a healthy child. Population programmes discussed women as 'targets' of family planning and were surprised that many women did not choose to become 'acceptors' of contraceptives. As the economic value of children to subsistence families was recognized, many population proponents began to support programming to reduce women's drudgery and increase their income.

The welfare ethic provides an easy approach for development agencies; it garners support at home, as it continues to do with pictures of famine in Africa; it takes less effort to give something away, such as food, than to organize local groups to earn it; and it does not threaten the status quo.

To the WID advocate, such programmes simply reinforce the stereotypes of weak and dependent women and their children. In contrast, WID proponents support income activities to help poor women since

Table 2.1: *Viewpoints of Women-in-Development Proponents: Issues and Responses*

	Proponents		
Issues	**Advocates**	**Practitioners**	**Scholars**
Economic development	Adverse impact Integrate women	Efficiency	Count women's economic activities Class/gender
Equality	Legal rights	Income as liberating	Patriarchy major constraint
Empowerment	Form women's organizations	Women-only projects	Global feminism Distinct values
Education	Access to professional schools	Non-formal education	Scientific and technical Revise content for sex bias
Employment	Affirmative action Basis for status	Micro-enterprise	Sexual division of labour
Welfare	Seen as dependency creating	Participation in health, population and housing programmes	Dual roles Female sphere
Efficiency	Integration	Sectoral programmes	Not feminist

they consider economic activity as the key to improving women's status. They are not alone: many NGOs that solicit contributions on a welfare basis—because that is what moves the public—have nonetheless instituted multifaceted community development programmes often featuring income activities for women.

The major problem with the welfare approach is not these frankly charitable programmes but the tendency of the welfare attitude to 'misbehave' by permeating and eventually dominating programmes theoretically designed to generate income for poor women (Buvinic, 1986).[4] Three programmatic characteristics of these poverty-alleviation programmes predict this outcome. The first characteristic is the setting up of women-only programmes through intermediary organizations whose primary expertise is running welfare projects for women. Second, assumptions are made by these organizations about group membership and cooperation; these tend to exclude the poorest women, who were meant to be the beneficiaries of these programmes. Finally, a major drawback of early poverty-oriented women-focused programmes was that the organizations chosen to implement them were themselves outside the mainstream of development programming.

EFFICIENCY AS THE BASIS FOR WID PROGRAMMING

The original concept of WID was based on the adverse impact of inappropriate economic development programmes that undercut women's economic activities by treating them only as mothers. The solution to this inequity was to design programmes so that women were integrated into them; the result would be more successful programming for the poor. Thus efficiency became the primary argument used by practitioners as they tried to convince the development community that development projects would be more likely to attain their goals if women were an integral part of both design and implementation.

SCHOLARS

Scholars of women in development are a much more diverse group than either the advocates or the practitioners. Constrained neither by the existing governmental systems nor by agency bureaucracies, they are free to utilize ideologies or images of the future to test and judge contemporary issues. All are grounded in feminism; those writing within the two major economic persuasions of liberal and Marxist economics have provided valuable critiques of these theories.

Feminist scholars are clearly grounded in the current wave of the women's movement that has as its uniting principle its attack on the inequities in a world run by men for men.

Two sets of basic issues have dominated the field, one revolving around the counting and valuing of women's work, the other around the efforts of adapting or changing development theories to accommodate feminist thought.

DOCUMENTING WOMEN'S WORK

Women in development advocates, echoing the US feminists' emphasis on economic independence for women as the key to freeing women from male dominance, had argued that development was having a negative impact on women's traditional economic activities. This position set off a search of the scholarly literature for documentation of women's work that could be utilized in the writing of policy papers.

As WID practitioners began to design projects for women, their agencies became not only important consumers of data about women but funders of research as well.

ADAPTING DEVELOPMENT THEORY

Scholarly critiques of the development community in general and of women in development in particular have come primarily from three sources: Marxist feminists, women in the developing countries, and scholars identifying with the female-sphere approach.

Women as a category has been challenged by Marxist feminists, who argue that biological sex is turned into gender relationships between men and women through cultural, social, economic and political forces that vary by class; following the logic of class conflict, women across classes have no common interests. Feminists have pointed out that women of all classes, and in all societies including socialist nations, are disadvantaged; for them, patriarchy is the source of subordination. Both Marxist and mainstream feminists would alter the structures of oppression toward equality, but the female-sphere theorists would celebrate difference.

Two different perspectives, both emanating from the female-sphere approach, have questioned the pursuit of equality of work as the basis for an egalitarian society. The first is based on the tradition of women's autonomy within the private world, leaving the public world to men. The second perspective questioning male values comes from scholars such as Elise Boulding who argue that as a result of centuries of autonomy, women have developed a female culture geared to nurturing and survival.

Influenced by these arguments and perturbed by evidence that development projects supplying more resources may free women from patriarchal control but not from poverty or child care, more and more feminists are searching for alternative visions.

Macroeconomic policies and women has become a critical topic of research. The debt crisis has made obvious the connection between global trends and women's poverty even when exact causality is difficult to establish. DAWN (Development Alternatives with Women for a New Era) chronicles the systemic crises that threaten both environment and economic activity—and hence women—at the local level but which are caused by policies that encourage exploitation of land and natural resources, open global capital markets and militarism.

The three women's conferences for the Decade for Women introduced large numbers of women to the formal UN process. Even more, these conferences fostered the internationalization of the women's movement; out of Nairobi emerged a variety of global networks based on Third World women to complement and balance the earlier American and European organizing efforts. There is widespread agreement among them that only through connecting women's views of human priorities to national and global issues can women gain access to meaningful resources. This move to consider the impact of macropolicies on women at the microlevel requires that women's groups bring this perspective into national politics, where little support now exists.

CONCLUSION

This series of commentaries on critical issues of women in development is meant to illustrate two trends. First, there is a growing similarity of ideas being proposed by women coming from various perspectives. Women's roles are multifaceted, women's identities are multilinked. There is strength in gender diversity; there is also strength in women's shared culture and values.

The second trend is toward greater awareness of political power and of the need to assess political institutions through a gender-sensitive lens. If two decades ago the emphasis was on economics as a path for women to attain greater equity, today the emphasis is on politics: local, national and global.

The Fourth UN World Conference on Women, held in Beijing in September 1995, advanced this political agenda by demanding that women's rights be recognized as human rights. Challenging the separation of family/traditional/customary law and civil/public law that has privileged male control of households, women demanded the same punishment for crimes of battering or murder within the family as outside. Control over their own fertility and rights to land and housing also flow from the recognition of women as equal citizens under law. This declaration of women's rights was supported by thousands of women's organizations around the world and was articulated at the parallel NGO Forum by many of the 23,000 women attending. Once again, the international networking among participants themselves and with the 4500 delegates to the official conference strengthened both scholarship and action as women move with greater equality into the twenty-first century.

3. ACCUMULATION, REPRODUCTION AND WOMEN'S ROLE IN ECONOMIC DEVELOPMENT: BOSERUP REVISITED

LOURDES BENERÍA AND GITA SEN

More than a decade has passed since Ester Boserup's *Woman's Role in Economic Development* was published.[1] Probably no single work on the subject of women and development has been quoted as often.

In the literature on development the specific role of women had been largely ignored, particularly the question of how development affects women's subordinate position in most societies. Boserup pointed out a variety of subjects that are systematically related to the role of women in the economy.

First, she emphasized gender as a basic factor in the division of labour, prevalent across countries and regions: 'Even at the most primitive stages of family autarky there is some division of labor within the family, the main criteria for the division being those of age and sex ... Both in primitive and in more developed communities, the traditional division of labor within the family is usually considered 'natural' in the sense of being obviously and originally imposed by the sex difference itself.'[2] Despite the existence of stereotyped sex roles and the universality of women's concentration in domestic work, Boserup pointed out significant differences in women's work across countries and regions. She criticized the 'dubious generalization' that attributes the provision of food to men in most communities; women too have been food providers in many areas of the world. She emphasized the fundamental role women played in African agriculture in contrast to their lesser role in Asian countries and in Latin America as well. While there are many similarities in women's work in the industrialized urban sector, rural work exhibits diverse patterns associated with the particular characteristics of each area.

Second, Boserup provided some explanations for and analysed a variety of factors behind these differences. One of the most frequently quoted parts of her analysis is her comparison between the 'female' and 'male' systems of farming, which correspond to the African system of shifting agriculture and the Asian system of plow cultivation. In Africa, low population density, easy access to land and less class differentiation than is found in Asian societies resulted in a division of labour where men cleared the land for cultivation and women actually cultivated the subsistence crops. In Asia—a region characterized by high population density—a ready supply of landless labourers available for hire and the 'technical nature of farming operations under plough cultivation' discouraged women's involvement in agricultural tasks and encouraged segregation of the sexes, including the seclusion of women in some areas.[3]

Boserup's analysis pointed to the correlations between women's work and factors such as population density and landholding. Although she was not always explicit about precise connections, she did suggest the existence of a relationship between these factors and different forms of women's subordination. For example, she argued that polygamy made it possible for a man to control more land and labour, because each wife was assigned a plot of land to cultivate. Her analysis pointed to an economic basis for polygamy and the bride price. Though it did not explain polygamous arrangements in which wives seem to represent a cost rather than an economic resource for the husband, it created a challenge for others to do so.

Third, Boserup's book began to delineate the negative effects that colonialism and the penetration of capitalism into subsistence economies have often had on women. She pointed out that European colonial rule, rather than being a 'liberalizing' factor for African women, contributed to their loss of status. Women often lost their right to land as a result of 'land reforms introduced by European administrators'.[4] These reforms were based on the European belief that cultivation was properly men's work. She argued that the introduction of modern technology and cash crops benefited men rather than women by creating a productivity gap between them; women were relegated to the subsistence sector of food production using traditional methods of cultivation.

Fourth, Boserup, among others, emphasized that 'subsistence activities usually omitted in the statistics of production and income are largely women's work'.[5] Although there is a tendency for official statistics to under-report all subsistence activities, whether carried out by men or women, some of these activities tend to be specific to women, particularly domestic work and participation in agriculture as 'unpaid family labor'.[6] In addition, the conventional theoretical concepts that underlie statistical categories are ideologically biased toward an undervaluation of women's work.[7] Boserup, therefore, raised an issue that is essential to a proper understanding of women's participation in economic life.

Finally, Boserup's comparative analysis projected the different sexual divisions of labour encountered in farming systems onto patterns of women's participation in non-agricultural activities. For example, she called attention to the influence of farming systems on migration patterns and on the participation of men and women in urban labour markets. African women's involvement in food cultivation generated a pattern of predominantly male migration, leaving women and children in the village. In contrast, the Latin American pattern in which women participated less in farming involved a high degree of female migration, due also to the employment opportunities for young women in urban centres. Boserup's scholarship inspired a great deal of the empirical and theoretical work that followed.

THEORETICAL FRAMEWORK

One of the most common criticisms of Boserup's book is that it is repetitive. This problem becomes acute because the book fails to go beyond the data that it presents; Boserup rarely attempts to derive any overall theoretical or conceptual structure from her empirical data. These data are rich in insights about the patterns and variations in women's work across Africa and Asia, but most of her analysis is purely descriptive. Ad hoc introductions of values and ideology often take the place of explanations. In discussing the growing dominance of men over women in agriculture during Africa's colonial period, for example, Boserup contends that gender-based prejudice on the part of the colonialists caused them to teach advanced agricultural methods only to men.

When Boserup does use theoretical concepts, they tend to fall within the framework of neoclassical economics. In her discussion of the labour market and wage differentials between women and men, she suggests that the individual preference of employers and workers determines the nature of women's work, and hence their earnings. Boserup analyses demand in the labour market, stating that employers often prefer male over female labour; she analyses supply by stating that women prefer to work in home industries rather than in large enterprises.[8]

This emphasis on preferences constitutes a limited view. There are many cases in which employers prefer women over men: examples include tea plantations, textile-manufacturing firms, and labour-intensive industries operating in many areas of the Third World.[9] Many of these are in fact large enterprises. Therefore preference is not the adequate explanatory variable.

Boserup does go beyond a narrow focus on individual preference in her examination of hiring practices and wage formation in the export sector [but] her underlying neoclassical categories do not allow her to integrate her rich empirical observations within a coherent analytical framework. Similar limitations in her analysis result from her assumption of a unique development model.

MODEL OF DEVELOPMENT: MODERNIZATION VERSUS ACCUMULATION[10]

Boserup's general argument is that women workers are marginalized in the process of economic development because their economic gains as wage workers, farmers and traders are slight compared to those of male workers. Hence, policy efforts should be directed to redress this problem, so that women share more fully in the fruits of modernization. Underlying this is the view that modernization is both beneficial and inevitable in the specific form it has taken in most Third World countries—a notion that has been extensively criticized by radical social scientists over the last two decades.[11] The modernization approach has two negative effects on Boserup's analysis. First, she tends to ignore processes of capital accumulation set in motion during the colonial period, and the effects of such processes on technical change and women's work. Second, she does not systematically analyse the different effects of capital accumulation on women of different classes.

Of the many variants of modernization theory, Boserup's work is one based on technological determinism that uses cultural values as filler for conceptual holes in the analysis. [This] is clearest in her discussion of indigenous farming systems. Though Boserup argues that there is a negative correlation between the use of the plow and the extent of field-work done by women, the basis of this correlation is never clarified. Nor does she discuss the possibility that there may be deeper causal reasons for the empirically observed correlation. Instead, one is left to presume that technical variation exercises some mysterious, if powerful, impact on the division of labour by sex. This sort of unexplained correlation is rife in modernization theory. The processes of modernization—in this case, the effect of plow cultivation on women's work—are rarely explained. Rather, the more modern is usually held up as the model against which the more backward is judged. To Boserup's credit, she does not make this last step. Instead, she sees modernization operating concurrently with women's loss of economic independence.

However, this insight is not located in any coherent theory, but only in a sharp empirical intuition. Boserup holds cultural prejudices to blame for women's marginalization; overall the process of modernization is viewed as beneficial. Indeed, Boserup regards modernizing technical changes, such as the shift from hoe to plow cultivation, as the inevitable products of population growth.[12] But nowhere does she confront the causes of growing population density, particularly the Malthusian belief that population growth is somehow inherent in nature.

Viewing the Third World from this perspective involves ignoring effects on population growth and density of the alienation of land and its private appropriation during the colonial period. The direct effects were felt most sharply in regions such as Southern Africa where most of the land (inevitably, the best) was taken over by settlers, squeezing the indigenous population into shrinking reserves, and leaving high person-to-land ratios.[13] The indirect effects have been felt in most regions where the privatization of land, labour and subsistence have generated incentives for higher fertility among peasants.[14]

Such changes in the social organization of production and in the appropriation of the means of production also have powerful effects on the division of labour by sex and age. What appears to Boserup to be a technically determined correlation between plow cultivation and women's lower participation in fieldwork has its roots in the social relations of production and reproduction. In fact, the further one reads in Boserup's book, the more it appears that the crucial distinguishing feature between African and Asian farming is not, as she suggests, the tools used—hoe versus plow—but the forms of appropriation of land, of surplus and of women's reproductive capacity. The sexual division of labour is related to these factors.

Similarly, while Boserup discusses the economic roots of polygamy, she fails to examine the process of change in this system as the possibilities of capital accumulation multiply. In some pre-colonial African communities, a large number of wives gave a man status and possibly a greater voice in the village councils. But women had at least partial control over the product of their labour. With the coming of long-distance trade and private appropriation of land, women's labour could be used to produce a surplus, which formed a basis for accumulation of land and wealth.[15] In turn, class differentiation began to intensify, women came to have less and less control over the product of their labour, and additional wives became, in fact, simply additional field-workers who facilitated the accumulation of use-rights to more land. These changes probably indicated a major alteration in gender relations to the detriment of women. By failing to examine such matters, Boserup's argument remains divorced from any coherent analysis of the interconnections between the social process of accumulation, class formation and changes in gender relations.

Another example of the work's weak conceptual basis is Boserup's discussion of women's declining status under colonial rule. The biases of modernization theory are evident in her presumption that the introduction of commercial agriculture was generally beneficial, except for the consequent decline in women's status. This presumption ignores entirely the long history of resistance to forced cultivation of crops such as cotton and coffee in Africa and other Third World regions.[16] Cultivation involving the increased use of land and labour in the production of commercial crops was a major mechanism of the transformation of land relations and class differentiation, and it opened possibilities for exploitation by commercial capital.

Teaching the women better techniques in subsistence cropping, as Boserup suggests, would have been like treating cancer with a bandaid. That such teaching did not take place could hardly be the cause of women's worsening situation under conditions of rapid land alienation and class differentiation. Nor is Boserup correct in implying that all men benefited from commercial production. The possibilities of accumulation inherent in commercial farming undoubtedly enabled some men to raise themselves up the indigenous class hierarchy, but most men did not experience such mobility. The narrow truth of Boserup's thesis is that while some men could be integrated into the ruling class, almost no women could be, at least on their own. The concentration of women in subsistence farming undeniably caused this unevenness. That commercial cropping came to dominate over subsistence cropping was a product not of European patriarchal culture but of the process of capital accumulation. Thus, women's loss of status results from the interweaving of class relations and gender relations.

The single most powerful tendency of capitalist accumulation is to separate direct producers from the means of production and to make their conditions of survival more insecure and contingent. This tendency manifests itself in new forms of class stratification in rural areas—between rich peasants and capitalist farmers, on the one hand, and poor peasants and landless labourers on the other. Capitalist accumulation can have a variety of effects on women's work depending on the specific form accumulation takes in a particular region.

In some areas, the sexual division of labour may change and women's workload may be intensified. In other areas, women may lose effective control over productive resources and over the labour process and its product. A third possible effect of capital accumulation involves a new division of labour in which young women become migrant wage earners. The increasing internationalization of capital offers vivid examples of woman's place in the capitalist labour process. In some areas, capital accumulation may weaken traditional forms of patriarchal control over women and introduce new forms. Finally, class differentiation accompanying the capitalist transformation of a region provides a new basis for differentiation between women.

Modernization is not a neutral process, but one that obeys the dictates of capitalist accumulation and profit making. Contrary to Boserup's implications, the problem for women is not only the lack of participation in this process as equal partners with men; it is a system that generates and intensifies inequalities, making use of existing gender hierarchies to place women in subordinate positions at each different level of interaction between class and gender. This is not to deny the possibility that capitalist development might break down certain social rigidities oppressive to women. But these liberating tendencies are accompanied by new forms of subordination.

ANALYSIS OF SUBORDINATION: THE REPRODUCTIVE SPHERE

One of the most pervasive themes of the present feminist movement is the emphasis placed on the role of reproduction as a determinant of women's work, the sexual division of labour, and the subordinate/dominant relationships between women and men.[17] This emphasis is lacking in Boserup's book; her analysis does not contain a feminist perspective that speaks directly to the problem of women's subordination. To be sure, the book is about different forms subordination can take, but it fails to elucidate the crucial role of the household as the focal point of reproduction, nor does it explain the social relations among household members in the making of 'the woman problem' and in determining women's role in economic development.

Boserup's analysis of polygamy in Africa offers an illustration. Her analysis, as mentioned earlier, is grounded in economic factors, namely, the greater access to land and labour resources provided by each wife. Boserup's insight, however, is not accompanied by an analysis of the significance of this type of household arrangement for the dynamics of male domination, nor does it explain why polygamy can also be found in Middle Eastern countries where women are secluded and do not represent an addition to land and labour resources.

DOMESTIC WORK

Feminist attempts to understand the roots of women's oppression have resulted in a growing body of literature on domestic labour and household production, as well as on the patriarchal structure that controls them. The bulk of domestic work consists of the production of use values through the combination of commodities bought in the market and domestic labour time. The goods and services produced contribute to the reproduction of the labour force and to its daily maintenance. Domestic work performs a crucial role for the functioning of the economic system. It is linked with the market both by way of what it purchases and by what it provides. In the average household, this work is done by women and is unpaid. Women's unique responsibility for this work, their resulting weakness in the labour market and their dependency on the male wage both underlie and are products of asymmetric gender relations.

Women perform the great bulk of reproductive tasks. To the extent that they are also engaged in productive activities outside of the household, they are often burdened with the problems of a 'double day'. Yet nowhere does Boserup indicate how central women's primary involvement in household activities is to an understanding of their subordination and of their role in the economy.

REPRODUCTION AND PRODUCTION

The emphasis on reproduction and on analysis of the household sphere indicates that the traditional focus placed upon commodity production is insufficient to understand women's work and its roots in patriarchal relations. In order to understand fully the nature of sex discrimination, women's wages, women's participation in the development process and implications for political action, analysts must examine the two areas of production and reproduction as well as the interaction between them.

Within the Marxist tradition, Engels's view of the origins of women's subordination [does link] the productive sphere—the introduction of private property in the means of production and the need to pass it on from one generation to the next—with reproduction, that is, with the need to identify paternity of heirs through the institution of the family and the control of women's sexuality and reproductive activities.[18] The Engels thesis can be projected on to situations, such as those prevalent in industrialized societies, where large segments of the population do not own the means of production, but where there is still a hierarchy and class differences within the propertyless classes. It can be argued that to the extent reproduction implies the private transmission of access to resources—education, for example—the need to identify the individual beneficiaries of this transmission remains.[19]

Engels himself did not extend the analysis in that direction. For him, as for Marx, the production of the means of subsistence and the reproduction of human beings are the two fundamental levels of human activity. However, both assumed that the elimination of private property and women's participation in commodity production, made possible by industrialization, would set the preconditions for their emancipation. Thus the initial connection between production and reproduction found in Engels became blurred with the assumption that transformation of productive structures would automatically erase women's oppression. Traditional Marxist thinking and traditional leftist and liberal politics have followed a similar pattern. The new emphasis on reproduction is the result of the questions posed by feminists; it can be viewed as an elaboration of the simplifications inherent in Engels's initial formulation.

A variety of recent studies on women in Third World countries has focused on the interaction between production and reproduction to analyse women's work. Maria Mies's study of Indian women lace makers in Narsapur, Andhra Pradesh, for example, shows how the seclusion of women has conditioned their participation in nonhousehold production.[20] Mies argues that this highly exploitative system has in fact led to greater class differentiation within local communities as well as greater polarization between the sexes. The system is made possible by the ideology of seclusion that rigidly confines women to the home, eliminates their opportunities for outside work and makes them willing to accept extremely low wages. A strict focus on the productive aspects of lace making—this is Boserup's approach—to the exclusion of reproductive aspects, such as seclusion, presents only a partial picture of the nature of women's exploitation.

POPULATION CONTROL AND BIRTH CONTROL

Much of the literature on Third World countries has focused on the question of population control without directly addressing the problem of reproductive freedom for women or the possible contradictions between class and gender.[21] A feminist perspective can modify the analysis of population growth and control in the Third World.

The concept of reproductive freedom includes the right to bear or not to bear children and, by implication, the right to space childbearing. To the extent that children are potential labourers, or inheritors for the propertied class, decisions about childbearing affect not only the woman but her entire household. For example, in very poor peasant households that possess little land and are squeezed by usury and rent payments, the labour of children both on and off the peasant farm may be crucial to the ongoing ability of the household to subsist and maintain land. Pronatalist tendencies in rural areas may have a clear economic basis. Marxist writers have shown the conflict between the economic rationality of the individual household and social programmes of family planning and population control.[22]

Such programmes clearly cannot be a panacea for the basic problems of extreme poverty and inequality in landholding; the contradictions of class and capital accumulation in the countryside can be resolved only through systemic social change.

CONCLUSION

It is important to delineate the policy implications from this analysis. A long-term goal is the elimination of class and sex hierarchies through a radical transformation of society. We can no longer ignore what goes on within households. The feminist analysis of the Third World in the past decade has lent support and clarity to this vision.

4. GENDER AND DEVELOPMENT
KATE YOUNG

I want to point to some of the main ways in which a gender and development (GAD) approach differs from that of women and development (WAD). It must, however, be borne in mind that I will inevitably make the distinction between the two approaches clearer than it is in reality. In many areas there is considerable overlap between the two. Nonetheless it is worthwhile from the point of view of clarifying our understanding of the issues to make such an attempt. I will deal with six main points: the main object of the approach, the women's consciousness of discrimination/subordination, its holistic approach to social organization, the object of development, overall strategic approach and specific strategies.

(1) The focus in gender and development is not on women *per se* but on gender relations, i.e. the relations between women and men in a variety of settings. Many of these are what sociologists call ascribed relations, that is relations a person is involved in on the basis of their position in a network of kinship and affinity (i.e. relations by birth and through marriage); many of them are also achieved relations, that is relations established on the basis of a person's involvement in the economic, social or political life of her country. Both ascribed and achieved relations interlock with a matrix of other relations based on factors such as class, race, ethnicity, religion etc.

(2) The approach views women as active agents and not passive recipients of 'development' but does not assume that women have perfect knowledge or understanding of their social situation. That is to say it assumes that while women as individuals may well be aware of their subordinate position, this does not necessarily lead to an understanding of the structural roots of discrimination and subordination. As a corollary of this, the approach does not assume that men in their turn are aware of the social bases of male dominance, or that all men act actively to promote male dominance.

The GAD approach does not assume that women are in some way unquestionably or unassailably right in all forms of behaviours, in all their aims or objectives. It does not assume that men are invariably wrongheaded or wicked. It does assume that male privilege makes most men unlikely to ally themselves to the cause of women's advancement without powerful persuasion.

(3) The approach starts from a holistic perspective. That is, it looks at the totality of social organization, economic and political life in order to understand the shaping of particular aspects of society. As a result it does not focus merely on the reproductive aspect of social life—i.e. motherhood/childcaring—when trying to understand the particular patterning of women's lives. Nor does it focus solely on production and the distribution of goods and services made or produced in specialized work units like factories or hospitals when attempting to analyse the economic underpinning of social life. Rather it focuses on the 'fit' between family, household or the domestic life and the organization of both political and economic spheres. For example from a gender perspective, the structure of the working day in the sphere of production is only intelligible if the existence of the domestic sphere is taken as a given.

(4) Development is viewed as a complex process involving the social, economic, political and cultural betterment of individuals and of society itself. Betterment in this sense means the ability of the society and its members to meet the physical, emotional and creative needs of the population at a historically acceptable level. In examining the impact of economic development (planned or unplanned) on any particular society or group within a society, proponents of the gender and development approach ask the question: who benefits, who loses, what trade-offs have been made, [and] what is the resultant balance of rights and obligations, power and privilege between men and women, and between given social groups.

(5) The gender and development approach does not consider welfare, anti-poverty or equity approaches as three opposed alternatives. Rather it accepts that the welfare and anti-poverty approaches are often necessary preconditions for equity. The critical consideration then becomes: how to subvert welfare for equity. This of course raises a number of questions as to whether relying on fighting for reforms is sufficient or whether radical social change is imperative. Whichever choice is made necessarily throws up a whole series of other decisions and choices which themselves are necessarily shaped by the particular historical and geo-political situation.

(6) Strategies: WID concentrates on women's access to cash income (usually via the market), either as individuals or members of some

form of collectivity, as the base strategy. GAD is much less optimistic about the role of the market as distributor of benefit, and the
power that stems from having 'cash in hand'. WID puts emphasis
on the need for women to be organized into collective groupings
(cooperatives etc.) particularly for productive purposes so as to
increase their bargaining power in the economic system. For
example, women organized in a group often get better access to
credit since the group provides a better security risk for lenders.
GAD also stresses the need for organization but more in terms of
women's self-organization so as to increase their political power
within the economic system.

Unlike WID, GAD places equal emphasis on the necessary role of the
state in promoting women's emancipation. It points to the dual role of
the state in most developing countries as an employer of labour (often
the biggest) and allocator of social capital to socially necessary ends. It
underlines the duty of the state to provide social capital for the care and
maintenance of the future generation, i.e. the role of social expenditure—education, health, training—in providing the conditions for future
economic growth. In so doing it implicitly rejects the view that producing (physically as well as socially) the future generation is entirely the
concern of individuals, for the view that it is a social matter. Support is
sought at all levels of the state—local, regional, central—rather than
[from] central government alone. This strategy has to confront the fact
that women are politically weak and have little bargaining power at the
national, regional or even local level. [GAD] requires that strategies must
go beyond concerns with economic self-sufficiency to the need for political self-reliance.

   GAD also looks to the role of local communities to provide support for
women and in some ways sees organization of women at this level as the
precursor of organization at higher levels. Since women are frequently
impeded from organizing even at this level because of constraints
located at the level of the family, GAD has to include consideration of the
bases of support for women's emancipation within families and kinship
groups, as well as of resistance to it. In this area contradictions between
the interests of men and women are often not as critical as those
between the generations.

   Given that GAD assumes that political and economic power are closely
enmeshed, the first step in women's advancement is to provide the
conditions for men and women to surmount poverty. But the main
constraint here is that the poor are rarely able to tackle the conditions
which create their poverty in the first place—these are usually well
beyond their reach. As a result the GAD approach would stress attempt-

ing to build into welfare or basic needs programmes an element of consciousness-raising. Welfare in this sense is seen as a means not an end. The consciousness-raising has to encompass not only the nature of the structures creating poverty for some and wealth for others, the mal-distribution of social wealth and capital, the unbalanced distribution of political power, but also the structures of inequality between men and women which weaken both in their common struggle for survival and for betterment. Such work has to include the importance of organizing, of creating alliances and coalitions, of exerting influence, of communica-tion and public education. In other words every attempt has to be made to create the political will in the country which will enable welfare to be subverted for equity and reform for radical restructuring.

NOTE

This is the abridged text of a talk delivered by Kate Young at the Canadian Council for International Cooperation (CCIC) in Ottawa (February 1992), when she was a fellow of the Institute of Development Studies at the University of Sussex. We are reprinting it here with the permission of the author, now Executive Director of WOMANKIND Worldwide, a development agency promot-ing the advancement of women through support for women's groups in a number of developing countries in a variety of ways.

5. WOMEN, THE ENVIRONMENT AND SUSTAINABLE DEVELOPMENT

R. Braidotti, E. Charkiewicz, S. Häusler and S. Wieringa

WOMEN, ENVIRONMENT AND SUSTAINABLE DEVELOPMENT (WED) IN HISTORICAL PERSPECTIVE

In the early 1970s a growing interest in women's relations with the envi-ronment in the countries of the South emerged within the development discourse.

The oil 'crisis', initiated by the oil-producing countries in 1973, as well as the large-scale effects of drought in the Sahel, sharply jolted the North into a realization that natural resources were not infinitely exploitable. Development planners began to give serious attention to the need for more systematic global-energy planning for the future.

It was clear that in the coming decades the majority of the South's peoples would depend for their energy needs on wood fuel and that oil or other energy sources would be simply too costly for them. Women, in their role as users of wood, were to become the target group for a two-fold strategy to grapple with the future trends of diminishing resources of wood energy: (a) reduce wood-fuel consumption by introducing wood-saving stoves; and (b) initiate large-scale afforestation to increase wood supply.

A powerful image emerged of poor people in the South, with too many children, using too much fuel; the poor were seen to have no choice but to destroy their own environment. Whereas this may be true for some areas, it cannot be generalized. As Madhu Sarin, an experienced stove-promoter working in the Himalayas pointed out, deforestation in this area was due much more to commercial tree-felling and the extension of agriculture into forest land than to domestic fuel consumption (Sarin 1991).

By the mid-1970s, due to Boserup's work, an interest in women's role in agriculture as well as in rural development at large had emerged. In light of global economic problems, increasing environmental degradation and the feminization of poverty in the South the debate on the specific effects of these processes on women gained momentum.

At the NGO conference held parallel to the 1972 UN Conference on the Human Environment in Stockholm, the initiatives of local people in India to protect their forests—the now widely-known Chipko Movement—were reported by Sundarlal Bahuguna, the movement's leader. The success of the Chipko women's activities later inspired other local initiatives in the South, and also those wishing to stimulate bottom-up, people-oriented development work.

At the Nairobi Forum 1985, held parallel to the UN Women and Development Conference, women's actions and special role in environmental management were presented in case studies that documented women's involvement in forestry, agriculture, energy and so on, based on the experiences of women living in the South. Women were portrayed as environmental managers whose involvement was crucial to the achievement of sustainable development. These studies were powerful tools to further the WED debate and stimulate international recognition of women's problems in relation to natural resource management.

The Brundtland Report, *Our Common Future*, published in 1987, promoted long-term strategies for achieving sustainable development (defined as development that meets the needs of the present without compromising future generations' ability to meet theirs) and highlighted the importance of environmental issues in the development process. In the years following publication of the Brundtland Report, the WED debate focused on the imperative for women's involvement in strategies and programmes aimed at 'sustainable' development. Gradually, 'women, environment and development' became 'women, environment and sustainable development'.

In the late 1980s national and international events organized on the WED theme gained increased momentum. The images of poor women in the South as victims became transformed into images of strength and resourcefulness. In the wider debate on sustainable development women were increasingly promoted as 'privileged environmental managers' and depicted as possessing specific skills and knowledge in environmental care.

IDEAS OF WOMEN, ENVIRONMENT AND SUSTAINABLE DEVELOPMENT

The WED debate encompasses several main streams of thought. One stream stresses the managerial aspects of minimizing negative effects of the process of economic development by targeting women as recipients of development assistance and simultaneously considering the effects of development on the environment. This approach is propagated by development agencies. Other approaches tend toward anti-development or transformational stances and assert that the model of western development is fundamentally flawed, as its effect on women, the environment and the South's peoples makes evident. This line of thought calls for transformations towards alternative development. Crucial in the different lines of argumentation is the respective conception of the woman/nature relation.

An economistic line of thinking conceptualizes WED from the viewpoint of women's work: the sexual division of labour that has led to women's particular role in managing natural resources. This role is seen as a product of the historical evolution of patriarchy which has assigned men roles in economic production and women the lower-valued roles connected with economic reproduction.

A more 'cultural' stream of thought sees women's position as essentially closer to nature because within the sexual division of labour their work has always entailed a close relationship with nature. Women are depicted as 'naturally' privileged environmental managers who, over generations, have accumulated specific knowledge about natural processes that is different and more appropriate than that of men in general. This approach perceives the woman/nature relation as one of reciprocity, symbiosis, harmony, mutuality and inter-relatedness due to women's close dependence on nature for subsistence needs. Women have successfully used both lines of argument as the basis for political struggles, in accordance with different strategies.

DIFFERENT CONCEPTUALIZATIONS OF WED IN THE LITERATURE

In reconceptualizing women's work, Maria Mies (1986), coming from a Marxist background, developed her argument by defining women's role in child-bearing and -rearing as work, and within a Marxist/feminist perspective this was an important contribution. Furthermore, for Mies, reproduction, that is, providing the basic necessities for family survival, constitutes women's closer relation to nature. Through this double role women's understanding of nature is superior to men's. Women not only work closer to nature, women 'are' nature because they give birth and nurture their children, hence they are doubly exploited within patriarchal society globally.

Shiva (1989) draws on Hindu religion and philosophy which describes the 'feminine principle' (*prakriti*) as the source of all life. She equates the feminine principle with women in real life and constructs the practical relation that women have with nature in Indian rural reality as the embodiment of the feminine principle. This relation needs to be recovered as a base for a sustainable mode of development. In India, according to Shiva, this mode existed before the era of colonialism. Under colonialism, and later under the influence of the development process, a capitalist mode of development and green-revolution technology has penetrated India's rural economies, a process that destroyed the economic base of small-scale local survival agriculture. Shiva condemns the change to large-scale, mechanized and ultimately unsustainable market-oriented agriculture. This process facilitated the marginalization of the majority of the South's small-scale farmers, particularly poor women.

Shiva sees the dominant mode of development as western, patriarchal and based on a reductionist model of science and technology that serves the global market and is effectively destructive for women, nature and all 'others'—non-western peoples. Shiva sets up a model of opposition between the destructive western, white, male, patriarchal development model and the traditional Indian agricultural system that works in harmony with nature. The western model propagates monocultural plantation techniques in both forestry and agriculture in service of the market and capital accumulation. The traditional Indian economic model is described as having preserved a mutual relationship with nature through the cultivation of multicultural plantations meant for local subsistence production, using only what nature produces within the traditional farming system.

In common with Mies, Shiva's thinking stems from a search for an alternative development model. Both conclude that to recover the systems of subsistence agriculture globally is the solution. The western development model's commoditization of nature, as well as women's and non-western people's labour, has resulted in capital accumulation in the affluent 'developed' countries and poverty in the 'developing' countries.

For Mies, northern women's major role lies in denouncing, and abstaining from, unnecessary consumption with the ultimate aim of undermining capitalism. Shiva cites women's prominent role within the Indian Chipko movement as evidence that the life-creating and -preserving 'feminine principle' embodied by these women must be reclaimed as the source for an alternative global development model.

Staying Alive (1989), in which Shiva developed her argument, has been influential in shaping WED, as well as environmental and alternative development thinking, especially in northern NGOs and social movements, and in development agencies. Shiva has been much less influential in her own Indian context. The problem is the essentialism she has constructed in the concrete relation of women with nature in subsistence agriculture as a theoretical category—the feminine principle as the life-giving force. She propagates the idea that only poor, rural women, bearing the brunt of the environmental and developmental crisis in their daily struggle for survival, know, and have known, how to survive since time immemorial and therefore have the solutions to the crisis.

Shiva idealizes Indian subsistence agriculture and recreates a past where people lived in perfect harmony with nature, and women were highly respected in society. But this romantic past may never have existed. Subsistence agriculture in India replaced tribal people's cultures, often by violent means. Indian history shows that the agricultural system was introduced on the sub-continent only with Aryan invasion. In India, there is a large number of tribal peoples outside the caste system who, even today, are not integrated into society. Shiva's model of traditional society fails to account for highly exploitative structures along the axes of race, class and caste within Indian society today; she also ignores patriarchal structures. Instead, she lays blame for the environmental crisis wholly on 'the state' and the global economy. Shiva's total neglect of class in Indian society has brought her much criticism, especially from Indian Marxist scholars.

Both Mies and Shiva propagate a global model of subsistence agriculture. The question is, however, would [this] model alone, even though attractive in certain aspects, be a viable option in the present situation, especially if we think, for example, of the densely populated countries of Europe as well as India?

Yet what Shiva (and many other scholars too) has brought out in her argument is a fundamental questioning of the western model of development as the only possible one. Instead, she outlines the validity of subjugated and marginal people's knowledges in the search for sustainable models for development and environmental protection. She illustrates that such knowledge is sophisticated rather than 'primitive', being based on generations of close observation of natural processes, albeit often relevant only in a specific local setting. She also introduces the question of different values and perceptions: what is real material poverty and what is only culturally perceived as poverty? Are rural people living off local resources 'backward' *vis-à-vis* urban people in the North who are overconsuming global energy and natural resources at unsustainable levels? In this respect she contributes to a challenge of the epistemological assumptions underlying the dominant development model and highlights its violence to people and nature and destructive effects on local cultures and lifestyles.

DEVELOPMENT AGENCIES' CONCEPTUALIZATION OF WED

Mainstream development organizations' line of argumentation on WED is cast within the frame of an improvement of present development practice. Usually the neglect of women and destruction of the environment within the development process are compared. This argument stresses the institutional nature of the problem. If only women and the environment were considered in development practice the environmental crisis could be solved. Consideration of both 'poor Third World women' and the environment is seen as crucial for the attainment of sustainable development. Rarely is a connection made between macro-economic and political processes: overconsumption of natural resources by the few in the North and poverty of the many in the South.

In both the Mies/Shiva and many NGOs' arguments and those propagated by development agencies, women's and environmental interests to a certain extent become identical: the cause of the restoration of the environment becomes the cause of (poor Third World) women. The two lines of argument differ in their proposed solution to environmental degradation: on the one hand that the basic parameters of the development model need to be radically rethought; and on the other that they simply need to be improved.

Recent WED publications depict women as privileged environmental managers because of their intimate knowledge of natural processes due to their closer relationship with nature; women are seen as the answer to the crisis; women have the solutions; they are privileged knowers of natural processes.

This valorization of women's ways of knowing may seem positive to us, but the accuracy of promoting women as exclusive and privileged knowers of natural processes is doubtful. In the rural economies of the

South, men also possess such knowledge, except related more closely to their own traditional areas of work. Within the developmentalist framework women are seen as *the most valuable resource* in achieving sustainable development.

This thinking has prompted development planners seriously to consider women's roles in environmental projects; in virtually all environment-related project documents there is at least rhetoric about women, but the instrumentalization of women for the sustainable use of the environment and environmental recovery needs to be questioned seriously.

Criticism of the WED approach expounded by Shiva (1989) and subscribed to by many NGOs, North and South, comes largely from members of northern women's (and environmental) movements who, for some decades, have grappled with the woman/nature connection in their emancipatory struggles. These critics argue that to equate women with nature has reinforced women's continued subordination to men. While in the South's cultures the male/female relation has traditionally often been seen as complementary, in the North's perspective this relation has been one of superiority/inferiority since the middle ages. Therefore women from the South find identifying with nature less difficult and hence use this type of argument as a basis for their struggles.

From within the development context and in a different vein, Melissa Leach (1991) takes the approach of gender and development (GAD) as a point of departure for her WED argument. She argues that more appropriate development policy-making is needed and sees the woman/nature link in a differentiated way. Leach examines gender relations, not simply women, and how they interact with the responsibilities, rights and activities in natural-resource management and use over time. She analyses a case study from Sierra Leone where the introduction of cocoa and coffee cash-crop production altered the whole pattern of agricultural production. By demonstrating the changes effected on household   rice production, time allocation of different groups, land-use rights and resource-use access on the one hand, and gender relations on the other, she is able to show their interdependent nature. This approach allows for an identification of differences between groups of women as well as men, which a focus on women alone would obscure.

Bina Agarwal (1991) develops an approach to WED that encompasses many elements of the WED debate outlined above in a holistic way. She combines the levels of material reality and ideological constructs of meanings in her analysis of the Indian experience of the environmental crisis, its causes, effects and responses to it. She argues that women are both victims of this crisis in gender-specific ways as well as important actors in resolving it. Agarwal, like Shiva, draws on experience in India, but unlike Shiva she asserts the need to contextualize the fact that poor rural women have emerged as main actors in the environmental movements in India because, due to their marginality, they have had to maintain a reciprocal link with nature. For Agarwal, the woman/nature link has been socially and culturally constructed, not biologically determined (Agarwal, 1989:60).

From this position Agarwal calls for struggles over material as well as symbolic resources. She suggests as a two-pronged strategy the need to grapple with groups who control resources, and ways of thinking about resources, with the help of media, educational, religious and legal institutions. Feminists, she suggests, should challenge and transform notions about gender as well as struggling against the actual sexual division of labour; and environmentalists should challenge and transform the representations of the relationship between nature and people as well as the actual methods of appropriating natural resources for the benefit of the few. She concludes by stressing the need for a transformative rather than a welfarist approach to economic development.

Agarwal's argument is most in line with our own thinking on WED because she contextualizes the material situation of women within the ideological construction of the woman/nature connection, pointing out that in reality this construct caters to vested interests.

From yet another point of departure, the Development with Women for a New Era (DAWN) network presented another southern women's position. Starting from an analysis of women's experiences of environmental degradation in different regions in the South, Wiltshire (1992) contests the northern developmentalist myth that the poor are destroying their environment, that population growth is responsible for environmental degradation, and that local people in the South need to be taught by northern 'experts' how to recover their environment. Wiltshire refrains from romanticizing the woman/nature connection, but a certain essentialism can be read into earlier DAWN statements on the 'poor Third World woman' as the intersection of all forms of domination—based on sex, nationality, race, class and caste—resulting in her privileged perspective in defining parameters for an alternative development paradigm.

The thrust of Wiltshire's argument is, however, an attack on the international economic order and affluent lifestyles in the North, and of élites in the South. She stresses the imperative for democratic, decentralized and people-centred approaches to natural-resource use.

6. WOMEN IN NATURE
Vandana Shiva

NATURE AS THE FEMININE PRINCIPLE

Women in India are an intimate part of nature, both in imagination and in practice. At one level nature is symbolized as the embodiment of the feminine principle and at another she is nurtured by the feminine to produce life and provide sustenance.

From the point of view of Indian cosmology, in both the exoteric and esoteric traditions, the world is produced and renewed by the dialectical play of creation and destruction, cohesion and disintegration. The tension between the opposites from which motion and movement arises is depicted as the first appearance of dynamic energy (Shakti). All existence arises from this primordial energy which is the substance of everything, pervading everything. The manifestation of this power, this energy, is called nature (Prakriti).[1] Nature, both animate and inanimate, is thus an expression of Shakti, the feminine and creative principle of the cosmos; in conjunction with the masculine principle (Purusha), Prakriti creates the world.

NATURE AND WOMEN AS PRODUCERS OF LIFE

With the violation of nature is linked the violation and marginalization of women, especially in the Third World. Women produce and reproduce life not merely biologically, but also through their social role in providing sustenance. All ecological societies of forest-dwellers and peasants, whose life is organized on the principle of sustainability and the reproduction of life in all its richness, also embody the feminine principle. Historically, however, when such societies have been colonized and broken up the men have usually started to participate in life-destroying activities or have had to migrate; the women, meanwhile, usually continue to be linked to life and nature through their role as providers of sustenance, food and water. The privileged access of women to the sustaining principle thus has a historical and cultural, and not merely biological, basis. The principle of creating and conserving life is lost to the ecologically alienated, consumerist élite women of the Third World and the over-consuming West, just as much as it is conserved in the lifestyle of the male and female forest-dwellers and peasants in small pockets of the Third World.

Maria Mies has called women's work in producing sustenance the *production of life* and views it as a truly productive relationship to nature, because 'women not only collected and consumed what grew in nature but they *made things grow*'.[2] This organic process of growth in which women and nature work in partnership with each other has created a special relationship of women with nature, which, following Mies, can be summarized as follows:

(a) Their interaction with nature, with their own nature as well as the external environment, was a reciprocal process. They conceived of their own bodies as being productive in the same way as they conceived of external nature being so.

(b) Although they appropriate nature, their appropriation does not constitute a relationship of dominance or a property relation. Women are not owners of their own bodies or of the earth, but they cooperate with their bodies and with the earth in order 'to let grow and to make grow'.

(c) As producers of new life they also became the first subsistence producers and the inventors of the first productive economy, implying from the beginning social production and the creation of social relations, i.e. of society and history.

Productivity, viewed from the perspective of survival, differs sharply from the dominant view of the productivity of labour as defined for processes of capital accumulation. 'Productive' man, producing commodities, using some of nature's wealth and women's work as raw material and dispensing with the rest as waste, becomes the only legitimate category of work, wealth and production. Nature and women working to produce and reproduce life are declared 'unproductive'.

With Adam Smith, the wealth created by nature and women's work was turned invisible. Labour, and especially male labour, became the fund which supplies us originally with all the necessities and conveniences of life. As this assumption spread to all human communities, it introduced dualities within society, and between nature and man. No more was nature a source of wealth and sustenance; no more was women's work in sustenance 'productive' work; no more were peasant and tribal societies creative and productive. They were all marginal to the framework of the industrial society, except as resources and inputs. The transforming, productive power was associated only with male western labour and economic development became a design of remodelling the world on that assumption. The devaluation and derecognition of nature's work and productivity has led to the ecological crises; the devaluation and derecognition of women's work has created sexism and inequality between men and women. The devaluation of subsistence, or rather sustenance economies, based on harmony between nature's work, women's work and man's work has created the various forms of ethnic and cultural crises that plague our world today.

The crisis of survival and the threat to sustenance arises from ecological disruption that is rooted in the arrogance of the West and those that ape it. This arrogance is grounded in a blindness towards the quiet work and the invisible wealth created by nature and women and those who produce sustenance. Such work and wealth are 'invisible' because they are decentred, local and in harmony with local ecosystems and needs. The more effectively the cycles of life, as essential ecological processes, are maintained, the more invisible they become. Disruption is violent and visible; balance and harmony are experienced, not seen. The premium on visibility placed by patriarchal maldevelopment forces the destruction of invisible energies and the work of women and nature, and the creation of spectacular, centralized work and wealth. Such centralization and the uniformity associated with it works further against the diversity and plurality of life. Work and wealth in accordance with the feminine principle are significant precisely because they are rooted in stability and sustainability. Decentred diversity is the source of nature's work and women's productivity; it is the work of 'insignificant' plants in creating significant changes which shift the ecological equilibrium in life's favour. It is the energy of all living things, in all their diversity, and together, the diversity of lives wields tremendous energy. Women's work is similarly invisible in providing sustenance and creating wealth for basic needs. Their work in the forest, the field and the river creates sustenance in quiet but essential ways. Every woman in every house in every village of rural India works invisibly to provide the stuff of life to nature and people. It is this invisible work that is linked to nature and needs, which conserves nature through maintaining ecological cycles, and conserves human life through satisfying the basic needs of food, nutrition and water. It is this essential work that is destroyed and dispensed with by maldevelopment: the maintenance of ecological cycles has no place in a political economy of commodity and cash flows.

The existence of the feminine principle is linked with diversity and sharing. Its destruction through homogenization and privatization leads to the destruction of diversity and of the commons. The sustenance economy is based on a creative and organic nature, on local knowledge, on locally recycled inputs that maintain the integrity of nature, on local consumption for local needs, and on the marketing of surplus beyond the imperatives of equity and ecology. The commodity and cash economy destroys natural cycles and reduces nature to raw materials and commodities. It creates the need for purchase and sale to centralized inputs and commodity markets. When production is specialized and for export, surplus becomes a myth. There is only indebtedness, of peoples and nations. The debt trap is part of global commodity production and sale which destroys nurturing nature and nurturing economies in the name of development.

Sustenance, in the final analysis, is built on the continued capacity of nature to renew its forests, fields and rivers. These resource systems are intrinsically linked in life-producing and life-conserving cultures, and it is in managing the integrity of ecological cycles in forestry and agriculture that women's productivity has been most developed and evolved. Women transfer fertility from the forests to the field and to animals. They transfer animal waste as fertilizer for crops, and crop by-products to animals as fodder. They work with the forest to bring water to their fields and families. This partnership between women's and nature's work ensures the sustainability of sustenance, and it is this critical partnership that is torn asunder when the project of 'development' becomes a patriarchal project, threatening both nature and women. The forest is separated from the river, the field is separated from the forest, the animals are separated from the crops. Each is then separately developed, and the delicate balance which ensures sustainability and equity is destroyed. The visibility of dramatic breaks and ruptures is posited as 'progress'. Marginalized women are either dispensed with or colonized. Needs go unfulfilled, nature is crippled. The drama of violence and fragmentation cannot be sustained and the recovery of the feminine principle thus becomes essential for liberating not only women and nature, but also the patriarchal reductionist categories which give rise to maldevelopment.

The revolutionary and liberational potential of the recovery of the feminine principle consists in its challenging the concepts, categories and processes which have created the threat to life, and in providing oppositional categories that create and enlarge the spaces for maintaining and enriching all life in nature and society. The radical shift induced by a focus on the feminine principle is the recognition of maldevelopment as a culture of destruction. The feminine principle becomes a category of challenge which locates nature and women as the source of life and wealth, and as such, active subjects, maintaining and creating life processes.

There are two implications that arise from the recognition of nature and women as producers of life. First, that what goes by the name of development is a maldevelopment process, a source of violence to women and nature throughout the world. This violence does not arise from the misapplication of an otherwise benign and gender-neutral model, but is rooted in the patriarchal assumptions of homogeneity, domination and centralization that underlie dominant models of thought and development strategies. Second, that the crises that the maldevelopment model has given rise to cannot be solved within the paradigm of the crisis mind. Their solution lies in the categories of thought, perception and action that are life-giving and life-maintaining. In contemporary times, Third World women, whose minds have not yet been dispossessed or colonized, are in a privileged position to make visible the invisible oppositional categories that they are the custodians of. It is not only as victims, but also as leaders in creating new intellectual ecological paradigms, that women are central to arresting and overcoming ecological crises. Just as ecological recovery begins from centres of natural diversity which are gene pools, Third World women, and those tribals and peasants who have been left out of the processes of maldevelopment, are today acting as the intellectual gene pools of ecological categories of thought and action. Marginalization has thus become a source for healing the diseased mainstream of patriarchal development. Those facing the biggest threat offer the best promise for survival because they have two kinds of knowledge that are not accessible to dominant and privileged groups. First, they have the knowledge of what it means to be the victims of progress, to be the ones who bear the costs and burdens. Second, they have the holistic and ecological knowledge of what the production and protection of life is about. They retain the ability to see nature's life as a precondition for human survival and the integrity of inter-connectedness in nature as a precondition for life. Women of the Third World have been dispossessed of their base for sustenance, but not of their minds, and in their uncolonized minds are conserved the oppositional categories that make the sustenance of life possible for all. The producers of life alone can be its real protectors. Women embedded in nature, producing life with nature, are therefore taking the initiative in the recovery of nature.

To say that women and nature are intimately associated is not to say anything revolutionary. After all, it was precisely just such an assumption that allowed the domination of both women and nature. The new insight provided by rural women in the Third World is that women and nature are associated *not in passivity but in creativity and in the maintenance of life*.

This analysis differs from most conventional analyses of environmentalists and feminists. Most work on women and environment in the Third World has focused on women as special victims of environmental degradation. Yet the women who participate in and lead ecology movements in countries like India are not speaking merely as victims. Their voices are the voices of liberation and transformation which provide new categories of thought and new exploratory directions. In this sense, this study is a post-victimology study. It is an articulation of the categories of challenge that women in ecology movements are creating in the Third World. The women and environment issue can be approached either from these categories of challenge that have been thrown up by women in the struggle for life, or it can be approached through an extension of conventional categories of patriarchy and reductionism. In the perspective of women engaged in survival struggles which are, simultaneously, struggles for the protection of nature, women and nature are intimately related, and their domination and liberation similarly linked. The women's and ecology movements are therefore one, and are primarily counter-trends to a patriarchal maldevelopment. Our experience shows that ecology and feminism can combine in the recovery of the feminine principle, and through this recovery, can intellectually and politically restructure and transform maldevelopment.

Maldevelopment is seen here as a process by which human society marginalizes the play of the feminine principle in nature and in society. Ecological breakdown and social inequality are intrinsically related to the dominant development paradigm which puts man against and above nature and women. The underlying assumptions of dialectical unity and cyclical recovery shared by the common concern for the liberation of nature and of women, contrast deeply with the dominant western patriarchal assumptions of duality in existence and linearity in process. Within the western paradigm, the environmental movement is separate from the women's movement. As long as this paradigm with its assumptions of linear progress prevails, 'environmentalism' and 'feminism' independently ask only for concessions *within* maldevelopment, because in the absence of oppositional categories, that is the only 'development' that is conceivable. Environmentalism then becomes a new patriarchal project of technological fixes and political oppression. It generates a new subjugation of ecological movements and fails to make any progress towards sustainability and equity. While including a few women as tokens in 'women and environment', it excludes the feminine visions of survival that women have conserved. Fragmented feminism, in a similar way, finds itself trapped in a gender-based ideology of liberation—taking off from either the 'catching-up-with-men' syndrome (on the grounds that the masculine is superior and developed), or receding into a narrow biologism which accepts the feminine as gendered, and excludes the possibility of the recovery of the feminine principle in nature and women, *as well as* men.

7. THE GENDER AND ENVIRONMENT DEBATE: LESSONS FROM INDIA

BINA AGARWAL

What is women's relationship with the environment? Is it distinct from that of men's? The growing literature on ecofeminism in the West, and especially in the United States, conceptualizes the link between gender and the environment primarily in ideological terms. An intensifying struggle for survival in the developing world, however, highlights the material basis for this link and sets the background for an alternative formulation to ecofeminism, which I term 'feminist environmentalism'.

SOME CONCEPTUAL ISSUES

ECOFEMINISM

Ecofeminism embodies within it several different strands of discourse, most of which have yet to be spelled out fully, and which reflect, among other things, different positions within the western feminist movement (radical, liberal, socialist). As a body of thought ecofeminism is as yet underdeveloped and still evolving, but carries a growing advocacy. My purpose is not to critique ecofeminist discourse in detail, but rather to focus on some of its major elements, especially in order to examine whether and how it might feed into the formulation of a Third World perspective on gender and the environment. Disentangling the various threads in the debate, and focusing on those more clearly articulated, provides us with the following picture of the ecofeminist argument(s):[1] (1) There are important connections between the domination and oppression of women and the domination and exploitation of nature. (2) In patriarchal thought, women are identified as being closer to nature and men as being closer to culture. Nature is seen as inferior to culture; hence, women are seen as inferior to men. (3) Because the domination of women and the domination of nature have occurred together, women have a particular stake in ending the domination of nature, 'in healing the alienated human and non-human nature'.[2] (4) The feminist movement and the environmental movement both stand for egalitarian, non-hierarchical systems. They thus have a good deal in common and need to work together to evolve a common perspective, theory and practice.

In the ecofeminist argument, therefore, the connection between the domination of women and that of nature is seen basically as ideological, as rooted in a system of ideas and representations, values and beliefs, that places women and the non-human world hierarchically below men. It calls upon women and men to reconceptualize themselves, and their relationships to one another and to the non-human world, in non-hierarchical ways.

We might then ask: in what is this connection between nature and women seen to be rooted? The idea that women are seen as closer to nature than men was initially introduced into contemporary feminist discourse by Sherry Ortner who argued that 'woman is being identified with—or, if you will, seems to be a symbol of—something that every culture devalues, defines as being of a lower order of existence than itself ... [That something] is 'nature' in the most generalized sense ... [Women are everywhere] being symbolically associated with nature, as opposed to men, who are identified with culture.'[3] In her initial formulation, the connection between women and nature was clearly rooted in the biological processes of reproduction although, even then, Ortner did recognize that women, like men, also mediate between nature and culture.

Ortner has since modified her position which was also criticized by others (particularly social anthropologists) on several counts, especially because the nature–culture divide is not universal across all cultures, nor is there uniformity in the meaning attributed to 'nature', 'culture', 'male' and 'female'.[4] Still, some ecofeminists accept the emphasis on biology uncritically and reiterate it in different ways. An extreme form of this position is that taken by Ariel Kay Salleh who grounds even women's consciousness in biology and in nature. She argues: 'Women's monthly fertility cycle, the tiring symbiosis of pregnancy, the wrench of childbirth and the pleasure of suckling an infant, these things already ground women's consciousness in the knowledge of being coterminous with nature. However tacit or unconscious this identity may be for many women ... it is nevertheless "a fact of life".'[5] Others such as Ynestra King and Carolyn Merchant argue that the nature–culture dichotomy is a false one, a patriarchal ideological construct which is then used to maintain gender hierarchy. At the same time they accept the view that women are ideologically constructed as closer to nature because of their biology.[6]

Merchant, however, in an illuminating historical analysis, shows that in pre-modern Europe the conceptual connection between women and nature rested on two divergent images, coexisting simultaneously, one which constrained the destruction of nature and the other which sanctioned it. Both identified nature with the female sex. The first image, which was the dominant one, identified nature, especially the earth, with the nurturing mother, and culturally restricted 'the types of socially and morally sanctioned human actions allowable with respect to the earth.

One does not readily slay a mother, dig into her entrails for gold, or muti-late her body ...'[7] The opposing image was of nature as wild and uncon-trollable which could render violence, storms, droughts and general chaos. This image culturally sanctioned mastery and human dominance over nature.

Between the sixteenth and seventeenth centuries, Merchant suggests, the Scientific Revolution and the growth of a market-oriented culture in Europe undermined the image of an organic cosmos with a living female earth at its centre. This image gave way to a mechanistic world-view in which nature was reconceived as something to be mastered and controlled by humans. The twin ideas of mechanism and of dominance over nature supported both the denudation of nature and male domi-nance over women. Merchant observes:

> The ancient identity of nature as a nurturing mother links women's history with the history of the environment and ecological change ... In investigating the roots of our current environmental dilemma and its connections to science, technology and the economy, we must reexamine the formation of a world-view and a science that, by reconceptualizing reality as a machine rather than a living organ-ism, sanctioned the domination of both nature and women.

Today, Merchant proposes, juxtaposing the egalitarian goals of the women's movement and the environmental movement can suggest 'new values and social structures, based not on the domination of women and nature as resources but on the full expression of both male and female talent and on the maintenance of environmental integrity'.[8]

Ecofeminist discourse, therefore, highlights (a) some of the important conceptual links between the *symbolic* construction of women and nature and the ways of *acting* upon them (although Merchant alone goes beyond the level of assertion to trace these links in concrete terms, histor-ically); (b) the underlying commonality between the premises and goals of the women's movement and the environmental movement; and (c) an alternative vision of a more egalitarian and harmonious future society.

At the same time the ecofeminist argument as constructed is problem-atic on several counts. First, it posits 'woman' as a unitary category and fails to differentiate among women by class, race, ethnicity and so on. It thus ignores forms of domination other than gender which also impinge critically on women's position.[9] Second, it locates the domination of women and of nature almost solely in ideology, neglecting the (inter-related) material sources of this dominance (based on economic advan-tage and political power). Third, even in the realm of ideological constructs, it says little (with the exception of Merchant's analysis) about the social, economic and political structures within which these constructs are produced and transformed. Nor does it address the central issue of the means by which certain dominant groups (predicated on gender, class, etc.) are able to bring about ideological shifts in their own favour and how such shifts get entrenched. Fourth, the ecofeminist argument does not take into account women's lived material relationship with nature, as opposed to what others or they themselves might conceive that relationship to be. Fifth, those strands of ecofeminism that trace the connection between women and nature to biology may be seen as adhering to a form of essentialism (some notion of a female 'essence' which is unchangeable and irreducible).[10] Such a formulation flies in the face of wide-ranging evidence that concepts of nature, culture, gender and so on are historically and socially constructed and vary across and within cultures and time periods.[11]

In other words, the debate highlights the significant effect of ideological constructs in shaping relations of gender dominance and forms of acting on the non-human world, but if these constructs are to be challenged it is necessary to go further. We need a theoretical understanding of what could be termed 'the political economy of ideological construction', that is, of the interplay between conflicting discourses, the groups promoting particular discourses, and the means used to entrench views embodied in those discourses. Equally, it is critical to examine the underlying basis of women's relationship with the non-human world at levels other than ideology (such as through the work women and men do and the gender division of property and power) and to address how the material realities in which women of different classes/castes/races are rooted might affect their responses to environmental degradation. Women in the West, for instance, have responded in specific ways to the threat of environmental destruction, such as by organizing the Greenham Common resistance to nuclear missiles in England and by participating in the Green movement across Europe and the United States. A variety of actions has similarly been taken by women in the Third World. The question then is: are there gendered aspects to these responses? If so, in what are these responses rooted?

Vandana Shiva's work on India takes us a step forward. Like the ecofeminists, she sees violence against nature and against women as built into the very mode of perceiving both. Like Merchant, she argues that violence against nature is intrinsic to the dominant industrial/developmental model, which she characterizes as a colonial imposition. Associated with the adoption of this developmental model, Shiva argues, was a radical conceptual shift away from the traditional Indian cosmological view of (animate and inanimate) nature as *Prakriti*, as 'activity *and* diversity' and as 'an expression of *Shakti*, the feminine and creative principle of the cosmos' which 'in conjunction with the masculine principle (*Purusha*) ... creates the world'. In this shift, the living, nurturing relationship between man and nature as earth mother was replaced by the notion of man as separate from and dominating over inert and passive nature. 'Viewed from the perspective of nature, or women embedded in nature', the shift was repressive and violent. 'For women ... the death of *Prakriti* is simultaneously a beginning of their marginalisation, devaluation, displacement and ultimate dispensability. The ecological crisis is, at its root, the death of the feminine principle ...'.[12]

At the same time, Shiva notes that violence against women and against nature are linked not just ideologically but also materially. For instance, Third World women are dependent on nature 'for drawing sustenance for themselves, their families, their societies'. The destruction of nature thus becomes the destruction of women's sources for 'staying alive'. Drawing upon her experience of working with women activists in the Chipko movement—the environmental movement for forest protection and regeneration in the Garhwal hills of northwest India—Shiva argues that 'Third World women' have both a special dependence on and a special knowledge of nature. This knowledge has been systematically marginalized under the impact of modern science: 'Modern reductionist science, like development, turns out to be a patriarchal project, which has excluded women as experts, and has simultaneously excluded ecology and holistic ways of knowing which understand and respect nature's processes and interconnectedness as *science*'.[13]

Shiva takes us further than the western ecofeminists in exploring the links between ways of thinking about development, the processes of developmental change, and the impact of these on the environment and on the people dependent upon it for their livelihood. These links are of critical significance. Nevertheless her argument has three principal analytical problems. First, her examples relate to rural women primarily from northwest India, but her generalizations conflate all Third World women into one category. Although she distinguishes Third World women from the rest, like the ecofeminists she does not differentiate between women of different classes, castes, races, ecological zones and so on. Hence, implicitly, a form of essentialism could be read into her work, in that all Third World women, whom she sees as 'embedded in nature', *qua women* have a special relationship with the natural environment. This still begs the question: what is the basis of this relationship and how do women acquire this special understanding?

Second, she does not indicate by what concrete processes and institutions ideological constructions of gender and nature have changed in India, nor does she recognize the coexistence of several ideological strands, given India's ethnic and religious diversity. For instance, her emphasis on the feminine principle as the guiding idea in Indian philo-sophic discourse in fact relates to the Hindu discourse alone and cannot be seen as applicable for Indians of all religious persuasions.[14] Indeed, Hinduism itself is pluralistic, fluid and contains several coexisting discourses with varying gender implications.[15] But perhaps most impor-tantly, it is not clear how and in which historical period(s) the concept of the feminine principle *in practice* affected gender relations or relations between people and nature.

Third, Shiva attributes existing forms of destruction of nature and the oppression of women (in both symbolic and real terms) principally to the Third World's history of colonialism and to the imposition of western science and a western model of development. Undeniably, the colonial experience and the forms that modern development have taken in Third World countries have been destructive and distorting economically, institutionally and culturally. However, it cannot be ignored that this process impinged on pre-existing bases of economic and social (includ-ing gender) inequalities.

Here it is important to distinguish between the particular model of modernization that clearly has been imported/adopted from the West by many Third World countries (with or without a history of colonization) and the socio-economic base on which this model was imposed. Pre-British India, especially during the Mughal period, was considerably class/caste stratified, although varyingly across regions.[16] This would have affected the patterns of access to and use of natural resources by different classes and social groups. Although much more research is needed on the political economy of natural resource use in the pre-colo-nial period, the evidence of differentiated peasant communities at that time cautions against sweeping historical generalizations about the effects of colonial rule.

By locating the 'problem' almost entirely in the Third World's experi-ence of the West, Shiva misses out on the very real local forces of power, privilege and property relations that predate colonialism. What exists today is a complex legacy of colonial and pre-colonial interactions that defines the constraints and parameters within which and from which present thinking and action on development, resource use and social change have to proceed. In particular, a strategy for change requires an explicit analysis of the structural causes of environmental degradation, its effects and responses to it. The outline for an alternative framework, which I term feminist environmentalism, is suggested below.

FEMINIST ENVIRONMENTALISM

I would like to suggest here that women's and men's relationship with nature needs to be understood as rooted in their material reality, in their specific forms of interaction with the environment. Hence, insofar as there is a gender and class/caste/race-based division of labour and distribution of property and power, gender and class (caste/race) structure people's interactions with nature and so the effects of environmental change on people and their responses to it. And where knowledge about nature is experiential in its basis, the divisions of labour, property and power which shape experience also shape the knowledge based on that experience.

For instance, poor peasant and tribal women have typically been responsible for fetching fuel and fodder and in hill and tribal communities have also often been the main cultivators. They are thus likely to be affected adversely in quite specific ways by environmental degradation. At the same time, in the course of their everyday interactions with nature, they acquire a special knowledge of species varieties and the processes of natural regeneration. (This would include knowledge passed on to them by, for example, their mothers.) They could thus be seen as both victims of the destruction of nature and as repositories of knowledge about nature, in ways distinct from the men of their class. The former aspect would provide the gendered impulse for their resistance and response to environmental destruction. The latter would condition their perceptions and choices of what should be done. Indeed, on the basis of their experiential understanding and knowledge, they could provide a special perspective on the processes of environmental regeneration, one that needs to inform our view of alternative approaches to development. (By extension, women who are no longer actively using this knowledge for their daily sustenance, and are no longer in contact with the natural environment in the same way, are likely to lose this knowledge over time and with it the possibility of its transmission to others.)

In this conceptualization, therefore, the link between women and the environment can be seen as structured by a given gender and class (/caste/race) organization of production, reproduction and distribution. Ideological constructions such as of gender, of nature, and of the relationship between the two, may be seen as (interactively) a part of this structuring but not the whole of it. This perspective I term 'feminist environmentalism'.

In terms of action such a perspective would call for struggles over both resources and meanings. It would imply grappling with the dominant groups who have the property, power and privilege to control resources, and these or other groups who control ways of thinking about them, via educational, media, religious and legal institutions. On the feminist front there would be a need to challenge and transform both notions about gender and the actual division of work and resources between the genders. On the environmental front there would be a need to challenge and transform not only notions about the relationship between people and nature but also the actual methods of appropriation of nature's resources by a few. Feminist environmentalism underlines the necessity of addressing these dimensions from both fronts.

8. THE AFRICAN CONTEXT: WOMEN IN THE POLITICAL ECONOMY
MARGARET SNYDER AND MARY TADESSE

The African women who witnessed the independence of their countries possessed rich traditions as leaders, as participants in women's movements and, along with men, in liberation struggles. They had tangible records of economic activity, largely in peasant societies but also in monetized 'modern' cultures. None the less, the introduction of cash crops and technologies, of education and wage-employment opportunities, had usually bypassed them. As men had been drawn into the modern sectors, women's productivity was eroded during the pre-independence era, the colonial perception of women as home-makers eclipsing women's substantial political and economic activity.

AFRICAN WOMEN'S LEGACY

Historical evidence indicates that African women's participation in economic life was deeply rooted everywhere on the continent. While generalizations are risky in a region so vast and so varied as Africa, we can state that in a large number of early African societies the gender division of labour allocated responsibility for cultivation to women, who could barter or sell their excess produce, while men engaged in hunting. The division of labour was different in other societies; for example, in Ethiopia men ploughed the fields and women weeded and harvested along with them. In parts of West Africa too, women and men farmed side by side.

The burden of food production generally fell to women, despite exceptions like the cocoa-growing areas of Nigeria. 'In most of Africa, women were the backbone of rural farming,' said Achola Pala-Okeyo of Kenya.[1] They usually cultivated community-owned land allocated to them by male political or lineage heads, to whom they in turn paid over some of their produce.

Besides agriculture, women engaged in commercial activity locally and with European merchants, as recorded as early as the eighteenth century in West Africa. Whilst the merchant princesses of West Africa remain legendary for their wealth and overseas trade, it is true that almost all the women in that area engaged in some kind of trade. Women in other parts of the continent also traded or bartered in the local markets. Thus, for most women on the continent, petty trade or agriculture was the source of livelihood.

Clearly, in traditional African societies, whilst it cannot be said that all women had equality with men, despite class differences, a balance of economic responsibility did prevail between women and men, and the work of both was valued in a largely non-competitive division of labour. Parallel gender-based institutions were common in such an environment, and men's and women's groups each managed their own affairs. In south-western Nigeria, for example, there were women's courts to impose fines and women were the market authorities who fixed prices and settled quarrels. In Cameroun, the best of the Bemileke female farmers belonged to a special women's society. Both men and women participated in some functions of overall government and women at times reached positions of high authority.[2]

THE COLONIAL PERIOD

Profound changes came with colonialism and its attendant technologies, cash cropping and a wage economy. Colonial officials tended to visualize women in terms of a Victorian image of what a woman ('a lady') should be, instead of observing women's actual functions. From that perspective they envisioned women's responsibilities as limited largely to nurturing and conserving society, while men engaged in political and economic activities. Colonials equated 'male' with 'breadwinner' and, as a result, introduced technologies to men and recruited men for paying jobs which often took them off the farm. Anthropologists and other researchers did little to rectify the one-sided view; they themselves were inclined to underestimate women's productivity.[3]

As the international market economy encroached more rapidly on Africa, major setbacks to women arose from male migration to mines, plantations and towns. Whether men left by choice, by necessity or by force, their migration left women on the farm doing both men's and women's work. Those women often had many dependants—children, elders and the ill—to care for without enough adult workers. In the colonial system, as in many other systems at the time, men were favoured with opportunities for education, employment and access to resources.

But perhaps the most serious setback for women came when land consolidation and settlement schemes gave title deeds to men as 'heads of household' even when they were absent from the farm. This was often in direct contradiction to the use-rights that were customary and that encouraged women's productivity.[4] With the titles came men's right to the proceeds of the land, including the products of women's labour that women had previously contributed to family maintenance. The prestige accorded to women's work in the parallel-society system of earlier eras was consequently downgraded, even though women often worked continuously and for many more hours than the men.

The confrontations that arose were rooted in women's traditional and central position in economic life. It should have come as no surprise to the colonial administrators that African women's farm and merchant groups mobilized to protest against those colonial policies which appeared to jeopardize their economic activity. Recognizing the reality of the encroaching capitalist economy, women organized to preserve their chances to meet their responsibilities for the well-being of their families. The colonial officials held firm, regarding these women's efforts to preserve subsistence crops as reactionary and detrimental to the development of a market economy.

In the 1940s and 1950s, for example, women in Cameroun, Côte d'Ivoire, Sierra Leone and Uganda resisted the introduction of cash crops such as coffee, sisal and tea, to which the most fertile lands were being allocated and which added weeding and other tedious tasks to their already heavy workloads. The 'Women's War' was an anti-tax rebellion against the colonial powers by women in southern Igboland in Nigeria.[5] Kenyan women protested against unjust labour regulations as early as 1902.[6]

Women continued to persist in their economic activities during colonial times, despite the formidable odds they faced. One example is the way they mobilized to form corn-mill societies in western Cameroun in the 1950s. Over time 200 such societies were formed with a total membership of 18,000. They used grinding mills that were owned in common, fenced their fields, and constructed water storage units and cooperative stores.[7] In some countries, when the introduction of cash crops could not be prevented, women devised alternative strategies for meeting their family responsibilities, such as requesting wages for their labour or threatening to leave their husbands.[8]

In other words, 'for generations women established some form of collective actions to increase group productivity, to fill-in socio-economic gaps wherever the colonial administration failed, or to protest policies that deprived them of the resources to provide for their families'.[9]

But despite such well-organized efforts, colonialism and its market economy continued to revolutionize the family division of labour, and the family itself. Pala-Okeyo identifies the colonial period as the beginning of the deterioration of food production in Africa.[10] That observation and the need to feed growing populations would underlie the selection of rural development and food production as the initial emphases of ECA (Economic Commission for Africa) programmes directed to women in the early 1970s.

INDEPENDENCE MOVEMENTS

Women's historic protests against economic policies laid the groundwork for them to join with men in the struggle for independence from colonialism and became the foundation of the women and development movement. More than eleven thousand women were jailed during the MauMau Emergency of the 1950s.[11] Women fought side by side with men in Algeria, Angola, Zambia, Mozambique and Guinea-Bissau. The heroism of Mbuya Niyanda of Zimbabwe and Mama Chikamoneka of Zambia is legendary in their countries. Women constituted over 25 per cent of the cadres of the Zimbabwe African National Union Liberation Army (ZANLA) and a full one-third of some of the opposition fighting forces in the 1980s in Ethiopia.

The independence movements of the 1950s and 1960s allowed the roots of the women and development concept and movement to take hold. After the experience of struggle, women were determined to be fully participating citizens of their new nations. Though this wish is not yet fully realized, the solidarity groups and organizations they evolved from their work still 'rank among the most important components of African civil society'.[12]

It was against this background of women's history of leadership, of their strength in adversity and of their economic activities and community participation that the United Nations Economic Commission for Africa invited women to be advisers and participants in development activities just after it was founded in 1958.

B. Discourse/Language of WID

Examines terminology and categories used in development literature, i.e. 'Development', 'Third World', 'modernization', 'women'. Also includes a discussion of voice in the WID literature.

9. UNDER WESTERN EYES: FEMINIST SCHOLARSHIP AND COLONIAL DISCOURSES

CHANDRA TALPADE MOHANTY

Any discussion of the intellectual and political construction of 'third world feminisms' must address itself to two simultaneous projects: the internal critique of hegemonic 'Western' feminisms, and the formulation of autonomous, geographically, historically and culturally grounded feminist concerns and strategies. The first project is one of deconstructing and dismantling; the second, one of building and constructing. While these projects appear to be contradictory, the one working negatively and the other positively, unless these two tasks are addressed simultaneously, 'third world' feminisms run the risk of marginalization or ghettoization from both mainstream (right and left) and Western feminist discourses.

It is to the first project that I address myself. What I wish to analyse is specifically the production of the 'third world woman' as a singular monolithic subject in some recent (Western) feminist texts. The definition of colonization I wish to invoke here is a predominantly *discursive* one, focusing on a certain mode of appropriation and codification of 'scholarship' and 'knowledge' about women in the third world by particular analytic categories employed in specific writings on the subject which take as their referent feminist interests as they have been articulated in the US and Western Europe. If one of the tasks of formulating and understanding the locus of 'third world feminisms' is delineating the way in which it resists and *works against* what I am referring to as 'Western feminist discourse', an analysis of the discursive construction of 'third world women' in Western feminism is an important first step.

Clearly Western feminist discourse and political practice is neither singular nor homogeneous in its goals, interests or analyses. However, it is possible to trace a coherence of *effects* resulting from the implicit assumption of 'the West' (in all its complexities and contradictions) as the primary referent in theory and praxis. My reference to 'Western feminism' is by no means intended to imply that it is a monolith. Rather, I am attempting to draw attention to the similar effects of various textual strategies used by writers which codify Others as non-Western and hence themselves as (implicitly) Western. It is in this sense that I use the term *Western feminist*. Similar arguments can be made in terms of middle-class urban African or Asian scholars producing scholarship on or about their rural or working-class sisters, which assumes their own middle-class cultures as the norm, and codifies working-class histories and cultures as Other. Thus, while this essay focuses specifically on what I refer to as 'Western feminist' discourse on women in the third world, the critiques I offer also pertain to third world scholars writing about their own cultures, which employ identical analytic strategies.

My critique is directed at three basic analytic principles which are present in (western) feminist discourse on women in the third world.

The first analytic presupposition I focus on is involved in the strategic location of the category 'women' *vis-à-vis* the context of analysis. The assumption of women as an already constituted, coherent group with identical interests and desires, regardless of class, ethnic or racial location, or contradictions, implies a notion of gender or sexual difference or even patriarchy which can be applied universally and cross-culturally. (The context of analysis can be anything from kinship structures and the organization of labour or media representations.) The second analytical presupposition is evident on the methodological level, in the uncritical way 'proof' of universality and cross-cultural validity are provided. The third is a more specifically political presupposition underlying the methodologies and the analytic strategies, i.e., the model of power and struggle they imply and suggest. I argue that as a result of the two modes—or, rather, frames—of analysis described above, a homogeneous notion of the oppression of women as a group is assumed, which, in turn, produces the image of an 'average third world woman'. This woman leads an essentially truncated life based on her feminine gender (read: sexually constrained) and her being 'third world' (read: ignorant, poor, unedu-cated, tradition-bound, domestic, family-oriented, victimized, etc.). This, I suggest, is in contrast to the (implicit) self-representation of Western women as educated, as modern, as having control over their own bodies and sexualities, and the freedom to make their own decisions.

The distinction between western feminist re-presentation of women in the third world and Western feminist self-presentation is a distinction of the same order as that made by some Marxists between the 'mainte-nance' function of the housewife and the real 'productive' role of wage labour, or the characterization by developmentalists of the third world as being engaged in the lesser production of 'raw materials' in contrast to the 'real' productive activity of the first world. These distinctions are made on the basis of the privileging of a particular group as the norm or referent. Men involved in wage labour, first world producers, and, I suggest, Western feminists who sometimes cast third world women in terms of 'ourselves undressed' (Michelle Rosaldo's [1980] term), all construct themselves as the normative referent in such a binary analytic.

'WOMEN' AS CATEGORY OF ANALYSIS, OR: WE ARE ALL SISTERS IN STRUGGLE

By women as a category of analysis, I am referring to the crucial assumption that all of us of the same gender, across classes and cultures, are somehow socially constituted as a homogeneous group identified prior to the process of analysis. This is an assumption which characterizes much feminist discourse. The homogeneity of women as a group is produced not on the basis of biological essentials but rather on the basis of secondary sociological and anthropological universals. Thus, for instance, in any given piece of feminist analysis, women are characterized as a singular group on the basis of a shared oppression. What binds women together is a sociological notion of the 'sameness' of their oppression. It is at this point that an elision takes place between 'women' as a discursively constructed group and 'women' as material subjects of their own history.[1] Thus, the discursively consensual homogeneity of 'women' as a group is mistaken for the historically specific material reality of groups of women. This results in an assumption of women as an always already constituted group, one which has been labelled 'powerless', 'exploited', 'sexually harassed', etc., by feminist scientific, economic, legal and sociological discourses. (Notice that this is quite similar to sexist discourse labelling women weak, emotional, having math anxiety, etc.) This focus is not on uncovering the material and ideological specificities that constitute a particular group of women as 'powerless' in a particular context. It is, rather, on finding a variety of cases of 'powerless' groups of women to prove the general point that women as a group are powerless.

In this section I focus on specific ways in which 'women' as a category of analysis is used in Western feminist discourse on women in the third world. Each of these examples illustrates the construction of 'third world women' as a homogeneous 'powerless' group often located as implicit *victims* of particular socio-economic systems.

This mode of defining women primarily in terms of their *object status* (the way in which they are affected or not affected by certain institutions and systems) is what characterizes this particular form of the use of 'women' as a category of analysis. In the context of Western women writing/studying women in the third world, such objectification (however benevolently motivated) needs to be both named and challenged. As Valerie Amos and Pratibha Parmar argue quite eloquently, 'Feminist theories which examine our cultural practices as "feudal residues" or label us "traditional", also portray us as politically immature women who need to be versed and schooled in the ethos of Western feminism. They need to be continually challenged ...' (1984, 7).

WOMEN AND THE DEVELOPMENT PROCESS

The best examples of universalization on the basis of economic reductionism can be found in the liberal 'Women in Development' literature. Proponents of this school seek to examine the effect of development on third world women, sometimes from self-designated feminist perspectives. At the very least, there is an evident interest in and commitment to improving the lives of women in 'developing' countries. Scholars such as Irene Tinker and Michelle Bo Bramsen (1972), Ester Boserup (1970), and Perdita Huston (1979) have all written about the effect of development policies on women in the third world.[2] All three women assume 'development' is synonymous with 'economic development' or 'economic progress'. As in the case of Minces's (1980) patriarchal family, Hosken's (1981) male sexual control and Cutrufelli's (1983) Western colonization, development here becomes the all-time equalizer. Women are affected positively or negatively by economic development policies, and this is the basis for cross-cultural comparison.

For instance, Perdita Huston (1979) states that the purpose of her study is to describe the effect of the development process on the 'family unit and its individual members' in Egypt, Kenya, Sudan, Tunisia, Sri Lanka and Mexico. She states that the 'problems' and 'needs' expressed by rural and urban women in these countries all centre around education and training, work and wages, access to health and other services, political participation and legal rights. Huston relates all these 'needs' to the lack of sensitive development policies which exclude women as a group or category. For her, the solution is simple: implement improved development policies which emphasize training for women fieldworkers, use women trainees, and women rural development officers, encourage women's cooperatives, etc. Here again, women are assumed to be a coherent group or category prior to their entry into 'the development process'. Huston assumes that all third world women have similar problems and needs. Thus, they must have similar interests and goals. However, the interests of urban, middle-class, educated Egyptian housewives, to take only one instance, could surely not be seen as being the same as those of their uneducated, poor maids? Development policies do not affect both groups of women in the same way. Practices which characterize women's status and roles vary according to class. Women are constituted as women through the complex interaction between class, culture, religion and other ideological institutions and frameworks. They are not 'women'—a coherent group—solely on the basis of a particular economic system or policy. Such reductive cross-cultural comparisons result in the colonization of the specifics of daily existence and the complexities of political interests which women of different social classes and cultures represent and mobilize.

Thus, it is revealing that for Perdita Huston, women in the Third World countries she writes about have 'needs' and 'problems', but few if any have 'choices' or the freedom to act. This is an interesting representation of women in the third world, one which is significant in suggesting a latent self-presentation of Western women which bears looking at. She writes: 'What surprised and moved me most as I listened to women in such very different cultural settings was the striking commonality— whether they were educated or illiterate, urban or rural—of their most basic values: the importance they assign to family, dignity and service to others' (1979: 115). Would Huston consider such values unusual for women in the West?

What is problematical about this kind of use of 'women' as a group, as a stable category of analysis, is that it assumes an ahistorical, universal unity between women based on a generalized notion of their subordination. Instead of analytically *demonstrating* the production of women as socio-economic political groups within particular local contexts, this analytical move limits the definition of the female subject to gender identity, completely bypassing social class and ethnic identities. What characterizes women as a group is their gender (sociologically, not necessarily biologically, defined) over and above everything else, indicating a monolithic notion of sexual difference. Because women are thus constituted as a coherent group, sexual difference becomes coterminous with female subordination, and power is automatically defined in binary terms: people who have it (read: men), and people who do not (read: women). Men exploit, women are exploited. Such simplistic formulations are historically reductive; they are also ineffectual in designing strategies to combat oppressions. All they do is reinforce binary divisions between men and women.

What would an analysis which did not do this look like? Maria Mies's work illustrates the strength of Western feminist work on women in the third world which does not fall into the traps discussed above, Mies's study of the lace makers of Narsapur, India (1982), attempts to analyse carefully a substantial household industry in which 'housewives' produce lace doilies for consumption in the world market. Through a detailed analysis of the structure of the lace industry, production and reproduction relations, the sexual division of labour, profits and exploitation, and the overall consequences of defining women as 'non-working housewives' and their work as 'leisure-time activity', Mies demonstrates the levels of exploitation in this industry and the impact of this production system on the work and living conditions of the women involved. In addition, she is able to analyse the 'ideology of the house-wife', the notion of a woman sitting in the house, as providing the neces-sary subjective and sociocultural element for the creation and maintenance of a production system that contributes to the increasing pauperization of women, and keeps them totally atomized and disorga-nized as workers. Mies's analysis shows the effect of a certain historically and culturally specific mode of patriarchal organization, an organization constructed on the basis of the definition of the lace makers as 'non-working housewives' at familial, local, regional, statewide and interna-tional levels. The intricacies and the effects of particular power networks are not only emphasized but form the basis of Mies's analysis of how this particular group of women is situated at the centre of a hegemonic, exploitative world market.

This is a good example of what careful, politically focused, local analy-ses can accomplish. It illustrates how the category of women is constructed in a variety of political contexts that often exist simultane-ously and are overlaid on top of one another. There is no easy general-ization in the direction of 'women' in India, or 'women in the third world'; nor is there a reduction of the political construction of the exploitation of the lace makers to cultural explanations about the passiv-ity or obedience that might characterize these women and their situa-tion. Finally, this mode of local, political analysis which generates theoretical categories from within the situation and context being analysed, also suggests corresponding effective strategies for organizing against the exploitation faced by the lace makers. Narsapur women are not mere victims of the production process, because they resist, chal-lenge and subvert the process at various junctures. Here is one instance of how Mies delineates the connections between the housewife ideol-ogy, the self-consciousness of the lace makers, and their inter-relation-ships as contributing to the latent resistances she perceives among the women.

> The persistence of the housewife ideology, the self-perception of the lace makers as petty commodity producers rather than as workers, is not only upheld by the structure of the industry as such but also by the deliberate propagation and reinforcement of reac-tionary patriarchal norms and institutions. Thus, most of the lace makers voiced the same opinion about the rules of *purdah* and

seclusion in their communities which were also propagated by the lace exporters. In particular, the *Kapu* women said that they had never gone out of their houses, that women of their community could not do any work other than housework and lace work etc. but in spite of the fact that most of them still subscribed fully to the patriarchal norms of the *gosha* women, there were also contradictory elements in their consciousness. Thus, although they looked down with contempt upon women who were able to work outside the house—like untouchable *Mala* and *Madiga* women or women of other lower castes—they could not ignore the fact that these women were earning more money precisely because they were *not* respectable housewives but workers. At one discussion, they even admitted that it would be better if they could also go out and do coolie work. And when they were asked whether they would be ready to come out of their houses and work in one place in some sort of a factory, they said they would do that. This shows that the *purdah* and housewife ideology, although still fully internalized, already had some cracks, because it has been confronted with several contradictory realities. (p. 157)

It is only by understanding the *contradictions* inherent in women's location within various structures that effective political action and challenges can be devised. Mies's study goes a long way toward offering such analysis. While there are now an increasing number of Western feminist writings in this tradition,[3] there is also, unfortunately, a large block of writing which succumbs to the cultural reductionism discussed earlier.

As discussed earlier, a comparison between Western feminist self-presentation and Western feminist re-presentation of women in the third world yields significant results. Universal images of 'the third world Woman' (the veiled woman, chaste virgin, etc.), images constructed from adding the 'third world difference' to 'sexual difference', are predicated upon (and hence obviously bring into sharper focus) assumptions about Western women as secular, liberated and having control over their own lives. This is not to suggest that Western women *are* secular, liberated and in control of their own lives. I am referring to a *discursive* self-presentation, not necessarily to material reality. If this were a material reality, there would be no need for political movements in the West. Similarly, only from the vantage point of the West is it possible to define the 'third world' as underdeveloped and economically dependent. Without the overdetermined discourse that creates the *third* world, there would be no (singular and privileged) First World. Without the 'third world woman', the particular self-presentation of Western women mentioned above would be problematical. I am suggesting, then, that

the one enables and sustains the other. This is not to say that the signa-
ture of Western feminist writings on the third world has the same authority as the project of Western humanism. However, in the context of the
hegemony of the Western scholarly establishment in the production and
dissemination of texts, and in the context of the legitimating imperative
of humanistic and scientific discourse, the definition of 'the third world
woman' as a monolith might well tie into the large economic and ideological praxis of 'disinterested' scientific inquiry and pluralism which are
the surface manifestations of a latent economic and cultural colonization
of the 'non-Western' world. It is time to move beyond the Marx who
found it possible to say: they cannot represent themselves; they must be
represented.

10. BARGAINING WITH PATRIARCHY

DENIZ KANDIYOTI

Of all the concepts generated by contemporary feminist theory, patriarchy is probably the most overused and, in some respects, the most
undertheorized. This state of affairs is not due to neglect, since there is a
substantial volume of writing on the question, but rather to the specific
conditions of development of contemporary feminist usages of the term.
While radical feminists encouraged a very liberal usage, to apply to virtually any form or instance of male domination, socialist feminists have
mainly restricted themselves to analysing the relationships between
patriarchy and class under capitalism. As a result, the term patriarchy
evokes an overly monolithic conception of male dominance, which is
treated at a level of abstraction that obfuscates rather than reveals the
intimate inner workings of culturally and historically distinct arrangements between the genders.

I would like to propose an important and relatively neglected point of
entry for the identification of different forms of patriarchy through an
analysis of women's strategies in dealing with them. I will argue that
women strategize within a set of concrete constraints that reveal and
define the blueprint of what I will term the 'patriarchal bargain'[1] of any
given society, which may exhibit variations according to class, caste and
ethnicity. These patriarchal bargains exert a powerful influence on the
shaping of women's gendered subjectivity and determine the nature of
gender ideology in different contexts. They also influence both the
potential for and specific forms of women's active or passive resistance

in the face of their oppression and are susceptible to historical transformations that open up new areas of struggle and renegotiation of the relations between genders.

By way of illustration, I will contrast two systems of male dominance, rendered ideal-typical for the purposes of discussing their implications for women. The types are based on examples from sub-Saharan Africa, on the one hand, and the Middle East, South Asia and East Asia on the other. My aim is to highlight a continuum ranging from less corporate forms of householding, involving the relative autonomy of mother–child units evidenced in sub-Saharan polygyny, to the more corporate male-headed entities prevalent in the regions identified by Caldwell (1978) as the 'patriarchal belt'. In the final section, I analyse the breakdown and transformation of patriarchal bargains and their relationship to women's consciousness and struggles.

AUTONOMY AND PROTEST: SOME EXAMPLES FROM SUB-SAHARAN AFRICA

I had one of my purest experiences of culture shock in the process of reviewing the literature on women in agricultural-development projects in sub-Saharan Africa (Kandiyoti, 1985). The literature was rife with instances of women's resistance to attempts to lower the value of their labour and, more important, women's refusal to allow the total appropriation of their production by their husbands.

Wherever new agricultural schemes provided men with inputs and credit, and the assumption was made that as heads of household they would have access to their wives' unremunerated labour, problems seemed to develop. In the Mwea irrigated rice settlement in Kenya, where women were deprived of access to their own plots, their lack of alternatives and their total lack of control over men's earnings made life so intolerable to them that wives commonly deserted their husbands (Hanger and Moris, 1973). In Gambia, women's customary duties with respect to labour allocation to common and individual plots protected them from demands by their husbands that they provide free labour on men's irrigated rice fields. Men had to pay their wives wages or lend them an irrigated plot to have access to their labour. In the rainy season, when women had the alternative of growing their own swamp rice, they created a labour bottleneck for the men, who simply had to wait for the days women did not go to their own fields (Dey, 1981).

In Conti's (1979) account of a supervised smallholder settlement project in Upper Volta, the men were provided with land and credit, leaving the women no independent resource base and a very inadequate infrastructure to carry out their daily household chores. The result was vocal protest and refusal to cooperate. Roberts (n.d.) similarly illustrates the strategies used by women to maximize their autonomy in the African context. Yoruba women in Nigeria, for instance, negotiate the terms of their farm-labour services to their husbands in order to devote more time and energy to the trading activities that will enable them to support themselves and ultimately give up such services.

In short, the insecurities of African polygyny for women are matched by areas of relative autonomy that they strive to maximize. Men's responsibility for their wives' support, while normative in some instances, is in fact relatively low. It is the woman who is primarily responsible for her own and her children's upkeep, including meeting the costs of their education, with variable degrees of assistance from her husband. Women have very little to gain and a lot to lose by becoming totally dependent on husbands, and hence they quite rightly resist projects that tilt the delicate balance they strive to maintain. In their protests, wives are safeguarding already-existing spheres of autonomy.

Documentation of a genuine trade-off between women's autonomy and men's responsibility for their wives can be found in some historical examples. Mann (1985) suggests that despite the wifely dependence entailed by Christian marriage, Yoruba women in Lagos accepted it with enthusiasm because of the greater protection they thought they would receive. Conversely, men in contemporary Zambia resist the more modern ordinance, as opposed to customary, marriage, because it burdens them with greater obligations for their wives and children (Munachonga, 1982). A form of conjugal union in which the partners may openly negotiate the exchange of sexual and labour services seems to lay the groundwork for more explicit forms of bargaining. Commenting on Ashanti marriage, Abu (1983, p. 156) singles out as its most striking feature 'the separateness of spouses' resources and activities and the overtness of the bargaining element in the relationship'. Polygyny and, in this case, the continuing obligations of both men and women to their own kin do not foster a notion of the family or household as a corporate entity.

Important variations in African kinship systems with respect to marriage forms, residence, descent, and inheritance rules (Guyer and Peters, 1987) are grounded in complete cultural and historical processes, including different modes of incorporation of African societies into the world economy (Mbilinyi, 1982; Murray, 1987; S. Young, 1977). Nonetheless, it is within a broadly defined Afro-Caribbean pattern that we find some of the clearest instances of non-corporateness of the conjugal family both in ideology and practice, a fact that informs marital and market-place strategies for women. Works on historical transformations (for example, Etienne and Leacock, 1980) suggest that colonization eroded the material basis for women's relative autonomy (such as usufructary access to communal land or traditional craft production) without offering attenuating modifications in either market-place or marital options. The more contemporary development projects discussed above also tend to assume or impose a male-headed corporate family model, which curtails women's options without opening up other avenues to security and well-being. The women perceive these changes, especially if they occur abruptly, as infractions that constitute a breach of their existing accommodations with the male-dominated order. Consequently, they resist them openly.

SUBSERVIENCE AND MANIPULATION: WOMEN UNDER CLASSIC PATRIARCHY

These examples of resistance stand in stark contrast to women's accommodations to the system I will call 'classic patriarchy'. The clearest instance of classic patriarchy may be found in a geographical area that includes North Africa, the Muslim Middle East (including Turkey, Pakistan and Iran), and South and East Asia (specifically, India and China).[2]

The key to the reproduction of classic patriarchy lies in the operations of the patrilocally extended household, which is also commonly associated with the reproduction of the peasantry in agrarian societies (E. Wolf, 1966). Even though demographic and other constraints may have curtailed the numerical predominance of three-generational patrilocal households, there is little doubt that they represent a powerful cultural ideal. It is plausible that the emergence of the patriarchal extended family, which gives the senior man authority over everyone else, including younger men, is bound up in the incorporation and control of the family by the state (Ortner, 1978), and in the transition from kin-based to tributary modes of surplus control (E. Wolf, 1982). The implications of the patrilineal–patrilocal complex for women not only are remarkably uniform but also entail forms of control and subordination that cut across cultural and religious boundaries, such as those of Hinduism, Confucianism and Islam.

Under classic patriarchy, girls are given away in marriage at a very young age into households headed by their husband's father. There, they are subordinate not only to all the men but also to the more senior women, especially their mother-in-law. The extent to which this represents a total break with their own kin group varies in relation to the degree of endogamy in marriage practices and different conceptions of honour. Among the Turks, there are lower rates of endogamy, and a husband is principally responsible for a woman's honour. Among the

Arabs, there is much greater mutuality among affines, and a women's natal family retains both an interest and a say in protecting their married daughter's honour (Meeker, 1976). As a result, a Turkish woman's traditional position more closely resembles the status of the 'stranger-bride' typical of pre-revolutionary China than that of an Arab woman whose position in the patriarchal household may be somewhat attenuated by endogamy and recourse to her natal kin.

Whether the prevalent marriage payment is dowry or bride-price, in classic patriarchy women do not normally have any claim on their father's patrimony. Their dowries do not qualify as a form of pre-mortem inheritance since they are transferred directly to the bridegroom's kin and do not take the form of productive property such as land (Agarwal, 1987; Sharma, 1980). In Muslim communities, for a woman to press for her inheritance rights would be tantamount to losing her brothers' favour, her only recourse in case of severe ill-treatment by her husband or of divorce. The young bride enters her husband's household as an effectively dispossessed individual who can establish her place in the patriliny only by producing male offspring.

The patrilineage totally appropriates both women's labour and progeny and renders their work and contribution to production invisible. Woman's lifecycle in the patriarchally extended family is such that the deprivation and hardship she experiences as a young bride is eventually superseded by the control and authority she will have over her own subservient daughters-in-law. The cyclical nature of women's power in the household and their anticipation of inheriting the authority of senior women encourages internalization of this form of patriarchy by the women themselves. In classic patriarchy, subordination to men is offset by the control older women attain over younger women. However, women have access to the only type of labour power they can control, and to old-age security, through their married sons. Since sons are a woman's most critical resource, ensuring their life-long loyalty is an enduring preoccupation. Older women have a vested interest in the suppression of romantic love between youngsters to keep the conjugal bond secondary and to claim sons' primary allegiance. Young women have an interest in circumventing and possibly evading their mother-in-law's control. There are culturally specific examples of how this struggle works to the detriment of the heterosexual bond (Boudhiba, 1985; Johnson, 1983; Mernissi, 1975; M. Wolf, 1972), but the overall pattern is similar.

The class or caste impact on classic patriarchy creates additional complications. Among the wealthier strata, the withdrawal of women from non-domestic work is frequently a mark of status institutionalized in various seclusion and exclusion practices, such as the purdah system and veiling, reinforcing women's subordination and their economic dependence on men. However, the observance of restrictive practices is such a crucial element in the reproduction of family status that women will resist breaking the rules, even if observing them produces economic hardship (Mies, 1982).

In classic patriarchy, the cyclical fluctuations of their power position, combined with status considerations, result in women's active collusion in the reproduction of their own subordination. They would rather adopt inter-personal strategies that maximize their security through manipulation of the affections of their sons and husband. As M. Wolf (1972) suggests, this strategy can even result in the aging male patriarch losing power to his wife. Though these individual power tactics do little to alter the structurally unfavourable terms of the overall patriarchal script, women become experts in maximizing their own life chances.

THE DEMISE OF PATRIARCHAL BARGAINS: RETREAT INTO CONSERVATISM OR RADICAL PROTEST?

The material bases of classic patriarchy crumble under the impact of new market forces, capital penetration in rural areas (Kandiyoti, 1984) or processes of chronic immiseration. While there is no single path leading to the breakdown of this system, its consequences are fairly uniform [resulting] in the earlier emancipation of younger men from their fathers and their earlier separation from the paternal household. While this process implies that women escape the control of mothers-in-law and head their own households at a much younger age, it also means that they themselves can no longer look forward to a future surrounded by subservient daughters-in-law. For the generation of women caught in between, this transformation may represent genuine personal tragedy, since they have paid the heavy price of an earlier patriarchal bargain but are not able to cash in on its promised benefits.

Thus, when classic patriarchy enters a crisis, many women may continue to use all the pressure they can muster to make men live up to their obligations and will not, except under the most extreme pressure, compromise the basis for their claims by stepping out of line and losing their respectability. Their passive resistance takes the form of claiming their half of this particular patriarchal bargain—protection in exchange for submissiveness and propriety.

The response of many women who have to work for wages in this context may be an intensification of traditional modesty markers, such as veiling. Younger women adopt the veil, Azari (1983, p. 68) suggests, because 'the restriction imposed on them by an Islamic order was a small price to be paid in exchange for the security, stability and presumed respect this order promised them'.

This analysis of female conservatism as a reaction to the breakdown of classic patriarchy does not exhaust the range of possible responses available to women. It is intended merely to demonstrate the place of a particular strategy within the internal logic of a given system.

CONCLUSION

Systematic analyses of women's strategies and coping mechanisms can help to capture the nature of patriarchal systems in their cultural, class-specific and temporal concreteness and reveal how men and women resist, accommodate, adapt and conflict with each other over resources, rights and responsibilities. Such analyses dissolve some of the artificial divisions apparent in theoretical discussions of the relationships between class, race and gender, since participants' strategies are shaped by several levels of constraints. Women's strategies are always played out in the context of identifiable patriarchal bargains that act as implicit scripts that define, limit and inflect their market and domestic options. The two ideal-typical systems of male dominance discussed provide different baselines from which women negotiate and strategize, and each affects the forms and potentialities of their resistance and struggles.

NOTES TO PART 1

Chapter 2

1. The UN Commission on the Status of Women was originally formed as a subcommission of the Human Rights Commission at the inaugural meeting of the United Nations in 1945. Fierce lobbying, led by women from the Inter-American Commission of Women, resulted in its upgrading to commission status in June 1946. Its first meeting as a full commission was held in 1947.
2. The women's caucus, Women in Development, was set up within the Society for International Development (SID/WID).
3. The politics of these three world conferences was an explosive combination of the UN North–South agenda and international feminism. The most contentious issue at all three meetings related to the equating of zionism with racism, colonialism and imperialism as causes of underdevelopment. Many women objected to this politicization of the conferences, arguing that such critical international debate belonged in the General Assembly. Others insisted that women had as much right as men to debate the PLO or apartheid and rejected the complaint that discussing subjects unrelated to the conference topic could only deflect whatever impact the conference hoped to make. *Signs* [*1*(1); *6*(3); *6*(4); *7*(3); *8*(2); *11*(3)] includes comments on all conferences.
4. M. Buvinic (1986) 'Projects for Women in the Third World: Explaining Their Misbehaviour', *World Development*, Vol. XIV: 653–64, May.

Chapter 3

1. Ester Boserup, *Woman's Role in Economic Development* (London: George Allen & Unwin, 1970).

2. Ibid., p. 15.
3. Ibid., p. 26.
4. Ibid., pp. 54, 60.
5. Ibid., p. 163.
6. Adult men may also engage in unpaid family labour where extended families prevail.
7. Lourdes Benería, (ed.), 'Accounting for Women's Work', in *Women and Development: The Sexual Division of Labor in Rural Economies* (Geneva: International Labour Organisation, n.d.).
8. Boserup, p. 113.
9. International Labour Organisation (ILO), *Conditions of Work of Women and Young Workers in Plantations* (Geneva: ILO, 1970); Noeleen Heyzer, 'From Rural Subsistence to an Industrial Peripheral Workforce: Female Malaysian Migrants in Singapore', in Lourdes Benería (ed.), and Dorothy Elson and Ruth Pearson, 'Nimble Fingers Make Cheap Workers: An Analysis of Women's Employment in Third World Export Manufacturing', *Feminist Review* (Spring 1981): 87–107.
10. The modernization approach to economic development is based on a perception of social change as a linear movement from backwardness to modernity. Specifically, it calls for the adaptation of technology, institutions and attitudes to those existing in the advanced capitalist countries of the West. The theory does not emphasize changes in class relations or the contradictory effects of the capitalist development process, nor does it acknowledge the possibility of alternative development models. In contrast, the capital accumulation approach analyses the growth of interconnected processes of production—both quantitative and qualitative—motivated by profits, extension of the market, growing social division of labour and modes of production, and the proletarianization of the labour force. Private ownership of resources, and hence of the surplus generated in production (profits, rent and interest), leads to class differentiation between owners and non-owners of the means of production. Private ownership also signals the private appropriation of productive wealth, and growing inequalities in the distribution of income and power.
11. Paul Baran, *The Political Economy of Growth* (New York: Monthly Review Press, 1959); André G. Frank, *Capitalism and Underdevelopment in Latin America: Historical Studies of Chile and Brazil* (New York: Monthly Review Press, 1967); Samir Amin, *Unequal Development* (New York: Monthly Review Press, 1976).
12. See Ester Boserup's earlier work, *The Conditions of Agricultural Growth* (London: George Allen & Unwin, 1965). In this book, exogeneously given population growth provides the major impetus for technical change in agriculture. Her argument is intended to be anti-Malthusian—rising population density in a region is followed, not by the Malthusian checks of war or famine, but by technological adaptation (shorter fallow, higher cultivation intensity, the shift from hoe to plow) designed to facilitate greater food production.
13. Robert Palmer and Neil Parsons (eds), *The Roots of Rural Poverty in Central and Southern Africa* (Berkeley and Los Angeles: University of California Press, 1977).
14. Mahmood Mamdani, *The Myth of Population Control* (New York: Monthly Review Press, 1972).
15. Penelope Ciancanelli, 'Exchange, Reproduction and Sex-subordination

among the Kikyu of East Africa', *Review of Radical Political Economics* 12, No. 2 (1980): 25–36.

16. A.T. Nzula, I.I. Potekhin and A.Z. Zusmanovich, *Forced Labour in Colonial Africa*, Robin Cohen (ed.), trans. Hugh Jenkins (London: Zed Press, 1979).

17. Reproduction here refers not only to biological reproduction and daily maintenance of the labour force, but to social reproduction—the perpetuation of social systems. Related is the view that in order to control social reproduction (through inheritance systems, for example) most societies have developed different forms of control over female sexuality and reproductive activities. This control is the root of women's subordination.

18. Friedrich Engels, *The Origins of the Family, Private Property and the State* (New York: International Publishers, 1975).

19. See Lourdes Benería, 'Reproduction, Production and the Sexual Division of Labor', *Cambridge Journal of Economics* 3, No. 3 (1979): 203–25, for an elaboration of the point. This notion can explain, for example, why sexual mores are less strict among the poor than among middle- and upper-class people in many urban as well as rural areas.

20. Maria Mies, 'The Dynamics of the Sexual Division of Labor and the Integration of Women Into the World Market', in Benería (ed.).

21. Martha Gimenez, 'Population and Capitalism', *Latin American Perspectives* 4, No. 4 (1977): 5–40; Mamdani; Bonnie Mass, 'Puerto Rico: A Case Study of Population Control', *Latin American Perspectives* 4, No. 4 (1977): 66–81.

22. Mamdani.

CHAPTER 6

1. 'Prakriti' is a popular category, and one through which ordinary women in rural India relate to nature. It is also a highly evolved philosophical category in Indian cosmology. Even those philosophical streams of Indian thought which were patriarchal and did not give the supreme place to divinity as a woman, a mother, were permeated by the prehistoric cults and the living 'little' traditions of nature as the primordial mother goddess.

2. Maria Mies, *Patriarchy and Accumulation on a World Scale*, London: Zed Books, 1986, pp. 16–17, 55.

CHAPTER 7

1. See especially Ynestra King, 'Feminism and the Revolt', *Heresies* 13, Special Issue on Feminism and Ecology (1981): 12–16; 'The Ecology of Feminism and the Feminism of Ecology', in *Healing the Wounds: The Promise of Ecofeminism*, (ed.) Judith Plant (Philadelphia: New Society Publishers, 1989), 18–28; 'Healing the Wounds: Feminism, Ecology, and the Nature/Culture Dualism', in *Reweaving the World: The Emergence of Ecofeminism*, ed. Irene Diamond and Gloria Orenstein (San Francisco: Sierra Club Books, 1990), 98–112; Ariel Kay Salleh, 'Deeper Than Deep Ecology: The Eco-Feminist Connection', *Environmental Ethics* 16 (Winter 1984): 339–45; Carolyn Merchant, *The Death of Nature: Women, Ecology, and the Scientific Revolution* (San Francisco: Harper & Row, 1980); and Susan Griffin, *Women and Nature: The Roaring within Her* (New York: Harper & Row, 1978). Also see discussions and critiques by Michael E. Zimmerman, 'Feminism, Deep Ecology and Environmental Ethics', pp. 21–44 and Karen J. Warren, 'Feminism and Ecology: Making Connections', pp. 3–20, both in *Environmental Ethics* 9 (Spring 1987); Jim Cheney, 'Ecofeminism and Deep Ecology', *Environmental Ethics* 9 (Summer 1987):

115–45; and Helen E. Longino's review of Merchant in *Environmental Ethics* 3 (Winter 1981): 365–69.

2. King, 'Ecology of Feminism', 18.
3. Sherry Ortner, 'Is Male to Female As Nature Is to Culture?' in *Women, Culture, and Society*, ed. Michelle Z. Rosaldo and Louise Lamphere (Stanford: Stanford University Press, 1974), quotes on pp. 72, 73.
4. See the case studies, and especially Carol P. MacCormack's introductory essay, in *Nature, Culture and Gender*, ed. Carol P. MacCormack and Marilyn Strathern (Cambridge: Cambridge University Press, 1980), 13. Also see Henrietta L. Moore, *Feminism and Anthropology* (Minneapolis: University of Minnesota Press, 1989).
5. Salleh, 340.
6. See Merchant, 144.
7. Ibid., 2, 3.
8. For this and the previous quote see ibid., xx–xxi, xix.
9. King in 'Feminism and the Revolt' (unlike in her earlier work) does mention the necessity of such a differentiation but does not discuss how a recognition of this difference would affect her basic analysis.
10. For an illuminating discussion of the debate on essentialism and constructionism within feminist theory, see Diane Fuss, *Essentially Speaking* (New York: Routledge, 1989).
11. See case studies in *Nature, Culture and Gender*.
12. Vandana Shiva, *Staying Alive: Women, Ecology, and Survival* (London: Zed Books, 1988), quotes on pp. 39, 42.
13. Ibid., 14–15.
14. Also see the discussion by Gabrielle Dietrich, 'Plea for Survival Book Review', *Economic and Political Weekly*, 18 Feb. 1989, pp. 353–4. Apart from the religion-specificity of the discourse on the feminine principle, an interesting example of the relationship between different religious traditions and the environment is that of sacred groves. These groves, dedicated to local deities and sometimes spread over 100 acres, were traditionally preserved by local Hindu and tribal communities and could be found in several parts of the country. Entry into them was severely restricted and tree cutting usually forbidden. (See Madhav Gadgil and V.D. Vartak, 'Sacred Groves of India: A Plea for Continued Conservation', *Journal of the Bombay Natural History Society* 72, No. 2 [1975].) These groves are now disappearing. Among the Khasi tribe of northeast India, elderly non-Christian Khasis I spoke to identify the main cause of this destruction to be the large-scale conversion of Khasis to Christianity which undermined traditional beliefs in deities and so removed the main obstacle to the exploitation of these groves for personal gain.
15. For instance, the Rig-Veda, the collection of sacred Sanskrit hymns preserved orally for over 3000 years, which constitutes the roots of Brahmanic Hinduism, is said to have been traditionally inaccessible to women and untouchable castes, both of whom were forbidden to recite the hymns on the ground that they would defile the magic power of the words (for elaboration see Wendy O. Flaherty's *Other People's Myths* [New York and London: Macmillan, 1990]). In contrast, the *Bhakti* movement, which began around the sixth century, sought to establish a direct relationship between God and the individual (without the mediation of Brahmin priests) irrespective of sex or caste and gave rise to numerous devotional songs and

poems in the vernacular languages. Many women are associated with the movement, one of the best-known being the sixteenth-century poet-saint, Mirabai. Today the *Bhakti* tradition coexists with the more ritualistic and rigid Brahmanic tradition. In fact a significant dimension of the growing Hindu fundamentalism in India in recent years is precisely the attempt by some to give prominence to one interpretation of Hinduism over others—a visible, contemporary struggle over meanings.

Similarly, several versions of the great epic, *Ramayana* have existed historically, including versions where the central female character, Sita, displays none of the subservience to her husband that is emphasized in the popular version (treated as sacred text) and which has moulded the image of the ideal Indian woman in the modern mass media. Feminist resistance to such gender constructions has taken various forms, including challenging popular interpretations of female characters in the epics and drawing attention to alternative interpretations. See for instance, Uma Chakravarty's essay 'The Sita Myth', *Samya Shakti* 1 (July 1983); and Bina Agarwal's poem 'Sita Speak', *Indian Express*, 17 Nov. 1985.

16. See Irfan Habib, 'Peasant and Artisan Resistance in Mughal India', *McGill Studies in International Development* 34 (McGill University, Center for Developing Area Studies, 1984), and his essay in *Cambridge Economic History of India*, Tapan Ray Chaudhuri and Irfan Habib (ed.) (Cambridge: Cambridge University Press, 1982).

CHAPTER 8

1. Achola Pala-Okeyo, *Towards Strategies for Strengthening the Position of Women in Food Production: an Overview and Proposals on Africa*, INSTRAW, Santo Domingo, 1985. See also Kathleen Staudt, 'Women Farmers in Africa: Research and Institutional Action 1972–1987', *CJAS*, Vol. 22; No. 3, 1988: 567–82, Ester Boserup, *Woman's Role in Economic Development*, St Martin's Press, New York, 1970.

2. Philomena Chioma Steady, 'African Feminism: a Worldwide Perspective', in Rosalyn Terborg-Penn (ed.), *Women in Africa*, Howard University Press, Washington DC, 1989, pp. 3–21.

3. Nearly all research during the colonial period was undertaken by expatriates and thus inclined to be influenced by the European perspective on women at the time.

4. Pala-Okeyo. See also Jane Parpart and Kathleen Staudt, *Women and the State in Africa*, Lynne Reiner, Boulder, 1990, pp. 12–13. On the question of forced labour see Steady, p. 11.

5. Judith Van Allen, '"Sitting on a Man": Colonialism and the Lost Political Institutions of Igbo Women', *CJAS*, Vol. 6, No. 2: 172.

6. Cora Ann Presley, 'The Mau Mau Rebellion, Kikuyu Women and Social Change', *CJAS* Vol. 22, No. 3: 502.

7. Margaret Snyder, 'Gender and the Food Regime: Some Transnational and Human Issues', in *Transnational Law and Contemporary Problems*, University of Iowa, 1991.

8. Ester Boserup, p. 64.

9. Snyder.

10. Pala-Okeyo, p. 11.

11. Presley.

12. Snyder.

Chapter 9

Terms such as *third* and *first world* are problematical both in suggesting over-simplified similarities between and among countries thus labelled, and in re-inforcing implicitly existing economic, cultural and ideological hierarchies which are conjured up using such terminology. I use the term '*third world*' with full awareness of its problems, only because this is the terminology available to us at the moment. [Eds: please note that in this chapter we use the author's preferred style – 'third world' and 'Western'.]

1. Elsewhere I have discussed this particular point in detail in a critique of Robin Morgan's construction of 'women's herstory' in her introduction to *Sisterhood Is Global: The International Women's Movement Anthology* (New York: Anchor Press/Doubleday, 1984). See my 'Feminist Encounters: Locating the Politics of Experience', *Copyright* 1, 'Fin de Siecle 2000', 30–44, especially 35–7.

2. These views can also be found in differing degrees in collections such as Wellesley Editorial Committee (ed.), *Women and National Development: The Complexities of Change* (Chicago: University of Chicago Press, 1977), and *Signs*, Special Issue, 'Development and the Sexual Division of Labor', 7, no. 2 (Winter 1981). For an excellent introduction of WID issues, see ISIS, *Women in Development: A Resource Guide for Organization and Action* (Philadelphia: New Society Publishers, 1984). For a politically focused discussion of feminism and development and the stakes for poor Third World women, see Gita Sen and Caren Grown, *Development Crises and Alternative Visions: Third World Women's Perspectives* (New York: Monthly Review Press, 1987).

3. See essays by Vanessa Maher, Diane Elson and Ruth Pearson, and Maila Stevens in Kate Young, Carole Walkowitz, and Roslyn McCullagh (eds), *Of Marriage and the Market: Women's Subordination in International Perspective* (London: CSE Books, 1981); and essays by Vivian Mota and Michelle Mattelart in June Nash and Helen I. Safa (eds), *Sex and Class in Latin America: Women's Perspectives on Politics, Economics and the Family in the Third World* (South Hadley, Mass.: Bergin and Garvey, 1980). For examples of excellent, self-conscious work by feminists writing about women in their own historical and geographical locations, see Marnia Lazreg (1988) on Algerian women, Gayatri Chakravorty Spivak's 'A Literary Representation of the Subaltern: A Woman's Text from the Third World', in her *In Other Worlds: Essays in Cultural Politics* (New York: Methuen, 1987), 241–68, and Lata Mani's essay 'Contentious Traditions: The Debate on SATI in Colonial India', *Cultural Critique* 7 (Fall 1987), 119–56.

Chapter 10

1. Like all terms coined to convey a complex concept, the term 'patriarchal bargain' represents a difficult compromise. It is intended to indicate the existence of set rules and scripts regulating gender relations, to which both genders accommodate and acquiesce, yet which may nonetheless be contested, redefined and renegotiated.

2. I am excluding not only Southeast Asia but also the Northern Mediterranean, despite important similarities in the latter regarding codes of honour and the overall importance attached to the sexual purity of women, because I want to restrict myself to areas where the patrilocal–patri-lineal complex is dominant.

REFERENCES TO PART 1

CHAPTER 5

Agarwal, Bina (1991) 'Engendering the Environmental Debate: Lessons Learnt from the Indian Subcontinent', CASID *Distinguished Speakers Series Monograph*, No. 8, Michigan State University.

Leach, Melissa (1991) 'Gender and the Environment: Traps and Opportunities', Paper prepared for Development Studies Association (DSA) Conference, Swansea, UK, 11–13 September.

Mies, Maria (1986) *Patriarchy and Accumulation on a World Scale. Women in the International Division of Labour*, London: Zed Books.

Sarin, Madhu (1991) 'Improved Stoves, Women and Domestic Energy', in *Environment and Urbanization*, Vol. 3(2), October.

Shiva, Vandana (1989) *Staying Alive*, London: Zed Books.

Wiltshire, Rosina (1992) 'Environment and Development: Grass Roots Women's Perspective', Development Alternatives with Women for a New Era (DAWN).

CHAPTER 9

Amos, Valerie, and Pratibha Parmar (1984) 'Challenging Imperial Feminism', *Feminist Review* 17:3–19.

Boserup, Ester (1970) *Women's Role in Economic Development*, New York: St Martin's Press; London: Allen and Unwin.

Cutrufelli, Maria Rosa (1983) *Women of Africa: Roots of Oppression*, London: Zed Press.

Hosken, Fran (1981) 'Female Genital Mutilation and Human Rights', *Feminist Issues* 1, no. 3.

Huston, Perdita (1979) *Third World Women Speak Out*, New York: Praeger.

Lazreg, Marnia (1988) 'Feminism and Difference: The Perils of Writing as a Woman on Women in Algeria', *Feminist Issues* 14, no. 1 (Spring): 81–107.

Mies, Maria (1982) *The Lace Makers of Narsapur: Indian Housewives Produce for the World Market*, London: Zed Press.

Minces, Juliette (1980) *The House of Obedience: Women in Arab Society*, London: Zed Press.

Rosaldo, M.A. (1980) 'The Use and Abuse of Anthropology: Reflections on Feminism and Cross-Cultural Understanding', *Signs* 53:389–417.

Tinker, Irene, and Michelle Bo Bramsen (eds) (1972) *Women and World Development*, Washington, DC: Overseas Development Council.

CHAPTER 10

Abu, K. (1983) 'The Separateness of Spouses: Conjugal Resources in an Ashanti Town', in C. Oppong (ed.), *Female and Male in West Africa*, London: George Allen & Unwin.

Agarwal, B. (1987) 'Women and Land Rights in India', Unpublished manuscript.

Azari, F. (1983) 'Islam's Appeal to Women in Iran: Illusion and Reality', in F. Azari (ed.), *Women of Iran: The Conflict with Fundamentalist Islam*, London: Ithaca Press.

Boudhiba, A. (1985) *Sexuality in Islam*, London: Routledge & Kegan Paul.

Caldwell, J.C. (1978) 'A Theory of Fertility: From High Plateau to Destabilization', *Population and Development Review* 4:553–77.

Conti, A. (1979) 'Capitalist Organization of Production through non-Capitalist Relations: Women's Role in a Pilot Resettlement Project in Upper Volta', *Review of African Political Economy* 15/16:75–91.

Dey, J. (1981) 'Gambian Women: Unequal Partners in Rice Development Projects', in N. Nelson (ed.), *African Women in the Development Process*, London: Frank Cass, pp. 109–22.

Etienne, M. and E. Leacock (eds) (1980) *Women and Colonization*, New York: Praeger.

Guyer, J.I. and P.E. Peters (1987) 'Introduction to Conceptualizing the Household: Issues of Theory and Policy in Africa', *Development and Change* 18:197–213.

Hanger, J. and J. Moris. (1973) 'Women and the Household Economy', in R. Chambers and J. Moris. (eds), *Mwea: An Irrigated Rice Settlement in Kenya*, Munich: Weltforum Verlag.

Johnson, K.A. (1983) *Women, the Family and Peasant Revolution in China*, Chicago: Chicago University Press, pp. 209–44.

Kandiyoti, D. (1984) 'Rural Transformation in Turkey and its Implications for Women's Studies', in *Women on the Move: Contemporary Transformations in Family and Society*, Paris: UNESCO.

—— (1985) *Women in Rural Production Systems: Problems and Policies*, Paris: UNESCO.

Mann, K. (1985) *Marrying Well: Marriage, Status and Social Change Among the Educated Elite in Colonial Lagos*, Cambridge: Cambridge University Press.

Mbilinyi, M.J. (1982) 'Wife, Slave and Subject of the King: The Oppression of Women in the Shambala Kingdom', *Tanzania Notes and Records* 88/89:1–13.

Meeker, M. (1976) 'Meaning and Society in the Near East: Examples from the Black Sea Turks and the Levantine Arabs', *International Journal of Middle East Studies* 7:383–422.

Mernissi, F. (1975) *Beyond the Veil: Male–Female Dynamics in a Muslim Society*, New York: Wiley.

Mies, M. (1982) 'The Dynamics of Sexual Division of Labour and the Integration of Women into the World Market', in L. Benería (ed.), *Women and Development: The Sexual Division of Labour in Rural Societies*, New York: Praeger.

Munachonga, M.L. (1982) 'Income Allocation and Marriage Options in Urban Zambia: Wives Versus Extended Kin', Paper presented at the Conference on Women and Income Control in the Third World, New York.

Murray, C. (1987) 'Class, Gender and the Household: The Developmental Cycle in Southern Africa', *Development and Change* 18:235–50.

Ortner, S. (1978) 'The Virgin and the State', *Feminist Studies* 4:19–36.

Roberts, P. (n.d.) 'Rural Women in Western Nigeria and Hausa Niger: A Comparative Analysis', in K. Young (ed.), *Serving Two Masters*, New Delhi: Allied Publishers.

Sharma, U. (1980) *Women, Work and Property in North West India*, London: Tavistock.

Wolf, E. (1966) *Peasants*, Englewood Cliffs, NJ: Prentice-Hall.

—— (1982) *Europe and the People Without History*, Berkeley: University of California Press.

Wolf, M. (1972) *Women and the Family in Rural Taiwan*, Palo Alto, CA: Stanford University Press.

Young, I. (1981) 'Beyond the Unhappy Marriage: A Critique of the Dual Systems Theory', in L. Sargent (ed.), *Women and Revolution*, London: Pluto Press.

Young, S. (1977) 'Fertility and Famine: Women's Agricultural History in Southern Mozambique', in R. Palmer and N. Parsons (eds), *The Roots of Rural Poverty in Central and Southern Africa*, London: Heinemann.

Part 2
Households and Families

INTRODUCTION TO PART 2
LYNN DUGGAN

In many ways households are the nucleus of women's subordination, a condition that may change in form but which survives shifts from agriculture to industrial societies, and from feudal to capitalist modes of production. Part 2 provides an introduction to a gender analysis of dynamics between men and women and among women themselves within households. As noted in Part 1, modernization proponents emphasize that capitalism tends to release women from feudal obligations and restrictions, as men's power over their wives and children is reduced when wage labour gives women and children options outside the household-based economies. The new system, however, brings new power constellations, such as those of capitalist firms and welfare states, and greater concentration of wealth in general.

A. WOMEN'S UNPAID WORK

Historical and recent experience shows that women's family work does not subside when women enter into wage work. Regardless of whether or not they are responsible for generating cash income, women perform the lioness's share of household food preparation, cleaning and child-care work, work which in rural settings usually involves carrying water and finding firewood or other fuel. Typically, unpaid work is not considered 'productive' activity or is simply overlooked by economic analysts and policymakers, as well as by the men who benefit directly from this gender division of labour. In 1995, as part of the Beijing Platform for Action, the UN passed a resolution assigning member governments the responsibility to estimate the value of non-market work and include this in satellite accounts to national income or other official accounts. As of this writing, Trinidad and Tobago has passed legislation to implement this UN decision; it remains to be seen whether other nations will carry out the resolution and to what use these estimates will be put.[1] Although this is but a first step toward recognizing the value of women's unpaid work, the importance of such devalued, often stigmatized labour has, by this move, been formally acknowledged, and caregiving and subsistence agricultural production are gradually being taken into account in evaluating the impacts of economic growth on a population's well-being.

Reading
We begin Part 2 with an excerpted article by Lourdes Benería (Chapter 11). The author explains briefly the ways in which subsistence, informal, domestic and volunteer work have been underestimated and ignored. She reviews

the progress that has been made toward generating more accurate estimates of these activities.

B. HOUSEHOLDS AND CAPITALISM

As mentioned in the Introduction to Part 1, Ester Boserup (1970) is the first to have hypothesized that capitalist economic development tends to increase the productivity of tasks that men usually engage in, as they acquire access to new methods, tools and machinery; in the process, the household balance of power is shifted away from women. Margaret Mead (1976) also calls attention to the power inequalities that arise from the tendency for men to control markets and mechanization while women work in unpaid subsistence agriculture.

Little research has been done on the relationship between women's work in subsistence agriculture and men's agricultural entrepreneurship. Although production for exchange and export leads to greater specialization and efficiency, this also increases households' vulnerability to the world market. Those households in which subsistence production is greatest are best able to withstand downturns in the economy and business risks of all kinds. As Marjorie Cohen points out in her 1985 article on Canadian economic history, agricultural production for trade tends to expand women's workload, because it is usually women who are assigned the responsibility for their families' subsistence needs.

In their pioneering article included in Part 1 above, Lourdes Benería and Gita Sen (1981) support and give class content to Boserup's conclusion that development benefits men disproportionately. Sen and Caren Grown (1987) note that families offer a vantage point from which to resist the encroachment of capitalist values and more individual-based organizations of production. Precapitalist households are usually more expansive, with communal structures that afford more scope for human ties, as well as greater insurance against risk. With increased migration and urbanization, extended families that acted as insurance systems for old-age security and other types of risk are often replaced by nuclear and female-headed units (Becker, 1981; Brown, 1981; Folbre, 1994; Abraham, 1993; D'Amico, 1993; Blumberg, 1993; Castro, 1993; Islam, 1993; Mencher, 1993).

Research by Deere (1977, 1978) and Wiegersma (1981), on Peruvian and Vietnamese peasant households, challenges the notion that capitalism exacerbates gender inequality. Their work supports the Marxist perspective that the destruction of feudal constraints often gives women more degrees of freedom. This debate, rich with implications of the expansion of world capitalism for women, need not be reduced to 'right and wrong' perspectives, but can instead be used to illuminate underlying patterns and experiences common to women in different regions and nations.

In the early 1980s Marxist and socialist-feminist economists also debated the usefulness of the concept of a 'patriarchal mode of production', seeking to extend Marxism beyond its market- and production-centric focus to include and value reproductive care-giving and home-making work (Folbre,

1986; Koopman, 1991; Wiegersma, 1991). On the one hand, this theoretical framework can be used to sum up extensive empirical evidence of unequal exchanges between men and women in work and consumption; mothers and girls, for example, receive less of their daily nutritional requirements than men and boys when food is not abundant, and Third World women work longer hours than men. On the other hand, a 'modes of production' approach focuses attention on material exploitation, putting physical productive and reproductive work at the centre of the analysis. It provides no framework to value the emotional effort involved in caring for children and others. Psychological and emotional dimensions of male domination are implicitly ranked lower than other types of domination.

As it has with Marxian theory, an evolving feminist literature has critiqued the assumptions contained in mainstream, neoclassical economic models of households and gender divisions of labour. Nobel Laureate Gary Becker founded the school of 'New Home Economics' in the 1960s, a body of theory that views households as tiny factories that exist to make efficient use of inputs to 'produce' children and to maximize the well-being of family members. Beckerian neoclassical economic models purport to show that men receive higher returns to their investments in education and training and specialize in labour-force work because they are more efficient at this than are women. Women are correspondingly more efficient at home-making and child-rearing.

Neoclassical economists do not model the origins of gender differences in access to education, resources and power, nor do they look at the complex dynamics within families, relegating such studies to sociologists and anthropologists. The mainstream economic theory of gendered labour is hence tautological; women earn less in the labour force because they specialize in child-rearing; they specialize in child-rearing because they earn less in the labour force.

As with their models of household production, when neoclassical economists theorize intrahousehold distribution they use another simplifying assumption, that of altruistic behaviour within the household (Becker, 1981). Empirical studies have shown, however, that the percentage of income that a household spends on children and its allocations of food and medical care vary, based on the proportions of income earned by women and men (Hoddinott, 1992). Given men's and women's different socialization, women tend to allocate more income to children's needs. Fapohunda (in Dwyer and Bruce, 1988) suggests that researchers should investigate the preconditions that encourage or discourage income-pooling among household members.

In the last several decades, economists have begun to use bargaining models to interpret expenditure patterns and other household decisions (Manser and Brown, 1979; McElroy, 1992; Seiz, 1991; Agarwal, 1994). Such models abandon the assumption of altruism to focus instead on the relative power of household members to influence household decisions. Members' 'threat points', for example, may be defined as the income, skills, and resources these individuals would fall back on in the event that the household should dissolve. Research has begun to frame individuals' fall-back positions within the context of parameters such as the policy-setting that structures men's and women's options and bargaining power. Examples include laws pertaining to marital property, child custody, child-support payments and domestic violence, as well as the extent to which such laws are enforced (McElroy, 1992). For empirical studies of gender dynamics in household decisions see, for example, Blumberg (1993), Hoddinott (1992) and the studies cited in Dwyer and Bruce (1988), as well as the special issues of *Development and Change* (1987) and *World Development* (1989).

Readings
Diane Wolf's sociological comparison (Chapter 12) of two Asian countries challenges the notion of a unified household survival strategy. Chapter 13 on the reasons for declining food security in rural African households also dissects household dynamics to show that men's and women's enterprises and incomes are largely separate. Koopman uses the patriarchal mode-of-production framework noted above to examine the implications of women's responsibility for household food production while men control export crops and land.

We have included Gita Sen's landmark piece (Chapter 14) examining the control of Indian women's sexuality. Sen explores the ways in which pervasive threats of sexual harassment and rape impact women's place in families, communities and labour markets.

C. VIOLENCE IN HOUSEHOLDS

Perhaps the most graphic expression of unequal household power relations is physical violence against subordinate family members. In the absence of institutions that equalize men's and women's access to cash income and property, women are frequently unable to divorce or leave abusive partners, especially if they have children to support. An in-depth look at spouse abuse is provided in *Sanctions and Sanctuary* (1992), a collection of anthropological and sociological essays on intrahousehold violence in Third World societies. This text examines aspects of social organization in countries with varying degrees of wife-beating. Cultural practices associated with less violence against women include a larger role for women in choice of marital partners, bonds of solidarity among village women, cultural norms that disdain expressions of anger, a greater role for women as principal food providers and the near absence of alcohol.

As Kandiyoti points out (Chapter 10), women's compromises with male power structures often have the effect of pitting generations of women against one another. Tensions between mothers-in-law and daughters-in-law are endemic in most Asian cultures, where sons are women's main source of status and security. Mothers' most important bonds are thus with their sons, whose emotional ties to their mothers may be stronger than those with their wives, depending on the extent to which marriages are arranged or based on filial choice. Margery Wolf's (1972) landmark text provides a detailed examination of patrilocal marriage and its implications for women.

Reading

Rita Gallin's article on family structure in a Taiwanese village (Chapter 15) looks at some of the ways in which mothers' need to rely on their sons for old-age insurance impinges on the sons' relationships with their wives. Rather than muting antagonisms between mothers-in-law and daughters-in-law, the pressures that come with increased industrialization and international trade may intensify conflict within the family, as is also noted by Dalsimer and Nisonoff in Chapter 24). The increased incidence of dowry deaths in India illustrates this tendency.

D. FEMALE-HEADED HOUSEHOLDS

As markets bring rapid change to methods and sites of production, options for women in traditional societies, such as their access to labour-force work and thus income, may increase, as noted above. In countries in which women's roles are not strictly constrained, when alternatives to child-rearing and household production have arisen, fertility rates (births to women of child-bearing age) have fallen. As education requirements for children have increased, and acreage in family-based agriculture has diminished, households have come to benefit less from their children's labour, another factor that tends to reduce birth rates. Who Pays for the Kids? (1994) illuminates the gender-power dimension of this type of demographic transition; as children's employment options increase and ownership of land is reduced, fathers have less power to control their offspring by threatening disinheritance, so reducing men's economic incentives to have children. Women's options are not as numerous as men's, so women generally have fewer disincentives or alternatives to child-rearing.

In the face of the enormous changes accompanying the world market's invasion of traditional societies, transforming both women's autonomy and men's relative material stake in children's labour, the incidence of female-headed households has grown. In Latin America the percentage of female-headed units ranges from 14 per cent to 30 per cent across countries, and in the Caribbean, from 25 per cent to 45 per cent (Folbre, 1994). In some urban areas of Latin America and parts of Africa the rate exceeds 50 per cent.

Oestergard (1992) estimates that, at any point in time, one-third of the world's households are female-headed, either temporarily, due to a male partner's migration, or permanently, due to separation, abandonment, divorce or death. Rates of female-headship in today's less industrial countries are much higher than those that prevailed in presently industrial countries at comparable income levels. These households are disproportionately represented among the poorest of the poor. A recent anthology edited by Joan Mencher and Anne Okongwu (1993) focuses on female headship in various developing and industrial countries. The authors compare households' income-generating activities and the attitudes and conditions that give rise to single motherhood.

Reading

From the growing literature in this area, we have included Sylvia Chant's piece on female-headed households in Queretaro, a Mexican shanty town (Chapter 16). The author examines the causes of single motherhood, the economic differences in households headed by males and females, and the authority patterns in dual- and single-parent families, suggesting possible effects of female-headed households on gender roles in Latin America.

NOTE

1.   For further information contact the International Women Count Network, Box 11795, Philadelphia, PA 19101.

FURTHER READING

Abraham, Eva (1993) 'Caught in the Shift: The Impact of Industrialization on Female-Headed Households in Curacao, Netherlands Antilles', in J.P. Mencher and A. Okongwu (eds) (1993).

Agarwal, Bina (1994) *A Field of One's Own: Gender and Land Rights in South Asia*, Cambridge and New York: Cambridge University Press.

Agarwal, Bina (1990) 'Neither Sustenance nor Sustainability: Agricultural Strategies, Ecological Degradation and Indian Women in Poverty', in Bina Agarwal (ed.) *Structures of Patriarchy*, New Delhi: Kali for Women.

Ahmad, Nigar and Shahnaz Ahmead (1990) 'A Day in the Life of Masi Jheelo', in L. Dube and R. Patriwala (eds) (1990).

Becker, Gary S. (1981). *A Treatise on the Family*, Cambridge, MA: Harvard University Press.

Blanc-Szanton, M. Cristina (1990) 'Gender and Intergenerational Resource Allocation among Thais and Sino-Thai Households', in L. Dube and R. Patriwala (eds) (1990).

Blumberg, Rae Lesser (1993) 'Power versus "Purse Power": The Political Economy of the Mother-Child Family III', in J.P. Mencher and A. Okongwu (eds) (1993).

Boserup, Ester (1970) *Women's Role in Economic Development*, New York: St Martin's Press.

Brown, Carol, (1981) 'Mothers, Fathers, and Children: From Private to Public Patriarchy', in Lydia Sargent (ed.) *Women and Revolution*, Boston: South End Press.

Brydon, Lynne and Sylvia Chant (1989) *Women in the Third World: Gender Issues in the Rural and Urban Areas*, New Brunswick, NJ: Rutgers University Press.

Castro, Mary Garcia (1993) 'Similarities and Differences: Female-Headed Households in Brazil and Colombia', in J.P. Mencher and A. Okongwu (eds) (1993).

Chant, Sylvia (1996) *Gender, Urban Development and Housing*, New York: United Nations Development Programme.

Chen, Marty (1990) 'Poverty, Gender and Work in Bangladesh', in R.I. Dube and R. Patriwala (eds) (1990).

Chen, Martha A. (1991) *'Women and Wasteland Development in India'*, Harvard Institute of International Development, Cambridge, MA.

Clark, Mari H. (1984) 'Woman-Headed Households and Poverty: Insights from Kenya', *Signs*, Vol. 10, No. 2.

Cohen, Marjorie (1995) 'The Razor's Edge Invisible: Feminism's Effect on Economics', *International Journal of Women's Studies*, Vol. 8, No. 3.

Collins, Jane L. and Martha Gimenez (eds) (1990) *Work Without Wages: Comparative Studies of Domestic Labor and Self-Employment*, Albany, NY: SUNY Press.

Counts, D.A., J.K. Brown and J.C. Campbell (eds) (1992) *Sanctions and Sanctuary: Cultural Perspectives on the Beating of Wives*, Boulder, CO. Westview Press.

D'Amico, Deborah (1993) 'A Way Out of No Way: Female-Headed Households in Jamaica Reconsidered', in J.P. Mencher and A. Okongwu (eds) (1993).

Deere, Carmen D. (1977) 'Changing Relations of Production in Peruvian Peasant Women's Work', *Latin American Perspectives*, Vol. 4.

Deere, Carmen D. (1978) 'The Differentiation of the Peasantry and Family Structure: A Peruvian Case Study', *Journal of Family History*, Vol. 3.

Deere, Carmen Diana and Magdalena, Leon (eds) (1987) *Rural Women and State Policy: Feminist Perspectives on Latin American Agricultural Development*, Boulder, CO: Westview Press.

Dey, Jenny (1981) 'Gambian Women: Unequal Partners in Rice Development Projects?' *Journal of Development Studies*, Vol. II.

Dube, L. and R. Patriwala (eds) (1990) *Structures and Strategies: Women, Work and Family*, New Delhi: Sage Press.

Fapohunda, Eleanor R. (1988) 'The Nonpooling Household: A Challenge to Theory', in J. Bruce and D. Dwyer (eds), *A Home Divided: Women and Income in the Third World*, Palo Alto, CA: Stanford University Press.

Floro, Maria Sagario (1991) 'Market Orientation and the Reconstitution of Women's Role in Philippine Agriculture', *Review of Radical Political Economics*, Vol. 23, No. 3–4.

Folbre, Nancy (1983) 'Of Patriarchy Born: The Political Economy of Fertility Decisions', *Feminist Studies*, Vol. 9, No. 2.

Folbre, Nancy (1986) 'Hearts and Spades: Paradigms of Household Economics', *World Development*, Vol. 14, No. 2.

Folbre, Nancy (1991) 'Women on their Own: Global Patterns of Female Headship', in Rita Gallin and Ann Fergeson (eds) *Women and Development Annual*, Vol. 2, Boulder, CO: Westview Press.

Folbre, Nancy (1994) *Who Pays for the Kids? Gender and the Structures of Constraint*, London and New York: Routledge.

Guyer, Jane (1984) 'Women in the Rural Economy: Contemporary Variations', in M.J. Hay and S. Stichter, (eds) (1984).

Hay, M.J. and S. Stichter (eds) (1984) *African Women South of the Sahara*, Harlow, UK: Longman Group.

Hetler, Carol B. (1990) 'Survival Strategies, Migration and Household Headship', in L. Dube and R. Patriwala (eds) (1990).

Hoddinott, John (1992) 'Household Economics and the Economics of Households', Paper presented at the International Food Policy Research Institute—World Bank Conference on Intrahousehold Resource Allocation, 12–14 February, Washington, DC: International Food Policy Research Institute.

Islam, Mahmuda (1993) 'Female-headed Households in Rural Bangladesh: A Survey', in J.P. Mencher and A. Okongwu (eds) (1993).

Jahan, Roushan (1988) 'Hidden Wounds, Visible Scars: Violence Against Women in Bangladesh', in Bina Agarwal (ed.) *Structures of Patriarchy*, New Delhi: Sage Press.

Johnson, Elizabeth (1975) 'Women and Childbearing in Kwan Mun Hau Village: A Study in Social Change', in M. Wolf and R. Witke (eds), *Women in Chinese Society*, Stanford CA: Stanford University Press.

Katz, Elizabeth (1991) 'Breaking the Myth of Harmony: Theoretical and Methodological Guidelines to the Study of Rural Third World Households', *Review of Radical Political Economics*, Vol. 23, Nos. 3–4.

Kisseka, Mary and Hilary Standing (eds) (1989) *Sources of Sexual Behaviour: A Review and Annotated Bibliography*, London: Overseas Development Administration.

Koopman, Jeanne (1991) 'Neoclassical Household Models and Modes of Household Production: Problems in the Analysis of African Agricultural Households', *Review of Radical Political Economics*, Vol. 23, Nos 3–4.

Leslie, Joanne (1988) 'Women's Work and Child Nutrition in the Third World', *World Development*, Vol. 16, No. 11.

Maher, Vanessa (1981) 'Work, Consumption and Authority within the Household: A Moroccan Cafe', in K. Young, C. Wolkowitz, and R. McCullagh (eds), *Of Marriage and the Market*, London: CSE Books.

Manser, Marilyn and Murray Brown (1979) 'Bargaining Analyses of Household Decisions', in C. Lloyd, E. Andrews and C. Gilroy (eds), *Women in the Labor Market*, New York: Columbia University Press.

McCrate, Elain (1987) 'Trade, Merger and Employment: Economic Theory on Marriage', *Review of Radical Political Economics* Vol. 19, No. 1.

McElroy, Marjorie (1992) 'The Policy Implications of Family Bargaining and Marriage Markets'. Paper prepared for the International Food Policy Research Institute/World Bank Conference on Intrahousehold Resource Allocation: Policy Issues and Research Methods, 12–14 February 1992, Washington, DC: International Food Policy Research Institute.

McElroy, Marjorie and Mary Jean Horney (1981) 'Nash-bargained Household Decisions: Toward a Generalization of the Theory of Demand', *International Economic Review*, Vol. 22, No. 2.

Mead, Margaret (1976) 'A Comment on the role of Women in Agriculture', in Irene Tinker and Michele Bo Bramen (eds) *Women and World Development: The Complexities of Change*, Washington, DC: The Overseas Development Council.

Mencher, Joan (1989) 'Women Agriculture Labourers and Land Owners in Kerala and Tamil Nadu: Some Questions about Gender and Autonomy in the Household', in M. Krishnaraj and K. Chanana (eds) *Gender and the Household Domain*, New Delhi: Sage Press.

Mencher, Joan (1993) 'Female-headed, Female-supported Households in India: Who Are They and What Are Their Survival Strategies?', in Mencher, J.P. and A. Okongwu (eds) (1993). *Where Did All the Men Go?* Boulder, CO: Westview Press.

Mencher, J.P. and A. Okongwu (eds) (1993) *Where Did All the Men Go?* Boulder, CO: Westview Press.

Mitchell, William E. (1992) 'Why Wape Men Don't Beat Their Wives: Constraints Toward Domestic Tranquility in a New Guinea Society', in D.A. Counts, J.K. Brown and J.C. Campbell (eds) (1992).

Nash, Jill (1992) 'Factors Relating to Infrequent Domestic Violence Among the Nagovisi', in D.A. Counts, J.K. Brown and J.C. Campbell (eds) (1992).

Obbo, Christine (1980) *African Women: Their Struggle for Economic Independence*, London: Zed Press.

Ostergard, Lise (ed.) (1992) *Gender and Development: A Practical Guide*, London and New York: Routledge.

Radcliffe, Sarah A. (1991) 'The Role of Gender in Peasant Migration: Conceptual Issues from the Peruvian Andes', *Review of Radical Political Economics*, Vol. 23, Nos 3–4.

Robertson, Claire C. (1984) 'Women in the Urban Economy', in M.J. Hay. and S. Stichter (eds) (1984).

Saradamoni, K. (ed.) (1992) *Finding the Household: Conceptual and Methodological Issues*, New Delhi: Sage Press.

Seiz, Janet (1991) 'The Bargaining Approach and Feminist Methodology', *Review of Radical Political Economics*, Vol. 23, Nos 1–2.

Sen, Gita and Caren Grown (1987) *Development, Crises, and Alternative Visions: Third World Women's Perspectives*, New York: Monthly Review Press.

Singh, Andrea and Kelles Viitaen (eds) (1987) *Invisible Hands: Women in Home-based Production*, Sage Press, New Delhi.

White, Luise (1984) 'Women in the Changing African Family', M.J. Hay and S. Stichter (eds) (1984).

Wiegersma, Nancy (1981) 'Women in the Transition to Capitalism: Nineteenth to Mid-Twentieth Century Vietnam', *Research in Political Economy*, Vol. 4.

Wiegersma, Nancy (1988) *Vietnam: Peasant Land, Peasant Revolution. Patriarchy and Collectivity in the Rural Economy*, New York: St Martin's Press.

Wiegersma, Nancy (1991) 'Peasant Patriarchy and the Subversion of the Collective in Vietnam', *Review of Radical Political Economics*, Vol. 23, Nos. 3–4.

Wolf, Margery (1972) *Women and the Family in Rural Taiwan*, Stanford, CA: Stanford University Press.

Wolf, Margery (1975) 'Women and Suicide in China', in M. Wolf and R. Witke (eds) *Women in Chinese Society*, Stanford, CA: Stanford University Press.

Yoon, Soon-Young S. (1990) 'Super Motherhood: Rural Women in South Korea', in Dube, L. and R. Patriwala (eds) (1990).

11. ACCOUNTING FOR WOMEN'S WORK: THE PROGRESS OF TWO DECADES[1]

LOURDES BENERÍA

The problem of underestimation of women's work in labour force statistics and national income accounts has been pointed out repeatedly since the 1970s (Boserup, 1970: Weinerman and Lattes, 1981; Benería, 1982; Dixon-Mueller and Anker, 1988; Folbre and Able, 1989; UN, 1989). This underestimation has been observed particularly in four general areas of activity: (a) subsistence production; (b) informal paid work; (c) domestic production and related tasks; (d) volunteer work. Even by accepted definitions of labour force, there has been a tendency to underestimate female labour force participation rates in the first and second areas–as with the case of unpaid family workers in agriculture or with participants in the informal labour market; the main problem in this case consisted in designing more comprehensive and accurate methods of data collection although some conceptual issues regarding the definition of subsistence production also had to be dealt with. In the case of domestic production and related tasks, the problem has been more conceptual; in the conventional view, this type of production was not included in any national accounting statistics because it was defined as falling outside of the economic realm unless performed as some form of remunerated activity. Similarly, in the case of volunteer work the problem has also been conceptual and definitional.

Boserup (1970) was one of the first authors to point out the importance of women's subsistence activities, particularly in rural areas in predominantly agricultural countries, and the underestimation of such activities in the conventional methods of national-income accounting. The influence of the international women's movement since the 1970s, however, and the subsequent work carried out in international organizations and academic institutions, have been instrumental in providing the impetus to analyse and emphasize all aspects of the invisibility of women's work, including domestic production.

The need to deal with the undercounting of women's work at all levels was given important recognition in the 1985 Nairobi Conference that ended the UN Decade for Women, as was reflected in its report *Forward-looking Strategies for the Advancement of Women*. By strongly recommending appropriate efforts to measure the contribution of women's paid and unpaid work 'to all aspects and sectors of development', the report officially sanctioned the process by which the underestimation of women's economic activities had been analysed while the conceptual and practical obstacles to overcome the problem had gradually weakened. Since then, strong support for a more systematic inclusion of statistics on women's work in national accounts has been expressed by other international organizations, many government officials and non-governmental institutions (UN, 1989: UN Office at Vienna, 1989). The effort has been undertaken at the two levels which are most relevant, that is, labour force and production statistics.

ASSESSING THE PROBLEM

Labour force statistics and national-income accounts were historically designed to gather information about the level of economic activity and changes over time, and to provide a basis for economic policy and planning. In capitalist economies, the market has always been viewed as the core of economic activity. Similarly, participation in the labour force and the inclusion of production in national accounts have been defined in relation to their connection to the market or to the performance of some work for 'pay or profit' (as defined by the International Conference of Labor Force Statisticians in 1954). The typical story about the decrease in GNP when a man marries his housekeeper is well known by readers of introductory economics textbooks even if, as a wife, her household activities might not have changed or might even have increased. The reason for this is the notion that unremunerated work was not to be included in national income, and the person performing it not to be counted as a member of the labour force because they were not part of the market or paid exchanges of goods and services and therefore not viewed as economically significant. The notion, however, has been applied differently to various areas of economic activity:

SUBSISTENCE PRODUCTION
An important exception to this rule was subsistence production. As early as 1947, Kuznets had warned about the need to improve the then still-quite young system of national income accounts to include subsistence production: methods to estimate its value and the proportion of people

engaged in it were recommended by the UN system of national income accounts during the 1950s, particularly for countries in which this sector had a relatively important weight in the economy. Thus, countries such as Nepal, Papua New Guinea. Tanzania and others developed methods of estimating subsistence production in varying degrees during this period. By 1960 a working party of African statisticians recommended that estimates of rural household activities would be useful and could be added to those of subsistence production in agriculture, forestry and fishing (Waring, 1988).

This effort was consolidated with the 1966 definition of labour force recommended by the International Conference of Labor Statisticians which included *all persons of either sex who furnish the supply of economic goods and services* (ILO, 1976; emphasis mine). Whether this supply was furnished through the market was not relevant. This exception to the market criterion was addressed particularly to the case of subsistence production although what constituted 'economic goods and services' was not entirely clear.

For the purpose of recording women's economic activities, the 1966 definition of labour force did not end the problem. Despite the conceptual and practical progress made to include subsistence production in national accounting, the statistical information on women working in this sector was problematic for a variety of reasons having to do with methods of data collection, enumeration procedures as in cases of application of concepts such as 'family labour', and the perception of respondents—men and women—regarding women's work and their primary area of concentration (Benería, 1982).

National income accounts likewise differed in their definition of economic goods and services regarding unremunerated production. As Blades (1975) showed based on a survey of 70 countries, an effort to incorporate subsistence production *in agriculture* in GDP accounts was gradually made in most countries but the statistical estimation of subsistence activities was subject to a great variation by country. Once the market criteria did not apply clearly, what was considered an economic activity became arbitrary, and differences between countries developed regarding their inclusion in national accounts of activities such as home gardening, water carrying and food processing (Dixon-Mueller and Anker, 1988).

All of these factors resulted in a tendency to undercount the proportion of the population in the labour force and the value of goods and services included in national accounts. The problem has affected women in particular, given their high concentration in subsistence activities and their specific role in the domestic sphere—which often makes difficult the drawing of a clear line between domestic and subsistence activities.

Over the years, this has resulted in significant statistical disparities between countries—creating difficulties for comparative analysis. Given the general acceptance of the need to include subsistence production in labour force and national income statistics, the problem presently could be identified as one of defining with greater clarity what are 'economic goods and services', a task that has been taken up by experts and appropriate organizations.

THE INFORMAL SECTOR

A different type of problem is represented by the lack of statistical information on workers engaged in the underground and informal sector of the economy or any form of paid work not registered statistically. The absence of appropriate and systematic data collection can in this case be overcome only through an effort to recognize the importance of this sector in many countries and, in the case of women, the high participation of the female population in it. Projects have been undertaken, but they have been of an *ad hoc* nature (SSP/UCECA, 1976; Portes *et al.* 1989; Roberts, 1991).

The difficulties of such a task are not to be underestimated; they derive from the underground character of a [substantial] proportion of this sector as well as from its unstable, precarious and unregulated nature. Periodic and more systematic country surveys, could, however, realistically be elaborated to provide estimates of this sector's weight in labour force and GNP statistics. Along these lines, the UN has prepared general conceptual and methodological guidelines for the measurement of women's work in the sector–industry, trade and services—and carried out useful pilot studies in Burkina Faso, Congo, the Gambia and Zambia (UN Statistical Office/ECA/INSTRAW, 1991a and 1991b). In each case, micro-economic survey data have been combined with macro-economic data.

DOMESTIC WORK

In the case of domestic production and related activities, the problem was of a different nature; unlike subsistence production, this type of work was not viewed as a substitute for market-oriented goods and services and not defined as an 'economic activity'. Until recently there was therefore no attempt to include it in national accounts and labour force statistics because it was seen as falling outside the boundary of these accounts.

The practice was not questioned until the late 1970s. Boserup (1970), for example, argued strongly for the inclusion in national accounts 'of food items obtained by collecting and hunting, of output of home crafts such as clothing, footwear, sleeping and sitting mats, baskets, clay pots, calabashes, fuel collected by women, funeral services, hair cuts, entertainment, and traditional administrative and medical services' together with 'pounding, husking and grinding of foodstuffs and the slaughtering of animals' (pp. 162–3). She saw these activities, however, mostly as subsistence production, not as domestic work; although she mentioned the omission of the 'domestic services of housewives' from national accounts, she was less vociferous about it than in the case of subsistence production. Thus, she emphasized the need to include production for own consumption, which she pointed out was larger in the economically less-developed and agricultural countries than in the more industrialized countries. Yet, as labour has become more expensive in the high-income countries, self-help activities such as construction, carpentry and repairs have increased considerably; this is likely to result in an increase in the number of hours spent on unpaid household work.

Production therefore shifts out of the household at some stages in the economic development process while at least part of it might return to the domestic sphere later—regardless of who performs it. If household production is not being accounted for, growth rates are likely to be over-estimated when this production shifts to the market [and] underesti-mated when it shifts from the market to the household. Given the predominant division of labour and women's role in the household the problem affects women's work in particular. Self-help work, however, such as construction and repairs, also involves men. In any case, the problem of over- or underestimation would disappear if all domestic work and related activities were accounted for. This includes tasks that are carried out simultaneously—as when a housewife cleans the house or goes shopping and takes care of children at the same time.

Since the late 1970s, the absence of statistical information about domestic work has been under scrutiny in many circles and for a variety of reasons. What seemed to be a far-fetched and quite unacceptable notion a decade earlier, has become a matter of serious and constructive work, with specific practical implications, even though much remains to be done.

VOLUNTEER WORK

A different area of undercounted work by women is that of volunteer work. The wide range of tasks in this category creates both conceptual and methodological problems. Conceptually, it refers to work whose beneficiaries must not be members of the immediate family. In addition, there cannot be any direct payment and the work must be part of an orga-nized programme. That is, volunteer work is different from domestic work even though there might be some close connections between the two—such as in the case of voluntary work performed in one's neigh-bourhood—which might make the boundaries difficult to draw. In addi-tion, while some voluntary tasks might easily be viewed as production, such as that of free job training and voluntary home-building organizations, others are more difficult to classify, such as some of those associated with charitable work. Even in the latter case, some accounting of these tasks seems important, particularly if the tasks are free substitutes for what would otherwise be remunerated market work. Gender asymmetries with regard to volunteer work are abundant. As argued by women in New Zealand when they mobilized around this issue in 1984, while (mostly male) monetary contributions to charity are tax-deductible, time contributions (mostly female) are not. The result of this mobilization was the inclusion of a question about time dedicated to volunteer work in the 1986 Census of Population (Waring, 1988).

Much remains to be done to account for women's volunteer work, particularly given that in many areas it has been increasing significantly. Such is the case with survival activities among the poor resulting from the drastic deterioration of living standards of countries with structural adjustment packages. The participation in collective kitchens, for example, raises questions about the conventional definition of volunteer work since the beneficiaries often include both immediate family and neighbourhood members.

CONCLUSION

Numerous reasons have been given for recording unremunerated production and improving the accuracy of statistical information in other areas. These range from the need to base national and international policies and planning on the most accurate assessment of reality, to recognizing the contribution of women to all aspects of development to constructing more comprehensive indices of welfare. A variety of studies carried out in many countries over the years indicates that the value of unrecorded activities, a high proportion of which are performed by women, might range between one-third to one-half of measured GNP (Goldschmidt-Clermont, 1983 and 1989). Different UN documents have repeatedly pointed out that statistics on women's contribution to the economy can be useful for human-resources planning and estimations of potential output, agricultural policies, measures to be taken with regard to the informal sector, and the different adjustment and stabilization policies designed at time of economic crisis. Likewise, they can be useful for the study of savings and consumption patterns, the analysis of household dynamics, regional and comparative studies of men's and women's participation in production and studies of time use by gender (United Nations Office at Vienna, 1989). More accurate data can be useful to design appropriate policies regarding employment, income distribution, social security provisions, pay equity and others.

Systematic information about domestic production and related subsistence activities would shed light on the estimation of welfare levels and on the current discussion about the intensification of women's work resulting from the structural adjustment policies implemented in many countries during the past decade (Elson, 1991: Floro, 1992; Benería, 1992).

Conceptually at least, the battle against the invisibility of women's work seems largely to have been won, at least among those working on these issues; the remaining difficulties appear to be mostly of a practical nature even though, here too, some progress has clearly been made.

B. Households and Capitalism

This section looks at household gender and generational power distributions and their implications for women in the wider economy.

---

12. DAUGHTERS, DECISIONS AND DOMINATION: AN EMPIRICAL AND CONCEPTUAL CRITIQUE OF HOUSEHOLD STRATEGIES

DIANE L. WOLF

Feminists have cut through romantic assumptions about family and household unity, arguing that there exist instead multiple voices, gendered interests and an unequal distribution of resources within families and households (Hartmann, 1981; Thorne and Yalom, 1982). Attention is slowly turning to intra-household relations between genders and generations (Benería and Roldan, 1987; Greenhaigh, 1985; Guyer and Peters, 1987), yet we still know relatively little about intra-household processes, conflicts and dynamics, particularly within poor Third World peasant and proletarian households. Indeed, Third World household studies appear to be the only context in which the myth of family solidarity and unity is perpetuated, and this is seen most clearly in the concept of household strategies.

Those researching the conditions of poor people—both in social histories of advanced industrialized nations and in contemporary Third World countries—often refer to the sum total of behaviours at the household level as family or household survival strategies (hereafter referred to as household strategies) (de Janvry, 1987; Hareven, 1982;

Tilly and Scott, 1978; Stern, 1987; Sorensen, 1988; Findley, 1987). All demographically related acts, from the urban migration of household members in the Philippines, in Latin America and elsewhere (Arizpe, 1982; Findley, 1987; Harbison, 1981; Trager, 1981) to the allocation of labour in poor Javanese households (Firman, 1988; Guest, 1989; Hart, 1986; White, 1976), the early marriage of a daughter in rural Bangladeshi families (Abdullah and Zeidenstein, 1982), or the allocation of more food to male than to female children in Indian families (Rosenzweig and Schultz, 1986) are attributed to household strategies.

This chapter will focus on intra-household relations between parents and daughters in a Southeast and East Asian setting where gender relations differ considerably. This focus will further demystify 'the household', revising notions about internal household relations. Additionally, this analysis of intra-household processes will be utilized to illustrate the inadequacy of the concept of household strategies, and a number of erroneous assumptions therein. While not denying the utility of understanding what poor people or domestic groups must do in order to survive, I argue that, due to certain unwarranted assumptions about individuals and households, the concept of household strategies misrepresents intra-household behaviour, obscures intra-household stratification by gender and generation, and stifles the voices of the unempowered—usually females and the young.

The chapter will focus on women and their households in two Asian settings affected by the new international division of labour. Specifically, I will analyse the decision-making process in the family with regard to young women and factory employment in Java, Indonesia and Taiwan, and critically examine to what extent these processes reflect a household strategy.

PROBLEMS IN HOUSEHOLD RESEARCH

One of the main points in this article is that in household research, whether based on a neo-classical economic framework or a neo-Marxist one, individuals and households are merged and are discussed interchangeably, as though they are one and the same unit, and this problem is most clearly reflected in the concept of household strategies. The household is treated as 'an individual by another name', as though it has a logic and interests of its own (Folbre, 1986:5). On the other hand, any behaviour exhibited by an individual is de facto interpreted as motivated by household interests. The individual is treated like a household in miniature as though (s)he is directed by a gene of household with any and all behaviour assumed to reflect household needs.

A second and serious problem with the current usage of household strategies is that most individual or household-level behaviour is assumed by researchers to be part of a strategy without consulting the views of the social actors involved. Researchers rarely elicit respondents' explanations, motives for their behaviour, or the reasoning behind their decisions (Guest, 1989).

Researchers otherwise sensitive to the structural constraints faced by the poor often impose their own interpretations about strategies extrapolating from household-level or individual-level data. Without empirical information from those involved, they have had a free hand in interpreting behaviour in ways that reflect romantic and ideological views of the family or of family solidarity.

Before it is assumed that any and all individual- or household-level behaviour reflects certain motives, it is imperative to explore the expressed intentions of social actors. My point of departure, drawing upon Giddens's theory of structuration, is that social structures are both 'enabling and constraining' (1984: 169)—social actors are both affected by structural features of the political economy and in turn, through the process of reproduction, affect those very structures. Central to my argument is that social actors 'know a great deal about the conditions and consequences of what they do in day-to-day life' (Giddens, 1984: 281) and understand a good deal about 'the conditions of reproduction' (Giddens, 1984: 5) in their society. If asked, social actors can explain their behaviour and desires (Scott, 1985). The problem is that such responses might not fit models in which individual interests are already assumed.

EMPIRICAL CASE STUDIES

SETTING OF RESEARCH IN JAVA

My research site is a rural district (*kecametan*) in Central Java with a population of 83,500, located approximately sixteen miles south of Semarang, a large port city. In the early 1970s provincial and district-level government officials encouraged foreign and domestic urban investment in this area. Factories began locating in this rural district in 1972 and continue to do so.[1] The site is not a free trade zone, but has a mixture of multinational and domestically owned firms that are oriented towards both the national and global markets. The area is still rural, with the majority of the population engaged in some form of agricultural production.

Part of the continued attraction to this site is due to the low cost of available, docile female labour. In 1982, three-fourths of the approximately 6000-person industrial labour force consisted of females. Most of these women were single, between the ages of fifteen and twenty-four, and lived at home with their parents in the village. The familial context of workers allowed a more in-depth view of interactions between worker-daughters and their families.

RESEARCH DESIGN AND ANALYSIS

I lived in an agricultural village, Nuwun, located several miles from the factories with easy access to public transportation so as to study commuting workers, their non-factory village peers and their peasant families.[2] The decision to leave family, home, hearth and village on a daily basis to enter the industrial labour force represents an important individual transition which can also have a considerable impact on the family economy (Hareven, 1982; Tilly and Scott, 1978). To discern the determinants of factory employment, I interviewed all factory workers (n = 39) and all non-factory females ages fifteen to twenty-four (n = 90) and their families from Nuwun and a neighbouring village. In this unusual rural and industrial setting, households (co-residential groups sharing food and the kitchen) consisted of nuclear and extended families.

Class status interacted with individual and family life-cycle conditions in affecting the probability of seeking factory employment. If intra-household conditions were such that a productive member could be released for full-time work at a distance from home, it appeared that poor families allowed a daughter—or much less frequently a wife—to seek employment in the industrial capitalist sector. These conditions usually included few or no small children, and the availability of at least one other able-bodied female in the household, indicating a later stage of the family life-cycle, when children no longer needed constant care. The poorest families—those in poverty at an early, expanding stage of the family life-cycle—could not afford to forgo the daily labour or returns to the labour of one female productive member needed at home or on the farm.

From the quantitative analysis alone it could easily be concluded that if certain demographic and economic conditions exist within a household daughters seek factory employment to fortify the family economy. We could conclude that dutiful and sensible factory daughters in Java are driven by the 'family economy ideology' (Tilly and Scott, 1978)—altruism towards the family that persists even though the family and work are separate and work is remunerated; in addition, that factory employment is part of a household survival strategy for poor rural families who have few choices. Any notion of industrial employment as part of a household strategy collapses, however, when the household is opened up and the actors, and in this case, actresses, speak.

FACTORY EMPLOYMENT AND HOUSEHOLD DECISION-MAKING

I asked the parents (mostly mothers) of factory workers in Nuwun: 'In Java, who decides where an unmarried daughter should work?' Ten out of twenty parents said the child should decide, nine felt that the parents together with the child should decide and only one parent felt that the parents alone should decide. However, when asked 'Who in your household decided where *your* daughter should work?' *all* twenty parents responded that their daughter had decided alone, on her own.

Daughters had various ways of balancing parental approval with factory employment. Normatively, the ideal decision-making process was to ask parental permission (*minta ijin*) first and then apply for factory positions. While permission from the father seemed to be somewhat more important, most asked both parents. The more common sequence was to apply for positions first, receive a job, and *then* ask parental permission. While most parents agreed, not all consented to their daughter's decision. Parents who disagreed were either fathers or widowed mothers—both of whom are considered heads of households. At that point, daughters either went along with or went against their parents' wishes.

Many of the non-factory single females in 1982 belonged to the group of daughters whose parents would not consent to factory employment. In situations where the household could not afford to release her labour, parents emphatically forbade a daughter's factory employment. This particular group of daughters, most of whom were about thirteen or fourteen years old, obeyed their parents. However, at about age fifteen these young women did become factory workers, often when another sister took their place doing housework but, more importantly, when they became brave enough (*berani*) to defy parental orders.[3]

I found that dutiful daughters were the exception, not the rule. Surinah's widowed mother told this story:

> Actually, I didn't allow her to work in a factory but she forced it anyway. Her older brother also forbade it.[4] I didn't even know when she went looking for a job; I only found out after she started working. She said she wanted to have her own money. In my opinion, it's better if a daughter works at home, helping in the rice-fields (*sawah*).

Ratmi, a commuting factory daughter, recounted the common story of starting factory work against her father's wishes; he was so angry that he didn't speak to her for one month.[4] Another worker in Nuwun who had been forbidden by her parents to work in a factory secretly had sought work on her own:

> I saw my friends work in the factories and then I wanted to work there too. Before, my parents wouldn't allow it. I didn't ask their permission and I started work right away. I went secretly because if

my parents had known, they would have gotten angry with me because they had told me to go work in the *sawah*.

Qualitative data from a sample of fifteen migrant workers boarding in an industrialized village[5] revealed similar but even more dramatic dynamics, with daughters leaving home against parental wishes. Yularikah was told by a friend about the jobs at the biscuit factory. She signed up for work and received a job immediately. When asked how her parents felt, she said, 'Well, Father and Mother were forced to agree; they didn't have any choice since I decided to take the job.'

Clearly, seeking factory employment—an important transition normally assumed to greatly affect the family economy—was not necessarily made in tandem with parental visions of a daughter's role or a family economic plan. While younger daughters (ages thirteen to fourteen) accepted parental disapproval of factory employment, older daughters usually disobeyed and rebelled.[6] In not one case did a parent suggest to a daughter that she seek factory employment. Rather, most parents were on the defensive, responding and adapting to a daughter's decision.[7]

There is, of course, a class basis to this lack of parental control. Better-off families—a small minority in the village—controlled their children's activities and labour by giving them more education. Poor families had less ability to control grown offspring (White, 1976).

MOTIVES FOR SEEKING FACTORY EMPLOYMENT

An important and unexpected finding was that most young women were motivated to seek factory employment for individual social and economic reasons, not for the betterment of the family economy.[8] 'I wanted to be like my friends' said five workers. 'Almost all of my friends here work in a factory. In the late morning (*siang*), it's very quiet because they've all gone to work. I wanted to work too.'

Factory work was a higher-status job than agricultural labour or trade because, according to workers, their skin remained lighter, reflecting non-manual work. 'I wanted to work in a factory because it's not hot and you don't work hard', said one woman. This particular situation reflects some of the ideological contradictions of capitalist development. On the one hand, employment in an industrial capitalist firm was easier and economically more lucrative compared with agricultural labour or domestic service. In terms of workers' personal lives, industrial capitalism was a progressive change as it loosened familial control over their behaviour, brought them into contact with males and females from other villages, often led to romances, and gave them some earnings of their own. However, while factories were perceived as a more desirable work

environment, workers in factories had far less autonomy in the production process compared with traders in the market or agriculturalists, due
to the highly disciplined and controlled atmosphere of industrial capitalist production (Ong, 1987).[9]

Many workers sought factory employment to gain some financial
autonomy from their families. The economic rewards for such employment were, however, meagre and could not attempt to satisfy workers'
needs. Although such employment offered young women independence, low wages forced workers to remain economically dependent
upon their families.

Workers did not mention helping the family economy as a reason for
their employment; rather, they mentioned buying soap for themselves.
Most villagers purchased blocks of inexpensive, unscented soap. If the
family was poor, the same soap was used for bathing, washing clothing
and dishes. Factory workers bought bars of scented soap for bathing
only, costing more than half a day's wage. Buying their own bar of luxury
bath soap somehow signified independence and higher status, differen-
tiating them from other poor villagers. Comments such as 'I wanted to
work in a factory so that I could buy my own soap, like Parjiah', or, 'It's
nice to be able to buy my own soap' underscore the poverty of workers
and their families.

Given such poverty, I expected high remittances from factory wages to
the family economy. My findings of a high degree of income retention
rather than income pooling have been documented elsewhere (Wolf,
1988b). Unlike their Taiwanese counterparts who turn over 50 to 80 per
cent of factory wages to families, these Javanese factory daughters
controlled their own income, remitting little if anything from their
weekly wages to the family till, and often *asked* their parents for money.
Most participated in rotating savings association through which they
accumulated substantial sums of capital. That money was used to buy
their clothing, consumer goods for the household, and was made accessible to parents for life-cycle events (birth, death, circumcision,
marriage), emergencies and debts.

In 1986 I returned to Nuwun to find out if increasing participation in
the family economy by daughters was matched by a greater role in their
life decisions, the timing of marriage and the ability to choose one's own
spouse (Wolf, 1988a). Traditionally, Javanese females are married at a
young age in arranged marriages. I found that the majority of factory
daughters had chosen their own spouse. However, in not one case did a
daughter mention considering her family's economy in terms of the
timing of her marriage or her spouse (Tilly and Scott, 1978).

The relative autonomy of young Javanese females and their somewhat
self-centred concerns is far from resembling our image of docile Asian

females. Why might parents of a grown adolescent daughter not direct her labour? Why might they tolerate her rebellious decisions?

The Javanese kinship system traditionally accorded women some economic autonomy. Parents expect daughters to engage in economic activities and may not attempt to regulate strongly the economic motions of young and female members as they would in a more rigid, patriarchal system. In addition, factory females exhibited more autonomous and plucky behaviour than their mothers would have dared at the same age, because these young women are experiencing a new life-cycle state in Java for which there are few traditional norms—prolonged adolescence. Certainly, the mothers of these young women would have been more controlled by parents and would not have risked dissenting from them, but they would also have been married by age thirteen or fourteen. Increased education, the increasing age at marriage, a new period of adolescence, and young adulthood without economic dependants may well be encouraging more assertive behaviour among young women. Class position also affects behaviour. Since poor parents have little to bequeath to their children, they have less control over them compared with better-off landed families who can orchestrate children's movements more fully because of an eventual inheritance.[10]

To summarize, from a household perspective, economic-demographic characteristics were clearly important but not sufficient in explaining a daughter's employment trajectory. Parents appeared to react and adapt to daughters' decisions rather than direct or orchestrate them. The qualitative data argue against the assumption that poor Javanese households make decisions and develop a strategy, or that members of poor households automatically repress their own desires and needs for the collective good. This is not to argue that Javanese household members never adapt to each other (as did parents in this case) or pursue a united goal. When crop failure occurred in the mid-1980s, factory daughters' savings were used to sustain the family and prevent migration. The data suggest, then, that the economic behaviour of household members is fluid and dynamic and should be analysed rather than assumed. These findings challenge an overly structural or materialist approach to household behaviour.

TAIWANESE HOUSEHOLD STRATEGIES
From research on Taiwanese daughters and the Chinese family economy, we can see more clearly the formulation and execution of a parental strategy at the household level which draws heavily upon the organization of a patriarchal kinship system. Within this patrilineal and patrilocal system, daughters are socialized to be filial and to pay back the

debt they incurred to parents for bringing them up.[11] Parents socialize daughters 'to believe that they themselves [are] worthless, and that literally everything they [have]—their bodies, their upbringing, their schooling—belong[s] to their parents and [has] to be paid for' (Greenhalgh, 1985: 277; Wolf, M., 1972; Gates, 1987). While male and female children are born owing their parents this debt, males pay it off later in life by taking care of elderly parents. Since daughters permanently leave their natal home upon marriage, they must pay back their debt early in life. Because daughters were seen as 'short-term members' of the family, parents did not 'waste' resources in schooling them' (Greenhalgh, 1985: 270).

Without question, historically, parents controlled a daughter's labour—the decision to work, where to work, and her wages. In the 1920s and 1930s in Taiwan and elsewhere, parents controlled their daughters' labour and received her wage directly.[12] Fathers often signed labour contracts, turning their daughters into factory workers who were then treated as indentured servants (Kung, 1983: 17–27; Salaff, 1981: 40).[13]

Since daughters have been socialized to feel that they must pay back their debt to parents, it is not a question of whether to work, but when and where. While parents in the 1950s were hesitant to allow a daughter to leave home for factory work, eventually, factory employment became automatic for young women (Wolf, M., 1972: 99; Arrigo, 1980; Diamond, 1979).

In contemporary Taiwan, parents are still involved in a daughter's work-related decisions and parental opinions are obeyed. Indeed, Kung (1981 and 1983) and Greenhalgh (1985) found that parents make the decision as to when a daughter will stop schooling and where and when she will start working. When an occupation is selected, 'parents are insistent about having daughters abide by their decision' (Kung, 1983: 54). Parents exert authority over which factory she should work in if she is seeking employment or attempting to change factories, particularly if there is a wage differential between factories or if it involves living away from home (Kung, 1983: 54).

Worker's stories, such as: 'going to company Y was my father's idea; being just out of primary school I really didn't have many choices anyway'; or 'it was decided by my mother that I should go to the fish-net factory' (Kung, 1983: 58) demonstrate the difference in parental involvement and deference to parental authority in Chinese families compared with Javanese.[14] Since a daughter's labour and returns to it are seen as economic resources which families control (Salaff, 1981), parents do not demand money from daughters; there is an implicit contract and daughters fulfil their obligation by remitting 50–100 per cent of their wage.[15]

JAVANESE AND TAIWANESE FACTORY DAUGHTERS COMPARED

Changes in the international division of labour have not greatly changed female status within the family in either the Javanese or Taiwanese case, but have fortified the previous position of each, building upon the gender relations which existed before industrial capitalism. Javanese daughters operate within a context of a relatively higher level of female autonomy and they are able to bypass, resist, and defy parental control over their labour. Compared with the Javanese case, Taiwanese parents appropriate a daughter's labour as part of the family portfolio for the benefit of their brothers who will eventually provide for parents in their old age. Chinese daughters adhere to a high degree of subordination and deference to parents. As dutiful daughters they are controlled and used as a resource and, according to Greenhalgh (1985) and Niehoff (1987), even more exploited by parents due to changes in the global economy.[16]

While Chinese families may superficially fit the household strategy metaphor Hareven (1982: 6) suggested, of the movement of a school of fish, or perhaps even a flock of birds, it is clear that not all fish or birds are equal or willing, nor do they necessarily benefit from flying in a flock or swimming in a school. It is also obvious that Javanese families fall short of the bird or fish analogy. Let us now turn to the broader analytical implications of household strategies with these two different cases in mind.

IMPLICATIONS OF HOUSEHOLD STRATEGIES

DEFINITION

How are household strategies defined?

For a household strategy to be created, a decision must be made. Since such decisions are made with the collective good in mind, other household members must accept those decisions and carry them out. Individuals must sublimate their own wishes for this larger goal; 'personal autonomy is subsumed under the constraints imposed by family needs' (Fernandez-Kelly, 1982: 13)

DECISION-MAKING FOR HOUSEHOLD STRATEGIES

Certain people within the household make decisions and other less-empowered household members follow them. Since few family systems operate in democratic fashion (Todd, 1985), household strategies necessarily embody relationships of power, domination and subordination. We saw that Taiwanese parents, not households, make decisions about their daughters' education, labour and marriages, and that those daughters, because of a life-long socialization into their inferior positions, obey dutifully. We saw also that neither Javanese households nor Javanese parents control or decide how to allocate an adolescent daughter's labour.

FATHERS AS BENEVOLENT DICTATORS

Although we know rarely how it is that 'the household' makes its decisions, household economic theory carries a sexual bias in that the individual orchestrating this strategy is implicitly assumed to be male. He does the calculations and makes policy decisions, as the family economy manager and accountant (Findley, 1987: 31). Sorensen's (1988: 63) description of how Korean peasants make cropping decisions provides yet another example. Certainly this particular patriarchal power structure drives certain family systems, but as we saw in the Javanese case, not all (Todd, 1985).

In the new home economics models, Becker's concept of a benevolent dictator assumes that altruism is inherent in such decision-making power (Folbre, 1988: 248; Hannan, 1982; Becker and Murphy, 1988)—a wise Solomonian father-judge internalizes all family members' needs and rules with justice over his brood (Hart, 1978: 35).

The collective good, however, defined by the father or mother reflects particular interests which are not necessarily the interests of household members. Nerlove (1974: 207) noted that in patriarchal societies this often leads to more benefits for sons, particularly elder sons, and less education, food and health care for daughters, sometimes leading to higher female mortality. In her research on Mexican households, Roldan asks if their survival strategies provide the maximum benefit to each and every member of the household. From the perspective of the female industrial worker (engaged in industrial homework), 'the answer to this question must be negative' (1985: 271).

In our case study we saw that Chinese parents control a daughter's labour and attempt to extract as much capital as possible from her before she marries in *their* own interest. A Taiwanese factory daughter is exploited by patriarchal interests for as long as ten years. She is coerced and terrorized into drudgery and sometimes dangerous working conditions for fear of sanctions and loss of her one piece of security—the uterine family. Taiwanese factory daughters hand over their income to their parents and postpone their marriages, all for the interests of a household whose lineage doesn't recognize them.

THE MORAL ECONOMY OF THE HOUSEHOLD

In general, the lack of analysis of household relations, particularly in peasant studies, reflects a romanticized view of automatic and inevitable mechanical solidarity between members of poor families. Such an approach assumes that cohesion and coherence rather than conflict are at the basis of intra-household relationships. The peasant or semi-proletarian household is assumed to be a 'wholly co-operative unit' with its own 'moral economy' (Folbre, 1988: 253; Sorensen, 1988: 130). Those from both a neoclassical economic or Marxist economic background often assume that the competition, struggle or economic self-interest that pervades the capitalist market-place is left on the doorstep, and never enters the household. In the new home economics, 'altruism dominates family life; it drives out selfishness' (Hannan, 1982: 69). Pre-capitalist norms of mutual voluntary aid and concern for the group's good are thought to persist inside the house even as the cold winds of capitalism whip around its outer walls. According to Folbre, in peasant economy models and in Marxian analyses, the 'vision of pure altruism within the family' resembles nothing short of 'utopian socialism' (1988: 9). These assumptions allow neoclassical studies to be based on another assumption—a joint utility function, while more Marxist studies 'assume that reciprocity rules within the household' (Folbre, 1986: 254).

Portraying Third World households or families as cohesive units perpetuates the 'romantic mist' (Hannan 1982), from the world we have lost. The problem with these comforting, consensual images is that they miss entirely intra-household relations of power, subordination and perhaps conflict and dissent. Such research also tends to ignore everyday acts of resistance such as income-retention, non-compliance and conflict. Assumptions of household co-operation prevent researchers from considering (and therefore observing) that individual members may not exhibit altruism and may engage in passive non-strategic or overtly resistant, antagonistic, ambivalent, anti-strategic or even multi-strategic behaviour such as laziness, greed, selfishness, revenge or egocentrism.

WHOSE RATIONALITY?
Pronouncing household behaviour 'strategic' carries ethnocentric strains and imposes a particular world view on conditions vastly different from whence the concept came. It implies the kind of calculation, ratio-nalization and cost-benefit analysis financial advisers apply to our taxes and investments, or we apply to buying a car or a washing machine. The peasant, formerly the 'bumbling idiot of modernization theory enslaved by tradition, is here transformed into a hyper-rational strategist, playing the social game according to optimal strategies' (Gupta, 1987: 44). This is not to say that peasants don't calculate, but that we shouldn't assume that they do or that they calculate in the same way a Westerner might.

The term strategy itself implies militaristic reasoning and echoes language of the capitalist firm. Firms are individual, closed entities, economically independent of each other, competing with each other for a piece of the limited market and profit. However, poor households in the Third World are remarkably fluid in their boundaries and in their economic relations with other households. The struggle for household survival, unlike market profits, is not a zero-sum game. Additionally, the use of 'adaptive household strategies' reflects a Darwinistic ecological approach which portrays household behaviour in a manner similar to a sociobiological perspective (Sorensen, 1988). Clearly, the language used to describe household behaviour also needs serious remodelling.

THE VIEW FROM BELOW

Since researchers have tended to assume that most individual behaviour is part of a household strategy, the views and explanations of social actors are rarely elicited. In addition, researchers may have felt that respondents could not adequately explain their own behaviour. One reason why respondents' explanations are rarely investigated may be due to the assumption that household strategies tend to operate at the subconscious level, rendering empirical analysis difficult if not impossible. However, Giddens argues that the actions required in daily life and social reproduction (household strategies are one form of social reproduction) are not unconscious but lie within the realms of practical and discursive consciousness. Social actors *can* discuss their intentions, reasoning, choices and motives (Giddens, 1984:6); Javanese daughters and parents and Taiwanese parents were well able to express their motives and reactions.

Another reason why we rarely hear the voices of the strategists may be due to an assumption that, even if social actors can discuss their decisions, they cannot sufficiently understand or explain them. Put rather forcefully, social actors are often perceived either as 'cultural dopes' or mere 'bearers of a mode of production' (Giddens, 1979: 71).

A final and related explanation for this gap is that even if social actors can explain and discuss their behaviour, researchers may feel that respondents do not fully understand what they're doing, or do not understand it correctly. In other words, they may have 'false consciousness'.[17] These three reasons for the exclusion of those involved are paternalistic, and give researchers licence to impose their own interpretation upon the data.

BEYOND TAUTOLOGIES

'Peasants', a colleague once said to me, 'are by definition rational.' Similar tautological reasoning has led researchers to label all household behaviour 'strategic', echoing a functionalist, biological and ecological approach to adaptation. Whatever members of poor households do is necessarily a strategy, and strategies are whatever households do; nothing is presented comparatively as irrational, non-strategic or anti-strategic behaviour. Indeed Gupta (1987) points out that this approach severely circumscribes the complexity of behaviour and the range of individual responses. I am not suggesting that we focus solely on individuals, or that household-level research be abandoned. Javanese daughters may indeed repress their own wishes and adapt to household needs, but such conditions should be analysed more specifically in terms of age, family life-cycle stage, and type of problem or decision, and need to be seen more fluidly.

While sociologists and historians are beginning to recognize the need to examine differential power and divergent interests within the household (Salaff, 1988: 272, fn. 9), economists are considering ways to integrate power and control into the neoclassical household model (Lesthaeghe and Surkyn, 1988; Rosenzweig, 1986; Hannan, 1982). Indeed, Ellis's (1988) excellent text on *Peasant Economics* fully integrates Folbre's feminist critique (1986) of household models, an encouraging change which should affect future rural studies.

The question then becomes: how is it that Taiwanese parents can push a daughter into working selflessly for them to the extent that she will postpone her marriage, sell her youth to the company and still feel worthless? We need to better understand the social mechanisms, the struggles and the process within households which perpetuate domination or engender resistance. This will entail analysing gender ideology and relationships of power, particularly the processes through which power is exerted within the family or household, and linking these intra-household asymmetries and processes with political economic structural change. Benería and Roldan (1987), and Kandiyoti (1988), have succeeded in viewing such intra-household relationships dynamically in terms of a continuous process of negotiations, contracts, renegotiations and exchange within a broader political economic context. While such analyses represent a significant departure from the stasis in past studies, it is important to analyse empirically whether appropriating yet another set of economic terms accurately portrays intra-household dynamics.

While the deconstruction of households and the analysis of intra-household asymmetries has emerged in African and Latin American studies, considerable work is yet to be done in Asia, particularly Southeast Asia (Guyer and Peters, 1987; Watts, 1988). Qualitative and comparative data are needed, representing the voices, decisions, desires and acts of resistance of the unempowered, particularly females and the young. We also need a more appropriate and less static conceptual language which takes into account power differentials, different types of decisions and changes over the life-cycle. A comparative approach can help illuminate the differences among and commonalities between women and household practices, and can avert assumptions about the homogeneity of Third World women, Asian women or 'the patriarchal family' (Mohanty, 1988: 70). Opening up the household and analysing the interactions between social actors will erode the image of Third World women as passive victims (Moore, 1988: 79; Mohanty, 1988) and contribute to a portrayal of Third World women as active participants in social change in their own right.

13. THE HIDDEN ROOTS OF THE AFRICAN FOOD PROBLEM: LOOKING WITHIN THE RURAL HOUSEHOLD

Jeanne Koopman

As fundamental problems in Africa's food sector intensify under the strains of structural adjustment policies, African governments and international donors have become increasingly concerned about the political and economic implications of declining household food security and rising malnutrition (UNICEF, 1985; World Bank, 1988).

This chapter discusses the consequences of ignoring the gender aspects of Africa's food crisis: its goal is to emphasize the contributions of women farmers to household food security and aggregate food supply, to stress the importance of an analysis of gender-specific constraints on food production, and to explore the implications of gender-sensitive analysis for policy. It argues that a progressive and effective approach to Africa's food problems must not only direct resources to the great majority of resource-poor farmers, it must also be based on an adequate understanding of the intra-household separation and inter-relation of men's and women's enterprises and incomes. Because most women farmers produce food both to provision their families and to earn a personal income from food sales, women's food output is critical to both rural and urban food supplies. To ignore the tightening constraints on women's food production is to ignore trends that are threatening the health and well-being of large segments of the population.

STORMS VERSUS SEA CHANGES: POLICY FAILURES AND THE DECLINE OF TRADITIONAL AGRICULTURE

Africa's recurring food crises and the successive waves of research and policy initiatives following regularly in their wake can be compared to a series of tropical storms which, in capturing our immediate attention during their fury, tend to divert our analyses from the basic 'sea changes' in the resource base and social organization of traditional peasant agriculture.

The most important 'sea changes' in Africa's smallholder sector over the past several decades have been:

(1) declining soil fertility due to the reduction of fallowing (Hirschmann and Vaughn, 1984; Schoepf and Schoepf, 1988);

(2) continuing male withdrawal from agriculture and out-migration (Brown, 1980; Stichter, 1985); and

(3) increasing exhaustion of overworked women farmers (Bukh, 1979; Cloud and Knowles, 1988; Goheen, 1988; Koopman Henn, 1988).[1]

These fundamental trends are mutually reinforcing. Out-migration of husbands and sons deprives women food farmers of help in clearing new fields, thereby limiting their ability to cultivate more fertile land or to employ labour-intensive methods of soil regeneration. Declining fertility and smaller harvests reduce food farmers' ability to invest in fertility-restoring and labour-saving technology.

THE LIMITS OF A 'PROGRESSIVE FARMERS' APPROACH TO FOOD POLICY

A major problem with many food policies has been their implicit focus on the aspect of the food problem often considered politically most critical—feeding the cities. Since the urban population in most African countries represents only 15–40 per cent of the population (World Bank, 1989), some analysts and policymakers have argued that the stimulation of larger food surpluses from better-off farmers from modern farms operated by the urban élite, or from agro-industrial enterprises, can most effectively achieve national food self-sufficiency (Cohen, 1988). The basic problem with this approach is its inherent tendency to undermine the food security and food-related incomes of the *majority* of the rural population.

Policies that subsidise larger farmers and agro-industrial estates encourage the wealthier segments of the population to expand their control over rural resources, a process that tends to reduce the access of the poor to land and other critical resources. As a result, poorer men and women may be forced to seek seasonal employment on larger farms, even though this means neglecting their own farms at critical periods. Alternatively, men may be compelled to leave the villages altogether, even in periods of high rural unemployment. Policies that implicitly favour larger farmers and capitalist agro-industries rarely take their potential negative effects on resource-poor farmers into account. Evidence from several African countries that chronic malnutrition is becoming a serious problem for large segments of the rural population highlights the importance of a re-analysis of the effects of this type of policy on the rural majority (Pinstrup-Andersen, 1989; UNICEF, 1985).

BASIC CHARACTERISTICS OF AFRICAN AGRICULTURAL HOUSEHOLDS

Food production is, in fact, the major enterprise of nearly all rural African women. In some cases men also participate heavily, in others minimally or not at all. This section presents an outline of basic characteristics of African smallholder farming systems in which men and women pursue a significant number of separate agricultural and non-agricultural enterprises with each economically active adult managing the investment, labour, output and income from his or her enterprises on an individual basis.

Most African household production systems have the following characteristics:

(i) *In the production and processing of food crops, women's responsibilities and labour inputs normally exceed men's.* There are three basic variants of household food production systems: in the first, women are responsible for the production of all or most staple foods and for all other food crops; in the second, men and women cultivate staple food crops jointly in fields controlled by male household or compound heads, while women grow other essential food products in separate gardens; in the third (encountered far less frequently than the others), men are responsible for most food production, and women specialize in food processing and trade.

In the first variant, household food plots are usually considered women's fields. Men help with the clearing of large trees, but with little else. Women control the distribution of the harvest and derive their personal incomes from the sale of output which exceeds family consumption needs (Bukh, 1979; Funk, 1988; Goheen, 1988; Koopman Henn, 1988; Schoepf and Schoepf, 1988).

In the second variant, staple food crops are grown in household or compound fields, and although both women and dependent males help with planting, weeding and harvesting, the male household or compound head controls the output. Women, however, are still responsible for non-staple food production. Women's incomes are derived primarily from the processing and sale of crops from their individual fields (Cloud, 1986; Hemmings-Gapihan, 1982; Davison, 1988). In both variants, there is normally a clear demarcation between men's and women's crops, a distinction which determines who can claim the income from any marketed output (Guyer, 1984a; Roberts, 1988).

Even in the third variant, usually encountered where Islamic practices of female seclusion prevent most women from engaging in field work, young girls and older women may help on male fields, and married women may cultivate small gardens within compounds. Women are usually heavily engaged in food processing (Hill, 1972); non-Islamic women also specialize in the food trade (Guyer, 1984a).

(ii) *In an overwhelming majority of cases, men have ultimate control over the household's most basic productive resource–land* (Davison, 1988, presents ten case studies). In patrilineal inheritance systems, women gain access to land through their husbands. Daughters do not inherit land, divorced women farmers nearly always lose access to their ex-husband's land, and widows often lose a major portion of their deceased husband's land to his patrikin (Goody and Buckley, 1973; Hay, 1982; Wilson, 1982). In matrilineal systems (numerically less significant but still encountered in central and southern Africa), both men and women inherit land from their matrikin. Married women are usually pressured to cede effective land control to their husbands (Hirschmann and Vaughn, 1984), but they are often better able to retain access to land if divorced or widowed (Hill, 1975). In either system, women may be subject to arbitrary withdrawal of certain land rights, particularly with respect to land they allocate to market-oriented enterprises from which their husbands receive little or no monetary return (Hay, 1982; Hirschmann and Vaughn, 1984; Rose, 1988). In sum, male control of land increases significantly the uncertainty and risk in women's food-production activities.

(iii) *With the obvious exception of food produced for family consumption, most 'household income' is not pooled.* Husbands and wives keep separate budgets, make separate investments in their individual enterprises, and have gender-specific as well as joint responsibilities for different categories of family expenditures (Staudt, 1987; Guyer, 1988). In general, men are responsible for housing the family and women for feeding it. Men and women are individually responsible for their personal needs and for investment in their own productive enterprises (Bukh, 1979; Hemmings-Gapihan, 1982; Koopman Henn, 1978). Children's education and medical costs are usually joint expenditure items. It is here that the level of total 'family income' has its primary effect on 'family welfare' (Guyer, 1988).

(iv) *In nearly all African farming systems men alone control export-crop production and the resulting income.* If export crops are not grown, men normally control the production of the most lucrative food crops grown for market sale. Men's social seniority in household and lineage hierarchies and their ultimate control over land permit male household heads to mobilize considerable amounts of women's and male dependents' labour for the cultivation and processing of 'male crops'. Men nonetheless retain ultimate control over the monetary proceeds, deciding how much to spend on dependents' school fees, gifts to wives, other household needs and personal expenditures. This is an arena for bargaining, to be sure, but the real returns to wives and other dependents are inevitably far below the returns a man realizes for his own work (Carney, 1988; Crehan, 1984; Jones, 1986).

(v) *Male farmers also derive income from a wide range of non-agricultural enterprises and from casual or part-time wage labour*. Rural women's opportunities to engage in wage labour and non-agricultural enterprises are far more limited: most, like food processing, beer brewing and small-scale trade, are directly related to the food sector. Women's non-agricultural enterprises are sometimes organized explicitly to take advantage of seasonal increases in male incomes from export crops or other earnings. Wives' access to their husbands' incomes is more often realized through explicit or implicit market relations than through simple intra-household transfers (Guyer, 1988). Their economic opportunities are nonetheless highly conditioned by the state of the male economy.

(vi) *Women's incomes are lower than men's in large part because women are socially required to spend some 40 to 50 hours a week on domestic labour and subsistence food production before they can engage in income earning enterprises*. Men's unpaid family labour obligations are far fewer. Furthermore, a wife is rarely able to mobilise her husband's 'unpaid' labour for male controlled enterprises (Roberts, 1988; Guyer, 1984b). Consequently, women's total labour hours are much higher than men's, while their monetary incomes are much lower (Crehen, 1984; Engberg *et al.*, 1988; Koopman Henn, 1988). This essentially universal outcome seriously constrains women's investment capabilities, but it does not dampen their efforts to maintain individual enterprises and personal incomes.

PROBLEMATIC AGRICULTURAL HOUSEHOLD MODELS, PROJECTS AND POLICY

AGRICULTURAL HOUSEHOLD MODELS AND POLICY CONSTRAINTS ON WOMEN'S FARMS

Most smallholder food projects are based on an implicit model of the household which assumes that all economically active members operate as a single production and consumption unit.

Most African rural households are not, however, characterized by joint enterprise but by a series of individual enterprises in which the enterprise 'owner' manages the production process and controls the ultimate output. While jointly farmed household or compound fields do exist in many household production systems (those of the Sahel region, for example), their output is normally controlled by male household or compound heads. They are, furthermore, accompanied inevitably by individual fields or non-agricultural enterprises that sustain separate budgets (Cloud, 1986; Carney, 1988; Guyer, 1984a).

The prevalence of separate budgets rather than income pooling between spouses indicates that preferences as to what to produce, sell and consume differ. Guyer's conclusion that 'men and women have different spending preferences, not necessarily because they hold different values, but because they are in structurally different situations' (Guyer, 1988, p. 160) aptly sums up the importance of recognizing the structural differences between men's and women's economies within African households and of incorporating them into the formal models used to analyse policies and projects.

Differences between men's and women's enterprises and spending patterns are linked to food-security issues. As the previous section demonstrated, women's enterprises and incomes are more explicitly oriented toward the maintenance of household food security than are men's. While this does not, in itself, contradict the implicit assumption of standard models that total household income and family welfare are positively correlated, evidence on the relationship between children's nutrition and gender-specific incomes demonstrates that it is incorrect to assume that total household income is directly associated with nutritional welfare. Recent research has revealed a positive correlation between women's monetary incomes and children's nutrition. It has not been able to establish a similar correlation between increases in men's incomes and improvements in children's nutrition (Blumberg, 1988, surveys the evidence).

African policymakers and administrators tend to accept the model of the economically unitary household, perhaps because it supports their male constituents' desire to reinforce male control over household resources, in general, and women's labour, in particular. Patriarchal dominance over women's economic opportunities is so deep-rooted historically that it is widely regarded (particularly among men) as either 'natural' or as fully sanctioned by 'custom'. Even today it is not uncommon for men in positions of political or administrative power to suggest that a married woman should not have access to land, credit or other resources on her own account because it would undermine her husband's position as head of the family.

The constraints on women's access to resources are not limited to those emanating from patriarchal relations within households. They have regional, national and international political and economic determinants. At the national level, examples of institutional reinforcement of patriarchal dominance are manifold. State land-registration systems and state-sponsored resettlement schemes, for example, rarely allow married women to obtain individual titles to land (Carney, 1988; Feldman, 1984;

Goheen, 1988; Tadesse, 1982). While widows or divorced women are sometimes allowed to participate in settlement schemes or in state-sponsored irrigation projects as individuals, most women participate only as wives of a male household head. Married women often lose access to their traditional sources of independent income when they join a resettlement project (Bernal, 1988; Conti, 1979). They also face a significant risk of eviction in the event of divorce or widowhood (Brian, 1976; Jacobs, 1989).

Credit associations and export-crop marketing cum credit cooperatives often restrict their membership to household heads, thereby excluding all married and a majority of unmarried women (Goheen, 1988). State-sponsored projects to develop and diffuse modern technology have been heavily concentrated on men's export crops, but even innovations in food-production technology, such as improved seeds, tools and fertilizers, have in fact been targeted at men because it is men who receive the inputs as heads of households (Crehan, 1984; Lewis, 1981).

At the international level, donor-conceived and -funded projects have taken essentially the same ideological view of women as subject to male 'leadership' that informs African state policy. Most donor-provided resources are directed at households, with minimal attention to the nature of intra-household resource use and control. The failure of international agencies to recognize the separation of male and female enterprises has had the effect of drastically limiting women's access to productive resources for their own food production and non-agricultural activities (Staudt, 1985 and 1987).

Colonial governments and international donors have compounded the problems of African women farmers by promoting the western notion that the most appropriate role for women is that of a dependent housewife (Mies, 1986). Even though this view of women as housewives is in direct contradiction to the African assumption that women are responsible for producing most food for home consumption, western attitudes have had a regressive impact on post-colonial agricultural extension and educational services for rural women, which remain heavily oriented toward home economics skills rather than toward training in improved agricultural techniques (Staudt, 1982; Lewis, 1981).

African women farmers still cultivate their fields with the same backbreaking labour, the same hoes and the same range of inputs they used in the pre-colonial period.[2] As land fertility has declined and men have reduced their contributions to the traditional food sector, neither African states nor international donors have made notable progress in helping women farmers overcome the gender-specific constraints which have prevented them from gaining effective access to the resources and technology they need to raise their productivity and output. Thus, even though women are Africa's most experienced and committed food farmers, women and children have been the primary victims of Africa's continuing food crises.

WOMEN WITH RESOURCES: IMPLICATIONS FOR THE FOOD SECTOR

All farmers need secure access to land, credit and technology if the food crisis is to be resolved in a manner that will improve household food security. There is, nonetheless, a critical need to target women, not only because women are more involved in food production than men, but because they face gender-specific intra-household constraints that seriously impede their access to resources targeted at households.

Since the approach advocated here has been tried so rarely, and since women farmers face such daunting social and economic constraints, sceptics may ask: can it work? Do women have the motivation, the energy and the time to increase both food production and marketing even if they do obtain access to new resources? The rare cases in which women have in fact gained new resources show that they can indeed respond positively.

WOMEN'S RESPONSE TO IMPROVED MARKET ACCESS

A case study from southern Cameroon compared the production and marketing of food from two villages with significant differences in access to urban food markets. Market access for farmers in the first village was drastically improved in the early 1980s with the opening of a new highway. In the second village it was necessary, if one wanted to sell food, to headload it to a road situated 1.5 hours walk away and then to wait, possibly for several hours, for public transport. Since the production and marketing situation in the second village was very similar to that of the first before the construction of the highway, data on output, sales and incomes from the second village have been used to approximate the situation of farmers in the first village prior to the improvement in their access to food markets.[3]

With the availability of more efficient and less costly forms of market access, women farmers increased the time they allocated to the production and processing of marketed food by nearly 80 per cent (from 8.5 to 15.2 hours a week), thereby increasing their earnings from food sales by 136 per cent (Koopman Henn, 1989). Women also continued to work about 16 hours a week producing food for family consumption and about 30 hours a week on domestic labour. Even though women's total labour time had been over 61 hours a week prior to the opening of the highway, they responded to the new marketing opportunities by increasing their weekly labour by about seven hours.

Women farmers' impressive response to improved market access contrasts strikingly with the response of men. Even though men's total labour time averaged less than 32 hours per week, only half the men in the village with improved market access increased their output of food products. (Men in this area gain the bulk of their incomes from cocoa production which, in 1985, the year of the survey, still paid a better return to male labour than most food-production activities). Among the men who did increase food production, none produced the variety of food products that women farmers cultivated and sold. Men only increased sales of the two traditionally 'male food crops' in southern Cameroon—plantain and bananas—crops with relatively low labour requirements and high returns to labour. There was no difference in men's total labour times between the two villages: the men who sold more food mobilized unpaid family labour to help increase their output and/or decreased the time they spent on alternative activities, particularly time spent clearing women's food fields (Koopman Henn, 1989).

The significant differences between men's and women's responses to improved food-marketing incentives revealed by this case study have several implications for policy. First, the data show that despite their heavy subsistence and domestic labour responsibilities, women farmers are able to increase food production when they have access to new resources. Second, men's failure to allocate additional labour to the food sector in response to the same incentives available to women indicates that even though men have more leisure time than women, they may well require significantly greater monetary incentives if they are to be motivated to increase food production. Men in rural Africa have a much wider range of income-earning opportunities than women and generally depend far less heavily on the food sector to generate monetary incomes. In the southern Cameroon case, for example, male farmers with excellent access to food markets obtained only 12 per cent of their total monetary income by selling food, while food sales generated 45 per cent of women's incomes even when they had very poor market access. Thus, women's primary involvement in the food sector and their strong motivation to increase production and sales should figure prominently in project design and policy analysis.

CONCLUSION

Until very recently women's food-production and marketing problems have received little attention from governments or donors. This chapter has argued that agricultural household models and project appraisal methods which assume that household resources are pooled and allocated to consumption and investment on the basis of shared preferences have contributed to the general failure to accord women access to improved productive resources. Models of this type have contributed to a serious misunderstanding of African rural household economies in which men and women conduct separate agricultural and non-agricultural enterprises and maintain separate budgets. When state and donor resources are targeted at households rather than at particular categories of farmers, they become subject to male control and rarely enable women to gain access to the inputs they require to improve the productivity of their food farms.

This chapter has attempted to demonstrate that women are highly motivated to increase food production to improve both household food security and their personal incomes. Declining soil fertility and the loss of men's and children's help in the food sector have, however, compounded the negative effects of the gender-specific constraints on women's farming. The failure of African and international authorities to help women overcome these constraints has contributed in a fundamental way to the general decline in Africa's per capita food production.

If women farmers are to increase their food output and sales, they must gain access to improved inputs, technology and credit. Whether or not this will happen remains an open question. Women's own attempts to improve their access to basic resources often meet fierce resistance at national, local and household levels.[4] The power of the social, ideological, political and economic forces that have impeded their access should not be underestimated. On the other hand, the persistent decline in food production and household food security experienced in many countries may finally force a new, gender-sensitive approach to food policy. There is the distinct possibility that repeated food crises will provoke an intensified political response from women farmers themselves. African women are unlikely to allow their families to suffer increasing food insecurity without protest, especially if they continue to see state resources being allocated to agro-industrial enterprises or to the large-scale farms of the élite while their own food farms are deprived of desperately needed inputs.

14. SUBORDINATION AND SEXUAL CONTROL: A COMPARATIVE VIEW OF THE CONTROL OF WOMEN
GITA SEN

A VIEW ACROSS CULTURES

Ask many an Indian man what he thinks of the movement for women's liberation in the West and his response would probably be, 'Oh, they need it there; western women are treated as sex objects by their men, with little recognition of their intellectual, emotional, or moral worth. We in India give our women a special place of honor and dominance in the home and family life; we respect our women.' Encounters with variants of the above self-satisfied pronouncement have forced upon me the realization that, as feminists, we urgently need a cross-cultural examination of the control over female sexuality.

Most Indian women would say that while, perhaps, we are not made to feel we are sex objects in the same manner as women in the West, we are certainly made constantly aware of ourselves as embodiments of sexuality. Whatever the justification for this, the implications for the restrictions on women's mobility, dress, behaviour or interpersonal ties are very similar in many parts of the country.

What we have then is the following interesting duality. In the West, the female body is constantly used as an advertizing medium for the sale of commodities—jeans, automobiles, washing machines, airlines—every consumer product where the choice of brand is believed to depend on the extent of sexual arousal of the consumer. The effect is to reinforce the objectification of woman as a purely sexual creature; all other human attributes are submerged. In India, on the other hand, use of the female anatomy for the purpose of selling commodities, while growing, is not quite so prevalent. Women are not turned into sexual objects principally *via the commodity form*. Sexual objectification is more direct and personal, its social roots lying in the historical antecedents of a peasant society.

In such a society, production has historically been privatized on the basis of patriarchal family units using family labour complemented by nonfamily labour. Patrilocality and patrilineality are the norm. Women of the landholding classes are secluded and their sexuality guarded not only as a mechanism to recruit and control their labour to the productive and reproductive tasks of the family, but especially to ensure the paternity of children. Children represent labour potential and are the heirs of the next generation.

It is an interesting puzzle why the patriarchal family should be so concerned about the precise paternity of the children borne by its female members. If the concern of the patriarchs is over children as potential labourers or as heirs, what does it matter who the *biological* father is, so long as the children are *socially* recognized as belonging to the patriarchal family? One possible answer is the tension among brothers or between males of different generations within the family. Control over children may be a crucial aspect of such intrafamily struggles for domination among males.

It is possible, however, that a more fundamental basis of the tension over biological paternity may lie in the relations between men and women. We have been accustomed to viewing paternity tensions as tensions among men, viz., 'to which man does this child belong?' However, if we examine the social origins of such 'appropriation' and treat it as historically evolved, we come to a different hypothesis about the social meaning of struggles over paternity.

This hypothesis states that in earlier, more egalitarian societies, it is most likely that women had both responsibility for *and* control over children. This would have been reinforced by the fact that, until recently, the only biological certainty in most societies was maternity, not paternity. However, as patriarchal household structures developed concomitant with the growth of economic surplus and the development of the state, the control of children (as over inanimate means of production) passed from women to some (if not all) men. This 'appropriation' of children by patriarchs occurred through the sexual control over women and was strongly reinforced by social and religious glorification of the 'chaste' woman. Indian religious mythology, for example, is full of stories of such embodiments of female 'chasity'; it is my hypothesis that many of these myths arose with the growth of patriarchal religious, cultural and economic domination over prior, more egalitarian, communities. Tensions over paternity therefore represent an ongoing assertion by patriarchs of their control over children. The expressed tension is really that between women and men, and only secondarily among men themselves.

It would be a mistake to infer from this that all women are in identical positions within the hierarchical structure of the patriarchal peasant household. Clearly, it is the sexuality of *young* women, daughters-in-law and daughters that is most in question. Even here, the position is not symmetrical; daughters-in-law must be sexually controlled in the interests of reproducing the patriarchal hierarchy within the household.[1]

Control of daughters on the other hand is undertaken to ensure their recruitment to other households via marriage, and thus to ensure the reproduction of the household within the nexus of the community's social life. The strictest guardians of the sexuality of young women are older women, mothers and mothers-in-laws, whose own relative position within the hierarchy is based on their ability to recruit and channel the labour and sexuality of younger women so as to reproduce patriarchal domination.

It would be a great mistake to imagine that the control of women's sexuality is as rigid within the kin network as it is outside. The extent to which sexuality is expressed within the family varies in different regions of India, but its existence is undeniable. The best known example is the relationship, involving a considerable degree of emotional and physical intimacy, between the daughter-in-law of the house and her husband's younger brothers in parts of North India. Much of this sexuality within kinship is unacknowledged as such, but there is a definite awareness among kin members about its nuances, the subtleties in tabooed relations, forms, etc. Sexuality is not therefore totally suppressed. Rather, it is channelled by and through the networks of the patriarchal family.

The role of men in such channelling is to dominate and control the public space. This control takes the forms of a more or less aggressive occupation of the space in which women, especially young women, are tolerated only within very rigidly defined and strict limits of movement, dress and action. Any transgression of these limits by a woman brings down swift and sometimes harsh retribution in the form of physical, often sexual molestation. Men police the limits, furthermore, by making women constantly aware of themselves as sexual objects, through looks, gestures, laughter and ribaldry. Harkening back to the duality with which we began, women then are no less sexual objects in India than they are in the West, but the form of objectification is different.

In India, for the most part, sexual control is very direct and only peripherally through the commodity form. The economic and cultural conjuncture of a peasant society that is turning capitalist throws up strange and highly contradictory ideological forms. The messages transmitted by Indian cinema, for example, about women and sexuality are a fascinating study in inconsistency, as they attempt to interpret and glamorize life in the cities for the benefit of a largely rural and small-town audience.

The growth of the film image of Indian woman-as-sex-object presents a paradox for our argument that the commodity form is less responsible here for the sex objectification of women. There is a rapidly growing use of female nudity, molestation and rape to titillate and attract male audiences, as well as a sharp increase in pornographic film during the last decade. Commercial Indian film has been using female sexuality precisely in order to sell a commodity—itself. But the apparent paradox is easily resolved when we note that cinema, while a commodity, is of a very unusual type. It is what we may call an 'ideological commodity'. At its most successful, it draws out and mirrors the cultural unconscious of its audience. For better or worse, whether we as feminists like it or not, male control of the public space is part and parcel of the Indian male's image of his world today. And it is this peculiarly male vision of gender relations, with its corollaries of direct, personalized sexual control of women, that is projected on the Indian screen. The example of film therefore buttresses, if anything, our argument about the personalized nature of sexual objectification and control in India.

CLASS DOMINATION AND SEXUAL IDEOLOGY

The direct control of women's sexuality in India, arising as it does from the social relations of patriarchal, family-based production, has its roots in the economics and culture of the landed classes.[2] Is sexual control unimportant then among those with no land? Women's experience appears to indicate otherwise. While seclusion and restrictions on mobility may not be as rigid among the class of landless wage-earners, they are not totally absent. Women agricultural labourers, construction workers or petty traders experience a degree of sexual control over their mobility that affects their entry into the market for wage labour and income earning.

Within the home and community of the landless, female chastity and female virtue are preponderant values guarded, as among the landholders, by older women and by men, young and old, in the public spaces. The relatively high incidence of free unions without formal marriage, or of wife-initiated separation bespeaks a degree of female autonomy within the conjugal bond; but this in no way implies an absence of sexual control.

To what can we attribute this concern with women's chastity in a situation where inheritance is largely irrelevant? Srinivas's theory of Sanskritization (Srinivas 1969) hypothesizes an attempt by those at the lower ends of the social, particularly caste, hierarchy to move upwards through the adoption of upper-caste norms, values and practices. A variant of this concept, of special relevance to women, is the idea that as agricultural households acquire more land or other access to income, they imbibe 'middle-class' values and withdraw their women from work outside the home, and even from work on the family farm.[3]

A counter theory is the orthodox Marxist one that the dominant ideology is that of the dominant class. Control by the ruling classes of the material means for the production of culture allows them to dominate and manipulate the ideas, beliefs and consciousness of the ruled. Such a domination fosters a more effective reproduction of the social hierarchy. Thus the two theories can be seen to approach the problem from opposing directions, the orthodox Marxist seeing the problem as one of domination and imposition, while Srinivas sees it as one of emulation and upward mobility.

Neither approach grants sufficient autonomy to the production of culture and beliefs by the ruled themselves. Neither can tell us enough about the material referents of the sexual control of women among the landless rural population in India. The orthodox Marxist theory of ideology cannot be simply applied in this case, since it is not at all clear what landholders have to gain from the sexual control of women among the landless. Arguments that it promotes divisions within the working class, thus lowering wages and militancy, are too general (perhaps tautological), and tend to confuse causality with factual assertion. Srinivas's theory of cultural assimilation, on the other hand, presumes an emulative pattern in the beliefs and culture surrounding sexuality that does not dissect the implicit hierarchies based on gender. The real question is *who* believes and *who* emulates, and *why*? And why do poor, landless women submit to sexual restriction in a situation where they do not, indeed cannot, rely on men for economic survival?

The answer to these questions must be two-fold. Male interest in the control of sexuality is probably rooted deep in the psychological make-up of oppressed manhood.[4] Common experience tells us that sex between human beings (like perhaps all human interaction) has dual, possibly dialectical, aspects—control appropriation versus communication. To the extent that male control of a woman's body is the dominant aspect (as opposed to the reciprocity inherent in communication), the sexual act is itself intrinsically linked to the transformation of woman into sexual object, not subject.

Though no formal studies have been done in India that I am aware of, the sharing of women's experiences tells us that such control/appropriation is the norm not only among the middle and upper classes, but also among poor people. For the latter, the absence of communication is compounded by very material problems such as lack of space and overcrowding. Perhaps, in addition, the extent of their oppression and subservience based on caste and class leads poor men to control and appropriate in the only sphere possible to them, the sexual.[5] Be that as it may, the consequent sexual objectification and control is experienced by poor women at various levels, from the conjugal bed to the village street. Sexual objectification and control in the public space has its counterpart, perhaps its roots, in objectification within the sexual act itself.

But why do poor, labouring women submit to this control? Responsibility for children under conditions of acute poverty makes women willing to submit to male sexual control in return for some economic resources, however meagre. Connection to a man also means a degree of protection, socially sanctioned and itself reflecting the community's control and channelling of women's sexuality, against sexual harassment by other men of the community. Such protection is much less effective against sexual molestation by members of the landed classes, a subject to which we will now turn.

Sexual demands by men from landed households are a regular and systematic aspect of the lives of poor women. Such oppression may take the form of regularized rape of women who are employed as casual agricultural labourers or as bonded permanent labourers on the owner's land. It may take the less onerous but no less demeaning form of undesired physical intimacy from landowners and supervisors who consider the women who work under them to be 'fair game'. The threat of joblessness and the ever-present spectre of hunger work effectively to ensure women's acceptance of molestation, unless there is a conscious attempt to organize against it.

This type of oppression is heightened during periods of class and caste tension. During times of militancy and organized resistance by either landless labourers or poor peasants, landowners and their hired goons often counter with organized orgies of gang rape and mass sexual violence. For poor women, their class is enmeshed with their gender in an unmistakeable way, since class violence here takes precisely the form of sexual violence. It punishes the militant women in the most direct and brutal manner, and it violates the militant men by appropriating the only arena in which they exercise authority—'their' women.

The class nature of sexual violence in India has been noted before (Mies 1980). Brutal as it is, the existence of such violence perpetrated by the ruling classes is perhaps easier to acknowledge than the sexual control inflicted by poor men upon the women of their own class. A socialist-feminist perspective does not allow us, however, to be blind to either, and even forces us to search out the links between the two.

In the course of organizing work among the women agricultural labourers in a district of Tamilnadu activists who were themselves village women found the medium of role-plays to be very useful in raising the consciousness of women in the village.

One such play dealt with the theme of sexual oppression by landowners. In the discussion that followed a debate ensued about the meaning and relevance of female chastity when it was a well-known, if unacknowledged, fact that such sexual impositions were fairly common. Some young village men on the periphery of the audience intervened, hotly demanding of the women how they could dare question 'chastity', and whether they all wished to be 'immoral'.

What had affected the men most was not the idea of the women having to face the violence of the landlords but the idea that the women might begin to question the notion of female 'virtue', thereby undermining their own, male, control over the women's sexuality.

SEXUAL CONTROL AND THE LABOUR MARKET

The theory of labour-market segmentation has been adopted without much modification to explain Indian women's 'secondary' position in [that] market (Mukhopadhyay, 1981). In a Third World context, the explanatory power of theories developed for labour markets in the West is limited. For women workers, in particular, I would hypothesize that restrictions to mobility arising from the control of sexuality play a crucial role in defining their secondary place.

Two examples will illustrate this argument. Women agricultural labourers are traditionally considered among the freest and most mobile of women workers. Given that many of them are casual labourers who have to search for work, sometimes on a daily basis, it has been assumed that they are free to move considerable distances and to accept work with little restriction.

In fact, the picture above is a rather roseate version of reality. Women labourers generally tend to work fairly close to their homes, or in work situations where co-workers are other women, or men from their own family/community. Women tend to work more in the 'private' or 'semi-public' spaces, and do few tasks considered demeaning to modesty (Kala, 1976).[6] The private space is defined, in the context of Kerala, as the house-site or owner's garden-area, while semi-public space is that which involves a short walk from home.

Only part of this work definition is based on considerations such as proximity to child care since most labouring women have either an older child, a neighbour or an older family member to look after small children. A significant part is the women's own, socially defined perceptions of 'virtue', and the importance they attach to it. Working in proximity to strange men often carries a moral stigma and a suspicion of promiscuity. Gulati (1981) documents such a perception for women construction workers in Kerala. Gangs of migrant labourers, who travel a great deal during the harvest periods, are often hired by contractors on a family basis. Usually, this is the only way in which women can be made to travel long distances from home.

A second illustration is derived from research on women petty traders in Madras city. Quite apart from the handicaps of insufficient capital and

connections needed to obtain a stall in the market, women suffer significantly from the control of sexuality. Their inability to travel, to associate
easily with male wholesalers, or to be in the market late at night, all act
as barriers to their income-earning capacity. This is compounded by the
daily sexual harassment faced by these women as a consequence of their
being in the public space (Lessinger, 1982).

My hunch is that the effect of the sexual control of women on their
labour-market position and income-caring capacity needs to be taken
more systematically into account. Certainly such phenomena are not
entirely unknown in the history of industrialization in the West.

Our conceptual concern is that sexual control is such a 'normal' and
accepted part of the work life of women that it has achieved the status of
an axiom. Our task as feminists is to raise it to the level of a practical and
theoretical problem.

CONCLUSION

In India today, the progressive feminist movement has two sections.
Those who focus mainly on the economic and class problems of poor
women, and those who focus more attention on issues like dowry and
bride-burning which seriously affect middle- and upper-class women.
While neither side underplays the importance of the work done by the
other, and while there are many points on which the two sides come
together, there is an unease in the alliance around the issues of class and
of the control of sexuality.

Facing up to the theoretical and practical importance of the control of
sexuality may place the alliance on firmer ground. The problems of
dowry, rape and bride-burning are the most visible and brutal effects of
the social control of female sexuality. But this is only the tip of the
iceberg. The way in which sexual control shapes gender relations among
workers, rural and urban, and defines poor women's subordination
within the family/community and in the workplace, is the iceberg itself.

C. Violence in Households

The chapter in this section examines the relationship between mothers' dependence on sons and sons' violence against their wives through the medium of a Taiwanese case-study.

15. WIFE ABUSE IN THE CONTEXT OF DEVELOPMENT AND CHANGE: A CHINESE (TAIWANESE) CASE

Rita S. Gallin

THE TRADITIONAL CHINESE FAMILY

The 'economic family', the *jia*, is the basic socio-economic unit in China. Such a family can take one of three forms: conjugal, stem or joint. The conjugal family consists of a husband, wife and their unmarried children; the joint family adds two or more married sons and their wives and children to this core group; and the stem family includes parents, their unmarried offspring, and one married son with his wife and children.

China's patrilineal kinship structure recognizes only male children as descent-group members with rights to the family's property.[1] In the past, and to a large extent today, residence was patrilocal; when a woman married, she left her natal home to live as a member of her husband's family, severing her formal ties with her father's household. Parents considered daughters a liability—as household members who drained family resources when they were children and who withdrew their assets of domestic labour and earning power when they married. Sons, in contrast, contributed steadily to the family's economic security during its growth and expansion and provided a source of support in old age. Parents strongly preferred male children.

Members of the older generation also favoured arranged marriages. Marriage brought a new member into the household, joined two people in order to produce children and established an alliance between families. The needs of the family therefore took precedence over the desires of the individual in the selection of a mate. When parents arranged marriages, they attempted to recruit women who would be compliant, capable workers who were able to produce heirs for the group and who came from families willing to forge bonds of cooperation and obligation.

The oldest male had the highest status, and women's status, although it increased with the birth of sons and age, was lower than that of any man. The roots anchoring this hierarchy were the mores of the 'three obediences', which required a woman to defer to father, husband and sons, and to the norms of piety (*xiao*), which obligated offspring to repay parents for nurturing them. Both principles served as forms of social control, perpetuating the family, the subordination of women to men and the domination of the young by the old.

HSIN HSING VILLAGE

Hsin Hsing is a nucleated village approximately 125 miles southwest of Taiwan's major city, Taipei, and located beside a road that runs between two market towns.

During the 1950s, no significant industries or job opportunities existed locally and land was the primary means of production. Almost all families were agriculturalists, deriving most of their livelihood from two crops of rice, marketable vegetables grown in a third crop and, in some cases, from farm labour hired out for wages. Men, working outside the home in the fields, dominated the public domain. Women managed the house and children, raised poultry, contributed to farm production by weeding fields and drying rice, and, in their 'spare time', wove fibre hats at home to supplement the family income.

By 1979, 85 per cent of resident families' incomes were derived from off-farm employment and almost half of the villagers 16 years or older no longer identified farming as either their primary or secondary activity. The movement of villagers off the land, however, was not limited to men. In 1979 one-half of the married women and four-fifths of the single women in the village worked for remuneration (R. Gallin, 1984a).

The wage employment of single women and men, not surprisingly, was accompanied by modifications in the way marriages were arranged. Parents' monopoly on mate selection disappeared, although the mainte-nance of family continuity required that parents still be involved in negoti-ations. Once these were completed, however, dating in the western sense usually occurred. Consequently, women and men married each other frequently after having already developed an emotional commitment.

WIFE-BEATING IN HSIN HSING

The cruelty of a Chinese mother-in-law toward her daughter-in-law is common knowledge and, during the 1950s, an older woman's treatment of a younger woman in Hsin Hsing was no different.[2] Women today frequently speak of the bitterness of their early years of marriage, when they were saddled with work under the close supervision and scrutiny of their mothers-in-law.

Many describe the capricious ways in which the older woman exercised her authority, by cursing, harassing and even, on occasion, beating.[3] A young woman had to be socialized and integrated into the household and, in the division of labour, this task fell to her mother-in-law (Baker 1979:43). To enforce obedience, and perhaps in retaliation for her own lifelong subjugation, an older woman might well resort to physical abuse of a daughter-in-law with whom she was dissatisfied.

Any number of women reported that men also had beaten their wives to keep them in line. These men had acted as agents of their mothers, who had demanded they bend their wives to the older women's will. One might ask why an older woman would find it necessary to impose her authority through her son. Enforcing compliance was considered to be the mother-in-law's prerogative; a daughter-in-law did not have sufficient power as an individual to defy her mother-in-law or disobey her commands.

The explanation for a mother-in-law's abrogation of authority to her son must, then, lie elsewhere. In Hsin Hsing, the most likely reason was rivalry for the affections of the son. An older woman had first come as a stranger to her husband's family and the birth of her son had improved her status within it and guaranteed her old age insurance. She had spent years nurturing her relationship with her son and tying him firmly to her. She saw the young wife as a competitor for claims on him, someone who would deprive her of his loyalty and support.

Older women had witnessed cases in which, despite the mother's stratagems to protect the filial bond between her son and herself, a real compatibility or unity of interest had developed between the husband and wife, so that the husband had listened to his wife's views and had accepted her advice. From the perspective of the mother, such an alliance represented a powerful and significant threat to her relations with her son, because the younger woman could use her husband to remove the older woman from the family.

To counter this threat, then, the mother-in-law enlisted her son as an ally in the abuse of his wife. Because he had been taught that the goal of marriage was the continuation of the family, and because he had close emotional ties with his mother, the man sacrificed his personal feelings toward his wife and beat her. The effect was that his acquiescence to his mother's demand reaffirmed and strengthened his solidarity with her, while his wife's resentment toward him for the beating negated and weakened his solidarity with her. The invigoration of filial ties and erosion of marital bonds contributed to the maintenance of the undivided family and the older woman's future economic and social security.

Undoubtedly, the ability of a mother-in-law to work her will so successfully reflected a young bride's lack of recourse. The husband was expected to and, as we saw, did side with his mother in dealings with his wife. Her neighbours were reluctant to interfere; 'husband–wife violence … [was] regarded as something "to shut the door on and listen to"' (Harrell, 1982:128). Nor could her father and brothers be counted on to intervene on her behalf.

The inaction of her relatives, in part, was due to the fact that they did not see her that often: marriage was usually village exogamous; people were poor; transportation facilities were not well developed; and visiting revolved primarily around village-based religious events. Unless the abuse of a woman was extreme, her natal family probably was not aware of a beating until long after the incident had occurred.[4] In part, however, their inaction was also due to the fact that most affines were unwilling to jeopardize a meaningful and utilitarian relationship; ties of affinity served as an important foundation for economic activities and were a source of support which supplemented that which was derived from patrilineal kin (Gallin and Gallin, 1985). It was therefore not in the family's interest to support a female relative who 'belonged' to a unit from which it hoped to elicit assistance.

An abused wife, then, had but two alternatives available to relieve her misery. She could endure it and look to the time when she would assume the role of the wife of the head of the house, or she could escape it by committing suicide. I do not know specifically whether any woman from Hsin Hsing chose this alternative, but Margery Wolf has pointed out that 'for peasant women suicide was … and still is … a socially acceptable solution to a variety of problems that offer no other' (1975:112).

Given this situation, did the pattern of wife abuse and the reasons that underlie it change with the transformation of the village's economy? One way to begin to answer this is to look at the way brides were integrated into the households of their husbands in the 1970s. We saw above that, in the 1950s, young women had few resources with which to contest the authority of their mothers-in-law. In the 1970s, in contrast, young brides were not as helpless in dealing with their mothers-in-law as the older women had been with theirs, because they brought decided emotional and economic advantages to the relationship (R. Gallin, 1984b, 1986).

First, the mutual affection that a young couple developed during the betrothal period represented in marriage a serious challenge to the mother–son bond on which an older woman depended to subjugate her daughter-in-law.

Second, by 1979 the value of a young woman's *sai-khia* (private money)—funds which represented a sizeable portion of the seed money for the conjugal family she and her husband would eventually establish and which he would head—outweighed the resources a man's mother had at her command.[5] An older woman, then, was no longer assured of the loyalty and support of her son in confrontations with his wife. Perhaps for this reason, mother-in-law undertook with moderation the integration of a new bride into the household. Although older women complained frequently about their daughters-in-laws' failings, they tended to avoid direct confrontations with them. It was better to side-step an issue than pit a son's ties to his mother against those to his wife, since at best, a son might remain neutral and withdraw from the fray, but at worst, he might defend his wife.

Ironically, it was the material resources which allowed young women to negotiate the new role relationship with their mothers-in-law that precipitated the following beating in 1979. The couple involved in the incident had been married about seven years and the husband drank and gambled heavily. Although he and his wife were members of a joint family, the woman knew that division of the large unit was inevitable and that, when it occurred, she would not be able to depend on her husband, certainly not as a stable source of support for their conjugal family.[6]

It was in her interest, therefore, to guard her *sai-khia*—to invest and cultivate it for future use. Consequently, when her husband demanded that she give him her private money she refused. Unable to extract the money from her through verbal abuse, he resorted to physical violence and beat her. Despite this, the young woman remained uncowed. She had very practical reasons not to give up her *sai-khia*: the future prosperity of her family, and, more importantly, the future prosperity of her two sons—which would determine the nature of her life in old age—depended on this money.

Like her counterparts in the 1950s, however, the young woman had little recourse to escape her husband's abuse. Divorce was not really a viable option; customary law required that sons remain with their father upon dissolution of a marriage and, without sons, who would take responsibility for her in her old age? Her father and brothers also were unlikely to offer protection or a haven to which she could retreat. The increasing importance of affinal ties in the world of a cash economy meant they would place their family's interests before her needs.[7]

Indeed, her natal family did not intercede to demand that her husband stop his abuse. Recognizing the delicacy of affinal ties, her father acted as his son-in-law's agent and also beat her. To reinforce his own family's security, he forced her to give her *sai-khia*—her bulwark against her future insecurity—to her husband.

CONCLUSION

On face value, it would appear that, in the absence of a well-developed social-security system, women's attempts to ensure their old-age security underlie wife abuse in Hsin Hsing.

This explanation masks, however, the fundamental cause of wife abuse in the village and constitutes victim-blaming. The perceived coalition of a young woman with her husband and the refusal of a wife to relinquish her private money were not the cause of wife-beating, though they provided significant excuses for it. In the cases described, young women were considered to have stepped outside the bounds of the cultural definition of femininity by challenging the traditional authority of both the older women and the man. To strengthen and sustain the hierarchical structure of subordination within the family, therefore, beating was believed to be justified. The abuse of women in Hsin Hsing was, in short, motivated by the need of the older women and the men to reaffirm their control over those women who, by cultural definition, were their subordinates.

D. Female-headed Households

The chapter within this section examines the social and economic characteristics of female-headed households in a Mexican shanty town.

---

16. SINGLE-PARENT FAMILIES: CHOICE OR CONSTRAINT? THE FORMATION OF FEMALE-HEADED HOUSEHOLDS IN MEXICAN SHANTY TOWNS

Sylvia Chant

In almost all urban areas throughout Latin America and other parts of the Third World, nuclear households headed by males appear to be the predominant family structure in low-income urban communities. However, in Latin America and the Caribbean, there are also significant numbers of households headed by women. The proportions of female-headed households vary from one place to another for reasons that shall be identified below, but a common denominator in studies which have attempted to account for the existence of the mother–child household has been the explanation that they are the result of male instigation. Furthermore, the family which the man 'leaves behind' is often thought to be worse off socially and economically in his absence, be it temporary or permanent.

Material collected in a survey of 244 low-income owner households in three irregular settlements in Querétaro, Mexico, shows first how female-headed households survive in comparison with male-headed households, and second clarifies the various reasons for the formation of single-parent units, indicating that they often result from female initiative.[1]

In the present study the term 'household' or 'family' will refer exclusively to the co-residential domestic unit, and the term 'matrifocal' will have a precise meaning, in this context, of a household with female leadership where the husband–father is absent permanently and plays no role in the household economy.

In three irregular settlements in Querétaro, a sample of owner households was randomly selected for interview.[2] Owner households were selected because one important aspect of the research project concerned the role of the family in housing improvement, which was less applicable to renters. This may suggest that we are dealing with a relatively privileged group of low-income households. Within Querétaro, however, the rental sub-market was far smaller than in other cities because of an abundance of land and the tolerance of squatting by the authorities during the 1970s. Two-thirds of the poor—defined by the urban development plan as those households surviving on less than two minimum wages (52 per cent of the total urban population)—lived in peripheral *barrios*. Within the study communities, the figures of rented accommodation are low. In Bolaños, for example, only 4 per cent of the population rent, 7 per cent in Los Andadores and 2 per cent in Las Américas. Therefore, we may assume in the present case that the sample is fairly representative of the lowest income groups in the city.

Within the total sample of 244 households, there were 167 male-headed nuclear families and twenty-two female-headed, single-parent units. The average age of male household heads was thirty-two years and of female heads forty years. The average size of a nuclear family was 6.2 people, and of a single-parent family 5.4 people.

WAGE OF THE HOUSEHOLD HEAD

One of the principal reasons offered for the disadvantageous position of single-parent households compared to nuclear families is the fact that women in Mexico on the whole earn less than men.

While the head's wage may be the principal source of income for the family, it is not, however, the only indicator of economic well-being. Contributions from other household members are also important. In nuclear households, there are an average of 1.2 workers, and the earnings of women and children make a negligible contribution to the total budget in comparison to the male head. But in single-parent families, which have an average of 1.6 workers, the head's contribution represents a lower proportion of the total income, and children in these families provide up to one-third of the weekly household budget. The Querétaro data indicate that in terms of per capita income, female-headed families are only marginally less well off than nuclear families.

SPENDING PATTERNS WITHIN HOUSEHOLDS

'Secondary poverty' is a term used to describe the situation of women and children in low-income families where the man withholds part of his wage for personal expenditure. The unequal allocation of economic resources means that women and children are often underfed or under-nourished. In the sub-sample of in-depth interviews carried out with twenty-two nuclear families, just over half (twelve) of the heads retained as much as 50 per cent of the wage for their personal use. Female heads, alternatively, seem to contribute all their wages to family welfare. Many female heads stressed that they were better off financially once their husbands had died or deserted because they could then plan their budgets more efficiently for the week ahead. Many women who lived with volatile husbands stressed that they could never budget effectively because of the variable amount that their husbands gave them for 'housekeeping' each week.

HOUSEHOLD MANAGEMENT

It seems there are important differences in the organization of domestic labour between the two types of family. A strict sexual division of labour in nuclear families dictates that a woman's place is in the home, and 69 per cent of female spouses in those structures were full-time house-wives, whereas in single-parent structures over 80 per cent of the women had paid employment. This has obviously major implications for the running of households.

In nuclear families, especially those with young children, in 55 per cent of the cases housework is carried out single-handedly by the women. When they are aided, help is solicited from daughters and not sons. The key issue here, however, is that there is a full-time house-worker, especially given that in irregular settlements, deficient housing and servicing poses major obstacles to comfort and hygiene. The fact that women in single-parent families have to take on both the role of wage-earner as well as housewife may mean, therefore, that the housework might not get done so efficiently. This problem is often solved in two ways. First, in all but two of the twenty-two cases of single-parent families, housework is shared by the children, and second, women who are employed effectively work a 'double-day' of labour in order to carry out household chores—they begin on the housework when they return home from their jobs. What is most important, however, in the single-parent units is that both boy and girl children participate actively in sharing the task of running the household, and this means ultimately that the time invested per house-worker in domestic labour in such units is roughly only half that invested by full-time housewives in nuclear families.[3] The fact that boys participate as well as girls contains important implications for the socialization of children.

THE SOCIALIZATION OF CHILDREN IN MALE- AND FEMALE-HEADED FAMILIES
Authority patterns in the families are important, because socialization (i.e. the process by which the children's characters are developed and moulded in accordance with dominant social and cultural values) has its origins in the family. It is not entirely clear how parental behaviour affects children's attitudes. On the one hand, it is suggested that boys become confused about their psychological identity in households where the father is absent, and this insecurity is sometimes thought to lead to exaggerated needs to demonstrate masculinity in later life. A more commonly held view, on the other hand, is that because Latin American fathers withhold affection from their sons, this leads to an inferiority complex, accompanied by frustration and anxiety, which results in the perpetuation of *machismo*.

The question of whether children's behaviour is largely imitative or develops as a reaction to their parents' attitudes is difficult to answer, given the limitations of the present study: longitudinal studies of the effect of family structure on subsequent generations were not carried out. However, two important features emerge from the field-work. The first is that frequently in families where husbands were understanding and responsible towards their spouses, men said that they had seen their own fathers treat their mothers badly, and that when their fathers had finally left home they had sworn not to treat their own wives and children in a similar fashion. Second, in female-headed families there tended to be less discrimination against female children, and girls were given opportunities equal to those of boys. In fact, female family heads stressed the need for girls to have education in case they should be deserted by their future husbands. On the surface, no pathological behaviour in children of female-headed families was apparent; they appeared, on the contrary, to be mature and responsible, probably as a result of early participation in household welfare. Children also tended to form an opinion of their mother as a capable person through her being the family's overall provider and mainspring.

THE FORMATION OF SINGLE-PARENT FAMILIES

The reasons why single-parent units are formed were explored in detail in the semi-structured interviews, of which there were only eleven cases. However, the sub-sample of households was selected with the aim of highlighting different sorts of responses, and they will allow us to appreciate the variety of reasons behind the formation of these units. Most women (five) had been deserted by their husbands and were on average eight years older than their counterparts in nuclear families. Abandonment is most likely to occur when the woman is approaching middle age. In three of these cases of desertion, the man had left in order to establish a home with another woman; in the other two cases, the man had left 'in search of work' and had never returned. Two female heads in the sub-sample were widows, and in the remaining four cases, the women themselves had taken the initiative and had left their husbands when they could no longer cope with a situation of violence, infidelity or a lack of financial commitment. In these cases the women had to move out of their husbands' home and find alternative accommodation for themselves and their children.

In the cases of desertion, one might suppose that, in accordance with the dominant view in the literature, the men were frustrated at their inability to provide adequately for the family and thus felt they could not enjoy a position of respect. However, what is most likely is that frustration on the part of the male leads him into behaviour that elicits disapproval from his wife, and a two-way process develops. In an effort to assert his masculinity, the man abuses his position and asserts himself through beating or withholding the wage packet. This in turn causes the wife to upbraid and undermine him (Fromm, 1959; Goode, 1963). In this way it may be suggested that the female is also contributing to 'breakdown'.

Non-viability of the nuclear family, as reflected in widespread divorce, separation and desertion, is perhaps the logical outcome of a situation where men and women are divided in their activities, interests and priorities, with women in a position of subservience. It has been suggested that female dependence and domesticity is actually antithetical to the development of strong emotional bonds (Arizpe, 1982; Hutter, 1981). What is important about the data from Querétaro is that they show that in as many as one-third of the cases, the split is precipitated by *female* initiative. This is a significant minority, given that it is difficult for the female partner to initiate a separation for a number of reasons. Not only is it unlikely that women can earn enough money to support their families, especially when the children are young, but also there are social stigmas attached to being a single parent in Mexico. The Roman Catholic Church, and its ideology of the suffering mother, is rigid in its view of the sanctity of marriage; women who complain about their husbands' behaviour to the local priest and ask for advice are more than likely to be told 'It's your cross and you have to bear it'. Single parents are viewed suspiciously by both men and women. To be a single woman may be conceived by others as an indication of weakness.

Generally, marriage is felt by women to be so binding that several nuclear families continued for many years in unhappy domestic situations. However, some women are prepared to take the initiative and to risk discrimination and a period of financial adjustment and hardship in order to avoid conflictive and insecure domestic situations.

THE EXTENSION OF FEMALE-HEADED UNITS

The survey data indicate that a significant number of single-parent households result from choice and achieve a high degree of economic security and stability within a relatively short period of time. Looking now at the total sample of households and considering extended families, there appear, however, to be two reasons which may lead to the extension of female-headed families.

In the first case, when households are young, women may find it difficult to cope with a full-time job in addition to housework and child care. In order to provide their families with greater economic security and to enable greater flexibility, female-headed units often incorporate relatives to help them manage survival. Extension of the family unit is more prevalent among households headed by women than households headed by men—one-third of the female-headed units in the total survey contained additional relatives, and this was the case in only one-fifth of the households headed by males.

Second, single-parent units often become extended at a later stage of the life cycle, when the children are grown up and getting married. In order not to forgo the economic support of sons and daughters, female heads may invite their prospective in-laws to come and live with them in their homes.

CONCLUSION

In this discussion of the differences between the economic and social welfare of female-headed and male-headed families in low-income communities on Querétaro, two important factors have emerged. First, in terms of economic welfare, household management and authority patterns, the male-headed, nuclear unit displays certain characteristics which are less desirable than those of female-headed households. Second, single-parent structures are often the outcome of a deliberate and positive choice by low-income women. However, as Harris (1982) points out, there is a 'cruel paradox' in that while the overall increase in the proportion of female-headed households in Latin America may be interpreted as an indication '... that women are beginning to free themselves from the more repressive and restricting aspects of *machista* culture...', their potential freedom is put in a strangle-hold by virtue of the fact that they are often found '... amongst the poorest strata where life is most precarious' (Harris, 1982: 6). Despite this, the data from Querétaro show that the formation of a female-headed unit, whether through male or female initiative, often results in family life becoming more secure and stable in a variety of ways. Sexual discrimination in the labour market often means that women earn low wages, but these earnings are boosted by economic cooperation from their children. Difficulties in carrying out the two full-time roles of worker and housewife are smoothed out by the help of both male and female children in the home. An absence of violence and of the abuse of authority within the family not only results in greater psychological security, but may also be conducive to both a reduction of *machismo* and of hostility between men and women. The fact that female-headed units often seek to incorporate kin is indicative, however, of the difficulties that single mothers face in a society which discriminates against women; nevertheless, the study shows that female-headed units contain several positive elements in the struggle for survival. Furthermore, we have also discussed single-parent families which exist without the safety net of a state welfare system, which may well improve the viability of single-parent households in other important respects.

Certainly, the heavy dependence of mothers on sons and daughters may be interpreted as imposing an obstacle to their children's education; however, the fact that female-headed units tend to form at a stage in the life cycle when many children from all kinds of families in the communities work part-time to further their studies means that the threat to the 'normal' development of the child's potential may be lessened.

Despite major structural constraints on the economic and social potential of female-headed families, single-parent units often fare better than male-headed nuclear households under the conditions described in this article. However, it is possible that single-parent families may not function so well in other situations. The majority of the poor in Querétaro have access to home ownership which gives greater scope for flexibility and security than renting. Future research ought to consider the position of families in rental accommodation in order to establish how effectively male- and female-headed families manage survival in other low-income tenure categories.

NOTES TO PART 2

CHAPTER 11

1. The original version of this chapter includes a summary of the 'contributions of a decade'.

CHAPTER 12

This chapter is a revised version of 'Father Knows Best about All in the Household: A Feminist Critique of Household Strategies', presented at the Sex and Gender session of the annual meeting of the American Sociological Association, 1988. Field research in Java was sponsored by LIPI and supported by a Title XII grant administered through the Program in International Agriculture, Cornell University (1981 to 1983) and the Graduate School Research Fund, University of Washington (1986).

1. When I conducted research in 1981–83 there were nine large-scale factories operating and three under construction. When I returned in 1986 three additional factories had been built and all fifteen seemed untouched by national and global economic crises. The largest factories (by number of workers) were two textile firms, followed by garments and food processing (bread, cookies, bottling), furniture and buses.
2. I conducted fieldwork for fifteen months from 1981 to 1983, and returned for a two-month follow-up in 1986.
3. In situations where a father is not present, an older brother or cousin takes over the patriarchal role, making decisions for, and attempting to protect, younger females in the household.
4. Silence and withdrawal is a more common way to express anger in Java, rather than openly and directly expressing discontent.
5. This industrialized village is different and separate from the agricultural villages studied–Nuwun and a neighbouring village.
6. This age difference in daughters' willingness to rebel may partially relate to the age requirements at most factories. Most only accepted females fifteen years old and above.
7. Certainly, better-off families had made calculations about their financial capabilities and, whenever possible, sent their children on to middle school and, in the rare case, to high school. Parents had hopes for one child becoming a civil servant and earning a steady wage unrelated to the agricultural cycle, which would help support parents in their old age. In these few families, parents made decisions about which child could continue schooling (and it was often a male child if a choice had to be made), and about their children's labour. With the prospect of a future inheritance in mind, grown children from better-off households tended to follow parental wishes.
8. It should be noted that young women's choices for income-earning were limited and usually less desirable compared with factory work: trade or agricultural labour, both of which were considered hard and seasonal labour, or domestic service, which was poorly paid and perceived as close to serfdom.
9. On the other hand it is important to note that domestic service was detested by young village women because of the high degree of control exerted by the employers, coupled with extremely low wages. Former domestics

described a situation in which they had to be prepared to work at any time of the day or night their employer demanded, for long hours, at very low pay.

10. While I am arguing that controls over the female within the family have weakened, working in a capitalist factory means that other, new forms of control over females outside the household have been reconstituted (Elson and Pearson, 1981; Ong. 1987). Such forms of control draw upon traditional generational and patriarchal relationships in Java as elsewhere in the world.

11. Margery Wolf (1972) points out that, before factory employment was common, some filial daughters took this burden to the extreme and became prostitutes, which parents accepted. See her chapter on 'Filial Daughters'.

12. Honig's historical research on women in the Shanghai cotton mills found that in some cases, women received their wages directly at least in the late 1930s, but most simply turned over all of their wages to their parents (1986: 170–1).

13. Honig writes that, in Shanghai in the 1920s and 1930s, young girls ages nine and ten were sent to work partly so that their brothers could go to school (1986: 168).

14. Although Chinese culture is on the whole patriarchal, there are regional differences.

15. This particular economic relationship has been carefully studied by several researchers, because even a 5 per cent increase in income retention by a factory daughter would indicate social change (Thornton *et al.*, 1984).

16. Salaff (1981) suggests that the nature of the Chinese family in Hong Kong creates values and practices which then in turn create a docile and disciplined workforce. This benefits the state, capitalists and the male working class (Roldan, 1985: 272).

17. I am not suggesting that anything and everything expressed by respondents be taken simplistically as data without analysis of ideology, consciousness or structure, but that women's voices and respondents' intents and explanations be included in the structural analyses of household behaviour.

CHAPTER 13

1. Malawi's 1977 census found that although 88 per cent of the population lived in rural areas, only 50 per cent of economically active men worked full-time (nine months or more per year) on their own farms, down from 76 per cent in 1966. In contrast, 90 per cent of all women were full-time farmers (Hirschmann and Vaughn, 1984).

2. This observation should not be taken to suggest that women have not been capable of making innovations in the range of farming techniques they practise nor in the varieties and types of crops they cultivate. The point being emphasized is women's virtual exclusion from access to state- and donor-provided inputs for the food production enterprises they manage as individuals.

3. The data are from field surveys conducted by the author in 1985 with the aid of a grant from the Social Science Research Council. See also Koopman Henn (1988 and 1989).

4. Carney (1988) provides an exceptionally instructive example.

CHAPTER 14

1. Reproduction involves both physical reproduction and the maintenance of social relations, in this instance, the patriarchal hierarchy.

2. There is a serious question of how to treat the rural semi-proletariat, i.e.

those who have a little land, but who must do wage labour as well. Since children are more important as workers and as old age security rather than as heirs in this case, the basis of the control of women's sexuality may be very similar to its basis among the landless poor.

3. This, of course, begs the question of the relation between sexual control and patriarchal control over land.

4. Franz Fanon's work springs readily to mind in this context.

5. This does not mean that the sexual realm is 'a haven in a heartless world' in any sense. Rather, it is a realm where the hierarchy and domination of gender relations are played out.

6. As is well-known, 'modesty' itself is socially defined; clothes considered modest for women in one region of India are often immodest in another. This fact, in itself, points to the social functions of the notion of modesty; there is nothing natural about it.

CHAPTER 15

1. Laws in both Taiwan and the People's Republic of China have attempted to alter this traditional pattern of inheritance by providing women with institutionalized access to the property of their families of origin. Women, however, seldom claim their inheritance, but rather accept their dowries as their patrimony.

2. The research covers the period from 1957 to 1982. The first field trip, in 1957–58, involved a seventeen-month residence in the village of Hsin Hsing. This was followed by two separate studies, in 1965–66 and 1969–70, of out-migrants from the area. The most recent research spanned two months in 1977, six months in 1979, and one month in 1982. Wife abuse was never a focus of the research and we did not interview villagers directly about the phenomenon. Interviews with approximately 300 people as well as our observations suggest that mothers-in-law in Hsin Hsing treated their daughters-in-law harshly and that the relationship between older and younger women in the family was an unhappy one.

3. During the summer of 1982, I interviewed 25 women aged 47 and older about changes in family life. In comparing their early years of marriage with those of their daughters-in-law, only one woman reported that she had been treated well by her mother-in-law; the remaining 24 reported that their mothers-in-law had been cruel to them. Of these 24, fully half said the older women 'beat' them, although only about 6 qualified their reports by indicating that their skin became 'black and blue' as a result. Unfortunately, I did not pursue the subject in the interviews, and I do not know how frequently the beatings occurred.

4. I use the term 'extreme' to describe cases of wife abuse in which a woman required medical treatment after she was beaten. No Hsin Hsing woman described such an occurrence, but Wolf (1975) speaks to the issue.

5. Cash and jewellery are given to a young woman as part of her dowry, the amount varying with the economic condition of her natal family. In contrast to the other items a woman takes with her to her husband's home at marriage, this cash and jewellery is considered to belong to her and not the family as a whole. Taiwanese call this 'private property' a woman's *sai-khia*. On family division, a woman's *sai-khia* is merged with the property inherited by her husband, and she loses control of her private fund. The practice of *sai-khia* was recognized in Hsin Hsing during the 1950s but was not

prevalent because of the poverty of the local people.

6. On the inevitability of family division, see Gallin and Gallin (1982b).

7. The reasons for this increase in affinal ties has been described in detail (Gallin and Gallin, 1985). As industrialization weakened community ties (Gallin and Gallin, 1982a), people made conscious efforts to broaden and intensify their relationships with those beyond the local area: Affines—who outnumber patrilineal kin and are dispersed over a wider area—are thus better suited to people's needs in a transformed economic environment than are members of the descent group.

CHAPTER 16

This chapter is based on fieldwork in Mexico carried out between June 1982 and June 1983. The work was funded by the Social Science Research Council of Great Britain (now the Economic and Social Research Council) in connection with a research project, directed by Drs Alan Gilbert and Peter Ward at University College London, entitled 'Public Intervention, Housing and Land Use in Latin American Cities'. The project was sponsored by the Overseas Development Administration.

1. Irregular settlement may be used to describe three main kinds of low-income neighbourhoods in Mexico:

(a) *Squatter settlements.* These are formed by invasion on either public or private land and legal title is, at least initially, non-existent.

(b) Ejidal *urban settlements.* An *ejido* is an area of land handed over by the state to a specific agricultural community. This land may not be sold or in any other way alienated. Despite that, many *ejidal* communities sell off lots illegally. Legal title does not pass into the hands of the settlers until a presidential decree makes possible expropriation.

(c) *Low-income subdivisions.* These arise as the result of land being sold to low-income families without services. The subdivision is irregular in the sense that it offends planning regulations.

The study settlements in Querétaro comprised:

(i) *Bolaños*—an *ejidal* settlement in the northeast of the city which had originated in 1970;

(ii) *Los Andadores*—a fraudulent subdivision in the south of the city dating from 1976; and

(iii) *Las Américas*—an *ejidal* urban settlement in the northwest of the city which began in the late 1970s.

2. The samples in each settlement were 30 per cent representative of a complete listing of all co-residential owner families.

3. Domestic labour in irregular settlements is time-consuming and arduous because housing is of poor quality and there are few basic services such as piped water, electricity and paved roads. Housework needs to be done very thoroughly in order to combat potential health risks arising from such problems as unpurified tanker water, an absence of rubbish collection and unhygienic improvised lavatory facilities. Domestic labour is often carried out single-handedly by female spouses in nuclear families, who frequently work an 11–hour day on household chores alone. When the work is carried out by one person, the housewife runs the risk of fatigue or injury, because much of the work is heavy. There is also a risk to other family members of cross-infection arising from the mixing of culinary, lavatory and cleaning duties in quick succession. Sharing chores in single-parent families helps to reduce health risks to individual workers by reducing their expenditure of time and

energy, and it also minimizes threats to hygiene.

REFERENCES TO PART 2

CHAPTER 11

Benería, Lourdes (1982) 'Accounting for Women's Work', in L. Benería (ed.), *Women and Development, The Sexual Division of Labor in Rural Societies*, New York: Praeger.

Benería, Lourdes (1992) 'The Mexican Debt Crisis: Restructuring the Economy and the Household', in L. Benería and S. Feldman (eds). *Economic Crises, Persistent Poverty and Women's Work*, Boulder, CO: Westview Press.

Benería, Lourdes and Stimpson, Catherine (1987) (eds), *Women, Households and the Economy*, New Brunswick, NJ: Rutgers University Press.

Blades, Derek W., *Non-monetary (Subsistence) Activities in the National Accounts of Developing Countries* (Paris: OECD, 1975).

Boserup, Ester (1970) *Woman's Role in Economic Development*, London: George Allen and Unwin.

Carrasco, Cristina *et al* (1992) *El Trabajo Doméstico y la Reproducción Social*, Madrid: Instituto de la Mujer.

Chadeau, Ann (1989) 'Measuring household production: Conceptual issues and results for France'. Paper presented at the Second ECE/INSTRAW Joint Meeting on Statistics of Women, Geneva, 13–16 November.

Dixon-Mueller, Ruth and Richard Anker (1988) *Assessing Women's Economic Contribution to Development*, Training in Population, Human Resources and Development Planning. World Employment Programme Paper No. 6, Geneva: ILO.

Elson, Diane (1991) 'Male bias in macro-economics: The case of structural adjustment', in Elson, D. (ed.), *Male Bias in the Development Process*, Manchester: Manchester University Press. pp. 164–190.

Floro, Maria Sagrario (1992) 'Work Intensity and Women's Time: A Conceptual Framework'. Paper presented at the URPE/ASSA conference, New Orleans, 3–5 January.

Folbre, Nancy and Marjorie Abel (1989 'Women's Work and Women's Household: Gender Bias in the US Census', *Social Research*, Vol. 56. No. 3, Autumn: 545–69.

Goldschmidt-Clermont, Luisella (1983) *Unpaid Work in the Household*, Geneva: ILO.

Goldschmidt-Clermont, Luisella (1989) 'Valuing Domestic Activities', Paper submitted to the Second ECE/INSTRAW Joint Meeting on Statistics of Women, Geneva, 13–16 November.

ILO (International Labor Office) (1976) *International Recommendations on Labor Statistics*, Geneva: ILO.

Kuznets, Simon (1954) *National Income and its Composition 1919–1938*, New York: National Bureau of Economic Research.

Langfeldt, Enno (1987) 'Trabajo no remunerado en el contexto familiar', *Revista de Estudios Económicos,* No. 1: 131–46.

Portes, Alejandro *et al.* (1989) *The Informal Economy*, Baltimore: Johns Hopkins University Press.

Pou, Francisca *et al.* (1987) La Mujer Rural Dominicana, Santo Domingo: CIPAE.

Roberts. Bryant (1991) 'Urban labor services and structural adjustment', in Guy Standing and Victor Tokman (eds). *Towards Social Adjustment*, Geneva:

International Labor Office, pp. 115–40.

SSP/UCECA (Secretaria de Programacion y Presupuesto/Unidad Coordinadora de Empleo. Capacitacion y Adriestramiento) (1976) *La Ocupacion Informal en Areas Urbanas*, Mexico. DF: December.

United Nations (1989) *Improving Statistics and Indicators on Women using Household Surveys*, Studies in Methods, Series F, No. 48, New York: Statistical Office/INSTRAW.

United Nations Office at Vienna, (1989) *World Survey on the Role of Women in Development*, New York: United Nations.

United Nations Statistical Office/ECA/INSTRAW (1991a) *Handbook on Compilation of Statistics on Women in the Informal Sector in Industry, Trade and Services in Africa*, Santo Domingo and New York: United Nations.

United Nations Statistical Office/ECA/INSTRAW (1991b) Synthesis of pilot studies on compilation of statistics on women in the informal sector in industry, trade and services in four African countries, Santo Domingo and New York: United Nations.

Wainerman. Catalina H., and Zulma, Recchini de Lattes (1981) *El Trabajo Femenino en el Banquillo de los Acusados*, Mexico, DF: Population Council/Terra Nova.

Waring, Marilyn (1988) *If Women Counted*, New York: Harper & Row.

CHAPTER 12

Abdullah, T. and S.A. Zeidenstein (1982) *Village Women of Bangladesh*, Oxford: Pergamon Press.

Arizpe, L. (1982) 'Relay Migration and the Survival of the Peasant Household', in H. Safa (ed.), *Towards a Political Economy of Urbanization in Third World Countries*, Delhi: Oxford University Press.

Arrigo, L.G. (1980) 'The Industrial Work Force of Young Women in Taiwan', *Bulletin of Concerned Asian Scholars* 12(2): 25–38.

Becker, G. and K. Murphy. (1988) 'The Family and the State', *Journal of Law and Economics* 31: 1–18.

Benería, L. and M. Roldan (1987) *The Crossroads of Class and Gender*, Chicago, IL: Chicago University Press.

Diamond, N. (1979) 'Women and Industry in Taiwan', *Modern China* 5: 317–40.

Ellis, F. (1988) *Peasant Economics*, Cambridge: Cambridge University Press.

Elson, D. and R. Pearson (1981) 'Nimble Fingers Make Cheap Workers: An Analysis of Women's Employment in Third World Export Manufacturing', *Feminist Review* Spring: 87–107.

Fernandez-Kelly, M.P. (1982) *For We Are Sold, I and My People: Women and Industry in Mexico's Frontier*, Albany, NY: SUNY Press.

Findley, S. (1987) *Rural Development and Migration: A Study of Family Choices in the Philippines*, Boulder, CO: Westview.

Firman, T. (1988) 'Labor Flows and the Construction Industry: the Case of Housing Development in Bandung, Indonesia', Unpublished PhD dissertation, University of Hawaii.

Folbre, N. (1986) 'Cleaning House: New Perspectives on Households and Economic Development, *Journal of Development Economics* 22: 5–40.

Folbre, N. (1988) 'The Black Four of Hearts: Toward a New Paradigm of Household Economics', in J. Bruce (ed.), *A Home Divided: Women and Income in the Third World*, Stanford, CA: Stanford University Press.

Gates, H. (1987) *Chinese Working Class Lives: Getting By in Taiwan*, Ithaca, NY: Cornell University Press.

Giddens, A. (1979) *Central Problems in Social Theory*, Berkeley, CA: University of California Press.

Giddens, A. (1984) *The Constitution of Society*, Berkeley, CA: University of California Press.

Greenhalgh, S. (1985) 'Sexual Stratification: The Other Side of "Growth with Equity" in East Asia', *Population and Development Review* 11(2): 265–314.

Guest, P. (1989) *Labor Allocation and Rural Development: Migration in Four Javanese Villages*, Boulder, CO: Westview Press.

Gupta, A. (1987) 'The Choice of Technique and Theories of Practice', Unpublished paper, Jackson School of International Studies, University of Washington, Seattle.

Guyer, J. and P. Peters (eds) (1987) 'Conceptualising the Household: Issues of Theory and Policy in Africa', *Development and Change* (special issue), 13(2).

Hannan, M. (1982) 'Families, Markets, and Social Structures: An Essay on Becker's Treatise on the Family', *Journal of Economic Literature* 20: 65–72.

Harbinson, S. (1981) 'Family Structure and Family Strategy in Migration Decision-Making', in G. De Jong and R. Gardner, (eds). *Migration Decision Making*, New York: Pergamon Press.

Hareven, T. (1982) *Family Time and Industrial Time*, New York: Cambridge University Press.

Hart, G. (1978) 'Labor Allocation Strategies in Rural Javanese Households', Unpublished PhD dissertation, Cornell University.

Hart, G. (1986) *'Power, Labor and Livelihood: Processes of Change in Rural Java*, Berkeley, CA: University of California Press.

Hartmann, H. (1981) 'The Family as the Locus of Gender, Class and Political Struggle', *Signs* 6(3), 366–94.

Honig, E. (1986) *Sisters and Strangers: Women in the Shanghai Cotton Mills, 1919–1949*, Stanford, CA: Stanford University Press.

de Janvry, A. (1987) 'Peasants, Capitalism and the State in Latin American Culture', in T. Shanin (ed.), *Peasants and Peasant Society*, London: Basil Blackwell.

Kandiyoti, D. (1988) 'Bargaining with Patriarchy', *Gender and Society* 2(3): 274–90.

Kung, L. (1981) 'Perceptions of Work among Factory Women', in E.M. Ahern and H. Gates (eds), *The Anthropology of Taiwanese Society*, Stanford, CA: Stanford University Press.

Kung, L. (1983) *Factory Women in Taiwan*, Ann Arbor, MI: University of Michigan Press.

Lesthaeghe, R. and Surkyn, J. (1988) 'Cultural Dynamics and Economic Theories of Fertility Change', *Population and Development Review* 14: 1–45.

Mohanty, C. (1988) 'Under Western Eyes: Feminist Scholarship and Colonial Discourses', *Feminist Review* No. 30: 61–88.

Moore, H.L. (1988) *Feminism and Anthropology*, Cambridge: Polity Press.

Nash, J. (1983) 'Implications of Technological Change for Household Level and Rural Development', Working Paper No. 37, Women in International Development, Michigan State University.

Nerlove, M. (1974) 'Household and Economy: Toward a New Theory of Population and Economic Growth', *Journal of Political Economy* 82: 200–18.

Niehoff, J. (1987) 'The Villagers as Industrialist: Ideologies of Household Factories in Rural Taiwan', *Modern China* 13(3): 286–307.

Ong, A. (1987) *Spirits of Resistance and Capitalist Discipline: Factory Women in Malaysia*, Albany, NY: SUNY Press.

Roldan, M. (1985) 'Industrial Outworking, Struggles for the Reproduction of Working Class Families and Gender Subordination', in N. Redclift, and M. Enzo, (eds), *Beyond Employment*, pp. 248–85, New York: Basil Blackwell.

Rosenzweig, M. (1986) 'Program Interventions, Intrahousehold Distribution and the Welfare of Individuals: Modeling Household Behavior', *World Development* 14(2): 233–43.

Salaff, J. (1981) *Working Daughters of Hong Kong*, New York: Cambridge University Press.

Salaff, J. (1988) *State and Family in Singapore*, Ithaca, NY: Cornell University Press.

Scott, J. (1985) *Weapons of the Weak,* New Haven, CT: Yale University Press.

Sheridan, M. and J. Salaff (1984) *Lives: Chinese Working Women,* Bloomington, IN: Indiana University Press.

Smith, J., I. Wallerstein and H.D. Evers (eds) (1984) *Households and the World Economy*, Beverley Hills, CA: Sage Publications.

Sorenson, C. (1988) *Over the Mountains Are Mountains*. Seattle, WA: University of Washington Press.

Stern, M.J. (1987) *Society and Family Strategy*, Albany, NY: SUNY Press.

Thorne, B. and M. Yalom. (1982) *Rethinking the Family*, New York: Longman.

Thornton, A., Ming Cheng Chang and Te Hsiung Sun (1984) 'Social and Economic Change, Intergenerational Relationships, and Family Formation in Taiwan', *Demography* 21(4): 475–99.

Tilly, L. (1978) 'Women and Family Strategies in French Proletarian Families', Michigan Occasional Paper No. 4, Department of History, University of Michigan.

Tilly, L.A. and J. Scott (1978) *Women, Work and Family*, New York: Holt, Rinehart & Winston.

Todd, E. (1985) *The Explanation of Ideology: Family Structures and Social Systems*, New York NY: Basil Blackwell.

Trager, L. (1981) 'Rural-Urban Linkages and Migration: A Philippines Case Study', in G. Hainsworth (ed.), *Southeast Asia: Women, Changing Social Structure and Cultural Continuity*, Ottawa: University of Ottawa Press.

Watts, M. (1988) 'Putting Humpty-Dumpty Back Together Again? Some Comments on Studies of Households, Gender and Work in Rural Africa', Paper prepared for SSRC Workshop on 'Socio-economic Transformations, Demographic Changes and the Family in Southeast Asia', Honolulu.

White, B. (1976) 'Production and Reproduction in a Javanese Village', Unpublished PhD dissertation, Columbia University.

Wolf, D.L. (1984) 'Making the Bread and Bringing it Home: Female Factory Workers and the Family Economy in Rural Java', in G. Jones, (ed.), *Women in the Urban and Industrial Workforce*, Development Studies Center Monograph No. 33, Canberra: Australian National University Press.

Wolf, D.L. (1988a) 'Factory Daughters, the Family, and Nuptiality in Java', Paper presented to IUSSP conference on 'Women's Position and Demographic Change in the Course of Development', Oslo, June.

Wolf, D.L. (1988b) 'Female Autonomy, the Family, and Industrialization in Java', *Journal of Family Issues* 9(1): 85–107.

Wolf, D.L. (1992) *Factory Daughters: Gender, Household Dynamics, and Rural Industrialisation in Java*, Berkeley CA: University of California Press.

Wolf, M. (1972) *Women and the Family in Rural Taiwan,* Stanford, CA: Stanford University Press.

CHAPTER 13

Bernal, V. (1988) 'Losing Ground – Women and Agriculture on Sudan's Irrigated Schemes: *Lessons from a Blue Nile Village*', in J. Davison (ed.) (1988).

Blumberg, R.L. (1988) 'Income Under Female vs. Male Control: Differential Spending Patterns and the Consequences When Women Lose Control of Returns to Labor', World Bank Population and Human Resources Series, Washington, DC.

Brain, J.L. (1976) 'Less Than Second-Class: Women in Rural Settlement Schemes in Tanzania', in N.J. Hafkin and E.G. Bay (eds) *Women in Africa*, Stanford, CA: Stanford University Press.

Brown, B.B. (1980) 'Women, Migrant Labor and Social Change in Botswana', Working paper no. 41, African Studies Centre, Boston University, Massachusetts.

Bukh, J. (1979) *The Village Women in Ghana*, Uppsala: Scandinavian Institute of African Studies.

Carney, J.A. (1988) 'Struggles Over Land and Crops in an Irrigated Rice Scheme: The Gambia', in J. Davison (ed.) (1988).

Cloud, K. (1986) 'Sex Roles in Food Production and Distribution Systems in the Sahel', in Creevey L. E. (ed). *Women Farmers in Africa*, Syracuse: Syracuse University Press.

Cloud, K. and J.B. Knowles (1988) 'Where Can We Go from Here? Recommendations for Action', in J. Davison (ed.) (1988).

Cohen, R. (ed.) (1988) *Satisfying Africa's Food Needs: Food Production and Commercialisation in African Africulture*, Boulder, CO: Lynne Rienner.

Conti, A. (1979) 'Capitalist Organisation of Production through non-Capitalist Relations: Women's Role in a Pilot Resettlement in Upper Volta', *Review of African Political Economy*, No. 15–16.

Crehen, K. (1984) 'Women and Development in North Western Zambia: From Producer to Housewife', *Review of African Political Economy*, No. 27–8.

Davison, J. (ed.) (1988) '*Agriculture, Women, and Land: The African Experience*, Boulder, CO: Westview Press.

Engberg, L.E., Sabry, J.H., and Beckerson, S.A. (1988) 'A Comparison of Rural Women's Time Use and Nutritional Consequences in Two Villages in Malawi', in S.V. Poats, M. Schmink and A. Spring, *Gender Issues in Farming Systems Research and Extension*, Boulder, CO: Westview Press.

Feldman, R. (1984) 'Women's Groups and Women's Subordination: An Analysis of Policies Towards Rural Women in Kenya', *Review of African Political Economy*, No. 27–8.

Funk, U. (1988) 'Land Tenure, Agriculture and Gender in Guinea-Bissau', in J. Davison (ed.), (1988).

Goheen, M. (1988) 'Land and the Household Economy: Women Farmers of the Grassfields Today', in J. Davison, (ed.) (1988).

Goody, J. and J. Buckley (1973) 'Inheritance and Women's Labour in Africa', *Africa*, Vol. 43, No. 2.

Guyer, J.I. (1984a) 'Women in the Rural Economy: Contemporary Variations', in M.J. Hay and S. Stichter (eds) *African Women South of the Sahara*, London: Longman.

Guyer, J.I. (1984b) 'Naturalism in Models of African Production', *Man*, Vol. 19, No. 3: 371–88.

Guyer, J.I. (1988) 'Dynamic Approaches to Domestic Budgeting: Cases and Methods from Africa', in D. Dwyer and J. Bruce (eds) *A Home Divided:*

Women and Income in the Third World, Stanford, CA: Stanford University Press.

Hay, M.J. (1982) 'Women as Owners, Occupants, and Managers of Property in Colonial Western Kenya', in M.J. Hay and M. Wright (eds) *African Women and the Law: Historical Perspectives*, Boston, MA: Boston University.

Hemmings-Gapihan, G.S. (1982) 'International Development and the Evolution of Women's Economic Roles: A Case Study from Northern Gulma, Upper Volta', in E.G. Bay (ed.) (1982).

Hill, P. (1972) *Rural Hausa: A Village and a Setting*, Cambridge, MA: Cambridge University Press.

Hill, P. (1975) 'The West African Farming Household', in J. Goody (ed.) *Changing Social Structure on Ghana: Essays in the Comparative Sociology of a New State and an Old Tradition*, London: International African Institute.

Hirschmann, D. and M. Vaughn (1984) *Women Farmers of Malawi: Food Production in the Zomba District*, Berkeley, CA: Institute of International Studies, University of California.

Jacobs, S. (1989) 'Zimbabwe: State, Class, and Gendered Models of Land Resettlement', in J.L. Parpart and K.A. Staudt (eds) *Women and the State in Africa*, Boulder, CO: Lynne Rienner.

Jones, C.W. (1986) 'Intra-Household Bargaining in Response to the Introduction of New Crops: A Case Study from Northern Cameroon', in J.L. Moock, (ed.) *Understanding Africa's Rural Household and Farming Systems*, Boulder, CO: Westview Press.

Koopman Henn, J. (1978) 'Peasants, Workers, and Capital: The Political Economy of Labor and Incomes in Cameroon', unpublished PhD dissertation, Harvard University, Massachusetts.

Koopman Henn (1988) 'Intra-Household Dynamics and State Policies as Constraints on Food Production: Results of a 1985 Agroeconomic Survey in Cameroon', in S.V. Poats, M. Schmink, and A. Spring (eds) *Gender Issues in Farming Systems Research and Extension*, Boulder, CO: Westview Press.

Koopman Henn (1989) 'Food Policy, Food Production, and the Family Farm in Cameroon', in P. Geschiere and P. Konings (eds) 'Proceedings: Conference on the Political Economy of Cameroon–Historical Perspectives', Part II, Research Reports No. 35, African Studies Centre, Leiden, The Netherlands.

Lewis, B. (1981) 'Invisible Farmers: Women and the Crisis in Agriculture, AID Office of Women in Development', Washington DC.

Mies, M. (1986) *Patriarchy and Accumulation on a World Scale*, London: Zed Books.

Pinstrup-Andersen, P. (1989) 'Assuring a Household Food Security and Nutrition Bias in African Government Policies', Paper presented at the Ninth World Congress of the International Economic Association, Athens, Greece, 28 August–1 September.

Roberts, P.A. (1988) 'Rural Women's Access to Labor in West Africa', in S.B. Stichter and J.L. Parpart (eds) *Patriarchy and Class: African Women in the Home and the Workforce*, Boulder, Colorado: Westview Press.

Rose, L. (1988 '"A Woman Is Like a Field": Women's Strategies for Land Access in Swaziland', in J. Davison, (ed.) (1988).

Schoepf, B.G. and C. Schoepf (1988) 'Land, Gender, and Food Security in Eastern Kivu, Zaire', in J. Davison (ed.) (1988).

Staudt, K. (1982) 'Women Farmers and Inequities in Agricultural Services', in E.G. Bay (ed.). (1982).

Staudt, K. (1985) 'Women, Foreign Assistance and Advocacy Administration', New York: Praeger.

Staudt, K. (1987) 'Uncaptured or Unmotivated? Women and the Food Crisis in Africa', *Rural Sociology*, Vol. 15, No. 1.

Stichter, S. (1985) *Migrant Labourers,* Cambridge: Cambridge University Press.

Tadesse, Z. (1982) 'The Impact of Land Reform on Women: The Case of Ethiopia', in L. Benería (ed.) *Women and Development: The Sexual Division of Labor in Rural Societies*, New York: Praeger.

UNICEF (1985) *Within Human Reach, A Future for Africa's Children*, New York: UNICEF.

Wilson, F.R. (1982) 'Reinventing the Past and Circumscribing the Future: *Authenticité* and the Negative Image of Women's Work in Zaire', in E.G. Bay (ed.) (1982).

World Bank (1988) *The Challenge of Hunger in Africa*, Washington DC: World Bank.

World Bank (1989) *World Development Report 1989*, New York: Oxford University Press.

CHAPTER 14

Gulati, L. (1981) *Profiles in Female Poverty*, Delhi: Hindustan Publishing Company.

Lessinger, J. (1982) 'On the Periphery of Trade: Male–Female Competition in a South-Indian Market Place', Conference on *Women and Income Control in the Third World*, Columbia University, Mimeo.

Mies, M. (1980) 'Capitalist Development and Subsistence Reproduction; Rural Women in India', *Bulletin of Concerned Asian Scholars* 12(1): 2–14.

Mukhopadhyay, S. (1981) 'Women Workers of India: A Case of Market Segmentation', *in Women in the Indian Labour Force*, pp. 93–119, Bangkok: ILO/ARTEP.

Srinivas, M.N. (1969) 'The Caste System in India', in *Social Inequality,* A. Beteille (ed.). pp. 265–72, Harmondsworth: Penguin Books.

CHAPTER 15

Baker, Hugh D.R. (1979) *Chinese Family and Kinship*, New York: Columbia University Press.

Gallin, Bernard and Rita S. Gallin (1982a) 'Socioeconomic Life in Rural Taiwan: Twenty Years of Development and Change' *Modern China* 8(2):205–46.

—— (1982b), 'The Chinese Joint Family in Changing Rural Taiwan', in Sidney Greenblatt, Richard Wilson and Amy Wilson (eds) *Social Interaction in Chinese Society*, New York: Praeger.

—— (1985) 'Matrilateral and Affinal Relationships in Changing Chinese Society' in *The Chinese Family and Its Ritual Behaviour*, Hsieh Jin-chang and Chuang Ying-Chang (eds) pp. 101–16, Taipei, Taiwan: Institute of Ethnology, Academia Sinica.

Gallin, Rita S. (1984a) 'The Entry of Chinese Women into the Rural Labor Force: A Case Study from Taiwan', *Signs* 9(3):383–98.

—— (1984b) 'Women, Family and the Political Economy of Taiwan', *Journal of Peasant Studies* 12(1):76–92.

—— (1986) 'Mothers-in-Law and Daughters-in-Law: Intergenerational Relations Within the Chinese Family in Taiwan', *Journal of Cross-cultural Gerontology* 1(1):31–49.

Harrell, Stevan (1982) *Ploughshare Village*, Seattle, WA: University of Washington Press.

Wolf, Margery (1975) 'Women and Suicide in China', in *Women and Chinese*

Society, Margery Wolf and Roxane Witke (eds) pp. 111–41, Stanford, CA: Stanford University Press.

CHAPTER 16

Arizpe, Lourdes (1982) *Etnicismo, Migración y Cambio Económico*, México DF: El Colegio de México.

Fromm, Erich (1959): 'Sex and Character', in Ruth Nanda Anshen (ed.): *The Family: Its Function and Destiny*, New York: Harper & Row, pp. 399–419.

Goode, William J. (1963) *World Revolution and Family Patterns*, New York: The Free Press.

Harris, Olivia (ed.) (1982) *Latin American Women*, London: Minority Rights Group.

Hutter, Mark (1981) *The Changing Family: Comparative Perspectives*, New York: John Wiley.

Part 3
Women in the Global Economy

INTRODUCTION TO PART 3

Laurie Nisonoff

Women work. Women of all ages and marital statuses—single, married, divorced or widowed—work. Women in nearly all circumstances of class or status work, and have always worked. However, as explained by Lourdes Benería in Chapter 11, much of the work that women have done and continue to do is invisible, or is either assumed to be 'natural' or of little value. These assumptions exist, in part, because most tasks and even occupations done primarily by women take place within the household and are not seen as productive (in economic terms creating goods or services that are paid for) or as making direct contributions to the economy of either a household or a nation (Chapter 11). Over the last 25 years, there has been a significant debate about whether women's subordinated status influences how their work is regarded, or whether the lack of respect for certain tasks reserves such jobs for relatively lower-status workers, i.e., women. The result is, in both cases, the degradation of both women and their work.

As economies have industrialized, women have often followed their 'traditional' tasks from the private household into the public industrialized sphere of production. This can be seen in the predominance of women in transforming raw material (cotton, flax, wool) into cloth and garments, planting crops and preparing food, and educating or succouring younger, older and weaker members of the community. Over the past 200 years, the women in North America and Europe who have performed these 'women's' tasks have received lower pay for their care-giving work. This transformation of the work of women in many developing nations has, however, taken place more rapidly due, in part, to government-sponsored development plans and, in part, to global economic phenomena (see Chapters 3, 12, 17, 19 and 32).

In the years since World War II, governments of some developing nations have sought to transform their countries from poor, stagnant economies dependent on the export of raw materials into industrialized nations capable of rapid growth and material prosperity which planners hoped would eventually 'trickle down' throughout the society. The two principal policies have been import-substitution—the local production of formerly imported goods such as automobiles and steel—and export-led industrialization employing local low-wage workers to produce inexpensive export items such as clothing.

Since the consumption-goods markets in the Third World reflect the tastes of wealthy minorities of the population, import-substituting production is generally capital-intensive, requiring expensive manufacturing processes and plants, as well as 'skilled' workers. Export-led growth is, in contrast, often a much less costly process to initiate, requiring fewer expensive materials,

less manufacturing equipment, and lower-waged workers. Men have constituted the predominant labour force in import-substitution and women in the
export-led sector.

While both of these strategies were used quite often in the immediate
post-war era, the past decade has witnessed a decided shift to the export-led
method, especially under the impact of structural adjustment (Part 4).
Studies of the implications for women of these processes have centred on
their role in the global economy and their experiences in the informal sector.
The latter (discussed below) falls between formalized state-registered and
taxed economic enterprises and the household or farm economy.

A. WOMEN AND INDUSTRIALIZATION

During the Industrial Revolution of the late eighteenth and nineteenth
centuries, many European and North American women found employment in
the industrial sector, particularly in the textile and garment industries. These
women formed a visible section of the paid labour force, and often played a
crucial role in organizing for regulations that were subsequently sanctioned
by the state and established in legislation (e.g. wages, hours, working conditions, pensions and benefits). The firms subject to these regulations were
(and are) often defined as the formal economy. Many other women produced
goods and services in their homes, where their contributions were not
always visible to census gatherers or policymakers (Part 2).

The increasing post-WWII focus on export-led development in the Third
World has had a profound impact on the working lives of women. Capital and
production were increasingly internationalized, and multinational corporations (MNCs) began to subdivide the labour process. At one time, garment
production concentrated in centres such as New York or Paris to take advantage of many small support firms (e.g., button-makers, or sub-contractors for
part of the production process). By the 1930s, production had become more
geographically diverse and union officials and scholars began to discuss the
phenomenon of 'runaway shops'. Declines in transportation costs (airplanes
and shipping), changes in tax codes and materials, and innovations in electronic communications meant that sales, design and skilled cutting of pieces
could remain in the central location while the 'piecework'—the assembly and
sewing of garments—could be done elsewhere to take advantage of cheaper
labour and special development programmes. The first of these schemes
was the post-war 1948 Operation Bootstrap in Puerto Rico, which exploited
the island's US commonwealth status for lower taxes, and also made land
and capital available (with subsidized low prices) (Acevedo, 1990).

Helen Safa's (1981) classic article places this new phenomenon in its
historic context. She notes that the US garment and textile industries had
first employed displaced, but skilled, farm women and then immigrant
labour. This search for cheap labour continues: the history of the industrialization process can be traced by following these industries around the world
from the nineteenth century when they originated in Lancashire, England and

the New England region of the US to their present location in the newest free trade zone.

Operation Bootstrap included, however, an explicit government role in this process. When the Puerto Rican experience with export-led development proved financially successful for mainland firms, although significantly less so for the long-term economic development of the island, US tariff laws were amended to make it feasible to export partially completed goods to take advantage of low wages and pay only import duties on the value added abroad (which was small due to the low wages) when the goods returned to the US for completion and marketing. Export-processing zones were established in many regions of the Third World. Import duties and local and environmental laws were often suspended, and land, plants, infrastructure (such as airports and modern roads) and capital were provided at low or no cost.

The zone along the US-Mexico border has been the subject of many studies by social scientists and business people. Some twin plants have been established wherein the US-side plant performs the capital-intensive tasks and provides high-wage jobs. The plant in Mexico, called a *maquiladora*, offers low-wage employment that involves the labour-intensive tasks of electronic assembly or sewing garments. Many *maquiladoras* were eventually established but the more capital-intensive tasks continued to be performed in the US, often outside the border region. The early *maquiladoras* employed a predominantly young female labour force. However, the 1990s have seen the growth of employment in automobile parts and electronic-component manufacturing, jobs usually reserved for men (Rendon and Salas, 1995). The zone approach has been so successful in creating low-wage work in the Third World that, since the 1980s, Great Britain and the US have established free enterprise zones within their own borders to encourage industrial investment in impoverished regions.

Throughout the 1980s, social scientists and activists debated whether jobs in the zones were good for women—liberating them from patriarchal homes and providing them with wages—or served as another level of exploitation. This question of whether women were 'pulled' to new opportunities or 'pushed' out of the home to provide wages for either their natal or marital families parallels historical debates over early industrialization in Europe and the United States, debates which remain unresolved.

The authors of our first selection, Diane Elson and Ruth Pearson, have written several of the earliest and most comprehensive analyses of the new phenomenon: Third World women working in 'world market factories producing manufactures exclusively for export to the rich countries'. They highlight the incorrect assumption that women are 'unskilled' and therefore worthy of only low wages. Both in this selection and in their *Feminist Review* (1981) article Elson and Pearson analyse the historical construction of men's tasks as skilled (i.e., learned in public apprenticeships on the job), in contrast to women's tasks, which are viewed as unskilled (learned at home from mothers or other women).

Several significant contributions to this literature were published in 1983: a key anthology by June Nash and María Patricia Fernández-Kelly, Fernández-

Kelly's (1983a) monograph, Wendy Chapkis and Cynthia Enloe's edited collection, and an introductory pamphlet by Annette Fuentes and Barbara Ehrenreich. The latter two provide short first-hand accounts of women's work experiences and resistance activities around the globe. A film of the same year, *The Global Assembly Line* (Gray, 1983), illustrates the effect of the movement of jobs upon women in the Philippines, Mexico and the US. It includes interview footage of both management and union officials as well as dramatic strike and lockout scenes. Kamel (1990) suggests methods to incorporate the film into classroom and community-organizing activities.

Among other important monographs that explore the complicated realities of women workers' lives, those of Aiwha Ong (1987) and John Humphrey (1987) reveal the worldwide nature of the global factory and provide details of the relationship between the home lives and work lives of factory women. Humphrey studies both men and women in seven Brazilian factories and explores the process by which gender roles established in the family are transmitted and maintained in the workplace. Ong's study of Malay peasant women in Japanese-owned factories in Malaysia portrays the multiple cultural influences of religion, patriarchy and modern capitalism encountered by these women. The women's working conditions are negotiated 'for them' by their fathers and brothers. These women are famous for generating perhaps the most resourceful resistance to new tasks and increased demands: claims of 'spirit possession' that require time-consuming ceremonies to 'free' them or the machines. Women were thus able to negotiate the overlapping layers of culture and patriarchy to gain a modicum of control over their work lives. Bill Maurer (1991) contributes another ethnographic example, from Dominica, to 'elucidate the connections among gender, sexuality and work' and focuses on the 'problematization of the distinction between sex as "natural" and gender as "cultural" in much feminist thought'.

While most of the literature focuses on the poor conditions faced by women workers in the free trade zones and multinational firms, some authors, for example Linda Lim (Chapter 19), provide a contrasting perspective. Lim argues that MNCs have often provided higher wages and better employment opportunities relative to jobs with locally owned businesses or to women's uncompensated work in patriarchal households. Boserup (1970) stated that women appeared to lose employment possibilities as larger industrial firms replaced home industries. As Benería (1989) argues, the prominence in the literature of the impact of MNC employment on young women had 'tended to exaggerate' its importance, at least statistically, as only a small proportion of total women's employment is in these firms. She also offers compelling arguments for the importance of this phenomenon: in some countries (especially the Asian NICs) MNC employment is prevalent. There are indirect effects including: subcontracting chains to domestic firms that also employ women (see below), the discovery or acceptance of women as a new source of industrial labour by domestic firms, and the spread of capitalist consumerist behaviour into new households. Benería argues that it is more than women's low wages that is leading to the 'feminization of global capital'; she points to three factors: labour control and malleability; productivity; and 'flexible labor', which 'women provide ... through their predominance in temporary contracts as well as in part-time and unstable work' (1989:251). Guy Standing (1989) cites this flexibility as essential in both the formal and informal sectors, and in the economic restructuring of industrialized economies.

The issues of 'push versus pull' explanations of employment in the export sector and of whether filial piety or independence accompanies factory work have been explored by Janet Salaff (1981 and 1990). Kathryn Ward (1990) includes pieces on the interconnections of formal and informal work by Diane Wolf and Cynthia Truelove. Chapter 12 of this reader also explores this issue. Elson and Pearson's (1989) edited collection demonstrates the unevenness of the European experience, as European and US-based multinationals invest in the peripheries of the European Community. Jean L. Pyle in her work on Ireland (1990a, b and c) and Singapore (1994) posits that the state plays an essential role in determining whether new employment opportunities favour the employment of women or men. Seung-kyung Kim (Chapter 34) provides examples of workers' resistance to state policy (including martial law) in South Korea. Ward and Pyle (1995) provide a current assessment.

Susan Tiano (1990 and 1994) returns to the subject of *maquiladora* women and, using case-study data from assembly-processing work in several Mexican communities, addresses the debate as to whether this is a new kind of employment. Does it exacerbate the relative unemployment of men? Does it alleviate the lack of income due to the displacement of husbands, brothers and fathers from US agricultural employment, or are these women who have always made economic contributions to their households now simply working at a new location?

Readings
This section's selections illustrate these debates about women's experiences in the internationalization of labour. Elson and Pearson (Chapter 17) critique the supposedly 'natural womanly' qualities of 'nimble fingers', docility and subordination, noting that these attributes result from specific socialization processes. They pose the key question of whether wage work liberates women from gender subordination and discuss women's resistance to workplace and familial subservience.

Fernández-Kelly's account (Chapter 18) of her anthropological fieldwork in a US–Mexico border *maquiladora* allows us to see the labour process from the vantage point of the workers themselves, as well as to glimpse their impressions of the anthropologist. Working at the plant and studying the labour force, the author learns to appreciate how skilled this work is.

Chapter 19 provides a different point of view. While agreeing with many authors that the MNCs subject women to multiple layers of exploitation, Linda Lim suggests that within the interplay of these systems young women's employment in the MNCs might expand their limited freedom to confront the restrictions of their lives.

B. WOMEN IN THE INFORMAL SECTOR

The process of industrialization and the mechanization of agriculture in many Third World countries has resulted in unemployment and underemployment (people whose jobs do not fully occupy them, compensate them or use their skills), migration from the countryside to the cities and emigration abroad. Especially vulnerable to unemployment, women in the countryside and the cities create self-employment outside the formal sector, which has not provided a sufficient number of secure, stable and well-paid jobs. Portes *et al.* (1989) differentiate formality from informality by counting as formal-sector employment only those jobs that provide regulated wages, pensions and benefits. There is an extensive debate in the development literature about definitions and their applicability to different situations (Peattie, 1987; Kabra, 1995). Lourdes Arizpe, in the 1977 article excerpted in Chapter 20, was one of the first to integrate a feminist analysis into discussions of the informal economy.

Women in the informal economy are located primarily in particular inter-related areas: preparation of goods for sale in the market and marketing, domestic service, and sub-contracting and home production. Anthropologist Florence E. Babb's fieldwork on market women in the Andean city of Huarez in north-central Peru reveals a range of food preparation and clothing processes that, in part, move traditional housework out of the home. Babb also notes new tasks of buying and selling, transporting and bulk ordering that must be learned from other market women. Unlike domestic workers, market women perceive themselves, even under the stress of structural adjustment, as a group with different interests from the male market entrepreneurs, the government and consumers, and they act accordingly.

Gracia Clark's work on the relationship between Ghanaian women producers and marketers suggests that the market women's flexible arrangements allow them to continue to supply food 'through stresses of political upheaval, economic crisis, and seasonal and extended drought' (1992:21). Market women play an important role in Jamaican 'higgling' (trading); Witter's anthology (1989) and Faye V. Harrison's (1991) study present a range of experiences and theoretical insights. A special issue of *Cultural Survival Quarterly* (Rothstein 1992) contains contemporary reports on the key role of women's market activities in Africa, Nicaragua and other parts of Latin America; Stephen, Sullivan, Trask and Trask raise the problem of indigenous women in Mexico and Hawaii 'marketing' their 'ethnicity'. Nash's (1993) anthology continues this debate on the role of craft production and marketing in the lives of peasant artisans.

Elsa M. Chaney and Maria Garcia Castro's edited collection (1989) presents a theoretical model for understanding the situation of domestic workers. The authors note that: the work of domestic workers is undervalued; domestics are recruited from among poor and often indigenous women with minimal education, who are considered inferior in culture, language, dress and race; they work in isolation and are 'invisible' to other domestic workers, to trade unions and to society; they are not protected by labour legislation; and they are distrustful of women in professional and feminist groups due to their ambivalent relationship with their middle-class women employers. This collection includes five chapters written by domestic workers. The film *Maids and Madams*, made in South Africa in 1985 for British television, illustrates the complex relationships between domestic servants and their employers, other domestic workers, trade unions and society.

Ximena Bunster and Elsa Chaney (1985) provide an excellent case-study of 50 women in Lima, Peru, who have tried various domestic- and market-employment opportunities in a capital city that has experienced enormous in-migration. Chapters focus on the different ages of women involved in the extensive rural-to-urban movement. Since the Gulf War, the international press and feminist scholars have raised questions, similar to those posed in Chaney's two co-authored books, about ethnic difference and the isolation of young women from the Philippines and other Southeast Asian nations who are hired as domestic workers and then stranded and abused in Kuwait and the Arab Emirates. Research on this topic is beginning (see Delia Aguilar, 1996).

Another type of informal-sector work is industrial home work, in which women produce industrial goods at home or in small workshops. Large formal-sector firms often sub-contract portions of the production process to smaller firms or to workshops which may operate outside the auspices of the state. Benería and Roldan (1987) and Benería (1987) reveal an extensive network of non-traditional home work and workshops in Mexico City. They note that MNCs take advantage of women workers' vulnerability by using this type of production (without the costs of higher factory wages, machinery and plants) to increase their profits. The women move through various sub-sectors of formal and informal employment because of familial and house-hold responsibilities, their lives vividly detailed over the course of the 1980s. Economic downturns in the Mexican economy in the 1990s have, however, resulted in lower wages for factory workers, making this cost-cutting strategy less common and virtually eliminating this type of informal-sector work as a source of employment at present (Rendon and Salas, 1995).

Sometimes women themselves, especially under the pressure of economic crises such as structural adjustment or the transformation from a planned economy, begin small entrepreneurial activities (e.g. garment production and repair). These micro-enterprises often begin as a method of self-employment but may grow to employ other workers. They are usually started with small infusions of capital. Blumberg (1995) and Osirim (1996) provide an analysis and examples of this phenomenon. There are many sources for this capital, including some new banks that specialize in making small loans to rural or urban women (Part 5). More commonly, rotating savings societies, found in many cultures and consisting of daily or weekly private collections of funds which are distributed to the members in rotation, provide lump sums of small capital to initiate or expand small enterprises.

While social scientists find it useful to make a distinction between formal and informal sectors, between enterprise zones and local entrepreneurs, or between home and marketing work, over the course of their working lives women move in and out of these areas without paying much heed to the differences, seeking to support themselves and their families. Firms in free trade zones often prefer younger and more formally educated women, and to avoid paying social benefits (such as state-mandated maternity leaves or pension plans) dismiss pregnant women or those over age thirty-five. Market women combine motherhood and selling responsibilities. Older women often make handicrafts and processed foodstuffs to be sold by others. For example, particular women in Nicaragua worked in a free trade zone in their youth, but later found employment in sales or the production of garments in their homes or small shops (Wiegersma, 1994).

Readings

Lourdes Arizpe's piece on women in the informal-labour sector (Chapter 20) was one of the first attempts to situate women within the long-standing debate in development theory over the boundaries and importance of this intermediate or transitional stage; she differentiates women's activities in Mexico by class and age.

Chapter 21, by Tripp, is from a recent collection (Rowbotham and Mitter 1994) and illustrates the rich variety of self-help responses of urban Tanzanian women to a post-structural adjustment economy. Such initiatives demonstrate the vital contribution the informal and independent sector plays in the support of families, communities and national economies.

FURTHER READING

WOMEN AND INDUSTRIALIZATION

Abraham-Van Der Mer, E. E. (1983) 'The Impact of Industrialization on Women: A Caribbean Case', in J. Nash and M. P. Fernandez-Kelly (eds) (1983).

Acevedo, L. A. (1990) 'Industrialization and Employment: Changes in the Patterns of Women's Work in Puerto Rico', *World Development*, Vol. 18: No. 2.

——(1995) 'Feminist Inroads in the Study of Women's Work and Development', in C. E. Bose and E. Acosta-Belen, *Women in the Latin American Development Process*, Philadelphia: Temple University Press.

Acker, J. C. (1988) 'Gender and the Relations of Distribution', *Signs*, Vol. 13: No. 3, Spring.

Arizpe, L. and J. Aranda (1988) 'The Comparative Advantages of Women's Disadvantages: Women Workers in the Strawberry Export Agribusiness in Mexico', in R. E. Pahl (ed.), *On Work: Historical, Comparative, and Theoretical Approaches*, New York: Basil Blackwood Inc.

Arrigo, L. G. (1985) 'Economic and Political Control of Women Workers in Multinational Electronics Factories in Taiwan: Martial Law, Coercion and World Market Uncertainty', *Contemporary Marxism*, 11.

Bell, P. F. (1991) 'Gender and Economic Development in Thailand', in P. and J. Van Esterik (eds), *Gender and Development in Southeast Asia*, Canadian Council for Southeast Asian Studies XX, Vol. II.

Benería, L. (1989) 'Gender and the Global Economy', in A. MacEwan and W. K.

Tabb (eds), *Instability and Change in the World Economy*, New York: Monthly Review Press.

Benería, L. and S. Feldman (1992) *Unequal Burdens: Economic Crises, Persistent Poverty and Women's Work*, Boulder, CO: Westview Press.

Berlin, M. (1985) 'Migrant Female Labor in the Venezuelan Garment Industry', in J. Nash and H. Safa (eds), *Women and Change in Latin America*, South Hadley, MA: Bergin and Garvey.

Boserup, E. (1970) *Women's Role in Economic Development*, New York: St Martin's Press.

Brown, W. (1992) 'Finding the Man in the State', *Feminist Studies*, Vol. 18, No. 1.

Buang, A. (1993) 'Development and Factory Women: Negative Perceptions from a Malaysian Source Area', in J. H. Momsen and V. Kinnaird (eds), *Different Places, Different Voices*, London: Routledge.

Cagatay, N. (1996) 'Gender and International Labor Standards in the World Economy', *Review of Radical Political Economics*, Vol. 28, No. 3.

Cagatay, N. and G. Berik (1990) 'Transition to Export-led Growth in Turkey: Is There Feminisation of Employment?', *Review of Radical Political Economics*, Vol. 22, No. 1.

Chapkis, W. and C. Enloe (eds) (1983) *Of Common Cloth: Women in the Global Textile Industry*, Amsterdam: Transnational Institute.

Dalsimer, M. and L. Nisonoff (1984) 'The New Economic Readjustment Policies: Implications for Chinese Urban Working Women', *Review of Radical Political Economics*, Vol. 16: No. 1.

Ecevit, Y. (1991) 'Shop Floor Control: the Ideological Construction of Turkish Women Factory Workers', in N. Redclift and M. T. Sinclair (eds), *Working Women: International Perspectives on Labour and Gender Ideology*, London: Routledge.

Elson, D. (ed.) (1991) *Male Bias in the Development Process*, New York: St Martin's Press.

Elson, D. and R. Pearson (1981) 'Nimble Fingers Make Cheap Workers: An Analysis of Women's Employment in Third World Export Manufacturing', *Feminist Review* 7.

Elson, D. and R. Pearson (eds) (1989) *Women's Employment and Multinationals in Europe,* Basingstoke, England: Macmillan.

Enloe, C. H. (1983) 'Women Textile Workers in the Militarization of Southeast Asia', in J. Nash and M. P. Fernández-Kelly (eds).

Fernández-Kelly, M. P. (1983a) *For We Are Sold, I and My People: Women in Industry in Mexico's Frontier*, Albany, NY: SUNY Press.

—— (1983b) 'Mexican Border Industrialization, Female Labor-force Participation and Migration', in J. Nash and M. P. Fernández-Kelly (eds) (1983).

——and Sassen, S. (1995) 'Recasting Women in the Global Economy: Internationalization and Changing Definitions of Gender', in C. E. Bose and E. Acosta-Belen (eds), *Women in the Latin American Development Process*, Philadelphia: Temple University Press.

Fuentes, A. and B. Ehrenreich (1983) *Women in the Global Factory,,* INC Pamphlet No. 2, Boston: South End Press.

Gallin, R. S. (1990) 'Women and the Export Industry in Taiwan: The Muting of Class Consciousness', in K. Ward (ed.), *Women Workers and Global Restructuring*, Ithaca, NY: ILR Press.

Gray, L. (director and producer) (1986) *The Global Assembly Line*, Educational TV and Film Center, Los Angeles, CA.

Greenhalgh, S. (1988) 'Integrated Contrasts: Familial Roots of Sexual Stratification in Taiwan', in D. Dwyer and J. Bruce (eds), *A Home Divided: Women and Income in the Third World*, Stanford, CA: Stanford University Press.

Hatem, M. (1985) 'Conservative Patriarchal Modernization in the Arabian Gulf', *Contemporary Marxism* 11.

Humphrey, J. (1987) *Gender and Work in the Third World: Sexual Divisions in Brazilian Industry*, London and New York: Tavistock.

Inter-American Development Bank (1990) *Economic and Social Progress in Latin America*, Washington, DC: Johns Hopkins University Press and I-ADB.

Kamel, R. (1990) *The Global Factory: Analysis and Action for a New Economic Era*, Philadelphia: American Friends Service Committee.

Kidron, M. and R. Segal (1995) *The State of the World Atlas*, London: Penguin Books.

Lim, L. Y. C. (1990) 'Women's Work in Export Factories: The Politics of a Cause', in I. Tinker (ed), *Persistent Inequalities*, Oxford: Oxford University Press.

MacEwen Scott, A. (1990) 'Patterns of Patriarchy in the Peruvian Working Class', in S. Stichter and J. Parpart (eds) (1990).

Maurer, B. (1991) 'Symbolic Sexuality and Economic Work in Dominica, West Indies: The Naturalization of Sex and Women's Work in Development', *Review of Radical Political Economics*, Vol. 23, Nos 3 & 4, Fall and Winter.

Nash, J. (1988) 'Cultural Parameters of Sexism and Racism in the International Division of Labor', in J. Smith (ed.), *Racism, Sexism and the World System*, New York: Greenwood Press.

Nash, J. and M. P. Fernández-Kelly (eds) (1983), *Women, Men and the International Divison of Labor*, Albany, NY: SUNY Press.

Ong, A. (1983) 'Global Industries and Malay Peasants in Peninsular Malaysia', in J. Nash and M. P. Fernández-Kelly (eds) (1983).

——(1987) *Spirits of Resistance and Capitalist Discipline: Factory Women in Malaysia*, Albany, NY: SUNY Press.

Phongpaichit, P. (1988) 'Two Roads to the Factory: Industrialisation Strategies and Women's Employment in Southeast Asia', in B. Agarwal (ed.), *Structures of Patriarchy*, New Delhi: Kali for Women.

Pyle, J. L. (1990a) 'Export-Led Development and the Underemployment of Women: The Impact of Discriminatory Development Policy in the Republic of Ireland', in Ward, K. (ed.) (1990).

——(1990b) 'Female Employment and Export-led Development in Ireland: Labour Market Impact of State-reinforced Gender Inequality in the Household', in S. Stichter and J. L. Parpart (eds) (1990).

——(1990c) *The State and Women in the Economy: Lessons from Sex Discrimination in the Republic of Ireland*, Albany, NY: SUNY Press.

—— (1994) 'Economic Restructuring in Singapore and the Changing Roles of Women, 1957 to Present', in N. Aslanbeigui, S. Pressman and G. Summerfield (eds), *Women in the Age of Economic Transformation*, London and New York: Routledge.

Rendon, T. and C. Salas (1995) *The Gender Dimension of Employment Trends in Mexico*, Conference paper presented at URPE at ASSA, Washington, DC, 6–8 January.

Rios, P. N. (1990) 'Export-Oriented Industrialization and the Demand for Female Labor: Puerto Rican Women in the Manufacturing Sector, 1952–1980', *Gender and Society*, Vol. 4, No. 3, September.

Rothstein, F. A. and M. L. Blim (eds) (1992) *Anthropology and the Global Factory: Studies of the New Industrialisation in the Late Twentieth Century*, New York: Bergin and Garvey.

——(1995) 'Gender and Multiple Income Strategies in Rural Mexico: A Twenty Year Perspective', in C. E. Bose and E. Acosta-Belen, *Women in the Latin American Development Process*, Philadelphia: Temple University Press.

Ruiz, V. and Tiano, S. (eds) (1991) *Women on the US–Mexico Border; Responses to Change*, Boulder, CO: Westview Press.

Safa, H. I. (1981) 'Runaway Shops and Female Employment: The Search for Cheap Labor', *SIGNS*, Vol. 7: No. 2.

——(1983) 'Women, Production and Reproduction in Industrial Capitalism: A Comparison of Brazilian and US Factory Workers', in J. Nash and M. P. Fernández-Kelly (eds) *Women, Men and the International Division of Labor*, Albany, NY: SUNY Press.

——(1995) *The Myth of the Male Breadwinner: Women and the Industrialization in the Caribbean*, Boulder, CO. and Oxford: Westview Press.

Saffioti, H. I. B. (1985) 'Technological Change in Brazil: Its Effect on Men and Women in Two Firms', in J. Nash and H. Safa, (eds) *Women and Change in Latin America*, South Hadley, MA: Bergin and Garvey.

Salaff, J. W. (1981) *Working Daughters of Hong Kong: Filial Piety or Power in the Family?*, Cambridge, England: Cambridge University Press.

——(1990) 'Women, the Family and the State: Hong Kong, Taiwan, Singapore— Newly Industrialized Countries in Asia', in S. Stichter and J. Parpart (eds) (1990).

Sanderson, S. E. (1985) *The Americas in the New International Division of Labor*, New York: Holmes and Meier Publishers Ltd.

Sassen-Koob, S. (1984) 'From Household to Workplace: Theories and Survey Research on Migrant Women in the Labor Market', *International Migration Review*, Vol. XVIII, No. 4.

Schmink, M. (1985) 'Women and Urban Industrial Development in Brazil', in J. Nash and H. Safa (eds), *Women and Change in Latin America*, South Hadley, MA: Bergin and Garvey.

Seguret, M. C. (1983) 'Women and Working Conditions: Prospects for Improvement', *International Labor Review*, Vol. 122: No. 3.

Sinclair, M. T. (1991) 'Women, Work and Skill: Economic Theories and Feminist Perspectives', in N. Redclift and M. T. Sinclair (eds), *Working Women: International Perspectives on Labour and Gender Ideology*, London and New York: Routledge.

Sklair, L. (ed.) (1988) *Maquiladoras: Annotated Bibliography and Research Guide to Mexico's In-Bond Industry, 1980–1988*, Monograph Series, 24, San Diego: Center for US–Mexican Studies, University of California at San Diego.

Standing, G. (1989) 'Global Feminization through Flexible Labor', *World Development*, Vol. 17, No. 7.

Stichter, S. and J. Parpart (eds) (1990), *Women, Employment and the Family in the International Division of Labor,* Philadelphia: Temple University Press.

Summerfield, G. (1994) 'Chinese Women and the Post-Mao Economic Reforms', in N. Aslanbeigui, S. Pressman, and G. Summerfield (eds), *Women in the Age of Economic Transformation: Gender Impact of Reforms in Post-socialist and Developing Countries*, London and New York: Routledge.

Tiano, S. (1990) 'Maquiladora Women: A New Category of Workers?', in K. Ward (ed.) (1990).

——(1994) *Patriarchy on the Line: Labor, Gender and Ideology in the Mexican Maquila Industry*, Philadelphia: Temple University Press.

United Nations (1995) *Women in a Changing Global Economy: 1994 World Survey on the Role of Women in Development*, New York: United Nations.

——(1995) *The World's Women 1995: Trends and Statistics*, New York: United Nations.

United Nations Development Programme (1995) *Human Development Report 1995*, Oxford and New York: Oxford University Press.

Ward, K. (ed.) (1990) *Women Workers and Global Restructuring*, Ithaca, NY: Cornell University Press.

Ward, K. and J. L. Pyle (1995) 'Gender, Industrialization, Transnational Corporations and Development: An Overview of Trends and Patterns', in C. E. Bose and E. Acosta-Belen (eds), *Women in the Latin American Development Process*, Philadelphia: Temple University Press.

Wiegersma, N. (1994) 'State Policy and the Restructuring of Women's Industries in Nicaragua', in N. Aslanbeigui, S. Pressman and G. Summerfield (eds), *Women in the Age of Economic Transformation*, London and New York: Routledge.

Wolf, D. L. (1990) 'Linking Women's Labor with the Global Economy: Factory Workers and Their Families in Rural Java', in K. Ward (ed.) *Women Workers and Global Restructuring*, Ithaca, NY: Cornell University Press.

WOMEN IN THE INFORMAL SECTOR

Aguilar, D. (1996) 'The Half-Hidden World of Filipina Migrant Labor: Servants to the Global Masters', *Against the Current*, Vol. XI: No. 1.

Babb, F. (1984) 'Women in the Marketplace: Petty Commerce in Peru', *Review of Radical Political Economics*, Vol. 16, No. 1.

——(1985) 'Producers and Reproducers: Andean Marketwomen in the Economy', in J. Nash and H. Safa (eds) *Women and Change in Latin America*, South Hadley, MA: Bergin and Garvey.

——(1987a) 'From the Field to the Cooking Pot: Economic Crisis and the Threat to Marketers in Peru', *Ethnology*, Vol. XXVI: No. 2.

——(1987b) 'Marketers as Producers: The Labor Process and Proletarianization of Peruvian Market Women', in D. Hakken and H. Lessinger (eds), *Perspectives in US Marxist Anthropology*, Boulder, CO: Westview Press.

——(1989) *Between Field and Cooking Pot: The Political Economy of Marketwomen in Peru*, Austin: University of Texas Press.

Benería, L. (1987) 'Gender and the Dynamics of Subcontracting in Mexico City', in C. Brown and J. A. Pechman (eds), *Gender in the Workplace*, Washington, DC: Brookings Institution.

Benería, L. and M. Roldan (1987) *The Crossroads of Class and Gender: Industrial Homework, Subcontracting, and Household Dynamics in Mexico City*, Chicago: University of Chicago Press.

Blumberg, R. L. (1995) 'Gender, Microenterprise, Performance and Power: Case Studies from the Dominican Republic, Ecuador, Guatemala and Swaziland', in C. E. Bose and E. Acosta-Belen (eds), *Women in the Latin American Development Process*, Philadelphia: Temple University Press.

Bolles, A. L. (1992) 'Common Ground of Creativity', *Cultural Survival Quarterly*, Vol. 16, No. 4, Winter.

Buechler, J. M. (1985) 'Women in Petty Commodity Production in La Paz, Bolivia', in J. Nash and H. Safa (eds), *Women and Change in Latin America*, South Hadley, MA: Bergin and Garvey.

Bunster, X. and E. Chaney (1985) *Sellers and Servants: Working Women in Lima, Peru,* New York: Praeger.

Castelberg-Koulma, M. (1991) 'Greek Women and Tourism; Women's Cooperatives as an Alternative Form of Organization', in N. Redclift and M. T. Sinclair (eds), *Working Women: International Perspectives on Labour and Gender Ideology,* London: Routledge.

Chaney, E. M. and M. Garcia Castro (1989) *Muchachas No More,* Philadelphia: Temple University Press.

Clark, G. (1992) 'Flexibility Equals Survival', *Cultural Survival Quarterly,* Vol. 16, No. 4, Winter.

Collins, J. L. and M. Gimenez (eds) (1990) *Work Without Wages: Comparative Studies of Domestic Labor and Self-Employment,* Albany, NY: SUNY Press.

Cook, Scott (1990) 'Female Labor, Commodity Production, and Ideology in Mexican Peasant-Artisan Households', in J. L. Collins and M. Gimenez (eds) *Work Without Wages: Comparative Studies of Domestic Labor and Self-Employment,* Albany, NY: SUNY Press.

Ecevit, Y. (1991) 'The Ideological Construction of Turkish Women Factory Workers', in N. Redclift and M. T. Sinclair (eds), *Working Women: International Perspectives on Labor and Gender Ideology,* London: Routledge.

Esim, Simel (1992) *Improving the Involvement of Women in the Egyptian Informal Sector,* Middle East and North Africa Country Department II, Country Operations Division, World Bank.

Hamermesh, M. (writer and director) (1985) *Maids and Madams,* Produced by C. Wargler, London: Channel 4 Television Co.

Harrison, F. (1991) 'Women in Jamaica's Urban Informal Economy: Insights from a Kingston Slum', in C. T. Mahonty, A. Russo, and L. Torres (eds), *Third World Women and the Politics of Feminism,* Bloomington: Indiana University Press.

Kabra, K. N. (1995) 'The Informal Sector: A Reappraisal', *Journal of Contemporary Asia,* Vol. 25, No. 2.

Koptiuch, K. (1992) 'Informal Sectorization of Egyptian Petty Commodity Production', in F. A. Rothstein, and M. L. Blim (eds), *Anthropology and the Global Factory: Studies of the New Industrialization of the Late Twentieth Century,* New York: Bergin and Garvey.

Lessinger, J. (1986) 'Work and Modesty: The Dilemma of Women Market Traders in South India', *Feminist Studies,* Vol. 12, No. 3, Fall.

Mohiuddin, Y. (1993) 'Female-headed Households and Urban Poverty in Pakistan', in N. Folbre, B. Bergmann, B. Agarwal and M. Floro (eds), *Women's Work in the World Economy,* New York: New York University Press.

Nash, J. (ed.) (1993) *Crafts in the World Market: The Impact of Global Exchange on Middle American Artisans,* Albany, NY: SUNY Press.

Osirim, M. J. (1996) 'The Dilemmas of Modern Development: Structural Adjustment and Women Microentrepreneurs in Nigeria and Zimbabwe', in J. Turpin and L. A. Lorentzen (eds), *The Gendered New World Order: Militarism, Development and the Environment,* New York and London: Routledge.

Peattie, L. (1987) 'An Idea in Good Currency and How It Grew: The Informal Sector', *World Development,* Vol. 15, No. 7.

Portes, A., M. Castells and L. Benton (1989) *The Informal Economy: Studies in Advanced and Less Developed Countries,* Baltimore, MD: Johns Hopkins University Press.

Portes, A. and R. Schauffler (1993) 'Competing Perspectives on the Latin American Informal Sector', *Population and Development Review* 19.

Rothstein, F. A. (ed.) (1992) 'Women's Work, Women's Worth: Women, Economics, and Development', *Cultural Survival Quarterly*, Vol. 16, No. 4, Winter.

Rowbotham, S. and S. Mitter (1994) *Dignity and Daily Bread*, London: Routledge.

Saraceno, C. (1992) 'Women's Paid and Unpaid Work in Times of Economic Crisis', in L. Beneria and S. Feldman (eds), *Unequal Burden: Economic Crises, Persistent Poverty, and Women's Work*, Boulder, CO. and Oxford: Westview Press.

Stephen, L. (1992) 'Marketing Ethnicity', *Cultural Survival Quarterly*, Vol. 16, No. 4, Winter.

Sullivan, K. (1992) 'Protagonists of Change', *Cultural Survival Quarterly*, Vol. 16, No. 4, Winter.

Trask, H. K. and M. Trask (1992) 'The Aloha Industry', *Cultural Survival Quarterly*, Vol. 16, No. 4, Winter.

Treulove, C. (1990) 'Disguised Industrial Proletarians in Rural Latin America: Women's Informal Sector Factory Work and the Social Reproduction of Coffee Farm Labor in Columbia', in K. Ward (ed.), *Women Workers and Global Restructuring*, Ithaca, NY: ILR Press.

Witter, M. (ed.) (1989) *Higglering/Sidewalk Vending/Informal Commercial Trading in the Jamaican Economy: Proceedings of a Symposium,* Mona, Jamaica: University of West Indies.

A. Women and Industrialization

This section focuses on women's work in industrial production: free trade zones, multinational corporations and domestically owned firms.

17. THE SUBORDINATION OF WOMEN AND THE INTERNATIONALIZATION OF FACTORY PRODUCTION

DIANE ELSON AND RUTH PEARSON

WORLD MARKET FACTORIES: THE LATEST PHASE OF THE INTERNATIONALIZATION OF CAPITAL

Since the late 1960s a new type of wage employment has become available to women in many Third World countries: work in 'worldmarket factories' producing manufactures exclusively for export to the rich countries (Hancock, 1980).

World market factories represent a relocation of production of certain kinds of manufactured product from the developed countries, where they continue to be consumed, to the Third World.[1] The factories typically produce on subcontract to the order of a particular overseas customer, and the customer arranges the marketing of the product. The world market factory may be owned by indigenous capitalists, be a wholly-owned subsidiary of its overseas customer, or be a joint venture of some kind between Third World businessmen and the overseas customer (Tang, 1980).

Some factories producing final consumer goods do no more than assemble parts supplied by their customers. Through the provision of material inputs, design capacity or working capital, the customer may control the production process to the extent that though the supplier has formal autonomy, in practice the customer is operating a new and more sophisticated version of the 'putting-out' system. The transfer of the goods across national boundaries, though ostensibly organized through market sales and purchases, may in substance be a transfer between two departments of an integrated production process.

In some cases there is some scope for local initiative, but in general the degree of autonomy enjoyed by the factories is limited for they lack the means to develop new technologies.

LABOUR-FORCE REQUIREMENTS

A critical factor in the location of world market factories is the availability of a suitable labour force, one which provides a ratio of output to costs of employment superior to that which prevails at existing centres of capital accumulation in the developed countries. This has been achieved by a combination of much lower costs of employment, and matching or even higher productivity than that achieved in developed countries. This is not being achieved through superior technology: it is the result of greater intensity of work, greater continuity of production; in short, greater control over the performance of the labour force.

Many Third World countries which in the past had enacted progressive labour legislation, often as a result of the contribution of trade union struggles to the fight against imperialism, have by now incorporated the official trade union organization into the state apparatus; and either suspended, or failed to enforce, major provisions of that legislation. Workers in [these] factories have been left exposed by the abrogation of their rights on such matters as minimum wage payments, contributions to insurance funds, limitations on the length of the working day and week, security of employment, redundancy conditions and payments, and the right to strike. Free Trade Zones[2] have particularly stringent controls on the activity of workers' organizations, but in some countries, particularly in South East Asia, such controls [are nationwide] and the power of the state is used vigorously to enforce them.

THE EMPLOYMENT OF WOMEN

Why is it young women who overwhelmingly constitute the labour force of world market factories? The reproduction in the factories of the sexual division of labour typical of labour-intensive assembly operations in developed countries rests upon some differentiation of the labour force which makes it more profitable to employ female rather than male labour. Female labour must either be cheaper than comparable male labour, have higher productivity, or some combination of both; the net result being that unit costs of production are lower with female [workers]. In general, the money costs of employing female labour in world market factories do seem to be lower than would be the costs of employing men but direct productivity comparisons are hard to make, since so few men are employed in comparable operations. In the few documented cases where men have been employed—in Malaysian electronics and Malawi textile factories—their productivity was lower than that of women in the same plants. Firms running world market factories seem firmly convinced that this would generally be the case.

What produces this differentiation? The answers that companies give when asked why they employ women, as well as the statements made by governments trying to attract world market factories, show that there is a widespread belief that it is a 'natural' differentiation, produced by innate capacities and personality traits of women and men, and by an objective differentiation of their income needs; men need an income to support a family, while women do not.

Women are considered not only to have naturally nimble fingers, but also to be naturally more docile and willing to accept tough work discipline, and naturally more suited to tedious, repetitious, monotonous work. Their lower wages are attributed to their secondary status in the labour market which is seen as a natural consequence of their capacity to bear children. The fact that only young women work in world market factories is also rationalized as an effect of their capacity to bear children—they will be either unwilling or unable to continue in employment much beyond their early twenties. Indeed the phenomenon of women leaving employment in the factory when they get married or pregnant is known as 'natural wastage', and can be highly advantageous to firms which periodically need to vary the size of their labour force to adjust to fluctuating demand for their output in the world market. There is a real differentiation between the characteristics of women and men as potential workers in world market factories [but] in our view it is far from being natural.

WHERE DO WOMEN GET THEIR SKILLS?

The famous 'nimble fingers' of young women are not an inheritance from their mothers, in the same way that they may inherit the colour of her skin or eyes. They are the result of the training they have received from their mothers and other female kin since early infancy in the tasks socially appropriate to woman's role. For instance, since industrial sewing of clothing resembles closely sewing with a domestic sewing machine, girls who have learnt sewing at home already have the manual dexterity and capacity for spatial assessment required. Training in needlework and sewing also produces skills transferable to other assembly operations.

It is partly because this training is socially invisible, privatized, that the skills it produces are attributable to nature and the jobs that make use of it are classified as 'unskilled' or 'semi-skilled'. Given that manual dexterity of a high order is an admitted requirement for many of the assembly jobs done by women in world market factories, and that women working in the electronics industry have to pass aptitude tests with high scores, it is clear that the categorization of these jobs as unskilled does not derive from the purely technical characteristics of the job. The fact that the training period required within the factory is short, and that once this is over workers do not take long to become highly proficient, does not detract from this conclusion. Little training and 'on the job' learning is required because the women are already trained. 'It takes six weeks to teach industrial garment making *to girls who already know how to sew*' (Sharpston, 1975, p. 105, emphasis added).

In objective terms, it is more accurate to speak of the jobs making a demand for easily trained labour, than for unskilled labour. But of course, skill categories are not determined in a purely objective way (Braverman, 1974). In particular, jobs which are identified as 'women's work' tend to be classified as 'unskilled' or 'semi-skilled', whereas technically similar jobs identified as 'men's work' tend to be classified as 'skilled' (Phillips and Taylor, 1980). To a large extent, women do not do 'unskilled' jobs because they are the bearers of inferior labour; rather, the jobs they do are 'unskilled' because women enter them already determined as inferior bearers of labour.

WOMEN'S SUBORDINATION

The social invisibility of the training that produces these skills of manual dexterity and the lack of social recognition for these skills is intrinsic to the process of gender construction in the world today. This is not only an ideological process, a matter of people ascribing lesser value to women's gender roles. It is a material process which goes on in our practices.

In claiming that it is a material process we do not intend to reduce it to an economic process, to be analysed only in terms of labour, but rather to emphasize that it cannot be changed simply through propaganda for more 'enlightened' views, but requires practical changes in daily living. We would suggest that this process of subordination of women as a gender can be understood in terms of the exclusion of women as a gender from certain activities, and their confinement to others; where the activities from which women as a gender are excluded are some of those which are constituted as public, overtly social activities, and the activities to which women as a gender are confined are some of those which are constituted as private, seemingly purely individual activities.

The constitution of activities as public or private, social or individual, of course differs over time, and between different kinds of society, and is itself a matter of struggle, not a pre-determined given. Activities in which the social aspect is dominant, which are overtly represented as social, confer social power. In our view it is a mistake to see private power as co-equal with social power. Social power is collective, reproducible through social processes, relatively autonomous from the characteristics of particular individuals; private power is individual, contingent on the specific characteristics of particular individuals, reproducible only by chance.

A distinction can usefully be made between relations which are gender ascriptive, that is, relations which are constructed intrinsically in terms of the gender of the persons concerned; and relations which are not gender ascriptive, but which can nevertheless be bearers of gender (Whitehead, 1979, p. 11). An example of the first is the conjugal relation: marriage is a relation necessarily involving the unions of persons of defi-nite and opposite gender; unions between persons of the same gender are not marriage. An example of the second is the sexual division of labour in the capitalist labour process. Though the capital–labour rela-tion is not gender ascriptive, it is nevertheless a bearer of gender (Phillips and Taylor, 1980).

Gender-ascriptive relations are clearly the fundamental sites of the subordination of women as a gender, and in them women's subordina-tion may take a literally patriarchal form, with women directly subject to the authority of the father, their own or their children's. But male hege-mony in gender-ascriptive relations does not always assume a patriarchal form. Rather it is a matter of the extent to which women's social being can only be satisfactorily established through the mediation of a gender-ascriptive relation, whereas the same is not true for men. This kind of gender subordination is not something which an individual woman can escape by virtue of choosing to avoid certain kinds of personal relation with men. For instance, it means that the absence of a husband is as significant as his presence for the establishment of a woman's social identity.

BEHIND THE MIRAGE OF DOCILITY

It is in the context of the subordination of women as a gender that we must analyse the supposed docility, subservience and consequent suit-ability for tedious, monotonous work of young women in the Third World. This is the appearance that women often present to men, partic-ularly men in some definite relation of authority to them, such as father, husband, boss. A similar appearance, presented by colonized peoples to their colonizers, was brilliantly dissected by Fanon, who showed how the public passivity and fatalism which the colonized displayed towards the colonizers for long periods concealed an inner, private rebellion and subversion. This passivity is not a natural and original state: to achieve it requires enormous efforts of self-repression (Fanon, 1969, p.48).

That self-repression is required for women to achieve an adequate level of docility and subservience can be demonstrated on an everyday level by differences in their behaviour when authority figures are present and absent. An example is the behaviour observed by Heyzer (1978) in a factory producing textiles in Singapore. Here the women workers were always on guard when the supervisors were around, and displayed a characteristic subservience; in the absence of supervisors behaviour changed. Far from displaying respectful subservience, workers mocked the supervisors and ridiculed them. The stress that such self-repression can impose and the 'non-rational' forms its relief may take are exemplified in the well-documented occurrence of outbreaks of mass hysteria among young women factory workers in South East Asia.

It is interesting that governments and companies are unwilling to trust completely the personal docility of women workers, reinforcing it with suspension of a wide variety of workers' rights. In spite of being faced with extensive use of state power to control labour unions and prevent strikes, women workers have at times publicly thrown off their subservience and taken direct action.

SECONDARY STATUS IN THE LABOUR MARKET

A major aspect of the gender differentiation of the labour force available for employment in world market factories is what is generally referred to in the literature as women's 'secondary status' in the labour market (Lim, 1978, p.11): women's rates of pay tend to be lower than those of men doing similar or comparable jobs; women form a 'reserve army' of labour, easily fired when firms want to cut back on their labour force, easily re-hired when firms want to expand again. This tends to be explained in terms of 'women's role in the family' or 'women's reproductive role'. In a sense this is true, but it is an ambiguous explanation, in that for many people 'women's role in the family' is an ahistorical fact, given by biology. What has to be stressed is that women's role in the family is socially constructed as a subordinated role—even if she is a 'female head of household'. For it is the female role to do the work which nurtures children and men, work which appears to be purely private and personal, while it is the male role to represent women and children in the wider society. It is the representative role which confers social power.

This kind of gender subordination means that when a labour market develops, women, unlike men, are unable to take on fully the classic attributes of free wage labour. A man can become a free wage labourer in the double sense that as a free individual he can dispose his labour-power as his own commodity and that, on the other hand, he has no other commodity for sale ... he is free of all the objects needed for the realisation of his labour-power. (Marx, 1976, p.273)

A woman is never 'free' in this way. She has obligations of domestic labour, difficulties in establishing control over her own body, and an inability to be fully a member of society in her own right. She may also obtain her subsistence from men in exchange for personal services of a sexual or nurturing kind, thus realizing her labour-power outside the capitalist labour process. It is this gender difference which gives women a 'secondary status' in the labour market. Our purpose is not to deny the social reality of this secondary status. It is to take up a critical stance towards it: nature does not compel the tasks of bringing up children to be the privatized responsibility of their mother while depriving her of the social power to secure, in her own right, access to the resources required for this, forcing her into a dependent position.

This secondary status arising from women's subordination as a gender means that women workers are peculiarly vulnerable to super-exploitation, in the sense that their wages may not cover the full money costs of the reproduction of their labour-power, either on a daily or a generational basis. It means also that women tend to get lower wages than men, even when those wages contribute to the support of several other people, as do the wages of many of the young women who work in world market factories (or indeed of many women workers in developed countries). Sending a daughter to work in such a factory is in some cases the only remaining strategy for acquiring an income for the rest of the family.

THE LIMITS TO LIBERATION THROUGH FACTORY WORK

Ever since large numbers of women were drawn into factory work in the industrial revolution in nineteenth-century England there has been a strong belief that wage work can liberate women from gender subordination. The fact that the social relations of factory work are not intrinsically gender ascriptive but rooted in an impersonal cash nexus gives some plausibility to such views. The end result would be a labour force undifferentiated by gender, with women and men doing the same jobs, in the same conditions, for the same wages, modified only by personal preferences or prejudices for this or that kind of employment or employee. There would be no objective basis for gender differentiation.

This argument fails to consider how it is that women have acquired the characteristics that make them initially the preferred labour force. If men are to compete successfully, they also need to acquire the 'nimble fingers' and 'docile dispositions' for which women are prized. For this, they would be required to undergo the same social experience as women. In order to compete successfully, men would need to experience gender subordination. But since men and women cannot both experience gender subordination simultaneously, this could happen only if women were to be freed from gender subordination; i.e. a reversal, rather than an elimination of gender differentiation. Competition between women and men in the labour market can tend to produce, in certain circumstances, signs of such a reversal (Engels, 1976, pp. 173–174), provoking the traditionalist critique of women's participation in wage work as an overturning of the natural order of things. But these signs of the reversal of gender roles are themselves a demonstration of the fundamental interdependence of the labour force characteristics of women and men. Though, as competitors in the labour market, women and men may at first appear as atomized individuals, they are never so completely separated. They are always linked through gender-ascriptive relations, and their labour market relations become bearers of gender. The important point about the development of capitalism is that it does offer a form of interdependence—the cash nexus—which is not gender ascriptive. But though capitalist production is dominated by the cash nexus, in the sense that it must be organized to make a profit, it cannot be organized solely through cash relations (through wages and prices) but requires a specific hierarchical managerial organization: the capitalist labour process. It has to be organized through the giving of orders, as well as the making of payments. Typically, [this] is defined as a male prerogative, while the role of women is defined as the carrying out of orders.

A great deal of the labour required to provide the goods and services needed for the reproduction of labour power can be socialized through the cash nexus. The monetization of labour processes formerly carried out domestically, and socialized through the gender-ascriptive relations of marriage, is one of the hallmarks of capital accumulation (Braverman, 1974, ch. 13). But the establishment of the social identity of children, their social integration, cannot be accomplished solely through the cash nexus. One implication of this is that the de facto position of women workers as major contributors to the family income does not automatically mean that they will become socially recognized as 'breadwinners', their secondary status in the labour market ended. The position of breadwinner is not constituted purely at the economic level; it is also constituted in the process of establishing the connection of the family with the wider society. The breadwinner must be the public representative of the family. Whitehead (1978) suggests that the wage itself, though clearly not a gender-ascriptive form, tends to become a bearer of gender, in the sense that wages of male and female family members are not treated as interchangeable but are ear-marked for different things.

The recognition of this limitation does not mean that we must therefore deny capitalism any liberating potential: the alternative, cash-based, forms of socialization it entails tend to undermine and disrupt other forms of socialization. They provide a material basis for struggle against the subordination of women as a gender; but there is no way that capitalist exploitation of women as wage workers can simply *replace* gender subordination of women. Exploitation of women as wage workers is parasitic upon their subordination as a gender.

THE DIALECTIC OF CAPITAL AND GENDER

We would like to distinguish three tendencies in the relation between factory work and the subordination of women as a gender: a tendency to *intensify* the existing forms of gender subordination; a tendency to *decompose* existing forms of gender subordination; and a tendency to *recompose* new forms of gender subordination.

There is evidence of all three at work in the case of women employed in world market factories. One way existing forms of gender subordination may be *intensified* is the case of a multinational corporation which believes in deliberately trying to preserve and utilize traditional forms of patriarchal power.

The enhanced economic value of daughters certainly provides a motive for fathers to exert more control, including sending them to work in the factories whether they wish to or not. On the other hand, the ability to earn a wage may be an important factor in undermining certain forms of control of fathers and brothers over young women. This does not mean that there is a reversal of the authority structure of the family. There is considerable empirical evidence that their wages do not confer greater status or decision-making power on the women, even though they may be the chief source of family income.

An example of the way existing forms of gender subordination may be *decomposed* [is posited in] Blake's observation (1979) of the importance of factory work as a way of escaping an early arranged marriage. But the ability to resist arranged marriage and opt for 'free-choice' marriage is two-edged. In the conditions of a society dominated by the capitalist mode of production, 'free-choice' marriage tends to take on the characteristics of the dominant form of choice in such societies, a *market* choice from among competing commodities. It is women themselves who take on many of the attributes of the competing commodities, while it is men who exercise the choice. This 'commoditized' form of making marriages is actively encouraged by the management styles of some of the large American multinational electronics companies which provide lessons in fashion and 'beauty care', rationalized as the provision of fringe benefits which appeal naturally to the 'feminine interests' of the young women workers. Such interests are indeed 'feminine' [when] many young women are competing in a marriage market. A young woman's face may quite literally be her fortune.

Though one form of gender subordination, [that] of daughters to their fathers, may crumble, another form, that of women employees to male factory bosses, is built up. Young female employees are almost exclusively at the bottom of [the] hierarchy; the upper levels are almost invariably male. The sexual element in the relation between female employee and male boss is not contained and shaped by kin relations. This is one of the reasons why factory girls are often regarded as not quite 'respectable'.

This *recomposition* of a new form of gender subordination can also intensify more traditional forms of subordination of wives to husbands. The fact that, if his wife works in a factory, she will be subject to the authority of other men, may be a powerful reason for a husband wishing to confine his wife to the home.

INSTABILITY OF EMPLOYMENT

The problem is not simply that young women may, through factory work, escape the domination of fathers and brothers only to become subordinate to male managers and supervisors, or escape the domination of managers and supervisors only to become subordinate to husbands or lovers. There is also the problem that the domination of managers and supervisors may be withdrawn—the woman may be sacked from her job—while the woman is without the 'protection' of subordination to father, brother, husband.[3] She may be left dependent on the cash nexus for survival, but unable to realize her labour-power in cash terms through working in the factory.

This problem is particularly acute for women who work in world market factories. The fact that the mass of capital continues to be accumulated in developed countries means that market demand, technical know-how and finance continue to be concentrated there, so that the factories, representing relatively small dispersions of capital accumulation, are inherently vulnerable to changes in the conditions of accumulation in developed countries.

The hiring and firing practices of particular firms add to the inherent precariousness and instability of employment. The preference of firms for young workers means that workers in their early twenties who have not left voluntarily are the first to be dismissed if it is necessary to retrench the labour force. Pregnancy is often grounds for dismissal, or women are dismissed on the grounds that they can no longer meet productivity or time-keeping norms. A deterioration in performance is, in fact, often the result of some disability caused by the work itself. Women employed in the garment industry on the Mexican Border tend[ed] to suffer from kidney complaints and varicose veins. Women using microscopes every day in the electronics industry suffer eye-strain and their eyesight deteriorates. The shift work which is common in electronics and textile factories can produce continual fatigue, headaches and general deterioration of health. The net result is that it is quite often workers who have already acquired new consumption patterns, responsibilities and, in many cases, debts, who lose their jobs, rather than those who have just entered factory life.

If a woman loses her job after she has reshaped her life on the basis of a wage income, the only way she may have of surviving is by selling her body. There are reports from South Korea that many former electronics workers have no alternative but to become prostitutes (Grossman, 1979, p.16). A growing market for such services is provided by the tourist industry, especially in South East Asia.

STRUGGLE AS WORKERS

In our view the development of world market factories provides a material basis for a process of struggle for self-determination. It does this by bringing together large numbers of women and confronting them with a common, cash-based, authority: the authority of capital. This is not the effect of most alternative forms of work for young Third World women.

The most obvious possibility for struggle which this suggests is a struggle as *workers* around such issues as wages and conditions of work. It is therefore, at first sight, disappointing to find a low level of formal participation in trade union activities by women employed in world market factories. But we need to bear in mind both the *limitations*, as well as the possibilities, of factory-based struggle about work-related issues, and the *shortcomings* of official trade union organizations in many parts of the world.

The limits within which workers in world market factories are confined are particularly narrow because of the ease with which operations might be relocated, and because the management so often enjoys the backing of particularly coercive forms of state power.

The ability to secure improvements tends to be conditioned by particular rates of accumulation at particular localities. It is noticeable that it is in countries like Hong Kong and Singapore where the rate of investment has been high that wage rates have tended to rise. A higher proportion of married, and older, women tends to be found in the factories in these countries, symptomatic of a tighter labour market.

An important consideration is the extent to which other social groups will support workers in particular factories in campaigns for better pay and conditions of work. [But] no matter how effective and far-reaching the support given to the workforce, the struggle for better pay and conditions of work remains contradictory. To a considerable extent, the success in this struggle is predicated upon the success of management in making profits.

Struggle at the level of the factory cannot be judged solely in terms of its effect on pay and conditions of work. It has to be judged [also] as a way of developing the capacities of those involved in it, particularly the capacity for self-organization. In this context, participation in collective action in the factory itself, even of a sporadic and spontaneous character, is more important than purely formal membership of a trade union. It also helps factory workers to understand the worldwide structure of the forces which shape their lives, and helps prepare them for struggle, not just in the factory where they work, but against the economic system of which it is a part.

STRUGGLE AS WOMEN

Struggles arising from the development of world market factories will, however, remain seriously deficient from the point of view of *women* workers if they deal only with economic questions of pay and working conditions, and fail to take up other problems which stem from the recomposition of new forms of the subordination of women as a gender: how to attract a husband or lover; how to deal with the contradictions of female sexuality—to express one's sexuality without becoming a sex-object; how to cope with pregnancy and child care (Blake, 1979, p.12). The concern of women workers with these problems is not a sign that they are 'backward' in consciousness as compared with male workers, but that for women, it is gender subordination which is primary, capitalist exploitation secondary and derivative.

The forms that workers' organizations have traditionally taken have been inadequate from women's point of view because they have failed to recognize and build into their structure the specificity of gender. New forms of organization are required that will specifically take up these problems, offering both practical, immediate action on them, and also revealing the social roots of what at first sight appears to be a series of individual, personal problems whose only common denominator lies in the supposed 'natural' propensities and capabilities of women as a sex.

The employment of women in world market factories does provide a material basis for 'politicizing the personal' because of the way it masses together women not simply as workers but as a gender.

A practical reality is given to the concept of women as a gender in the same way that a practical reality is given to the concept of labour in general (Marx, 1973, pp.103–105). This creates a basis for the struggle of women factory workers as members of a *gender*, as well as members of a class. Women workers in various parts of the Third World have formed sector-based organizations which link women in different factories operating in the same industry, and 'off-site' organizations to tackle issues like housing, education and sanitation, which remain the responsibility of women.

Of course, limitations and contradictions similar to those discussed in the case of activity to improve pay and working conditions in the factory beset the struggle to ameliorate other aspects of women workers' lives. Accordingly women's struggle as a gender should not be judged in purely instrumental terms. The development of conscious cooperation and solidarity between women on the basis of their common experience of gender subordination is even more important a goal than any particular improvement in the provision of jobs or welfare services to women, than any particular reform of legal status, than any particular weakening of 'machismo' or 'patriarchal attitudes'. Improvements which come about through capital accumulation or state policy or changing male attitudes can be reversed. Lasting gains depend upon the relationships built up between women themselves.

The most important task of sympathetic personnel in national and international state agencies is to work out how they can facilitate access to resources for organizations (and for activities) which are based on an explicit recognition of gender subordination and are trying to develop new forms of association through which women can begin to establish elements of a social identity in their own right, and not through the mediation of men. Such organizations do not require policy advisers to tell them what to do, supervise them and monitor them; they require protection from the almost inevitable onslaughts of those who have a vested interest in maintaining both the exploitation of women as workers, and the subordination of women as a gender.

18. *MAQUILADORAS*: THE VIEW FROM THE INSIDE

María Patricia Fernández-Kelly

Along the Mexican side of the United States–Mexico border, there has been a huge expansion of manufacturing activities by multinational corporations. This has incorporated large numbers of women into direct production in the last fifteen years. As a result of implementation of the Border Industrialization Program since 1965, more than one hundred assembly plants, or *maquiladoras*, have sprung up in Ciudad Juarez, across the border from El Paso, Texas. This set of programmes has made it possible for multinational firms to collaborate with Mexican state and private enterprise to foster the emergence of a booming export industry along the border. More than half of the plants are electric or electronic firms. Most of the rest are apparel assembly plants (see Newton and Balli, 1979).

The importance of the programme in recent years may be appreciated by noting that *maquiladoras* account for about half of US imports from underdeveloped countries under assembly-industry tariff provisions, as compared with only 10 per cent in 1970. The objective circumstances that have determined the growth of the *maquiladora* industry are the availability of what appears to be an inexhaustible supply of unskilled and semi-skilled labour, and extremely high levels of productivity.

The plants themselves are small, and most subcontract from corporations with their headquarters in the United States. Although nationally recognized brands are represented in Ciudad Juarez, the vast majority of these industries are associated with corporations that have regional rather than national visibility. The low level of capital investment in the physical plant often results in inadequate equipment and unpleasant working conditions.

While all *maquiladoras* employ an overwhelming majority (85 per cent) of women, the apparel industry hires women whose position in the city makes them especially vulnerable to exploitative labour practices. They tend to be in their mid-twenties, poorly educated and recent migrants to Ciudad Juarez. About one-third of the women head households and are the sole supports of their children.

LOOKING FOR A JOB: A PERSONAL ACCOUNT

What is it like to be female, single and eager to find work at a *maquiladora*? Shortly after arriving in Ciudad Juarez, and after finding stable lodging, I began looking through the pages of newspapers, hoping to find a want ad. My intent was to merge with the clearly visible mass of women who roam the streets and industrial parks of the city searching for jobs.

My objectives were straightforward. I wanted to spend four to six weeks applying for jobs and obtaining direct experience about the employment policies, recruitment strategies and screening mechanisms used by companies to hire assembly workers. I was especially interested in how much time and money an individual worker spent trying to get a job. I also wanted to spend an equal amount of time working at a plant, preferably one that manufactured apparel. This way, I expected to learn more about working conditions, production quotas and wages at a particular factory. I felt this would help me develop questions from a worker's perspective.

In retrospect, it seems odd that it never entered my head that I might not find a job. Finding a job at a *maquiladora* is easier said than done, especially for a woman over twenty-five. This is due primarily to the large numbers competing for jobs. At every step of their constant peregrination, women are confronted by a familiar sign at the plants—'no applications available'—or by the negative responses of a guard or a secretary at the entrance to the factories. But such is the arrogance of the uninformed researcher, I went about the business of looking for a job as if the social milieu had to conform to my research needs.

By using newspapers as a source of information, I was departing from the common strategy of potential workers in that environment. Most women are part of informal networks which include relatives, friends and an occasional acquaintance in the personnel-management sector. They hear of jobs by word of mouth.

Most job seekers believe that a personal recommendation from someone already employed at a *maquiladora* can ease the difficult path. This belief is well founded. At many plants, managers prefer to hire applicants by direct recommendation of employees who have proven to be dependable and hard working. By resorting to the personal link, managers decrease the dangers of having their factories infiltrated by unreliable workers, independent organizers and 'troublemakers'.

Appearing to take a personal interest in the individual worker at the moment of hiring, management can establish a paternalistic claim on the worker. Workers complain that superintendents and managers are prone to demand 'special services', like overtime, in exchange for granting personal 'favours' such as a loan or time off from work to care for children. Yet workers acknowledge a personal debt to the person who hired them. A woman's commitment to the firm is fused with commitment to the particular personnel manager or superintendent who granted her the 'personal favour' of hiring her. Anita expressed the typical sentiment: 'If the group leader demands more production [without additional pay], I will generally resist because I owe her nothing. But if the *ingeniero* asks me to increase my quota on occasion, I comply. He gave me the job in the first place! Besides, it makes me feel good to know that I can return the favour, at least in part.'

One firm advertised for direct production workers in the two main Juarez newspapers throughout the year, an indication of its high rate of turnover. I went into its tiny office in the middle of summer to apply for a job. As I entered, I wondered whether my appearance or accent would make the personnel manager suspicious. He looked me over sternly and told me to fill out a form [there and then] and to return the following morning to take a dexterity test. Most of the items were straightforward: name, age, marital status, place of birth, length of residence in Ciudad Juarez, property assets, previous jobs and income, number of pregnancies and general state of health. One, however, was unexpected: what is your major aspiration in life? All my doubts surfaced—would years of penmanship practice at a private school in Mexico City and flawless spelling give me away?

I assumed the on-the-job test would consist of a short evaluation of my skills as a seamstress. I was wrong. The next morning I knocked at the door of the personnel office where I filled out the application, but no one was there. In some confusion, I peeked into the entrance of the factory. The supervisor, Margarita, a dark-haired woman wearing false eyelashes, ordered me in and led me to my place at an industrial sewing machine. That it was old was plain to see; how it worked was difficult to judge. I listened intently to Margarita's instructions. I was expected to sew patch pockets on what were to become blue jeans from the assortment of diversely cut denim parts on my left. Obediently I started to sew.

The particulars of 'unskilled' labour unfolded before my eyes. The procedure demanded perfect coordination of hands, eyes and legs. I was to use my left hand to select the larger part of material from the batch next to me and my right to grab the pocket. There were no markers to show me where to place the pocket. Experienced workers did it on a purely visual basis. Once the patch pocket was in place, I was to guide the two parts under a double needle while applying pressure on the machine's pedal with my right foot.

Because the pockets were sewed on with thread of a contrasting colour, the edge of the pocket had to be perfectly aligned with the needles to produce a regular seam and an attractive design. Because the pocket was diamond shaped, I also had to rotate the materials slightly three times while adjusting pressure on the pedal. Too much pressure inevitably broke the thread or produced seams longer than the edge of the pocket. The slightest deviation produced lopsided designs, which then had to be unsewed and gone over as many times as it took to do an acceptable pocket. The supervisor told me that, once trained, I would be expected to sew a pocket every nine to ten seconds. That meant 360 to 396 pockets every hour, or 2,880 to 3,168 every day!

As at the vast majority of apparel-manufacturing *maquiladoras*, I would be paid through a combination of the minimum wage and piece-work. In 1978 this was 125 pesos a day, or US$5.00. I would, however, get a slight bonus if I sustained a calculated production quota through the week. Workers are not allowed to produce less than 80 per cent of their assigned quota without being admonished, and a worker seriously endangers her job when unable to improve her level of output. Margarita [indicated] a small blackboard showing the weekly bonus received by those able to produce certain percentages of the quota. They fluctuated between 50 pesos (US$2.20) for those who completed 80 per cent of the quota, to 100 pesos for those who completed 100 per cent. Managers call this combination of steep production quotas, minimum wages and modest bonuses an 'incentive programme'.

I started my test at 7:30 a.m. with a sense of embarrassment about my limited skills and disbelief at the speed with which the women in the factory worked. As I continued sewing, the bundle of material on my left was renewed and slowly grew in size. I had to repeat the operation many times before the product was considered acceptable. I soon realized I was being treated as a new worker while presumably being tested. I had not been issued a contract and therefore was not yet incorporated into the Instituto Mexicano del Seguro Social (the national social security system), nor had I been told about working hours, benefits or system of payment.

I explained to the supervisor that I had recently arrived in the city, alone, and with very little money. Would I be hired? When would I be given a contract? Margarita listened patiently while helping me unsew one of many defective pockets and then said, 'You are too curious. Don't worry about it. Do your job and things will be all right.' I continued to sew, aware of the fact that every pocket attached during the 'test' was becoming part of the plant's total production.

At 12:30, during the thirty-minute lunch break, I had a better chance to see the factory. Its improvised quality was underscored by the metal folding chairs at the sewing machines. I had been sitting on one of them during the whole morning, but until then I had not noticed that most of them had the Coca Cola label painted on their backs. I had seen this kind of chair many times in casual parties both in Mexico and in the United States. Had they been bought, or were they being rented? In any event, they were not designed to meet the strenuous requirements of sewing all day. Women brought their own colourful pillows to ease the stress on their buttocks and spines. Later, I was to discover that chronic lumbago is a frequent condition among factory seamstresses (Fernández, 1978).

My questions were still unanswered at 5 p.m. when a bell rang to signal the end of the shift. I went to the personnel office intending to get more information. Despite my overly shy approach to the personnel manager, his reaction was hostile. Even before he was able to turn the disapproving expression on his face into words, Margarita intervened. She was angry. To the manager she said, 'This woman has too many questions:

Will she be hired? Is she going to be insured?' And then to me, 'I told you already, we do piecework here; if you do your job, you get a wage; otherwise you don't. That's clear isn't it? What else do you want? You should be grateful! This plant is giving you a chance to work! What else do you want? Come back tomorrow and be punctual.'

I finally got a job at a new *maquiladora* that was adding an evening shift. I saw its advertisement in the daily newspapers and went early the following morning to apply at the factory, which is located in the modern Parque Industrial Bermudez. Thirty-seven women preceded me. Some had arrived as early as 6 a.m. At 10, the door that separated the front lawn from the entrance had not yet been opened, although a guard appeared once in a while to peek at the growing contingent of applicants. At 10:30 he opened the door to tell us that only those having personal recommendation letters would be permitted inside. This was the first in a series of formal and informal screening procedures used to reduce the number of potential workers. Thirteen women left immediately. Others tried to convince the guard that, although they had no personal recommendation, they knew someone already employed at the factory.

One by one we were shown into the office of the personnel manager, where we were to take a manual dexterity test. Later on, we were given the familiar application form. Demonstrating sewing skills on an industrial machine followed. At 3:30 p.m., seven hours after we arrived at the plant, we were dismissed with no indication that any of us would be hired. A telegram would be sent to each address as soon as a decision was made. Most women left disappointed and certain that they would not be hired. Two weeks later, when I had almost given up all hope, the telegram arrived. I was to come to the plant as soon as possible to receive further instructions.

Upon my arrival I was given the address of a small clinic downtown. I was to bring two pictures to the clinic and take a medical examination. Its explicit purpose was to evaluate the physical fitness of potential workers. In reality, it was a pregnancy test. *Maquiladoras* do not hire pregnant women in spite of their greater need for employment. During the first years of its existence, many pregnant women sought employment in the *maquiladora* programme knowing they would be entitled to an eighty-two day pregnancy leave with full pay. Some women circumvented the restrictions on employing pregnant women by bringing urine specimens of friends or relatives to the clinic. Plant managers now insist on more careful examinations, but undetected pregnant women sometimes get hired. The larger and more stable plants generally comply with the law and give maternity leave, but in small subcontracted firms women are often fired as soon as the manager discovers they are pregnant.

After my exam at the clinic, I returned to the factory with a sealed envelope containing certification of my physical capacity to work. I was told to return the following Monday at 3:30 p.m. to start work. After what seemed like an unduly long and complicated procedure, I was finally hired as an assembly worker. For the next six weeks I shared the experience of approximately eighty women who had also been recruited to work the evening shift.

WORKING AT THE *MAQUILADORA*

The weekday evening shift began at 3:45 and ended at 11:30 p.m. A bell rang at 7:30 to signal the beginning of a half-hour dinner break. Some women brought sandwiches from home, but most bought a dish of *flautas* or *tostadas* and a carbonated drink at the factory. On Saturdays the shift started at 11:30 a.m. and ended at 9:30 p.m., with a half-hour break. We worked, in total, forty-eight hours every week for the minimum wage, an hourly rate of about US$0.60.

Although wages are low in comparison to those of the US for similar jobs, migrants flock to zone 09, which includes Ciudad Juarez, because it has nearly the highest minimum wage in the country (only zone 01, where Baja California is located, has a higher rate). Legally, *maquiladoras* are also required to enrol their workers in the social-security system and in the national housing programme (Instituto Nacional a la Vivienda). As a result, investment per work hour reached US$1.22 in 1978. For women who have children, the medical insurance is often as important as the wage.

Newcomers receive the minimum wage but are expected to fulfil production quotas. My new job was to sew a narrow bias around the cuff openings of men's shirts. My quota of 162 pairs of sleeves every hour meant one every 2.7 seconds. After six weeks as a direct production operator, I still fell short of this goal by almost 50 per cent.

Sandra, who sat next to me during this period, assured me that it could be done. She had worked at various *maquiladoras* for the last seven years. Every time she got too tired, she left the job, rested for a while, then sought another. She was a speedy seamstress who acted with the self-assurance of one who is well-acquainted with factory work. It was difficult not to admire her skill and aloofness, especially when I was being continuously vexed by my own incompetence.

One evening Sandra told me she thought my complaints and manner of speech were funny and, at the end of what turned out to be a lively conversation, admitted to liking me. I was flattered. Then she stared at my old jeans and ripped blouse with an appraising look and said, 'Listen Patricia, as soon as we get our wage, I want to take you to buy some decent clothes. You look awful! And you need a haircut.' So much for the arrogance of the researcher who wondered whether her class background would be detected. Sandra became my most important link with the experience of *maquiladora* work.

Sandra lived with her parents in *las lomas* on the outskirts of the city. The area was rugged and distant, but the house itself indicated modest prosperity. There were four ample rooms, one of which was carpeted. The living room walls were covered with family photographs. There were an American television and comfortable chairs. There were two sinks in the kitchen as well as a refrigerator, blender, beater and new American-made washing machine (waiting until the area got its hoped-for running water). Sandra's father was a butcher who had held his job at a popular market for many years. Although in the past, when his three daughters were small, it had been difficult to stay out of debt, better times were at hand. He had only two regrets: his failing health and Sandra's divorce. He felt both matters were beyond his control. He considered Sandra a good daughter because she never failed to contribute to household expenses and because she was also saving so she could support her two children, who were currently living with her former husband. Sandra had left him after he beat her for taking a job outside the home.

Even with Sandra's help, I found the demands of the factory overwhelming. Young supervisors walked about the aisles calling for higher productivity and greater speed. Periodically, their voices could be heard throughout the workplace: 'Faster! Faster! Come on girls, let's hear the sound of those machines!'

My supervisor, Esther, quit her job as a nurse for the higher wages as a factory worker because she had to support an ill and aging father after her mother's death three years earlier. Although her home was nice and fully owned, she was solely responsible for the remaining family debts. She earned almost one thousand pesos a week in the factory, roughly twice her income as a nurse.

The supervisor's role is a difficult one. Esther, like the other supervisors, often stayed at the plant after the workers left, sometimes until one in the morning. She would verify quotas and inspect all garments for defects, some of which she restitched. She would also prepare shipments and select materials for the following day's production. Management held supervisors directly responsible for productivity levels as well as for workers' punctuality and attendance, putting the supervisors between the devil and the deep blue sea. Workers frequently believed that supervisors were the ones responsible for their plight at the workplace and regarded abuse, unfair treatment and excessive demands from them as whims. But while workers saw supervisors as close allies of the firm, management directed its dissatisfaction with workers at the supervisors. Many line supervisors agreed that the complications they faced on their jobs were hardly worth the extra pay.

Although my supervisor, Esther, was considerate and encouraging, she still asked me to repair my defective work. I began to skip dinner breaks to continue sewing in a feeble attempt to improve my productivity level. I was not alone. Some workers, fearful of permanent dismissal, also stayed at their sewing machines while the rest went outside to eat and relax.

I could understand their behaviour; their jobs were at stake. But presumably my situation was different. I had nothing to lose by inefficiency, and yet I felt compelled to do my best. I started pondering upon the subtle mechanisms that dominate will at the workplace, and about the shame that overwhelms those who fall short of the goals assigned to them. As the days passed, it became increasingly difficult for me to think of factory work as a stage in a research project. My identity became that of a worker; my immediate objectives, those determined by the organization of labour at the plant. I became one link in a rigidly structured chain. My failure to produce speedily had consequences for others operating in the same line. For example, Lucha, my nineteen-year-old companion, cut remnant thread and separated the sleeves that five other seamstresses and I sewed. Since she could only meet her quota if we met ours, Lucha was extremely interested in seeing improvements in my level of productivity and in the quality of my work. Sometimes her attitude and exhortations verged on the hostile. As far as I was concerned, the accusatory expression on her face was the best work incentive yet devised by the factory. I was not surprised to find out during the weeks I spent there that the germ of enmity had bloomed between some seamstresses and their respective thread cutters over matters of work.

Although [this] relationship was especially delicate, all workers were affected by each other's level of efficiency. Cuffless sleeves could not be attached to shirts, nor could sleeves be sewed to shirts without collars or pockets. Holes and buttons had to be fixed at the end. Unfinished garments could not be cleaned of lint or labelled. In sum, each minute step required a series of preceding operations completed effectively. Delay of one stage inevitably slowed up the whole process.

From the perspective of the workers, the work appeared as interconnected individual activities rather than as an imposed structure. Managers were nearly invisible, but the flaws of fellow workers were always present. Bonuses became personal rewards made inaccessible by a neighbour's laziness or incompetence. One consequence of these perceptions was that workers frequently directed complaints against other workers and supervisors. In short, the organization of labour at any particular plant does not automatically lead to feelings of solidarity.

On the other hand, the tensions did not inhibit talk, and the women's shared experiences, especially about longings for relief from the tedious-ness of industrial work, gave rise to an ongoing humorous dialogue. Sandra often reflected in a witty and self-deprecatory manner on the possibility of marriage to a rich man. She thought that if she could only find a nice man who would be willing to support her, everything in her life would be all right. She did not mind if he was not young or good looking, as long as he had plenty of money. Were there men like that left in the world? Of course, with the children it was difficult, not to say impossible, to find such a godsend. Then again, no one kept you from trying. But not at the *maquiladora*. Everyone was female. One could die of boredom there.

Sandra knew many women who had been seduced and then deserted by engineers and technicians. Other women felt they had to comply with the sexual demands of fellow workers because they believed otherwise they would lose their jobs. Some were just plain stupid. Things were especially difficult for very young women at large electronics plants. They needed guidance and information to stay out of trouble, but there was no one to advise them. During the first years of the *maquiladora* programme, sexual harassment was especially blatant. There were *inge-nieros* who insisted on having only the prettiest workers under their command. They developed a sort of factory 'harem'. Sandra knew of a man—'Would you believe this?'—who wanted as much female diversity as possible. All of the women on his crew, at his request, had eyes and hair of a different colour. Another man boasted that every woman on his line had borne him a child. She told me about the scandals, widely covered by the city tabloids, about the spread of venereal disease in certain *maquiladoras*. Although Sandra felt she knew how to take care of herself, she still thought it better to have only female fellow workers. The factory was not a good place to meet men.

Fortunately, there were the bars and the discotheques. Did I like to go out dancing? She did not think I looked like the type who would. But it was great fun. Eventually Sandra and I went to a popular disco, the Cosmos, which even attracted people from 'the other side' (the US), who came to Juarez just to visit this disco. It had an outer-space decor, full of colour and movement, and played the best American disco music. If you were lucky, you could meet a US citizen. Maybe he would even want to get married, and you could go and live in El Paso. Things like that happen at discotheques. Once a Jordanian solider in service at Fort Bliss had asked Sandra to marry him the first time they met at Cosmos. But he wanted to return to his country, and she had said no. Cosmos was defi-nitely the best discotheque in Juarez, and Sandra could be found dancing there amidst the deafening sound of music every Saturday evening.

The inexhaustible level of energy of women working at the *maquiladoras* never ceased to impress me. How could anyone be in the mood for all-night dancing on Saturdays after forty-eight weekly hours of industrial work? I had seen many of these women stretching their muscles late at night trying to soothe the pain they felt at the waist. After the incessant noise of the sewing machines, how could anyone long for even higher levels of sound? But as Sandra explained to me, life is too short. If you don't go out and have fun, you will come to the end of your days having done nothing but sleep, eat and work. And she didn't call that living. Besides, where else would you be able to meet a man?

Ah men! They were often unreliable, mean or just plain lazy ('wasn't that obvious from the enormous number of women who had to do factory work in Ciudad Juarez?'), but no one wanted to live alone. There must be someone out there worth living for—at least someone who did not try to put you down or slap you. Sandra could not understand why life had become so difficult. Her mother and father had stayed married for thirty years and they still liked each other. There had been some difficult times in the past, but they had always had each other. She knew a lot of older folks who were in the same situation. But it was different for modern couples.

At 11:15, Sandra's talks about men stopped, and we prepared to go home. We cleaned up our work area and made sure we took the two spools and a pair of scissors we were responsible for home with us to prevent their being stolen by workers the following morning. As soon as the bell rang at 11:30, we began a disorderly race to be the first to check out our time cards. Then we had to stand in line with our purses wide open so the guard could check our belongings. Women vehemently resented management's suspicion that workers would steal material or the finished products. The nightly search was an unnecessary humiliation of being treated as thieves until proven innocent by the guard.

Once outside the factory, we walked in a group across the park to catch our bus. There was a lot of laughing and screaming, as well as teasing and exchanging of vulgarities. Most of the time we could board an almost-empty bus as soon as we reached the main avenue. Sometimes, when we had to wait, we became impatient. In jest, a woman would push another worker toward the street, suggesting provocative poses for her to use to attract a passerby to offer a ride. When a car did stop, however, they quickly moved away. To joke was one thing, but to accept a ride from a man, especially late at night, was to look for trouble.

Individually, the factory women appeared vulnerable, even shy, but as a group, they could be a formidable sight. One night a man boarded the bus when we were already in it. His presence gave focus to the high spirits. Women immediately subjected him to verbal attacks similar to those they often received from men. Feeling protected by anonymity and by their numerical strength, they chided and teased him; they offered kisses and asked for a smile. They exchanged laughing comments about his physical attributes and suggested a raffle to see who would keep him. The man remained silent through it all. He adopted the outraged and embarrassed expression that women often wear when they feel victimized by men. The stares of whistling women followed him as he left the bus.

Although I saw only one such incident, I was told that it was not uncommon. 'It is pitiful', a male acquaintance told me; 'those girls have no idea of what proper feminine behavior is'. He told me he had seen women even paw or pinch men while travelling in buses and *ruteras*. According to him, factory work was to blame: 'Since women started working at the *maquiladoras* they have lost all sense of decorum'. The women see it as a harmless game fostered by the temporary sense of membership in a group. As Sandra liked to remind me, 'Factory work is harder than most people know. As long as you don't harm anybody, what's wrong with having a little fun?'

CONCLUSIONS

Textile and garment manufacturing are, of course, as old as factories themselves, but *maquiladoras* epitomize the most distinctive traits of the modern system of production. They are part of a centralized global arrangement in which central economies such as [that of] the US have become the locus of technological expertise and major financial outflows, while Third World countries increase their participation in the international market via the manufacture of exportable goods.

This global system of production has had unprecedented political and economic consequences. For example, the fragmentation of labour processes has reduced the level of skill required to perform the majority of assembly operations required to manufacture even the most complex and sophisticated electronics products. In turn, the geographical dispersion of production has curtailed the bargaining ability of workers of many nationalities *vis-à-vis* large corporations. At times, workers in Asia, Latin America and the Caribbean seem to be thrust into competition against one another for access to low-paying, monotonous jobs. Labour unions and strikes have limited potential in a world where factories can be transferred at ease to still another country where incentives are more favourable and wages cheaper.

It is evident from the testimony of workers that women seek *maquiladora* jobs compelled by their need to support families whether they be formed by parents and siblings or by their own children. Male unemployment and underemployment play an important part in this. Multinationals tend to relocate assembly operations to areas of the world where jobless people automatically provide an abundant supply of cheap labour. Sandra's longing for male economic support and regrets over the irresponsibility of men represent a personal counterpoint to a structural reality where men are unable to find remunerative jobs while women are forced, out of need, to join the ranks of the industrial labour force.

The same testimony demonstrates that *maquila* women would prefer to withdraw from the exhausting jobs available to them and give full attention to home and children. Husbands and fathers frequently press women to leave their jobs to adjust to a conventional understanding of what gender roles should be. Nevertheless, when women retire from wage labour to become housewives and mothers, they often face dire alternatives. Later, they may have to seek new forms of employment because of the inability of their men to provide adequately for their families. Older and with children to provide for, they then face special constraints in a labour market that favours very young, single, childless women. The life profile of *maquiladora* women is a saga of downward mobility, a fate contrary to the optimistic expectations of industrial promoters.

The segregation of the labour market on the basis of sex tends to weaken the bargaining position of both men and women as wage earners. But perhaps more important is the observation that the same segregation produces a clash between ideological notions about the role of women and their actual transformation into primary wage earners. This has given rise to tensions perceived both at the household and community levels. *Maquiladora* workers have become notorious in that they challenge conventional mores and values regarding femininity. Concerns about young women's morality, virtue and sexual purity are, in part, reflections of widespread anxiety and fear that, as a result of wage earning, women may end up subverting the established order. *Maquiladora* workers may see their riotous behaviour toward a man in a bus as an innocuous diversion. Others, however, see it as a clear sign that women are losing respect for patriarchy.

Maquiladoras are hardly a mechanism for upward mobility, hardly the bold entrance to middle-class respectability, hardly the key to individual economic autonomy. All these are issues that should be of concern to government officials and social planners. Yet, while *maquiladoras* have taken advantage of women's vulnerability in the job market, they have also provided a forum where new forms of consciousness and new challenges are present. For young *maquila* workers who are living with parents and siblings and have few or no children of their own, wage labour offers the cherished possibility of retaining at least part of their income for discretionary purposes.

19. CAPITALISM, IMPERIALISM AND PATRIARCHY: THE DILEMMA OF THIRD-WORLD WOMEN WORKERS IN MULTINATIONAL FACTORIES

LINDA Y. C. LIM

[There is] a central theoretical and political question that as yet remains unanswered: is the employment of women factory workers by multinational corporations in developing countries primarily an experience of liberation, as development economists and governments maintain, or one of exploitation, as feminists assert, for the women concerned?

CAPITALISM AND THE RELOCATION OF MANUFACTURING INDUSTRY TO DEVELOPING COUNTRIES

The relocation of manufacturing industry from developed to developing countries by multinational corporations engaged in 'offshore sourcing' is part of a new international division of labour and pattern of trade in manufactures.[1] This is the direct result of two developments in the world capitalist economy which began in the 1960s. First, growth in international trade intensified inter-capitalist competition among the developed nations. In particular, the ascendancy of Japan as a major industrial power and its rapid and highly successful penetration of western consumer markets led American and European manufacturers to invest in developing countries as a means of reducing costs in competition with the Japanese (Reynis, 1976). In the 1970s, the slowing down of growth in western and world markets further intensified these competitive pressures.

Second, the accelerating development of capitalist relations of production in a number of developing countries resulted in some of their indigenous entrepreneurs manufacturing for export to western markets, beginning in the 1960s. This placed them in direct competition with western manufacturers, who were forced to relocate to these same countries in order to be cost competitive in their own home markets. This trend continued through the 1970s on an ever larger and wider scale, particularly in Asian countries like Hong Kong, Taiwan, South Korea and Singapore, whose larger local firms have themselves become multinationals operating offshore manufacturing plants in other developing countries.

The crucial factor in the competition was and is the cost of production, which differs between mature and developing capitalist economies according to their stage of development. In the 1960s and early 1970s, the mature western economies experienced tight domestic labour markets—low unemployment rates, high wages and chronic labour shortages in many industries. Labour-intensive manufacturing industries—those which employ large numbers of workers in generally unskilled or low-skilled jobs—were the most affected, and these countries began to lose their international comparative advantage in industries such as garments, shoes, plastic toys and electronics assembly. The developing countries, on the other hand, had relatively abundant supplies of labour, reflected in the rural–urban migration of surplus labour off the farms; high urban-unemployment rates; and low wages. Cheap labour, combined in many cases with government-subsidized capital costs, including tax holidays and low-interest loans from government banks (Lim, 1978a), gave these countries a comparative advantage in world trade in labour-intensive products.

It is labour-intensive industries, then, that tend to relocate manufacturing plants to developing countries, becoming multinational in their operations. This is a rational competitive response to changing international comparative cost advantages. In a free world market, factors of production like capital and labour will tend to move to locations where they are most scarce and can command the highest returns from the employment in production. Through the nineteenth and early twentieth centuries, this was reflected in fairly free international migration of labour, but subsequent restrictive national immigration policies together with transportation costs and imperfect market information have increasingly inhibited the mobility of labour across international boundaries, except for the legal and/or illegal immigration of 'guest workers'. Capital, however, remains internationally mobile, especially from the developed to developing countries, a flow encouraged by policies of the latter's governments that offer profit tax holidays, duty-free imports and exports, unrestricted remittance of profits and repatriation of capital.

IMPERIALISM, NATIONALISM AND THE MULTINATIONAL CORPORATION

Imperialism—the system of military, political, economic and cultural domination of the Third World by its former colonial masters—was historically the outgrowth of capitalist development in the West. In the economic sphere, it is characterized by the exploitation of natural and human resources in the Third World by western capitalist enterprises. Although bourgeois economists were in agreement with classical

Marxists—including Lenin, Luxemburg and Marx—that imperialism, or western investment in developing countries, would be an agent of capitalist development in the Third World, modern-day theorists of imperialism—including dependency theorists and 'world-system' analysts following André Gunder Frank and Immanuel Wallerstein— argue that it retards such development.

Most of the latter analysis has been applied to the sectors of primary production for export and import-substituting industrialization in developing countries. But manufacturing for export by multinational subsidiaries also has its critics.[2] It is pointed out that workers' wages are much lower and their working conditions worse than in the multinationals' home countries; that few transferable skills or industrial linkages are generated; that there is heavy dependence on foreign capital, technology, skills, inputs and markets; that few taxes are paid in the host country; and high profits that accrue only to foreigners are mostly remitted overseas.

Although the above are true in most situations, it should be noted that manufacturing for export in developing countries is not the sole preserve of multinationals. Many local firms are also involved, and in some countries—such as Hong Kong, Taiwan and South Korea—and industries, such as garments, they may outnumber the multinationals. In general, Third World enterprises engaged in manufacturing for export to western markets are smaller, less capital intensive and more labour intensive than multinational subsidiaries and are concentrated in simple-technology industries with competitive markets and relatively low profit margins. Wages are usually lower and working conditions worse, sometimes much worse, than in the multinational sector. Skills are low, and there is dependence not only on foreign markets, to which access is less easy than for the multinationals, but also on foreign technology and inputs purchased on the world market. Tax payments and reinvestment rates may be higher than for multinational subsidiaries; but since earnings are less, absolute contributions may be lower.

Comparisons between multinational subsidiaries and local firms in export manufacturing in developing countries suggest that the former may contribute more to the host economy in terms of market access, output growth, total wage-bill, and skill and technology acquisition. Local firms may, however, contribute more to the national development of capitalist relations of production in the long run, in developing a class of indigenous entrepreneurs in the manufacturing sector. They may reinvest more, since they do not remit profits overseas and are less likely to transfer operations. But competition with multinational subsidiaries in factor, input and output markets may inhibit the development of independent indigenous enterprises and entrepreneurs (Lim, 1978b; Pang and Lim, 1977). A complementary relationship is possible, but it tends to maintain local firms in the dependent position of subcontractors and suppliers to foreign firms and markets.

Despite the validity of many of the criticisms against it, manufacturing for export does enhance the development of capitalist relations of production in developing countries, mainly by spurring the growth of industrial wage labour and an indigenous industrial capitalist class. Multinationals and local firms make somewhat different contributions to this process. Two more questions remain: What are the long-run prospects for a multinational-led, export-manufacturing sector in a developing country? Is this likely to lead to the development of an independent national capitalism in the developing country?

One of the criticisms commonly levelled at manufacturing for export by multinational corporations is that it is likely to be only a temporary phenomenon in developing host countries. Multinationals that relocate manufacturing capacity in these countries are 'footloose' because they are not bound to any particular location by a need for local markets or local input sources other than labour, which is abundantly available everywhere. Therefore, it is argued, they will tend to move away from a location if labour-market conditions or government policies change to make it less competitive. Although this has happened in individual firm cases, it has not yet threatened the viability of an entire export-manufacturing sector in any country.

On the contrary, in the less developed countries where most of the export-oriented multinational subsidiaries are concentrated—Hong Kong, Taiwan and Singapore—changing comparative costs, particularly the appearance of tight labour markets, have resulted in an upgrading of the industries producing for export. Multinationals, encouraged by host government policies, have begun relocating more capital-intensive, technology-intensive industrial products and processes from their home countries to these locations. Labour-intensive processes are replaced or shifted to more labour-abundant locations as comparative advantages continue to change between developed and developing countries and among developing countries themselves.

This suggests that, at least in some developing countries, the multinational-led export-manufacturing sector does mature over time, further developing capitalist relations of production. Wages rise, working conditions improve, more skills are imparted, more local linkages generated, more taxes paid and more profits reinvested locally. Although the countries where this is happening are still a minority in the Third World, they are the ones that have had the longest experience with multinational subsidiaries in manufacturing for export.

But what about local firms and the development of an independent national capitalism? As the multinational subsidiaries continue to grow and to upgrade and diversify their products, they generate more local linkages, make more input purchases from local suppliers and subcontract some of their simpler products and processes to local manufacturers. This may stimulate the growth of indigenous enterprises, though these remain in a dependent position *vis-à-vis* the multinationals. From the point of view of enhancing capitalist development, dependence may not be a problem if it results in accelerated growth and the emergence of an indigenous industrial capitalist class. A nationalist industrial policy that excludes multinationals may result in more independence but less growth and thus a smaller indigenous capitalist class since the advantages multinationals possess in stimulating supply sources and in providing technical and managerial training would be lost.

Although dependency theorists and others who argue that multinationals retard the development of capitalism in developing countries are right with respect to their criticisms of the early stages of labour-intensive manufacturing for export, the experience of some important developing countries suggests that bourgeois economists and classical Marxists alike might be right in the longer run, that multinationals do foster the development of capitalist relations of production and are often more successful in this than indigenous firms. The relocation of industry between countries continues if firms behave rationally in response to changing comparative advantages. Although multinationals may shift labour-intensive industries out of some developing countries as comparative costs change, so do national firms in these countries (as in the case of Singapore firms that shifted to cheaper-labour countries like Malaysia, Indonesia, Sri Lanka and Bangladesh); so long as new industries and processes are moved in, capitalist relations of production continue to develop and mature.

PATRIARCHY AND THE FEMALE LABOUR MARKET

Patriarchy is the system of male domination and female subordination in economy, society and culture that has characterized much of human history to the present day. In the economic sphere, it is reflected first in the sexual division of labour within the family, which makes domestic labour the sole preserve of women. Their involvement in production activities outside the home varies with different societies and different stages of development, but is, particularly in those countries where capitalist development has penetrated (Boserup, 1970), often accorded inferior status and reward compared to the activities of men.

In the pure capitalist model of 'bourgeois' economists, conditions of perfect competition prevail in the labour market, where workers are hired solely on the basis of their marginal productivity.[3] Competition and the progress of capitalist relations of production should eventually eliminate any differences between the sexes in the labour market.

This model is clearly invalid in the real-world capitalist labour market. Not only is participation in the wage-labour force lower for women than for men, but women are concentrated in a narrow range of occupations characterized by low wages, low productivity, low skill levels, high turnover, insecurity of tenure and limited upward mobility. Productivity differences between male and female workers are one explanation for this phenomenon, but they themselves reflect differential access to the determinants of productivity, such as education and skill training and different levels of technology in the jobs to which they are assigned. In addition, there is an element of pure discrimination by employers, discrimination unrelated to any productivity differences between male and female workers.

Patriarchal institutions and social relations are responsible for the inferior or secondary status of women in the capitalist wage-labour market. The primacy of the sexual division of labour within the family has several consequences for the woman who seeks wage employment. Socialized to accept this sex role in life, she has little motivation to acquire marketable skills; is often prevented by discrimination from acquiring such skills; and even after she has acquired them may be prevented by discrimination from achieving the employment or remuneration that those skills would command for a man.

Discrimination itself is based on the patriarchal assumption that woman's natural role is a domestic one and that she is therefore unsuited to many kinds of wage employment, either because her productivity will 'naturally' be lower than a man's in the same employment or because it will be affected adversely by her domestic responsibilities.

It is this comparative disadvantage of women in the wage-labour market that gives them a comparative advantage *vis-à-vis* men in the occupations and industries where they are concentrated. In the manufacturing sector of mature capitalist economies, women are concentrated in labour-intensive industries where the wages earned are often insufficient to support a family. It is assumed by employers and in general that women work only for 'pocket money' for luxuries or to make a secondary-income contribution to families where the principal breadwinner is a male.

Both the demand for and supply of female labour are determined by the culture of patriarchy, which assumes woman's role in the family as natural and consigns her to a secondary and inferior position in the wage-labour market. Even where women are acknowledged to be more productive than men, they are often paid less, and prevailing wages are always lower in female-intensive than male-intensive industries and occupations, even at equivalent skill levels. This is contrary to the prediction of neoclassical economic theory that higher productivity means higher, not lower, wages.

The industries in which women manufacturing workers are concentrated in mature capitalistic economies are the very industries that are losing their comparative cost advantage to newly industrializing countries. It is likely that these labour-intensive industries maintained their comparative advantage as long as they did because they employed the lowest-paid workers in those countries—women, often women of minority races. Thus it is female-intensive industries that have the greatest propensity to 'run away' from the developed countries and relocate manufacturing facilities in the Third World, where wages are even lower than those of women in the developed countries. In the developing countries as well, traditional patriarchal social relations ensure that women occupy a similarly secondary and inferior position in the wage-labour market and so are the preferred employees of multinational and local employers in labour-intensive export industries.

Although the relocation of manufacturing industry from mature to developing capitalist countries reflects changes in world capitalism, the employment of women in these industries reflects the influence of patriarchy on the female labour market in both mature and developing countries. Women's comparative disadvantage in the capitalist wage-labour market enhances the comparative advantage of firms that employ them in labour-intensive industries producing for the world market. This disadvantage—reflected in low wages—is greatest for women in countries where capitalist relations of production are least developed, since there they have the fewest opportunities for wage employment and the weakest bargaining power in the labour market. Patriarchal social relations are also strongest and most restrictive of female wage-employment where precapitalist modes of production, e.g. feudalism, persist. Thus, female employment in export manufacturing industries is most prevalent in those developing countries where capitalist relations of production are developing most rapidly, but traditional patriarchy is sufficiently strong to maintain women in an inferior labour-market position.

IMPERIALISM, PATRIARCHY AND EXPLOITATION

All workers employed in capitalist enterprises are exploited to produce profits for their employers, but the degree of exploitation differs among different groups of workers. In addition to being paid less than the value of the output they contribute, Third World women workers in multinational export factories are paid less than women workers in the multinationals' home countries and less than men workers in these countries and in their own countries as well, despite the fact that in relocated labour-intensive industries their productivity is frequently acknowledged to be higher than that of either of these other groups. Thus, Third World women workers are the most heavily exploited group of workers, relative both to their output contribution and to other groups. Although all are subject to capitalist exploitation, Third World women workers are subject additionally to imperialist and to patriarchal exploitation.

Imperialist exploitation—the differential in wages paid to workers in developed and developing countries for the same work and output—arises from the ability of multinationals to take advantage of different labour-market conditions in different parts of the world—a perfectly rational practice in the context of world capitalism. Patriarchal exploitation—the differential in wages paid to male and female workers for similar work and output—derives from women's inferior position in the labour market.

Although multinational employers in developing countries practice all the above forms of exploitation, they do so only in response to labour-market forces, specifically the international and sexual segmentation of labour markets. Differences in the degree of development of capitalist relations of production and natural restrictions on the international mobility of labour are responsible for differential wage rates between countries, whereas patriarchal institutions and attitudes limiting the employment opportunities open to women are responsible for differential wage rates between the sexes. Multinationals may consciously attempt to preserve these differentials from which they benefit, but in general they merely take advantage of [their existence].

It may be argued that the activities of multinationals in labour-intensive export manufacturing in developing countries might in the long run contribute to a reduction of national and sex wage differentials—in other words, a reduction of the imperialist and patriarchal components of capitalist exploitation of Third World women workers. To the extent that these [firms] contribute to the development of capitalist relations of production, particularly to the growth of demand for wage labour and to the upgrading of skills, wages will rise in the developing countries. If at the same time the relocation of industry from the developed countries reduces demand for labour in those countries, wage increases there will decline. Both factors will reduce over time the wage differential between the developed and developing countries—that is, the degree of imperialist exploitation.

Because multinationals engaged in export manufacturing in the developing countries employ mostly women workers, they increase the demand for female over male labour. Female wages will rise relative to male wages, and female unemployment rates will fall. Sex wage differentials will narrow. In some countries governments have already expressed concern about the lack of employment creation for men—whom they consider to be the principal breadwinners—in multinational export firms.

So far the narrowing of national and sex wage differentials has been imperceptible in most cases. In most developing host countries, multinationals manufacturing for export constitute too small a sector of the economy to have a significant impact on the national labour market. Even where, as in a handful of Asian countries, they are an important sector of the economy and have contributed to rising wages, wages have increased just as rapidly in the developed countries with generalized inflation. Furthermore, the relocation of industry has not reduced the overall demand for labour in the developed countries, where capitalist development continues in different sectors. With respect to sex wage differentials, although female wages have risen, high turnover of labour and the short average working life of women factory workers keeps their average wages low. The countries in which female wages have risen most rapidly are also those where male employment creation has been proceeding apace, and male wages have often increased even more rapidly in other sectors of the economy.

Continued imperialist and patriarchal exploitation in multinational factories in developing countries does not, however, imply that the women employed in these factories are worse off than they would have been without such employment. On the contrary, the vast majority are clearly better off, at least but not only in a narrow economic sense, for being subject to such exploitation. Wages and working conditions are usually better in multinational factories than in alternative employment for women in indigenous capitalist enterprises. Although in the relative economic sense defined previously they may be more exploited in the multinationals, in an absolute sense their incomes tend to be higher. This is true also when compared with women's traditional economic roles as housewives and unpaid family labour in farms and shops.

CAPITALIST DEVELOPMENT AND LIBERATION FROM PATRIARCHY

In developing as in mature industrial economies, the state of development of capitalist relations of production defines the employment opportunities available to wage labour. Patriarchal social structures and cultures divide these opportunities by sex, typically limiting female wage labour to a narrow range of inferior jobs. In this situation the entry of labour-intensive export manufacturing industries and of multinational corporations in particular into sex-segregated local labour markets has two somewhat contradictory effects. On the one hand, multinational and local employers can take advantage of women's inferior position to employ them at lower wages and poorer working conditions than exist for men in the same country and for women in developed countries. Both local firms and multinationals benefit from the gap between workers' wages in the developing country and final product prices in markets of developed countries.

On the other hand, in however limited a way, the availability of jobs in multinational and local export factories does allow women to leave the confines of the home, delay marriage and childbearing, increase their incomes and consumption levels, improve mobility, expand individual choice and exercise personal independence. Working for a local or foreign factory is for many women at least marginally preferable to the alternatives of staying at home, early marriage and childbearing, farm or construction labour, domestic service, prostitution or unemployment, to which they were previously restricted. Factory work, despite the social, economic and physical costs it often entails, provides women in developing countries with one of the very few channels they have of at least partial liberation from the confines and dictates of traditional patriarchal social relations.

Given their lack of access to better jobs, women usually prefer multinationals as employers over local firms since they offer higher wages and better working conditions and often have more 'progressive' labour practices and social relations (Lim, 1978b). Indeed, the more multinationals there are in any one country and the longer they have been established, the stronger becomes the workers' bargaining position. Exclusive employment of female production workers in labour-intensive export industries creates occasional labour shortages, resulting over time in rising wages, greater job security and improved working conditions for women in indigenous as well as multinational enterprises.[4] Greater competition for female labourers will tend to reduce the degree of exploitation found in women's work.

Whether or not market forces alone will expand women's employment alternatives beyond the traditional 'female ghettoes' of low wage, low skill, dead-end jobs depends on the state and rate of development of capitalist relations of production in the economy as a whole. In an economy that is rapidly growing, diversifying and upgrading itself in all sectors, high demand for labour might eventually propel women into skilled industrial and non-industrial jobs from which they have previously been excluded by custom, education or employment discrimination. This will improve the wages and working conditions of women who remain in factory employment as production workers, given the reduction in the numbers of women available for work.

So far, such a situation is an exceptional one among the many developing countries that host multinational corporations in female-intensive industries. Even where rapid growth occurs, employers may escape the tightening labour market by importing migrant [workers], by automation and by shifting labour-intensive processes to other countries, as they have done in the home countries of the multinationals and are now doing in rapidly developing countries like Singapore. In [Singapore], growth in other industries and sectors has prevented these actions from having a depressing effect on wages, and the government's high-wage policy has forced firms to shed or shift their labour-intensive activities. Also, when women ascend the job hierarchy, it is usually to take jobs vacated by male workers who have since advanced even higher in the hierarchy of skills and incomes. That is to say, although rapid growth may enable women to improve their position in the labour market in absolute terms, relative to men they remain in an inferior position.

Capitalism cannot wipe out patriarchy, though exploitation in capitalist enterprises can provide some women with an at least temporary escape from traditional patriarchal social relations.

EXPLOITATION AND LIBERATION: A DILEMMA FOR POLITICAL ACTION

Many of the studies of female employment in multinational export factories in developing countries focus their criticism on the multinational corporation as chief perpetrator of all the forms of exploitation that these women workers are subject to. Although the multinational does take advantage of national and sexual wage differentials and sometimes reinforces them, it is not responsible for creating them and cannot by its own actions eliminate them. National wage differentials are the result of differences in the development of capitalist relations of production between nations, whereas sex wage differentials originate in indigenous patriarchy.

Removing the multinational will, in the absence of a credible alternative form of development, drastically reduce employment opportunities for women in developing countries. This will weaken their labour-market position and subject them to even greater exploitation by indigenous capitalists and continued subordination to traditional patriarchy. A less radical solution—attempting to reduce imperialist exploitation by imposing reforms on the multinational or local employer—is unlikely to succeed even if host governments were willing. Export manufacturers operate in highly competitive international markets with generally elastic supply and, in important industries like garments and shoes, inelastic demand. Host governments and workers can neither demand nor enforce better wages and working conditions in profit-oriented multinationals that are mobile between countries. Local firms are often less competitive than multinationals in the world market and with their lower profits, are unlikely to be able to absorb the costs of such reforms.

Another possibility for reducing imperialist exploitation is through international action to restrict multinationals from exploiting market wage differentials between nations—for example, by standardizing certain terms and conditions of work in particular industries or occupations. This is clearly unrealistic, given the different stages of development of capitalism. Furthermore, workers in developed and developing countries tend to have opposing interests *vis-à-vis* the relocation of manufacturing industry. National interests inhibit the development of international labour solidarity. For example, protectionist groups of employers and labour unions in the multinationals' home countries have furthered their own self-interest by citing exploitation of women workers overseas as a reason why goods made by these workers should be prevented from reaching their destined markets by means of tariffs, quotas and other restrictive trade practices. This has the effect of pitting workers in mature and developing capitalist countries against each other.

Because patriarchal social relations are at the bottom of women's subjection to imperialist exploitation, it is logical to turn to an attack on traditional patriarchy as a means of improving the position of women. The successful elimination of patriarchal institutions and attitudes, discrimination, differential socialization by sex and the sexual division of labour within the family would equalize male and female employment opportunities and incomes. In developing countries, national identity is bound up with a traditional, often feudal, patriarchal culture. An attack on traditional patriarchy may be construed as an attack on national identity and thus arouse the forces of a reactionary nationalism against the liberation of women. Indeed, one of the dangers of multinational exploitation of Third World women workers is that it arouses local anti-imperialist sentiment that becomes identified—as in fundamentalist Islamic ideology in Iran—with traditionalism and opposition to wage employment by women.

Even if traditional patriarchy is undermined successfully and equality in the capitalist labour market achieved, women workers will remain subject, together with male workers, to capitalist exploitation in a capitalist economy. Capitalist employers themselves are unlikely to be indifferent to the elimination of sex differences in the labour market. Although employers of predominantly female workers may be expected to oppose sex equalization because it would reduce the supply and thus raise the wages of women workers in low-skill, labour-intensive and dead-end jobs, employers in male-intensive industries where labour is scarce may welcome the entry of female labour as a means of increasing the labour supply and reducing wages. The balance between these opposing interests, and the attitude of male workers themselves, depends on the state and rate of development of capitalist relations of production. A nation that is rapidly growing and upgrading into high-skill, high-wage industries and occupations, and experiences rising demand relative to supply of labour is likely to have greater sex equalization in the labour market than one which is growing only slowly or stagnating, with high unemployment and a dependence on low-wage, labour-intensive industries. In other words, rapid capitalist development is more conducive to sex equalization in the labour market but by itself cannot bring about such equalization.

Elimination of worker exploitation altogether can occur only if capitalism itself is eliminated. This presents enormous difficulties for the small developing country in a world dominated by capitalism and imperialism. Domestically, a necessary precondition is the unity of the working class, which is hampered by sex, race, regional and other differences. So long as patriarchal relations of production persist, male and female workers remain divided by occupational segregation and by the tendency for male workers to assume the position of a labour aristocracy. If development is slow and mainly in low-skill industries, male unemployment and low wages will limit this aristocracy to a small segment of the male workforce, rather than creating a male élite that opposes female workers. Thus, the elimination of patriarchy would facilitate the elimination of capitalism itself. The elimination of capitalist exploitation does not, however, necessarily facilitate the elimination of patriarchal exploitation. In some cases, the struggle against a capitalism identified with imperialist exploitation can lend itself to a reinforcement of traditional patriarchy and opposition to women's participation in the labour force.

CONCLUSION

Within the existing structure of economy and society, pro-capitalist and pro-imperialist strategies—for example, encouraging maximum investment by labour-intensive multinational factories—may serve an anti-patriarchal aim by increasing the demand for female labour and raising female wages absolutely and relative to male wages where, as in many developing countries, male wage employment is growing more slowly. Multinationals generally offer a better employment alternative to women than local enterprises in modern and traditional sectors of the economy and also provide a limited escape from the domestic roles imposed by traditional patriarchy. But there are limitations to the success of this strategy in raising women's wages permanently. Because female employment-creation in multinational factories is based on patriarchal exploitation, the elimination of these conditions may well bring about an elimination of the jobs themselves, given the international mobility of multinational capital and the availability of exploitable female labour in other countries. A similar limitation faces attempts to impose reforms on the multinationals through government policy actions or worker organization and labour-union activity on an enterprise, national or international scale.

In the larger national context, a pro-capitalist, pro-imperialist strategy on behalf of women workers can generate a 'backlash' from traditional patriarchy, making a general and genuine liberation more difficult. It also weakens worker solidarity where anti-imperialist and anti-capitalist struggles exist. On the other hand, these struggles are unlikely to succeed so long as the labour force and labour market remain divided by sex; these struggles would be strengthened by the undermining of patriarchal relations of production.

Ultimately, it is the existing structure of the economy and society that has to be changed if the exploitation of women in the labour force is to be eliminated. Capitalist market forces and employment based on imperialist exploitation cannot liberate women from patriarchal exploitation that is the very condition for their entry into wage labour in multinational factories producing for the world market. In the long run, capitalism and imperialism only perpetuate and may even reinforce patriarchal relations of production, which in turn reinforce capitalist and imperialist relations of production. Although the liberation of women workers as women and as workers can only come about through some combined struggle against capitalist, imperialist and patriarchal exploitation, the specific strategies to be undertaken depend on the particular historical, social, economic and political circumstances.

B. Women in the Informal Sector

*This section focuses on domestic service, industrial homework,
subcontracting and marketing work.*

20. WOMEN IN THE INFORMAL-LABOUR SECTOR: THE CASE OF MEXICO CITY

LOURDES ARIZPE

In recent years, the informal-labour sector has increasingly represented a testing point for theories of development. The proliferation of informal jobs in developing countries has been considered alternately a stage in the process of development and a blind alley leading a country back into underdevelopment. But social scientists and policymakers have rarely recognized that the majority of those left out of the formal occupational structure are women. It is, however, very difficult to establish the heuristic boundaries of the informal-labour sector, particularly with respect to women. Are we referring to the intermittent part-time activities of women outside the household both in cities and in rural areas? Men also engage in such activities, for example as street peddlers. Is the unpaid work of the wife and young unmarried daughters in a family enterprise such as a store, an informal job? If unpaid labour is to be included in the informal-labour sector, then women's voluntary community service and their unpaid domestic labour must also be taken into account. Moreover, since informal labour also comprises work not regulated through a contract, all low-income, non-contractual jobs registered as formal occupations, such as paid domestic service, belong to this classification. Many low-income and low-productivity jobs included in the formal occupational structure and registered in national censuses, even when such a contract does exist, can be considered as a continuation of informal jobs as well; [they] must be analysed within the informal labour sector.

THE NATURE OF THE INFORMAL-LABOUR SECTOR

An individualistic theoretical viewpoint would assume that the types of jobs taken, the sex distribution and the size of the informal-labour sector are a result of random individual decisions. Research based on such a viewpoint would centre on the way in which women weigh their options and decide on a course of action, but could not explain why those options alone were available. The usefulness of this individualistic approach is therefore limited. It can help show why certain women choose particular kinds of jobs at certain times, but not why women as a group tend to enter informal rather than formal employment. The answer can be found only in understanding how capitalistic development affects women's economic roles.

According to developmental theory, labour shifts from agriculture to the modern sector and is absorbed by manufacturing industries, following the pattern of industrial growth in developed countries.[1] In most Latin American countries, as well as those in Africa and Asia, however, data show that the displaced labour from agriculture enters the informal-labour sector, most often in the cities which provide a large market for such jobs, and remains there.[2] Whereas these informal activities constituted a secondary source of income for the peasant household, they become a primary source as agriculture is increasingly dominated by wage labour, and people become wholly dependent upon them economically. At best, workers go into the service sector rather than into manufacturing. Even in countries with moderate industrial growth, such as Brazil and Mexico, the jobs created by industrialization have been unable to compensate for the loss of employment in agriculture.[3] Rapid demographic growth has made this situation even more acute.

An alternative theoretical explanation to the expansion of the informal-labour market in Latin America is provided by the concept of marginality. Whereas the industrial reserve army in central capitalist economies provides an accommodating supply of labour, in underdeveloped countries labour absorption in industrial employment has not expanded in proportion to the increase of available labour, so that large numbers of workers have no possibility of finding formal employment. This marginal population, waiting to enter the formal occupational sector, survives by low-income, intermittent wage- or self-employment. In other words, workers are pushed into the informal-labour sector and into the services as a result of insufficient demand in the manufacturing sector. They are destined never to leave them.

Recent studies cast doubts on some aspects of this theory. There has been a slow but steady absorption of workers, even unskilled ones such as rural migrants, into the formal sector in Brazil, Argentina and Mexico, which have a moderate industrial growth rate.[4] Moreover, it has been argued by E. Hobsbawm that marginality has always existed in capitalist economies and that the difference between the industrial reserve army and the marginal population is not qualitative but quantitative. It has been suggested that 'marginals' do fulfil specific functions within the economy. In Brazil, for example, full-employment policies have not prevented street vendors from pursuing their activities.[5] In Mexico City, certain manufacturers, who could not place their products in supermarkets because of monopolistic trade practices, used street vendors successfully to increase sales. Finally, participation in the informal-labour sector does not automatically result from lack of jobs in the other sectors. Some informal activities are traditional in an urban society and usually fulfil specific functions. Indeed, participation in some traditional urban informal jobs seems to be unaffected by fluctuations in labour demand. Although increase in surplus labour adds a greater number of workers to those traditional informal activities, it also creates new ones.

WOMEN IN DEVELOPMENT: THEIR PARTICIPATION IN THE INFORMAL-LABOUR MARKET

Statistically, the distribution of women in the labour force tends to reflect the level of development of a country.[6] However, the overall rate of participation can vary simply because of differences in statistical definitions. As Boserup has observed, 'Official statistics in a developing country may show female activity rates increasing or decreasing over time without any real difference in the work performed by women being involved'.[7] Some countries take women's labour in agriculture into account, while others do not. Usually neither part-time work outside the home nor work for a family enterprise is included in national censuses. The Mexican census, for example, records only women's primary activity; since this is assumed to be domestic work, the frequent, and in many cases constant, involvement of women in the informal-labour sector does not appear in official statistics. Since women's domestic work is not classified as an economic activity, 79.9 per cent of women in Mexico appear to be 'economically inactive.'

By and large, women's productive activities decline when they are no longer involved in the agricultural tasks and the cottage industries of a peasant economy. This is particularly evident where rural–urban migration is involved.[8] By the same token, the introduction of new technology, both in the agricultural sector and in industries, displace women and restricts their access to new jobs.[9] During the first stage of industrialization, the types of industries that are established, mainly textiles and leather, are labour intensive and provide additional employment for women. When mechanization advances, employment goes predominantly to men. For example, whereas women in 1900 comprised 45.3 per cent of the Brazilian labour force, by 1970, notwithstanding industrial expansion, they represented [only] 21 per cent.[10] Industrial growth, in fact, intensifies sectorial sex inequality in both developed and developing economies. Cultural factors must then be taken into account to explain differential sex distribution in the economy, especially the sex labelling of jobs and women's attitudes toward work.[11] More specifically, age and marital status influence the possibility of formal or informal employment for women. In Mexico, for example, 'the level of participation of single females does seem to vary systematically with development levels, while the rates for ever-married females remain relatively unaltered by degree of development.'[12] This may mean that divorced, widowed or separated women work whether employment is expanding or not, while single women stay at home until industry offers them adequate jobs. Thus the increase in jobs does not benefit the most needy women who support their children, but the young women who will normally leave the labour force when they get married. In Latin America women's involvement in the labour force declines steadily after the age of twenty-five. Is this due to voluntary withdrawal, or to the unavailability of jobs for older women? I suggest that in Latin America, and perhaps in other developing regions, women's participation in formal employment declines with age while it increases in informal activities.

THE STRATEGIES OF WOMEN IN THE INFORMAL-LABOUR SECTOR OF MEXICO CITY

The informal activities of women in Mexico City range from private tutoring in foreign languages to dishwashing. A definite stratification of such tasks exists, related to at least two clearly defined social groups: middle-class women with educational and social advantages, and working-class and 'marginal' women with no schooling.

Mexican middle-class women generally consider work outside the home undesirable. According to social norms, their fulfilment, dignity and respectability lie in home and children. Only a minority, usually university graduates, accept salaried work, notably of a professional kind, as a part of a woman's life. Thus it is only women whose husbands do not earn enough who generally engage in part-time activities to earn money. Most can be done at home, or in other women's homes, such as baking, embroidery, sewing or knitting, private tutoring in languages or school subjects, and craftsmanship, such as dolls, boxes, paintings or leather work. Interestingly, all of these activities are normally done freely for friends and relatives; the only difference between such informal jobs and domestic or family tasks is wages.

Self-employment by middle-class women outside the home usually involves having a small restaurant, or a small shop that sells cakes, china, flowers, knitting, children's clothes, books and records. A more traditional business is the neighbourhood shop that sells everything from charcoal and candles to flour and sweets. The old shopkeeper who knows all the local gossip is still an institutional figure in some neighbourhoods today. The women who can afford it might establish small song, dance, gymnastics, yoga or 'personality' academies—a full-time activity for the owner, a part-time activity for women teachers. Significantly, the clientele and the workers in these establishments are almost exclusively women; they constitute an all-female supply-and-demand labour market.

Lower-class women, in contrast, carry out their activities primarily in the streets or in other women's homes. These involve personal services and trade, but most especially domestic service. Domestic service functions as an economic safeguard for migrant and poor urban women because it is always available. However, because it partakes of the traditional female preoccupations with house, children and kitchen, domestic work is not conceptualized as 'a job'. Since there is no contract, women can be fired with ease and can enter or leave domestic service at various times during their lives. Young women become chambermaids or nannies while they wait to marry; unmarried or separated mothers become domestics in order to support their children. Women between the ages of 35 and 50 can still get work as servants, provided they have no more than one child and no man; only rarely is the husband employed in the same house as gardener, chauffeur or handyman. It is extremely rare for old women to enter domestic service; the possibility of inefficient work and illness makes employers reluctant to hire them.

Would domestic workers accept an eight-hour work schedule with higher wages if they were offered alternative employment? Given the fact that a female servant's wages are far below the official minimum salary, that she must be available for work day and night with only Sundays off, and that she is often mistreated, one could reasonably assume that she would be eager for another type of job. Indeed, most young women in domestic service today say that they would like to find other types of jobs. However, free room and board for herself and sometimes for her small child often makes domestic work a woman's best option.

Some women live with their husband or children and provide part-time household services, such as washing clothes, windows and floors, mending clothes, looking after children or the house, and helping out at parties and celebrations. They go to the employer's house, sometimes to seven different houses a week, and return at night to their own homes. Such jobs are sought after and found through friends and relatives. Younger lower-class girls can sometimes get a job in a factory or a shop, especially if they have 'good appearance' (*buena presentación*), or they help in the family enterprise—a restaurant, market stall or shop.

Middle-aged and elderly women tend to go into petty trade or the sale of food in the streets. Whereas female petty trade usually involves edibles, such as sweets, chewing gum, fruit and chocolates, in keeping with the traditional image of women as providers of food, men vendors sell clothes, belts, jewellery and toys. Some women are provided with small carts by the city government; unauthorized street sellers, who move fast to avoid the police, are predominantly rural migrants, many of them Indians. Still other women sell food that they cook in charcoal burners outside their homes, near bus stations, sports grounds, university campuses or factories. These two types of street vending have proliferated in recent years. They tend, however, to offer an unnecessary service and to create their own demand, since a street vendor who sells what she just bought in the market two blocks away is not fulfilling a real demand. It is reasonable to suppose that if they had alternatives, these women would not engage in such activities.

Data from my own research on a group of underprivileged migrant Indian women in Mexico City suggest that they have few choices. These Mazahua peasants, who started migrating from their villages some 300 kilometres outside of Mexico City in the 1960s, cannot find alternative work. Because most of the men work only intermittently as construction peons, market porters and in similar low-paid, informal positions, women are obliged to earn additional income through street selling. Widows and divorced or abandoned women who have migrated to the city with their children are also street vendors. Their blatant poverty has aroused public attention and led to a repression of their activities by city police. City officials have wondered why these women have not conveniently disappeared into domestic service. Indeed, domestic service is used as a shield against protest over women's high unemployment rate and over the government's unwillingness to do anything about it. A simple analysis shows the limited range of occupational choices open to lower-class women. Most of these migrant women have children and/or husbands and are thus disqualified from residential domestic service. Even if they were willing to be separated from their families, their wages would be lower than those paid to urban women, and they would probably be ill-treated by their employers. Irregular domestic service is also unavailable to them because they lack the necessary skills and the social contacts to find such jobs. As dishwashers and kitchen help in restaurants, they know that they would be exploited, sometimes working up to 15 hours a day for extremely low pay. Young urban girls are usually preferred as waitresses. Finally, these migrant women lack the knowledge to sell in established markets; this requires an appropriate licence, an ability to cope with market administrators and inspectors, and established business contracts to obtain their merchandise at wholesale prices. Outright begging is subject to police harassment, and Mazahua women consider it degrading. They prefer to sell fruit or sweets in the streets, an activity which they know already from their peasant villages. The network of former Mazahua migrants in the wholesale fruit and vegetable section of the Merced, the main city market, gives Mazahua women access to wholesale prices. In addition, street selling can be taken up and left at any time, either in order to return to the village or to stay at home when a child or husband is ill. Another advantage is that small children remain with their mother while she sells, at times that are convenient to her and in places where she can talk and joke with her friends and relatives. Even more important, income from sales in 'good spots' is higher than her husband's unstable earnings as a construction worker or porter. Thus some husbands have stopped working altogether and only help out their wives by carrying the crates of fruit to the house, or by hiding the bulk of it in case the police arrest their wives. Others simply wait for their wives to bring home some money with which to get drunk. As this brief description suggests, given their occupational options, street selling provides the greatest advantages to these migrant women. Guided by decisions that are rational, they make the most out of their hopeless, underprivileged situation.

Another informal occupation open to women of all classes is prostitution [but] data are virtually nonexistent. According to one unpublished psychiatric study conducted in Mexico City, prostitutes are either extremely neurotic or mentally retarded, an explanation given in medical circles throughout the world. Although a serious attempt at a sociological survey was stopped by gangsterial opposition, bits of information suggest that young girls from middle-class families occasionally go into prostitution before marrying because they can make more money in one evening than in two weeks of secretarial work. For some, prostitution is a reaction against the tediousness and repression of their family life. The lack of reliable studies means that we can only speculate about the reasons why lower-class women become prostitutes. Judging from occasional data, it would seem that prostitution is a major informal source of income for women, but it is never taken into account in discussions of female economic participation or survival.

CONCLUSIONS

Informal activities in developing capitalist economies must be understood within the total pattern of employment in a given country. Whether temporarily or permanently, informal activities are usually taken up when formal jobs are unavailable. For women especially, the dividing line between formal and informal jobs is, as we have seen, tenuous. On the one hand, formal employment implies a long-term full-time contractual job, but this does not apply to paid domestic work or petty trade, and small-craft production, all of which have large numbers of female workers. These jobs are considered informal if they are carried out intermittently on an irregular basis. On the other hand, the boundary between women's wage labour in the informal sector and unpaid household and community tasks is even more tenuous. A woman not needing an income will do exactly the same tasks—baking, sewing, embroidery, crafts, and tutoring—without pay that other women who need an income do for a wage. Indeed, at the formal end of the spectrum, women servants who earn a salary are considered economically active and are included in the GNP; midway, women do the same tasks on an informal basis—part time and intermittently—and yet are paid for them without being considered economically active and without being included in the GNP; at the other end of the spectrum, housewives do full-time domestic work with no payment and are considered outside the economic system. All of these women are obviously doing exactly the same type of work. Thus there is a very real need to reconceptualize women's work.

The analysis of female work in Mexico City has suggested that when women are in economic need, they press the system for payment of their domestic services—but not those done for their own families. Instead women turn domestic duties into economic activities by offering such services to other women. This represents an all-female supply-and-demand market. At the same time, our analysis indicates that as long as women can enter paid domestic service, female unemployment will not be officially or publicly acknowledged. Government officials can claim that there is no female unemployment problem since lower-class women can always become servants.

As the data on Mexico City suggest, women withdraw from the labour force by the age of 30 to raise a family, but later on are unable to re-enter the labour force, primarily because of the unavailability of jobs. Since women with schooling have higher unemployment figures than their male counterparts, education, contrary to what is frequently argued, does not represent the determining factor in women's employment. Age is important; expanded job opportunities in Mexico have gone to young women between the ages of 15 and 30. After 30, the census indicates, women have more difficulty finding jobs than men. In such a situation, the notion that women should remain at home will tend to be reinforced, even by women themselves. Data showed an inverse correlation between women's unemployment and their participation in domestic tasks. Importantly, this means that female unemployment figures are far from accurate, since many women stay on sharing household duties rather than consider themselves unemployed when they are unable to find work.

When women who need to work cannot find jobs, they compensate for their unemployment by taking up informal activities. Middle-class women take up jobs they can carry out in their own homes or in those of other women. The largest number of women in Mexico City, though, the lower-class women, usually have to engage in informal activities even if their husband has a steady income. And, of course, elderly, divorced, widowed or single women depend entirely on informal activities. The ever-increasing number of women who sell fruits and sweets or snacks in the streets do not fill a demand within the urban economy, but create their own demand out of desperation, since they have no other economic alternative. Immigrant women in Mexico City have the most restricted range of options. The Mazahua women street sellers merely choose the activity that gives them the most advantages within their set of options. Indeed, if we were to ask them why they chose to work at such a low-income, harassed activity, most probably they would answer, 'Well, one must carry on one's little fight, mustn't one?' [*Pues tiene uno que hacer su luchita, ¿ no?*].

21. DEINDUSTRIALIZATION AND THE GROWTH OF WOMEN'S ECONOMIC ASSOCIATIONS AND NETWORKS IN URBAN TANZANIA

AILI MARI TRIPP

In many developing countries, one of the consequences of the world recession that started in the late 1970s and the economic restructuring programmes that followed has been an expansion of local women's organizations to cope with the new hardships they face as a result of the imposition of various austerity measures.[1] From the neighbourhood committees and communal kitchens of Peru, to the mothers' clubs of Brazil and the 1985 demonstrations of women in Sudan against rising prices, women have been active in responding to the new pressures they face. Similarly in urban Tanzania, women's economic associations and networks increased in number and expanded in size in the 1980s as more women became involved in income-generating activities. Tanzania, like many African countries, was severely affected in the late 1970s by pressures from the world economy and drops in export commodity prices, which contributed to a dramatic decline in the real wages of workers. This crisis, followed by a series of economic reforms which had a negative impact on industry, pushed large numbers of women, in particular, into informal income-generating activities.

Urban women formed organizations as one of the strategies they pursued to deal with the new economic difficulties they faced. These associations emerged in a context where the ruling party and government had increasingly curtailed their activities after independence in 1961 and discouraged the growth of new autonomous organizations, especially economic ones. This meant that while some well-established associations like the Young Women's Christian Association (YWCA) continued in the face of various proscriptions, most independent women's organizations were confined to being small and informal in character.

By the early 1990s, however, the government and party began to accommodate such voluntary associations to a greater extent, in part because they did not have the capacity to curtail their activities, but also because there was an increasing realization that a wider array of forces could be useful to the development process. The necessity for a greater plurality of organizations was reflected in the initiation of the debate in 1990 by former Party Chairman Julius Nyerere over whether Tanzania should move from a one-party to a multi-party system.

This study of women's associations and networks is based on fieldwork carried out by an assistant, Salome Mjema, and myself between 1987 and 1988 in Dar es Salaam, Tanzania's largest city. The research involved hundreds of unstructured interviews and several surveys, including one cluster survey of 287 residents in Manzese and Buguruni, two parts of Dar es Salaam, made up primarily of workers and the self-employed. We also talked to women leaders and members of a variety of formal and informal organizations. I have also drawn on interviews conducted by Marja-Liisa Swantz during 1989.

URBAN TANZANIAN WOMEN'S RESPONSES TO DEINDUSTRIALIZATION

For workers, the process of deindustrialization meant sharply declining real wages and layoffs. There had been an 83 per cent decline in the real income of wage earners between 1974 and 1988.[2] Prices increased 5.5 times from 1982 to 1988, while wages only doubled in this same period. For a low-income household food expenditure alone exceeded the minimum monthly salary eight times. Because wage earnings could no longer support the household, the burden fell largely on women to sustain the household. Because of low wages and discriminatory hiring practices, women were excluded from formal employment. As real incomes dropped for men, women were therefore more likely to initiate income-generating activities, frequently making them the main bread-winner in the family. In 1976, wages constituted 77 per cent of the total household income, while other private incomes accounted for only 8 per cent.[3] In contrast, by 1988, according to my survey in Dar es Salaam, informal incomes constituted approximately 90 per cent of the house-hold income, with wage earnings making up the remainder.

Thus, women, who in the past had contributed relatively little to the urban household income, were now critical to the very survival of the household through their involvement in projects. For low-income women these projects ranged from making and selling pastries, beer, paper bags, and crafts, to tailoring, hair braiding and even urban farming.

By the late 1980s it was women themselves who were often rejecting wage employment and seeking more beneficial incomes from self-employment. Women as a proportion of the employed workforce in Dar es Salaam had risen from 4 per cent in 1961 to 11 per cent in 1967 and 20 per cent in 1980. By 1984 the proportion had dropped to 19 per cent and if my survey is any indication it remained at 19 per cent up to 1987.[4] Between 1953 and 1980 few women left their jobs; according to my survey, however, the numbers more than doubled between 1980 and 1987. The most common reason both men and women (45 per cent) gave for leaving was low wages. The second most frequent response (17 per cent) was layoffs due to factory cutbacks or closures. Women were hit especially hard by these layoffs.

Participation in the informal economy had resulted in massive rever-sals in dependencies and reversals in the direction of resource flows at many different levels: away from the state towards private solutions to problems of income, security and social welfare; away from reliance on wage labour to reliance on informal incomes and farming; and a gradual shifting of migration patterns with increasing new movements out of the city into the rural areas. Similarly, relations and patterns of obligation in the household were being transformed with greater resource dependen-cies on women, children and the elderly, where only a decade earlier urban women had mostly relied on men for income, children on their parents and the elderly on their adult children.

The pervasiveness of urban women's involvement in business was unprecedented in a country like Tanzania. This major change went rela-tively unnoticed by the government, scholarly and donor circles since much of it was informal and therefore unrecorded. Moreover, women's informal work was often considered unimportant and petty because of the bias towards official employment. But gradually men were, at least privately, beginning to take note of these changes. As the head of the National Bank of Commerce told me in 1987: 'Women have become the largest private sector in Tanzania, but no one knows what they do.[5]

One indication of men's acceptance of women's increased involvement in micro-enterprises was the fact that 44 per cent of women with projects had received starting capital from their husbands. Several men indicated their apprehension, especially about the fact that women were making so much more than they. One way for women to avoid open conflict with their husbands over their new access to cash was not to disclose their full earnings to their spouse. This was also a way of ensuring control over their earnings, which had to be stretched to cover the household expenses.

The new economic importance of women to the household was also changing women's perceptions of themselves. As one woman, who had left employment as a secretary at a state-owned company to start a hair-dressing salon in 1984, explained:

> I started a business because I did not want to use my body to get money. I had four children to support and my salary was not enough. I wanted to use my own hands, brains and wanted to aim high. Whatever a man can do, I can do better. If you start aiming high, the sky is the limit ... Most women are in business and are no longer dependent on men.[6]

WOMEN AND THE LABOUR MOVEMENT

Women found the national labour union, the Trade Union of Tanzanian Workers (JUWATA), of little use in protecting their jobs or fighting for increased wages. Women had little impact in the national labour movement, in part because they were not involved in the sectors of labour most active in the union. Although all workers in the formal sector automatically belonged to the union, women generally did not participate in JUWATA actively. It was widely acknowledged that when women were forced to attend meetings they simply remained silent.[7] In part, this could be attributed to the political culture in Tanzania, where women in mixed gatherings often found it improper to speak in public. However, a more plausible reason was the fact that they rarely found the union leadership interested in taking up their particular concerns. In fact, by the 1990s it is doubtful that many workers, male or female, found the organization truly representing their interests.

WOMEN AND THE NATIONAL WOMEN'S UNION

Just as women could expect little assistance from the labour movement in protecting their interests on the job, similarly the party-affiliated national women's union, Umoja wa Wanawake wa Tanzania (UWT), was of little help in assisting women off the job in their pursuit of income-generating activities. The women's union, which had grown out of the independence movement, was since its inception in 1962 financially dependent on the party and was organized along the same lines. Although it had played an important role in galvanizing women in the struggle for independence, it did not start from women's own associations as a basis for organization, but rather superimposed its own notions of how women should be organized and what their concerns should be. While the UWT did attempt to address important needs in childcare, maternal health care, nutrition and income-generating projects, its top-down approach did not permit the popular mass base necessary in order to be truly effective and responsive to the needs of women.

The UWT's own organization that was aimed at helping women with income-generating projects, SUWATA (Shirika la Uchimi wa Wanawake Katika Tanzania), concentrated its efforts in rural areas virtually to the exclusion of urban women. In fact, virtually no foreign donor or government assistance was available to urban women for income-generating activities. Women preferred independent organizations, which they felt allowed for greater accountability, efficiency and individual input. Such organizations also served as barometers against which to measure the effectiveness of party and government organizing initiatives and performance.

WOMEN'S ASSOCIATIONS IN TANZANIA

Tanzanian women have a rich history of association which has largely been unrecorded because most women's associations have tended to be small, informal and loosely organized. These are the kinds of organizations which rarely attract the attention of social scientists (except for anthropologists), nor do they gain the proper recognition they deserve. Women historically came together to organize feasts, funerals, weddings, and provide collective assistance during childbirth and illness. They formed savings clubs, beer clubs, loose associations of instructresses of young girls (for puberty rites), ritual cult groups, informal social and religious groups, mutual support groups for cultivation and harvesting, and age and neighbourhood groups.[8] Women's economic associations in Tanzania, however, were never as large or varied as those found in West

Africa, the powerful unions of traders, for instance. Instead, their involvement in micro-enterprises was characterized by cooperation with a complex array of individuals who ranged from relatives and friends to neighbours and people from the wider communities.

Although there are a few independent national women's organizations, like the YWCA, the Legion of Mary, or the new Association of Businesswomen of Tanzania, both the party and the government served as militating factors against the formation of broader associations. Following a pattern found in much of Africa, the newly independent state led by the single party gradually co-opted, absorbed and even eliminated independent organizations, especially economic organizations like the agricultural cooperatives and the trade unions, which they felt posed the greatest threat to state-led development. The government in Tanzania, like many other African governments, is gradually becoming more tolerant of the non-governmental sector and is in many cases encouraging its growth. Non-governmental associations became especially important on the African political scene in the 1980s and became one of the most important forces promoting greater pluralism and democracy and more bottom-up approaches to development in contrast to the heavy top-down government-dominated approaches of the past.

While the party and government may have inhibited the growth of larger, more diverse women's organizations in the past, they were unable to prevent the growth of smaller informal organizations.

[That] growth is part of a broader urban response to economic crisis and to economic reform in which a wide variety of organizations is represented: e.g. rotating credit associations and independent cooperatives that accompanied the flourishing of the informal economy; and parents' organizations seeking to meet new childcare needs because of women's increased involvement in self-employment. Business associations expanded their activities, and new organizations like the Association of Businesswomen were formed to create an environment more conducive to the private sector. Such organizations focused on problems ranging from trade liberalization to the investment code, credit availability, devaluation, customs taxes and other issues. Some found themselves attempting to get the state to loosen up its restrictions on small informal enterprises and various sideline businesses. Others emerged to provide services and other resources the state could no longer deliver. For example, local defence teams took over where the police were corrupt or no longer effective. Finally, in this period, organizations which had previously been banned re-emerged since they could now take advantage of the few new political spaces which had opened up.

ROTATING SAVINGS SOCIETIES

One of the most pervasive forms of organization that emerged with the burst of economic activity was *upato* or rotating savings societies, to pool and save money. These associations are found throughout the world, not only the Third World but also the US, especially within newer immigrant communities, and in countries like Italy, England and Canada.[9]

Women historically participated in such societies in parts of Tanzania, but were more likely to pool clothes and food rather than money. These societies were especially prevalent along the coast and in Zanzibar. As low-income women increasingly had more self-generated income at their disposal in the late 1980s and early 1990s, such older mutual support forms of organization were revived in new arrangements. For example, if a woman [was] robbed, it was common to find a group of four to six of her women friends or neighbours getting together and taking wrap-around cloths they had set aside to give to her. The women would similarly help other members of the group in times of trouble.

Upato rotating savings societies were a more structured form of such organization that gained in popularity in the 1980s as more women became engaged in small businesses. They also became an important source of capital for reinvestment in small businesses. For women they were especially significant, since women had been excluded from access to credit in both rural and urban areas and frequently they did not have the collateral in the form of land or property with which to borrow from the Small-scale Industries Development Organisation, the Co-operative Rural Development Bank and the National Bank of Commerce, the Presidential National Trust Fund for Self-Reliance and other lenders.[10]

Upato evolved from an association of neighbourhood women to one organized among market sellers, workers in offices and factories, across communities, and among groups of friends or acquaintances spread throughout the city. *Upato* was fashionable not only among poor women but also among middle-income women. Men were even involved in the 1980s. Because Dar es Salaam has a rich mix of ethnic groups (46 were represented in my survey alone), people like the Chagga and Sambaa, which historically had not participated in such societies, were now involved.

Even though the societies were based on trust, many women actually sought to participate in societies outside their immediate family or circle of friends because of the difficulties that might arise if the society broke down because of non-payment. We found, for example, associations where the treasurer would know all the participants, but the participants had not known each other previously. To take another example in Manzese: one group of about ten women neighbours shared their daily activities, from cooking to cleaning pots, washing clothes, tending each others' children and even looking out for each others' projects. They were a lively group of friends. Nevertheless they were all involved in separate *upato* societies with women other than those in their immediate vicinity.

Zawadi was a typical participant of an *upato* society. She was in her early forties and had five children and three grandchildren. Most women who participated in *upato* societies were in the 35–50 age bracket, while self-employed women generally fell into the 20–35-year range. This can perhaps be attributed to the greater financial demands placed on women with small children who had a harder time saving. Zawadi had no education, although 61 per cent of women involved in *upato* societies had some (compared to self-employed women in general of whom only 49 per cent had some education). Like a large number of *upato* participants she belonged to the Zaramo ethnic group. There was, in fact, a greater number of participants from coastal ethnic groups like the Zaramo, Matumbi, Ndengereko, Zigua and Kwere relative to the general ethnic breakdown of women in the survey. Zawadi had never been employed but had started a project making *maandazi* pastries because her husband, who was a soldier in Songea, could no longer support the family. Zawadi prepared the mixture at night, woke up every morning at 4 a.m. to cook the pastries and took them at 7 a.m. to sell along the street to people on their way to work.

Almost half of all women surveyed who were self-employed and employed belonged to an *upato* group. All who were involved in *upato* societies were self-employed, even the ones who were employed. The most common reason given [for ending] participation was the fact that [a woman] no longer had a project. Not surprisingly, the majority had started soon after beginning income-generating projects, which was after 1985 for 80 per cent of the women I interviewed in 1988. Women who participated in *upato* societies made on average 26 per cent more than other self-employed women.

Zawadi belonged to an *upato* society of 20 women. This was considerably larger than most, where the average number of participants was twelve. In her society, each participant pooled 20Tsh (US$0.20) each day. Every five days one person claimed the kitty, which totalled 4000Tsh (US$40). Breaking the kitty every five days was the most common kind of arrangement, although there were other societies where people pooled money every 3, 4, 7, 10, 14 or 30 days. Zawadi was saving 600Tsh (US$6) each month, which represented the median amount saved by the women surveyed. But the range of money saved ranged from 150Tsh (US$1.50) to as much as 10 000Tsh (US$100) a month, with women saving roughly 20–30 per cent of their average monthly income obtained from small businesses. Zawadi was saving only about 10 per cent of her income because she alone was trying to support eight people including two of her daughters with children of their own.

One-fifth of the women in one *upato* society were involved in a second society. Even though these societies were usually made up solely of women or solely of men, occasionally a few men would be allowed to participate in an *upato* society of women or a few women in an *upato* society of men. In Zawadi's society only men who had secure businesses were allowed to participate, since men were generally considered more unreliable than women when it came to saving.

One person was appointed to collect the money and give it to each participant when her turn came around. In poor neighbourhoods like Buguruni she might visit each participant daily at her home or place of work if it was in the neighbourhood to make the collection, wrapping the money in the corner of the *khanga* (wrap-around cloth) that she wore or filling a small pail, basket or some other container with the money. This person, called *kijumbe* or secretary-treasurer, might claim a portion of the kitty for her service.

Women's involvement in *upato* societies not only reflects the increase in their involvement in income-generating activities; it is also an indication of their greater control over household resources. One of the main purposes of saving in such a society was to get the money out of the house so as to keep the men of the household from laying their hands on it. Since women had come to bear the greater burden of paying for most daily household expenses, money earned from income-generating projects needed to be guarded carefully. [They] were responsible for feeding the children and paying school fees and health-care costs. Women were usually the ones to save and initiate the building of a house in those households in a position to do so. They also used their *upato* savings to reinvest in their projects. Occasionally if they had money to spare, they would treat themselves to new *khangas* or get their hair fixed in one of the new hairdressing salons.

While women were often perceived by both men and women as more capable of saving than men, this was [because] it was primarily the woman's responsibility to make sure that the needs of the household and children were met.

WOMEN'S COOPERATIVES

Although most people owned and operated their own income-generating projects, this did not preclude becoming involved in larger associations and cooperatives. In Mlingotini, a small fishing village outside Dar es Salaam, women had been involved in transporting and selling coconuts to the city, growing and selling vegetables, making and selling pastries, and frying fish for sale. Twenty-one of these women formed a cooperative to mill rice, while continuing their own individual projects. Then in 1985, with the profits obtained from the mill, each woman contributed 150Tsh (US$1.50); collecting around 3000Tsh (US$30) they started a business transporting and selling fish to the city.

The leader of the cooperative said she had witnessed several changes over the years that preceded the formation of the cooperative. The women in her village were engaged in small businesses like never before and they were for the first time keeping all their own profits. She said: 'We women are getting clever. We didn't do that in the past.' She added that men would have liked to object to their wives' increased economic activity, 'but they keep quiet. They know they can't support the family and they need the woman's income. Some men are getting ambitious themselves and are trying to find businesses for themselves'.[11]

In villages on the outskirts of Dar es Salaam women were involved in similar collective endeavours: in Chiwanga women had organized to cultivate pineapples and later started a flour mill; in Mbegani women used money from a sewing project to start another flour mill; and in Mbweni, Pande and Mlingotini women had started their own cooperative shops, and a fish-smoking cooperative in Mlingotini.[12]

Cooperatives were not always women's first choice in organizational arrangements for their projects. Most women carried out their businesses alone or with one other person. Participating in a cooperative would have been only a secondary venture. Rarely would women have relied on [one] for their primary source of subsistence. Even better-off women formed cooperatives mainly as a way of gaining access to credit or loans since foreign donors as well as government agencies would approve funds only for cooperatives.

ASSOCIATION OF BUSINESSWOMEN IN TANZANIA

The creation of the Association of Businesswomen in Tanzania in January 1990 is another indication of the changing economic role of women in Tanzania. It was not only the poorer women who had begun to engage in income-generating businesses in the 1980s; professional and middle-income women were also leaving their salaried positions to go into business or were involved in sideline enterprises. They had established large tailoring businesses, dry cleaning companies, flour mills, secretarial-service companies, hair salons, export and import businesses, bakeries and other small manufacturing and service industries.

It is interesting that the businesswomen's association, although initiated by middle-class and big businesswomen, included as part of its constituency poor women involved in income-generating activities, and wanted to form with them a 'strong business community' of women.[13] The organization was seeking to gain recognition from the country's financial institutions, which had neglected women and their credit needs. [It] also planned to provide free expertise and conduct seminars for women on issues relating to marketing and other business skills. It began to investigate possibilities of acting as an intermediary agency to obtain loans for local women's organizations that found it difficult to make such applications themselves.

Not long after its inception, the organization found that economic possibilities for women were severely constrained by [their] weak representation in the political arena. Leaders of the association became vocal in criticizing the official party-affiliated women's union, arguing that this was not strong enough to represent the new interests of women in Tanzania. They began to express the need for stronger women's participation in parliament. The experience of the businesswomen's association suggests that the strengthened economic clout of better-educated middle-class women will eventually have important repercussions in the political arena, leading to greater political mobilization of women in the country.

PARENTS' ASSOCIATIONS

The lack of day-care centres had been one of the main obstacles in keeping women out of employment, but creating such centres had never been a priority of the government.[14] The Ministry of Labour and Social Welfare, along with the women's union UWT, was responsible for creating and supervising all day-care centres after 1976, but its efforts were minimal.[15] By 1980 there were only 2996 centres in the entire country with 94 in Dar es Salaam.[16] As more women of all income groups became self-employed, they became increasingly involved in initiating parent's organizations to form nurseries.

CREATING NEW NETWORKS

In addition to women's associations, women built networks around their businesses with people they trusted for information, advice and assistance of various kinds. Women generally owned their own projects (94 per cent). Forty per cent worked alone in their projects, 61 per cent were assisted by their children, while 50 per cent worked with one or two others in addition to their children. For the most part, when they did collaborate with someone else, they worked with another family member, distant relative or friend.

However, women increasingly found themselves having to go outside their closest family and kin to broaden their circle of contacts in order to do business. Neighbours in the city, usually of different ethnic origin, were fast becoming close associates. Often the same mutual obligations and expectations reserved for kin were extended to neighbours and friends, and the trust engendered by such relations became crucial when these same people were involved in a joint project.

Expressing great affection for their female friends and neighbours, women would often insist on being interviewed with them. Sometimes this involved going to great lengths to make arrangements so that all could be present. Relations with neighbours and friends, which in the past were reserved for helping each other with household tasks, tending children and plaiting each other's hair, were increasingly being extended to the area of micro-enterprises.

Urban life presented new opportunities for women to meet new people and establish information and resource networks. For example, living together in one house, as many families did, encouraged women neighbours to start projects together. It was not uncommon to find women living in the same house sharing a project like making local beer, while maintaining separate accounts. In one apartment complex, I visited four separate apartments where women were involved in sewing as a business; I was told that there were more women sewers in the building. They were all friends and had inspired each other to begin their projects to supplement their husbands' meagre wages. They helped each other out and insisted that they did not compete with one another. Other women found their formal jobs a place to exchange ideas and support for their projects. The hairdressing salon was another frequently mentioned place for meeting to discuss business.

Working arrangements with friends and neighbours were of various kinds and served different purposes. Friends would accompany each other to a restaurant or bar, one perhaps selling fried fish and chips and the other *mankongoro* soup. While companionship was obviously important, such an arrangement also enabled them to help each other in the more practical aspects of buying inputs and preparing the food for sale. Some reported they felt safer with a friend if they had to sell late into the night.

Women market sellers tended to sell in the same part of the market so they could help each other out with childcare if necessary and tend each others' stalls if one had to go away temporarily. They could also form a warning and support network to help each other evade the city council militia that came around to check licences. Since most women sold their wares without a licence, this could be a potential problem. Many women, for example, sold maize and flour in rows outside the market because they felt the unpredictability of their business did not warrant procuring a licence. Selling together gave them a sense of security and mutual support in case they were caught.

CONCLUSIONS

The decline of large-scale industry in Tanzania throughout the second half of the 1970s and the 1980s resulted in declining real wages and layoffs, putting greater pressures on household members to pursue income-generating projects. Similar patterns were found in many African countries. Urban women moved from a position of relatively little involvement in income-generating activities, to being, in many cases, the main economic support for the household. Women who were employed often had to leave their jobs because the pay was too low or they had to seek sideline incomes. Women's expanded economic role led to an increase in the variety of women's economic organizations and associations that could cater to women's new demands.

The forms of organization women adopted were indicative of their needs and priorities. These priorities were not always reflected in party-affiliated structures that offered superimposed blueprints of organizational structures. While the party and government had limited larger and more formal independent associations in order to ensure government control of the economy, women found little difficulty in organizing their own local informal associations. By the late 1980s it had become evident that the state's posture towards the non-governmental sector was untenable and its inability to restrict independent organizational activity coupled with a realization of the need to bring a broader array of forces into the development process gave way to a greater openness to organizations like the newly emerging Association of Businesswomen in Tanzania.

In order to understand women's response to the impact of deindustrialization upon relationships in Tanzanian society it is important to look not only at such visible formal organizations, but also at those embedded in the daily lives of women. Through such associations, women are transforming their lives in their day-to-day struggle to survive and at the same time changing the political landscape of the country.

NOTES TO PART 3

CHAPTER 17

1. The forces underlying the process of relocation are discussed in greater detail in Elson and Pearson, 1980, and Elson and Pearson, 1981.
2. Free Trade Zones are special areas which are exempt from normal import and export regulations, and also from many other kinds of regulation, such as protective labour legislation and tax laws.
3. It may seem paradoxical to talk of the protection afforded by subordination, but the paradox lies in the social relations themselves. When the social identity of women has to be established through their relation with men, the absence of father, brother or husband is often disadvantageous.

CHAPTER 19

1. See, for example, Leontiades, 1971; Adam, 1975; Moxon, 1974; UNIDO, 1979; Fröbel, Heinrichs and Kreye, 1980.

2. See, for example, Nayyar, 1978; Fröbel, Heinrichs and Kreye, 1978; Takeo, 1978; Landsberg, 1979; Sivanandan, 1980.

3. Marginal productivity is a theoretical concept central to neoclassical economic doctrine: it is the addition to a firm's total output value resulting from the employment of one additional worker or unit of labour.

4. Indigenous firms have to compete with multinationals in the labour market; multinationals are the leaders in setting wages and working conditions. In Singapore, the improvement of wages and working conditions in the female labour market is illustrated by the following: starting wages have been more that doubled in five years (ahead of inflation); fringe benefits have improved (for example, the extension of paid holiday time to two weeks in the year); part-time shifts have been instituted to suit housewives; the desired age of workers has risen from 16 to 23 years to up to 50 years; there has been a dramatic reduction in rotating shifts and microscope work in electronics factories; and a five-day week is typical. Singapore workers have become a 'labour-aristocracy' in the Southeast Asian region.

CHAPTER 20

1. The main exponent for this theory is W. W. Rostow (*The Stages of Economic Growth: A Non-Communist Manifesto* [Cambridge: Cambridge University Press, 1960]).

2. Rodolfo Stavenhagen, *Sociologia y subdesarrollo* (Mexico City: Nuestro Tiempo, 1972); F. H. Cardoso y Enzo Faletto, *Dependencia y desarrollo en America Latina* (México City: Siglo XXI, 1973); André Gunder Frank, *El Desarrollo del subdesarrollo* (México City: Escuela Nacional de Antroplogia e Historia, 1972).

3. Paul Singer, *Economía política de la urbanización* (México City: Siglio XXI, 1975); E. Suarez Contreras, 'Migración interna y oportunidades de empleo en la Cd. de Mexico', in *El perfil de México en 1980* (ed.) J. Martinez Ríos, Vol. 3 (México City: Siglio XXI, 1973).

4. Orlandina de Oliviera, *Absorción de mano de obra a la estructura ocupacional de la Ciudad de México* (México City: El Colegio de México, 1976).

5. Faria Vilmar, personal communication, February 1976.

6. Marta Tienda, 'Regional Differentiation and the Sector Transformation of the Female Labour Force: Mexico, 1970', (Ph.D. dissertation, University of Texas, 1974); Ester Boserup, 'Employment of Women in Developing Countries', paper presented at the International Population Conference, Liège, 1973.

7. Boserup, p. 388.

8. Ibid.

9. Elsa Chaney and Marianne Schmink, 'Las mujeres y la modernización: Acceso a la technologia', *La Mujer en América Latina*, Vol. 1 (México City: Sepsetentas, 1975).

10. Heleith Saffioti, 'Relaciones de Sexo y Clases Sociales', *La Mujer en América Latina*, Vol. 1 (México City: Sepsetentas, 1975).

11. Marianne Schmink, 'Dependent Development and the Division of Labor by Sex', paper presented at the Fifth National Meeting of the Latin American Studies Association, San Francisco, 1974, p. 18; Nadia Youssef, 'Social

Structure and the Female Labor Force: The Case of Women Workers in Muslim Middle Eastern Countries', *Demography* 8, No. 4 (November 1971): 427–39; and Boserup, p. 387.

12. Tienda, p. 16.

CHAPTER 21

1. See for example Victoria Daines and David Seddon, 'International Development Policy and the Recession', in *Survival Struggles, Protest and Resistance: Women's Responses to 'Austerity Programmes' and 'Structural Adjustment'*, n.d.; Jane Jacquette (ed.) *The Women's Movement in Latin America; Feminism and the Transition to Democracy*, Unwin Hyman, Boston, MA, 1989.

2. Bureau of Statistics (1989), *1988 Population Census: Preliminary Report*, Dar es Salaam: Ministry of Finance, Planning and Economic Affairs.

3. Bureau of Statistics (1977), *Household Budget Survey: Income and Consumption 1976–77*, Dar es Salaam: Ministry of Finance, Planning and Economic Affairs.

4. International Labour Organisation (1982), *Basic Needs in Danger. A Basic Needs Oriented Development Strategy for Tanzania*, Addis Ababa: International Labour Organisation, 1982 p. 143.

5. Aili Mari Tripp, interview 11 October 1987.

6. Aili Mari Tripp, interview 18 August 1987.

7. See M.H. Mgaya, 'A Study of Workers in a Factory', MA thesis, University of Dar es Salaam, 1976.

8. Marja-Liisa Swantz (1985) *Women in Development: A Creative Role Denied?* London: C. Hurst and Company, p. 160.

9. See for example, S. Ardener (1964) 'The Comparative Study of Rotating Credit Associations', *Journal of the Royal Anthropological Institute*, p. 94; Clifford Geertz (1962), 'The Rotating Credit Association: A "Middle Rung" in Development', *Economic Development and Cultural Change* 10(3); D.V. Kurtz (1973) 'The Rotating Credit Association: An Adaptation to Poverty', *Human Organisation* 32(1), C. Velez-Ibanez (1983) *Bonds of Mutual Trust: The Cultural Systems of Rotating Credit Associations among Urban Mexicans and Chicanos*, New Brunswick: Rutgers University Press.

10. Marjorie Mbilinyi (1990) 'A Review of Women in Development Issues in Tanzania', Report for World Bank, mimeo, pp.72–6; Anna K. Tibaijuka, Mary Kisanga, Joyce Hamisi and M. Abubakar (1979) 'Strategies to Enhance Women's Access and Effective Utilisation of Institutional Credit: Report on a Survey on Women's Land and Property Rights in Tanzania', Presidential Commission of Enquiry into Monetary and Banking Systems in Tanzania: Sub-Committee on Women's Credit Facilities, mimeo.

11. Aili Mari Tripp, interview 4 June 1988.

12. Marja-Liisa Swantz (1986) *The Role of Women in Tanzanian Fishing Societies: A Study of the Socioeconomic Context and the Situation of Women in Three Coastal Fishing Villages in Tanzania*, Institute of Development Studies Women's Study Group, University of Dar es Salaam, p. 57; Marja-Liisa Swantz, interview 23 April 1990.

13. *Daily News*, 19 March 1990.

14. Swantz, *Women in Development: A Creative Role Denied?* pp. 150–1.

15. Susan G. Rogers, 'Efforts Toward Women's Development in Tanzania: Gender Rhetoric vs. Gender Realities', in Kathleen Staudt and Jane Jacquette

(eds) (1982) *Women in Developing Countries: A Policy Focus*, New York: Haworth Press, pp. 28–9.
16. International Labour Organisation, *Basic Needs in Danger. A Basic Needs Oriented Development Strategy for Tanzania*, p. 145.

REFERENCES TO PART 3

CHAPTER 17

Blake, M. (1979) 'Asian Women in Formal and Non-Formal Sectors—Review and Proposals for Research—Education—Mobilisation', Occasional Paper No. 2, United Nations Asian and Pacific Centre for Women and Development.

Braverman, H. (1974), *Labour and Monopoly Capital*, London and New York: Monthly Review Press.

Elson, D. and R. Pearson (1980) 'The Latest Phase of the Internationalisation of Capital and its Implications for Women in the Third World', Discussion Paper No. 150, Institute of Development Studies, University of Sussex.

Elson, D. and R. Pearson (1981) 'Nimble Fingers Make Changed Workers: An Analysis of Women's Employment in Third World Export Manufacturing', *Feminist Review*, No. 7.

Engels, F. (1976) *The Condition of the Working Class in England*, St. Albans, UK: Panther.

Fanon, F. (1969) *The Wretched of the Earth*, Harmondsworth, England: Penguin.

Grossman, R. (1979) 'Women's Place in the Integrated Circuit', *Southeast Asia Chronicle*, No. 66 (joint issue with *Pacific Research*, Vol. 9, Nos 5–6).

Hancock, M. A. (1980) 'Women and Transnational Corporations: A Bibliography', Working Paper for East–West Culture Learning Centre, Honolulu.

Heyzer, N. (1978) 'Young Women and Migrant Workers in Singapore's Labour Intensive Industries', Paper presented to Conference on the Continuing Subordination of Women in the Development Process, Institute of Development Studies, University of Sussex.

Lim, L. (1978) 'Women Workers in Multinational Corporations in Developing Countries—The Case of the Electronics Industry in Malaysia and Singapore', *Women's Studies Program Occasional Paper* No. 9, University of Michigan.

Marx, K. (1973) *Gründrisse*, Harmondsworth, England: Penguin.

——(1976) *Capital*, Vol. 1, Harmondsworth, England: Penguin.

Phillips, A. and B. Taylor (1980) 'Sex and Skill. Notes Towards a Feminist Economics', *Feminist Review*, No. 6.

Sharpston, M. (1975), 'International Subcontracting', *Oxford Economic Papers*, March.

Tang, S. L. (1980) 'Global Reach and its Limits: Women Workers and their Responses to Work in a Multinational Electronics Plant', Mimeo, Department of Sociology, Chinese University of Hong Kong.

Whitehead, A. (1978) 'The Intervention of Capital in Rural Production Systems: Some Aspects of the Household', Paper presented at Conference 133 on the Continuing Subordination of Women in the Development Process, Institute of Development Studies, University of Sussex.

Whitehead, A. (1979) 'Some Preliminary Notes on the Subordination of Women', *IDS Bulletin*, Vol. 10: No. 3.

CHAPTER 18

Fernández, M. P. (1978) 'Notes from the Field', Ciudad Juarez, Mexico, Mimeo.

Newton, J. R. and F. Balli (1979) 'Mexican In-bond Industry', Paper presented to the Seminar on North–South Complementary Intra–industry Trade, UNCTAD United Nations Conference, DF: Mexico.

CHAPTER 19

Adam, Gyorgy (1975) 'Multinational Corporations and Worldwide Sourcing', in Hugo Radice (ed.), *International Firms and Modern Imperialism*, Harmondsworth, England: Penguin.

Boserup, Ester (1970) *Woman's Role in Economic Development*, London: Allen and Unwin.

Fröbel, Folker, Jürgen Heinrichs and Otto Kreye (1978) 'Export-Oriented Industrialization of Underdeveloped Countries', *Monthly Review* 30, No. 6: 22–7.

——(1980) *The New International Division of Labour: Structural Unemployment in Industrialised Countries and Industrialisation in Developing Countries*, Cambridge and New York: Cambridge University Press.

Landsberg, Martin (1979) 'Export-led Industrialization in the Third World: Manufacturing Imperialism', *Review of Radical Political Economics* 11, No. 4: 50–63.

Leontiades, James (1971) 'International Sourcing in the Less-developed Countries', *Columbia Journal of World Business* 6, No. 6: 19–26.

Lim, Linda Y. C. (1978a) 'Multinational Firms and Manufacturing for Export in Less-developed Countries: The Case of the Electronics Industry in Malaysia and Singapore', Ph.D. dissertation, University of Michigan, Ann Arbor.

——(1978b) *Women Workers in Multinational Corporations: The Case of the Electronics Industry in Malyasia and Singapore*, Michigan Occasional Papers, No. 9, Ann Arbor, Michigan: University of Michigan, Women's Studies Program.

Moxon, Richard W. (1974) 'Offshore Production in Less-developed Countries—A Case Study of Multinationality in the Electronics Industry', *Bulletin*, Nos 98–9 (July), New York University; Graduate School of Business Administration, Institute of Finance.

Nayyar, Deepak (1978) 'Transnational Corporations and Manufactured Exports from Poor Countries', *Economic Journal* 88: 58–84.

Pang Eng Fong and Linda Y. C. Lim (1977) *The Electronics Industry in Singapore: Structure, Technology and Linkages*, Economic Research Centre, University of Singapore, Research Monograph Series, No. 7.

Reynis, Lee Ann (1976) 'The Proliferation of US Firm Third World Sourcing in the Mid-to-Late 1960s: An Historical and Empirical Study of the Factors Which Occasioned the Location of Production for the US Market Abroad', Ph.D. dissertation, University of Michigan, Ann Arbor.

Sivanandan, A. (1980) 'Imperialism in the Silicon Age', *Monthly Review* 32, No. 3: 24–42.

Takeo, Tsuchiya (1978) 'Free Trade Zones in Southeast Asia', *Monthly Review* 29, No. 9: 29–39.

United Nations Industrial Development Organization (UNIDO) (1979) 'Redeployment of Industries from Developed to Developing Countries', Industrial Development Conference, 419, 3 October.

Part 4
International Women in Social Transformation

INTRODUCTION TO PART 4

NAN WIEGERSMA

Contemporary forces of social and economic transformation have destabilized and in many respects worsened women's lives. In Part 4, we look at women caught up in the throes of social changes such as structural adjustment, the extension of market capitalism to formerly socialist countries and the rise of religious fundamentalism. We consider first the impact of structural adjustment programmes on women (Chapters 22 and 23). Changes in state policies concerning women's health, reproductive rights and family policies under capitalism and socialism are covered next (Chapters 24 and 25), followed by a review of the impact of the AIDS epidemic on women and children in the Third World (Chapter 26).

The impact upon women of competing ideologies current in global politics is considered next. Chapter 27 examines the role of women in national liberation movements; two perspectives on women under the influence of Moslem fundamentalism, by Afshar and Hoodfar (Chapters 28 and 29), follow. Benería (Chapter 30) attempts to answer questions about the advantages and problems for women living under socialist systems, while Meurs (Chapter 31) shows the impact on women of the transformation from central planning to the market and capitalist private-property systems.

Global technological change and political-economic transformations have been rapid in the current era and women's lives have been affected by these changes in contradictory ways. In the newly industrializing economies of the Third World, as we explain in Part 3, women are the major participants in new export industries. With the extension of international markets, women have, on the other hand, lost economic resources and jobs disproportionately relative to men.

The dominant view of the United Nations (UN) staff, as expressed in *Women in a Changing Global Economy* (United Nations, 1994), is that the negative effects of economic transformation are short term and are caused by structural inequalities which limit women's access to resources. Legal and cultural constraints restrict women's response to new market incentives. This perspective has led UN agencies to work in two directions simultaneously: at the same time that both the International Monetary Fund (IMF) and the World Bank have been enforcing economic policies which have indirectly hurt women and children (see below), other UN bodies have been sponsoring legal and structural changes which have the aim of allowing women more access to economic resources (like land and credit). The UN expects that, in this way, in the long term women will be able to benefit from market reforms which have affected them adversely in the short run.

In Part 5 of the reader, we discuss the efforts of international agencies and

grassroots organizations to empower women, both economically and politically. Here we focus on the actual changes and real issues and problems of
women experiencing transformations of both state policies and
political–economic systems.

A. STRUCTURAL ADJUSTMENT AND WOMEN

The debt crises experienced by most underdeveloped countries in the 1980s
led to cutbacks in international lending. (The origins of these crises are
explained in our General Introduction.) In order to ensure loan repayment, the
bilateral and multilateral international lending agencies, predominantly the
IMF and the World Bank, proceeded to develop a number of
political–economic strategies, known collectively as structural adjustment,
which were then pressed upon less developed countries seeking the re-
financing of loans. These policies have taken economic directions which the
IMF/World Bank hoped would put countries experiencing financial trouble on
a more solid financial footing in the short run and improve their long-term
international market positions. They have included: (1) cutbacks in public
spending in order to balance government budgets and service past debts; (2)
monetary policies designed to fight inflation by restricting the money supply
(and incomes); (3) the selling of government enterprises (privatization) in an
attempt to balance government budgets and improve business production
efficiency; and (4) the shift of manufacturing and agricultural sectors toward
production for export instead of for the domestic market, in order to improve
international balances. The export processing zones, described in Part 3,
have been further developed because of this export orientation.

Developmental goals such as improvements in health and education have
been adversely affected by these policies, as have short-run food balances
and nutrition. Publications by UNICEF (Cornia, Jolly and Stewart, 1987) and
the UN (1989) describe how women and children have suffered unequally
under structural adjustment policies (SAPs). The claim and hope of UN officials that carefully designed policies could change this situation, that is give
SAPs a human face, seem overly optimistic. This view is shared by Manuh
(Chapter 27).

The assumptions concerning resources, choices and market perfection
underlying the SAPs, even in their more humanized form, are inconsistent
with the inequalities and market imperfections which constitute actual
conditions in less developed countries. The clearly unequal impact of the
adjustment process is predictable if we analyse the disadvantages for
women under structural adjustment: (1) the largest cutbacks in the public
sector are in health and education programmes which affect women (both
as teachers and health workers and as consumers) and their children particularly; (2) decreases in real wages and employment and increases in prices
of necessities affect women and children worst because they are already
the poorest of the poor.

A major geographical region of special concern relative to the impact
of structural adjustment is sub-Saharan Africa. Food balances have been

negatively affected in several countries when export crops have been favoured over subsistence production. Adding to the misery of the countries which have followed SAP directives, the increases in the availability of coffee and cocoa on international markets caused price declines and drastic reductions in the value of crops grown at the expense of subsistence crops. Chapter 13, on gender relations in sub-Saharan Africa, shows some of the complexity of gender effects where women are responsible for the acquisition of food for their families but where their husbands control necessary resources. Liberalized markets in the region have increased class and gender inequalities because only those with control over or access to resources could take advantage of market incentives. We recommend the film 'Man Made Famine' (1985), produced by the *New Internationalist*, on this subject.

The continuing impacts of structural adjustment on women are detailed in *Unequal Burden* (1992) edited by Benería and Feldman. The particular repercussions of SAP in the Caribbean are described in *In the Shadows of the Sun* edited by Deere *et al.* (1990).

Readings

Chapter 22, an excerpt from *In the Shadows of the Sun*, provides a general perspective on the effects of structural adjustment on the poor. The high percentage of female-headed households in the Caribbean accentuates the universal problem of women's poverty, made worse by SAPs. In the face of hardship, women do the best they can to maintain subsistence for their families by increasing their work in the formal sector wherever possible and/or through informal and community activities.

In chapter 23, Manuh shows the disadvantages to women of SAPs even in a country, Ghana, which has been described by the UN as a 'model of success'. A large percentage of employed working-class women lost employment in the country as a result of SAPs, and female traders' markets disappeared because of policies which gave credit only to the larger-scale male trading enterprises. The power and control of men over women were in these ways tightened by adjustment policies throughout sub-Saharan Africa.

B. STATE POLICY AND WOMEN'S HEALTH, SEXUALITY AND REPRODUCTIVE RIGHTS

Family policies in general and particularly the reproductive rights of women are decided upon within a cultural, religious and political–economic context. For example, when development planners have feared that population growth will outstrip that of output, these reproductive rights have often been restricted. Population-control efforts frequently use force or bribes (like money in exchange for sterilization) to control women's, or men's, reproductive potential. A different type of restriction on women's reproductive rights occurs when fundamentalist regimes limit access to family planning. Two recent works give an overview of global policies and conflicts in this area: Mueller (1993) and Sen and Snow (eds) (1994).

Further information on families and reproduction under two capitalist market systems can be found in the work of Jean Larson Pyle (1990, 1994). In Ireland the state has kept women out of the international labour force and has denied them access to birth control, reinforcing a traditional pro-natalist female role. In Singapore the government has moved from anti-natalist policies, prevalent when female labour was plentiful, to a pro-natalist stand now that there is a shortage of women's labour for use in export processing. These studies are recommended further reading on state policy and reproductive rights in the context of women's labour in the expansion of export processing. (See Part 2 for more information on how state policy influences intra-household power relations.)

Family policy under socialism is also influenced by socio-economic concerns and is likewise subservient to political–economic necessity. Hilda Scott's *Does Socialism Liberate Women?* (1974), is an influential source for understanding why Eastern European socialist state policy turned first in one direction, providing women with access to birth control, and then another, denial of access (because countries were concerned about declining population). Scott makes a convincing argument for government policy being determined by national, not women's, interests.

Important international forces, such as the increase in the intensity of nationalist movements, the advent of sexual tourism, and Cold War and post-Cold War militarism strongly affect women at the present time. Cynthia Enloe (1990) presents a feminist analysis of nationalism, militarism and women's sexuality on a world scale. Her work is an analysis of women in international politics, from those in the military to diplomatic wives. Central to her thinking is the engendered role of women in nationalist struggles. This global study is a pioneering work which warrants attention.

Military bases, established by the United States (US) in Third World countries during the Cold War period, created the conditions for the development of the sexual-tourism industry, which has, especially in Asia, grown to immense proportions. Wendy Lee (1991) analyses this particular extension of the global market-place and its disastrous impact on women.

Readings

Chapter 24 is a contemporary piece which shows Chinese socialist reproductive policy as a reflection of national, rather than women's interests. Dalsimer and Nisonoff describe the hardships women face under the concurrent privatization and one-child family plans. Women are at the pressure point when privatized holdings must be passed on by patrilineal inheritance, yet they have only one chance to produce a male heir.

A significant factor influencing state policy regarding reproductive rights is the international ideological climate for population control. This perspective is explained clearly in Chapter 25. Hartmann examines the contemporary international politics of population control, which show a tendency to blame both poverty and environmental degradation on women's fertility. The logical outgrowth of this stance is to limit population growth through contraceptive programmes, even though these are not supported with adequate general health-care institutions.

In the modern period, AIDS is increasingly affecting women's health. It has changed but not eliminated the sexual-tourism industry. Younger girls are often now used to reassure customers who fear infection from more experienced partners. AIDS has been spreading so rapidly in many less developed countries that policies with respect to its containment and the care of its victims have become important health issues. Many women are unaware that they are more likely to catch the disease through heterosexual transmission than are their male partners. In Chapter 26, Garcia-Moreno recounts how women sex workers in East Asia and in Africa are organizing to protect themselves, and how in Africa women are aiming to make AIDS a concern for all agencies working with women.

C. WOMEN AND IDEOLOGICAL CHANGE

The international women's movement has been growing in the midst of the conflicts between the major competing political ideologies of the last part of the twentieth century. New varieties of nationalism and new forms of religion have sprung up amidst the destruction of the Soviet bloc and the growth of global capitalism. Depending on the circumstances, either conflict or accommodation has characterized the interactions of feminist perspectives with such changes.

Religious ideologies have, in the late twentieth century, often challenged women's progress toward equality. It is from Protestantism that the 'fundamentalist' terminology was first derived; it was used to describe a return to basic Biblical tenets. Protestant fundamentalism has become an important and growing religious tendency in both the First and Third worlds, including several Latin American countries and in the Philippines. The Hindu fundamentalists, Hindutva have, meanwhile, been recruiting women to fight against feminism in India. Space does not permit us to review the ways in which these patriarchal religions have stepped up their attempts to limit women in their quest for equal access to resources and incomes. Moslem fundamentalism demands our attention, however, as a religion which determines state policy.

Islamic state fundamentalism is particularly important because it is, along with a considerably weakened socialism, the only prominent alternative ideology which has mounted a challenge to modern global capitalism. Its growth is also a particularly crucial issue for women because the religion captures state policy directly rather than simply resisting, bending or in other ways influencing political decision-making.

Readings

Delia Aguilar (Chapter 27) describes the conflicts and interconnections between feminism and the quest for national identity in the Philippine women's movement. She critiques a post-modernist-theory and -policy perspective which weights all issues and concerns equally, thereby leaving Third World women's movements with little focus.

The veil in Moslem countries has been used as a way to suppress women, first by traditional Moslem men and then more recently by nationalist movements (Enloe, 1990). In Chapter 28, Haleh Afshar shows how it has been used by Iranian leaders to constrict women's power and their spaces.

Hoodfar, in Chapter 29, looks at a different dimension of veiling; as a strategy to minimize conflicts in the life of working-class Moslem women. Because modern veiling can be a strategic choice where the fundamentalist movement does not control the state, the true impact on women of specific religious strictures should not be generalized throughout the Moslem world. Islamic fundamentalist state policies limit women's mobility, and their control over their own bodies (such as with what they wear), and restrict their access to education and economic resources. It is these constraints, rather than the act of veiling in itself, which are the central women's issues being confronted in fundamentalist-controlled countries.

D. WOMEN AND SOCIALIST TRANSFORMATIONS

The history of interconnections between women's liberation movements and those of socialism, as well as of their conflicts, is an important ongoing story. Since the advent of socialism, feminists have pointed out that the revolutionary-socialist primary focus on class analysis fails to analyse adequately the patriarchal family. This blind spot leads socialist leaders to neglect women's lack of access to productive resources such as land and raw materials.

With little acknowledgement of how class and patriarchy operate together within society, socialist leaders have often made policy decisions affecting relations of production that have had unintended and contradictory effects on class and family structure. The influence of Chinese patriarchy, for example, on the development of Chinese socialism has been discussed by Stacey (1983) while an analysis of how Vietnamese patriarchy subverted collective agriculture is included in works by Wiegersma (1988, 1991). These texts are recommended further reading in the misunderstanding and underestimating of the effect of patriarchy on collective processes, leading, thereby, to a misjudging of the results of socialist policies.

Women have often enthusiastically embraced socialist goals for reasons of clear self-interest. Sadly, women's political and economic advantages under socialism can be measured partially by what they lose when inequality increases as socialist economies are transformed. For example, the marketing of women's sexuality through pornography develops very quickly with economic transformation and the establishment of market capitalism. Legislation protecting women from night work or from pregnancy-related firings is quickly overturned and women's access to reproductive health care often threatened. A recent book on economic transformation and its impact on women around the world is that by Aslanbeigui et al. (eds) (1994).

Readings
Chapter 30, a short article by Benería, discusses the intersection of women's interests and the socialist vision. National-liberation movements have, historically, been supported by women who have fought in liberation struggles in

their own interests. Usually, after the national liberation struggle has been won, women have been expected to return to many of their former roles. In light of this experience, Benería develops a set of questions which feminists need to ask about alternative societies, which can help us envision a truly feminist and socialist form of social and political organization. In Chapter 31 Meurs describes problems arising for women under the transformation of socialized institutions like collective agriculture into private market-based institutions. Decollectivization is shown to lead to increased gender inequality as women's access to jobs is threatened more than men's. The author suggests ways to avoid some of these negative impacts of economic transformation on women.

FURTHER READING

THE IMPACT OF STRUCTURAL ADJUSTMENT ON WOMEN

Afshar, Haleh and Carolyne Dennis (1992) *Women and Adjustment Policies in the Third World*, New York: St Martin's Press.

Arizpe, L. *et al.* (1987) 'Effects of the Economic Crisis on the Living Conditions of Peasant Women in Mexico', in UNICEF, *The Invisible Adjustment: Poor Women and the Economic Crisis*, Chili: Santiago, Alfa Beta Impresores.

Aslanbeigui, Nahid, Steven Pressman and Gail Summerfield (eds) (1994) *Women in the Age of Economic Transformation*, New York and London: Routledge.

Benería, Lourdes and Shelley Feldman (1992) *Unequal Burden: Economic Crisis, Persistent Poverty and Women's Work*, Boulder, CO: Westview Press.

Bolles, Lynn (1992) 'Surviving Manley and Seaga: Case Studies of Women's Responses to Structural Adjustment Policies', *Review of Radical Political Economics*, Vol. 23, Nos 3–4.

Buvinic, M. (1986) 'Projects for Women in the Third World: Explaining their Misbehavior', *World Development*, Vol. 14, No. 5.

—— (1989) 'Investing in Poor Women: The Psychology of Donor Support', *World Development*, Vol. 17, No. 7.

Cornia, Giovanni, Richard Jolly and Frances Stewart (1987) *Adjustment With a Human Face*, Published for UNICEF, Oxford and New York: Oxford University Press.

Dalsimer, Marilyn and Laurie Nisonoff (1984) 'The New Economic Readjustment Policies: Implications for Chinese Urban Working Women', *Review of Radical Political Economics*, Vol. 16, No. 1.

Deere, Carmen *et al.* (eds) (1990) *In the Shadows of the Sun: Caribbean Development Alternatives and US Policy*. Boulder, CO: Westview Press.

Deere, Carmen Diana and Magdalena Leon (eds) (1987) *Rural Women and State Policy: Feminist Perspectives on Latin American Agricultural Development*, Boulder, CO: Westview Press.

Elson, D. (1989) 'The Impact of Structural Adjustment on Women: Concepts and Issues', in B. Onimode (ed.) *The IMF, the World Bank and the African Debt*, Vol. 2, London: Zed Books.

Lyon, Joy (1991) 'Evaluating Income Generating Projects for Women', in Nanneke Redclift and M. Thea Sinclair (eds), *Working Women: International Perspectives on Labor and Gender Ideology*, London: Routledge.

Meena, Ruth (1984) 'Foreign Aid and the Question of Women's Liberation', *The African Review*, Vol. 11, No. 1.

New Internationalist (1985) 'Man Made Famine', a film.

Schrijvers, Joke (1988) 'Blueprint for Undernourishment: The Mahaweli River Dev. Scheme in Sri Lanka', in Bina Agarwal *Structures of Patriarchy*, New Delhi: Kali for Women, and London: Zed Books.

Sparr, Pamela (1994) *Mortgaging Women's Lives: Feminist Critiques of Structural Adjustment*, London: Zed Books.

Van der Gaag, Nikki (1995) 'Women: Still Something to Shout About', *The New Internationalist*, No. 270, August.

United Nations (1989) 'Women, Debt and Adjustment', *1989 World Survey on the Role of Women in Development*, New York: United Nations.

—— (1994) 'Women in a Changing Global Economy', *1994 World Survey on the Role of Women in Development*, New York: United Nations.

Vickers, Jeanne (ed.) (1991) *Women and the World Economic Crisis*, London: Zed Books.

Wiegersma, Nan (1994) 'State Policy and the Restructuring of Women's Industries in Nicaragua', in Nahid Aslanbeigui *et al.* (eds) (1994).

THE IMPACT OF STATE POLICY ON WOMEN'S HEALTH, REPRODUCTIVE RIGHTS AND SEXUALITY

Bunster-Burotto, Ximena (1986) 'Surviving Beyond Fear: Women and Torture in Latin America', June Nash and Helen Safa (eds) *Women and Change in Latin America*, Bergin and Garvey Publishers, South Hadley, MA (publisher currently in New York).

Chee Heng Leng (1988) 'Babies to Order', in Bina Agarwal *Structures of Patriarchy*, New Delhi: Kali for Women, and London: Zed Books.

Croll, Elizabeth, Delia Davin and Penny Kane (eds) (1985) *China's One-Child Family Policy*, New York: St Martin's Press.

Dalsimer, Marlyn and Laurie Nisonoff (1987) 'The Implications of the New Agricultural and One-Child Family Policies for Rural Chinese Women', *Feminist Studies*, Vol. 13, No. 3.

Duggan, Lynn (1986) 'From Birth Control to Population Control: Depo-provera in Southeast Asia', in Kathleen McDonnell (ed.) *Adverse Effects: Women and the Pharmaceutical Industry*, Penang, Malaysia: International Organization of Consumers Unions.

Enloe, Cynthia (1990) *Bananas Beaches and Bases: Making Feminist Sense of International Politics*, Berkeley, CA: University of California Press.

Garcia-Moreno, Claudia (1992) 'Aids: Women Are Not Just Transmitters', in Tina Wallace and Candida March (eds) *Changing Perceptions*, Boston, MA: Oxfam.

Hartmann, Betsy and Hilary Standing (1985) *Food, Saris, and Sterilization*, London: BIAG.

—— (1995) *Reproductive Rights and Wrongs* (revised edn), New York: Harper and Row.

Kelkar, Govind (1988) 'New Agricultural Policies in Rural China and the Woman Question', in Bina Agarwal (ed.) *Structures of Patriarchy*, New Delhi: Kali For Women, and London: Zed Books.

Kisekka, Mere Nakateregga (ed.) (1992) *Women's Health Issues in Nigeria*, Zaria: Tamaza Publishing Co. Ltd.

Lee, Wendy (1991) 'Prostitution and Tourism in South-east Asia', in Nanneke Redclift, and M. Thea Sinclair, (eds) *Working Women: International Perspectives on Labor and Gender Ideology*, London: Routledge.

Mueller, Ruth Dixon (1993) *Population Policy and Women's Rights*, New York: Praeger.

Ostergard, Lise (ed) (1992) *Gender and Development: A Practical Guide*, London: Routledge.

Pyle, Jean Larson (1990) *The State and Women in the Economy*, Albany, NY: SUNY Press.

—— (1994) 'The Impact of State Policy on Women's Labor Force Participation in Singapore', in Aslanbeigui, N. *et al.* (eds) (1994).

Rothblum, Esther D. and Ellen Cole (eds) (1990) *Women and Mental Health in Africa*, New York: Haworth Press.

Scott, Hilda (1974) *Does Socialism Liberate Women?* Boston, MA: Beacon Press.

Sen, Gita (1984) 'Subordination and Sexual Control: A Comparative View of the Control of Women', *Radical Review of Political Economy* Vol. 16, No. 1.

—— and Snow, Rachel, C. (eds) (1994) *Power and Decision: The Social Control of Reproduction*, Boston: Harvard University Press.

Wichterich, Christa (1988) 'From the Struggle Against 'Overpopulation' to the Industrialization of Human Production', *Reproductive and Genetic Engineering*, Vol. 1, No. 1.

WOMEN AND IDEOLOGICAL CHANGE

Afshar, Haleh (ed.) (1987) *Women, State and Ideology,* Albany NY: SUNY.

—— (1988) 'Behind the Veil: The Public and Private Faces of Khomeini's Politics on Iranian Women', in B. Agarwal (ed.) *Structures of Patriarchy*, New Delhi: Kali for Women, and London: Zed Books.

Hatem, Mervat (1985) 'Conservative Patriarchal Modernization in the Arabian Gulf', *Contemporary Marxism*, Vol. 11.

Jayawardena, Kumari (1986) *Feminism and Nationalism in the Third World*, London: Zed Books.

Mahl (1995) 'Women on the Edge of Time (Algeria)', *The New Internationalist*, No. 270.

Najjar, Orayb Aref (1992) 'Between Nationalism and Feminism: The Palestinian Answer', in Jill M. Bystydzienski (ed.) *Women Transforming Politics*, Bloomington and Indianapolis: Indiana University Press.

Ong, Aihwa (1990) 'State Versus Islam: Malay Families, Women's Bodies, and the Body Politic in Malaysia', *American Ethnologist*, Vol. 17.

Tabari, Azar and Nahid Yeganeh (1982) *In the Shadow of Islam: The Women's Movement in Iran*, London: Zed Books.

WOMEN AND SOCIALIST TRANSFORMATIONS

Aslanbeigui, Nahid, Steven Pressman and Gail Summerfield (eds) (1994) *Women in the Age of Economic Transformation*, New York and London: Routledge.

Bengelsdorf, Carolee (1985) 'On the Problem of Studying Women in Cuba', *Race and Class*, Vol. 27, No. 2.

Chinchilla, Norma Stolz (1990) 'Revolutionary Popular Feminism in Nicaragua: Articulating Class, Gender, and National Sovereignty', *Gender and Society*, Vol. 4, No. 3.

Cole, Johnetta (1980) 'Women in Cuba: The Revolution within the Revolution', *Comparative Perspectives of Third World Women*, New York: Praeger.

Croll, Elizabeth (1986) 'Rural Production and Reproduction: Socialist Development Experiences', in E. Leacock and H. Safa (eds) *Women's Work*, South Hadley, MA: Bergen and Garvey.

Duggan, Lynn (1995) 'Restacking the Deck: Family Policy and Women's Fall-back

Position in Germany Before and After Unification', *Feminist Economics*, Vol. 1, No. 1.

Jayawardena, Kumari (1986) *Feminism and Nationalism in the Third World*, London: Zed Books.

Kelkar, Govind (1988) 'Two Steps Back? New Agricultural Policies in Rural China and the Woman', in Bina Agarwal, *Structures of Patriarchy*, New Delhi: Kali for Women, and London: Zed Books.

Kruks, Sonia F., Rayna Rapp and Marilyn B. Young (eds) (1989) *Promissory Notes: Women in the Transition to Socialism*, New York: Monthly Review Press.

Leven, Bozena (1994) 'The Status of Women and Poland's Transition to a Market Economy', in N. Aslanbeigui *et al.* (eds) (1994).

McMahon, Patrice C. (1994) 'The Effect of Economic and Political Reforms on Soviet/Russian Women', in Aslanbeigui, N. *et al.* (eds) (1994).

Meurs, Mieke (1994) 'From Hoes to Hoes: Agricultural Mechanization and Bulgarian Rural Women Under Central Planning', *Review of Radical Political Economics*, Vol. 26, No. 4, December.

Molyneux, M. (1982) 'Legal Reform and Socialist Revolution in the Democratic Republic of Yemen: Women in the Family', *International Journal of Sociology of Law*, Vol. 13, No. 2.

—— (1982) 'Socialist Societies Old and New', *Monthly Review*, Vol. 34, No. 3, July–August.

—— (1986) 'Mobilization without Emancipation', Fagen, Deere and Coraggio, (eds) *Transition and Development*, New York: Monthly Review Press.

Nazzari, Muriel (1983) 'The "Woman Question" in Cuba: An Analysis of Material Constraints on its Solution', in Gelpi, Hartsock, Novak, Strober (eds) *Women and Poverty*, Chicago: Univ. of Chicago Press.

Ridd, Rosemary and Helen Callaway (eds) (1987) *Women and Political Conflict: Portraits of Struggle in Times of Crisis*, New York: New York University Press.

Scott, Hilda (1974) *Does Socialism Liberate Women?*, Boston, MA: Beacon Press.

Stacey, Judith (1983) *Patriarchy and Socialist Revolution in China*, Berkeley, CA: University of California Press.

Wiegersma, Nancy (1988) *Vietnam: Peasant Land, Peasant Revolution: Patriarchy and Collectivity in the Rural Economy*. London: MacMillan Ltd.

—— (1991) 'Peasant Patriarchy and the Subversion of the Collective in Vietnam', in *Review of Radical Political Economics*, Vol. 23, nos 3–4, Fall.

—— (1994) 'State Policy and the Restructuring of Women's Industries in Nicaragua', in N, Aslanbeigui *et al.* (1994).

22. IMPACT OF THE ECONOMIC CRISIS ON POOR WOMEN AND THEIR HOUSEHOLDS
CARMEN DIANA DEERE, HELEN SAFA, PEGGY ANTROBUS
et al. (eds)

Poor women, especially those with families, have had to bear the major brunt of the regional economic crisis and the structural adjustment policies instituted in the Caribbean. The economic crunch has hit women harder than men because women's disadvantaged occupational distribution, and more limited access to resources, makes them more vulnerable; moreover their roles as producers and consumers are different. In addition, women have always assumed a primary role in household survival strategies, securing and allocating usually meagre cash and other resources to enable their families to make ends meet.

The economic crisis has made it extremely difficult for families to survive on a single wage, forcing additional women into the labour force to meet the rising cost of living and the decreased wage-earning capacity of men due to unemployment or wage cuts, or due to their absence as a result of migration. At the same time structural adjustment policies are forcing families to absorb a greater share of the cost of survival as a result of the cutbacks in social services, such as health and education, and the elimination or reduction of subsidies on food, transportation and utilities. By shifting more responsibility for survival from the state to the household, structural adjustment policies are increasing the burden on the poor, especially women.[1]

We shall examine the impact of the economic crisis and structural adjustment policies on poor women and their households in the Caribbean, focusing on Jamaica and the Dominican Republic, two of the countries most severely affected. In order to deal with balance of payments difficulties, both governments signed standby agreements with the International Monetary Fund (IMF): Jamaica in 1977–78, 1981 and 1984–85, and the Dominican Republic in 1983 and 1985. Similar structural adjustment policies were instituted in both countries, including cutbacks in social services, continuing devaluation of the national currency, liberalization of regulations regarding imports, removal of food subsidies and price controls on basic consumer goods, and the promotion of non-traditional exports.[2]

As a result of the crisis in the external sector, austerity measures and high debt-servicing payments, GDP per capita declined in both countries, but more precipitously in Jamaica than in the Dominican Republic, since the economic crisis generally has been more severe and of longer duration in Jamaica. In 1988, per capita Gross Domestic Product (GDP) in the Dominican Republic was US $1509, below that of Jamaica, which was $1843. Jamaica's GDP per capita in 1988 was, however, lower in real terms than it had been in either 1980 or 1970.[3] The resulting economic crunch has dramatically highlighted the structures of female subordination and exploitation which have long characterized both countries.

HOW THE CRUNCH IS FELT

The impact of the crisis and structural adjustment policies has been devastating for poor women due primarily to three factors: (1) a sharp fall in wages and rising female unemployment; (2) the unequal burden which the rising cost of living imposes on women; and (3) the reductions in public spending for services on which women rely.

GROWING HUNGER AND POORER HEALTH

The combined effect of the rising cost of living, particularly rising food prices, and decreased health care is that malnutrition as well as mortality from curable diseases is on the rise. UNICEF has documented the often dramatic changes in consumption and dietary patterns induced by the crisis, with severe implications for health and nutrition. There is a growing concentration on cheap sources of calories such as rice or yucca in the diet, and declining intakes of protein, such as milk or meat. Women and young girls are the family members most likely to be affected by declining food consumption, since preference is given to male wage earners.[4]

In Jamaica, a decline in the nutritional status of children under the age of four years, with the percentage of malnourished rising from 38 per cent in 1978 to 41 per cent in 1985, sums up the effects of these policies.[5] This trend was confirmed by hospital admissions; the proportion of children under five admitted to the Bustamante Children's Hospital for malnutrition and malnutrition/gastroenteritis, for example, rose from 2.7

per cent of all admissions in 1980 to 8.4 per cent in 1985. In addition, the percentage of pregnant women screened at prenatal clinics who were deemed anaemic rose from 23 per cent in 1981 to 43 per cent in 1985.[6] Moreover, the infant mortality rate has increased from 16 per thousand in 1980 to 18 per thousand in 1987.[7]

In the Dominican Republic, despite dramatic improvements in mortality and life expectancy rates starting in the 1950s, infant mortality in 1987 still stood at 65 per thousand, a figure which is surpassed only by Haiti. The rate of infant mortality tends to be generally under-reported and is considerably higher in rural areas and among the lowest income groups.[8] Maternal mortality, which also differs significantly in urban and rural areas and by income group, stood at 56 per 100,000 in 1980.[9] In one major maternity hospital in the capital of Santo Domingo, maternal mortality, while much lower than in rural areas, increased from 15 to 22 per 100,000 from 1981 to 1985.[10]

According to a study conducted by the Central Bank in 1976–77, 90 per cent of the Dominican population consume less than the recommended minimum of 2300 calories and 60 grams of protein per day, with the poorest significantly below this minimum standard. Among children aged one to four, the level of malnutrition in 1984 reached 40.8 per cent.[11] A 1981 US Agency for International Development (AID) study found the highest prevalence of malnutrition among infants aged five to eight months. The authors attribute this to a variety of causes: the abrupt cessation of breastfeeding as mothers are forced by economic circumstances to return to work, dilution of baby formulas to make them stretch, and lack of potable water used in infant feeding.[12] It is estimated that one-fourth of all babies born in the Dominican Republic are children of malnourished mothers.[13] In 1983, one-fourth of all children admitted to a major children's hospital in Santo Domingo died, not of incurable diseases but of the combined effects of poverty, ill health and poor health care.[14]

HOW HOUSEHOLDS SURVIVE

Caribbean women are not simply victims of economic hardship; they and their families are devising innovative strategies for dealing with it. Four main strategies can be detected: (1) women are entering the labour force in increasing numbers, particularly as workers in export-processing industries; (2) along with men, they are engaging in a wide variety of activities in the informal sector; (3) households are diversifying their survival strategies, changing living and consumption patterns; and (4) women are joining, and even predominating in, the international migration stream, especially to the United States. All of these constitute important economic and social changes of the last decade.

INCREASING LABOUR-FORCE PARTICIPATION

At first glance the growing number of women in the labour force may appear contradictory in view of increased unemployment and under-employment in the Caribbean generally. However, women are forced into the labour force precisely because of increased unemployment among men and because real wages of employed household members are decreasing, contributing to an overall reduction in household income. Women are able to find jobs even when men are not, because they work for lower wages, because the labour market in the Caribbean (as elsewhere) is highly segregated by gender, and because a high percentage of women work in the informal sector.

Several factors in the development process in the Dominican Republic have favoured the dramatic increase in the number of women entering the labour force (from 11 per cent in 1960 to 37.5 per cent in 1980), including urbanization, the growth of the service sector and the growth of export-processing industries. At the same time, changes have taken place in the female population in the last two decades which have made them more employable, including a rise in educational levels and a marked decline in fertility.[15] It would seem that many of these same factors help explain the high percentage of Jamaican women in the labour force. In the English-speaking Caribbean, however, women's participation rates have traditionally been high, and in Jamaica in 1985 stood at 62 per cent for women over 14 years of age.[16]

Export manufacturers have shown a preference for women workers because they are cheaper to employ, less likely to unionize and have greater patience for the tedious, monotonous work involved in assembly operations. Although Jamaica was initially targeted as the showpiece of the Caribbean Basin Initiative (CBI), export manufacturing never took off on the scale anticipated. The bulk of employment created in export manufacturing in Jamaica in recent years has occurred, not through the CBI (which excluded textiles and garments from its duty-free provisions) but through the preferences created by US Tariff Code 807 for apparel assembled overseas from US components.[17] Between 1981 and 1985, an additional 6800 women found employment in the manufacturing sector, so that the proportion of women employed in manufacturing rose from 7 to 8.7 per cent of the female labour force, the majority presumably employed in apparel production.

While data are unavailable on whether the increased number of women employed in export manufacturing are located in formal vs. informal-(domestic homeworkers) sector jobs, there is some evidence that garment manufacturers appear to be turning to the use of domestic homeworkers as a way of cutting their labour costs. By contracting out to homeworkers, they avoid the payment of fringe benefits and the costs of factory installations as well as any possible threat of unionization. Moreover, homeworkers offer manufacturers considerable flexibility in managing the size of their workforce, which can be scaled up or down with market fluctuations, clearly offering these women workers little stability of employment. The bulk of these manufacturers appear to be Jamaican nationals who are linked to US companies through subcontracting arrangements. Free-trade zones in Jamaica have had less appeal to US firms than have their counterparts in Haiti or the Dominican Republic. In 1987 total employment in foreign-owned firms in the Kingston Export Free Zone was only 8500, far lower than in the Dominican Republic.[18]

A study done for AID of the apparel industry in Jamaica revealed that US firms see unions as a major obstacle to investment, although only one of the twenty-two factories in the Kingston Export Free Zone is unionized.[19] Nonetheless, fear of labour unrest may explain the preference of US firms for subcontracting because there have been frequent public protests against such work abuses as low pay, excessive and forced overtime, occupational health hazards, arbitrary suspension and dismissal for protesting, and absence of trade union representation. Such complaints are common among workers employed in export manufacturing, and have also been voiced in the Dominican Republic.

The Dominican Republic has seen a dramatic growth in export manufacturing in recent years. The greatest increase has taken place precisely during the years of structural adjustment, when the number of firms in the free-trade zones increased from 103 in 1983 to 224 in 1988, and the number of employees more than quadrupled, reaching an estimated 85,000 in 1988.[20] The overwhelming majority (84 per cent) of these workers in export manufacturing are women.

One of the reasons for the explosion of export manufacturing in the Dominican Republic is the general wage reduction resulting from devaluation. Between 1981 and 1984 there was a 17 per cent reduction in the average real wage in manufacturing, despite increases in the minimum wage. At the rate of exchange prevailing in August 1986, the average wage in free-trade zones was approximately US $90 monthly.[21] In addition, succumbing to pressure from industrialists in the free-trade zones, the Dominican government granted them access to the parallel currency exchange market, which enabled them to buy local currency at an even more favourable rate. This new exchange-rate policy lowered operating costs by approximately 30 per cent, and is another major factor behind the rapid growth in activity in the zones in the last few years. Because of devaluation, average hourly wages are now at approximately the same level as in Haiti, the poorest country of the hemisphere.[22]

In addition to low wages and various government incentives, the weakness of the labour movement in the Dominican Republic attracts US investors to the free-trade zones. There are no unions in the zones and workers are fired and blacklisted with other plants if any union activity is detected. Women who have tried to take complaints of mistreatment or unjust dismissal to the government Labor Office have generally been rejected in favour of management. Workers complain of the lack of public transportation, proper eating facilities, adequate medical services and child care. Labour turnover is high, since many workers cannot withstand the pressure of high production quotas, strict discipline, sexual harassment and a 44 hour work week, with overtime sometimes imposed in addition.

In a study of Dominican free-trade zones conducted in 1981, it was found that most of the workers are under 30 years old, but in a departure from the global pattern of young, single women, over one-half are married and one-fourth are female heads of households.[23] Their need to work is demonstrated by the fact that nearly three-fourths of the female heads of households and nearly half of the married women claim they are the principal breadwinners for their families. In fact, employers in the Dominican Republic indicate a preference for women with children because they feel their need to work ensures greater job commitment.[24]

While growth in demand for female labour has been greatest in manufacturing, women in the Dominican Republic have also been employed as wage labourers in the new agro industries that have flourished recently due to the CBI. A 1985 study of rural women revealed that wages in these industries are even lower than in manufacturing, averaging three to six pesos daily in 1985, and the work is very unstable, concentrated in the harvest season. Many women also work as unremunerated family labour on small farms, some of which produce for agribusiness on a contract basis.[25]

In short, the growth of employment for women in domestic homework, in the free-trade zones and in agribusiness represents strategies by industries to reduce production costs at a time of intense international competition. The growth in export manufacturing employment also represents the adaptation by poor women to the need to augment their earnings. But while export promotion has increased the demand for female labour, it has also taken advantage of women's inferior position in the labour market and reinforced their subordination through poorly paid, dead-end jobs.

Women workers in the free-trade zones of both the Dominican Republic and Jamaica have received little or no support from their governments in their efforts to achieve better wages and working conditions. Both governments have attempted to control labour unrest in order to attract foreign investment. Under these circumstances it is understandable why workers have not organized nor protested more vehemently, although in March 1988 there were widespread strikes among Jamaican garment workers in favour of higher wages and better working conditions. Thus the failure to improve working conditions lies more with the lack of support women workers receive from government, political parties and unions than with the women themselves. At present (1990) these women workers have no adequate vehicles to express their grievances or to transform their sense of exploitation (which is very real) into greater worker solidarity. These difficulties are compounded for women employed in the urban and rural informal sectors.

Despite its disadvantages, most women still regard jobs in export processing, particularly the free-trade zones, as preferable to work in the informal sector. The informal sector in the Caribbean still includes a high percentage of domestic servants and petty vendors, as well as other self-employed workers whose activities range from food preparation for sale on the streets to home repairs and other services, as well as artisan production. Working in this sector generally provides no labour protection, minimum wages, social security or other benefits, but for growing numbers of men and women there is little alternative.

In Jamaica, the 38 per cent of women working in the informal sector is much higher than that of men (12 per cent).[26] Undoubtedly this reflects the high percentage of Jamaican women who work as 'higglers' or petty vendors, trading in homegrown foodstuffs and local manufactured goods. Women's involvement in the marketing of foodstuffs for the domestic market dates back to the days of slavery, and has traditionally provided them with the flexibility needed to manage their dual roles and a certain degree of independence. Studies on higglers in the English-speaking Caribbean suggest that women comprise over 80 per cent of the population engaged in trading and commercial activities.[27]

In recent years the role of higglers itself has been transformed, as some women now travel internationally, buying clothing and other consumer goods in Miami to sell in Jamaica or selling Jamaican goods in Haiti and other areas.[28] The complex web of inter-relationships in which these women engage at different levels and their creativity in managing their business is quite impressive—finding loans, identifying 'sure sells', bargaining wholesale purchases, devising book-keeping and accounting systems, learning the intricacies of air and boat travel, and learning new languages.[29]

In the Dominican Republic, the economically active population in the informal sector has grown from 39 per cent in 1980 to 45 per cent in 1983, with men outnumbering women. Unemployment in the 1980s would surely have been much higher were it not for the growth of this sector. Nevertheless, jobs in the informal sector pay 60 per cent less on average than those in the formal sector. Seventy per cent of women in the urban informal sector earn less than the estimated poverty level of income.[30] The majority of women working in the sector are employed in domestic service, which pays the lowest wages and has practically no labour protection.[31]

The growth of the informal sector in the Dominican Republic may also reflect state policy, since international development assistance has increasingly been encouraging the growth of micro-enterprises in Latin America and the Caribbean. Because of their capacity for absorbing labour and their very low costs, micro-enterprises have been identified as enjoying a comparative advantage in a highly competitive international market. Micro-enterprise development has thus been getting increasing support from both the public and private sector in terms of credit, access to raw materials and foreign exchange, and other privileges formerly reserved exclusively for the formal sector.[32]

THE INTENSIFICATION OF HOUSEHOLD SURVIVAL STRATEGIES

The increasing informalization of Caribbean economies has brought the household to the limelight, as it is here that strategies for generating incomes are conceived and coordinated by men and women, and across generations. In the context of the economic crisis, the household has acquired new importance as a centre for small-scale entrepreneurial activity, as women and men prepare foods for the market, organize and package agricultural produce, sew and embroider, do macramé and craft jewellery, grow and sell ornamental plants, collect aluminum cans and, as we have noted, engage in industrial homework for garment, electronic and computer industries. Women in poor Caribbean households have always sought to stretch family income by producing goods at home rather than purchasing them in stores and by making use of extended family and neighbourhood networks. The economic crisis has obliged women to intensify these activities in order to cope with declining household income, increasing prices and cuts in government services.

An understanding of Caribbean concepts of 'family' and 'community' is important here in understanding women's responses to the crisis. The structures of the family and of the community have emerged out of the history and culture of the region. They represent reconstructions of human communities out of the dehumanizing experience of slavery, the destruction, reconstruction and resistance of the African family, and the specific realities and requirements of the local economy.[33] For the majority of the black, working-class population of the Caribbean, the concept of family often extends beyond the household unit or nuclear family, beyond the neighbourhood or village, and even beyond the country, to encompass a network of mutually supporting members. Similarly, the concept of 'community' may transcend spatial dimensions to include people who are linked together in communities of interest—savings groups, the sports club or closely knit religious groups.

The persistence of these networks and associations has been important in building links among different social classes and in enabling women to respond creatively to the current crisis. For a central feature of women's survival strategies is the extent to which they draw on networks of family and community in times of hardship. These networks provide both a mode of survival and a source of affirmation—crucial for emotional support as well as for the empowerment of women.

However, by providing a retreat from an exploitative system, Caribbean forms of the family and community also facilitate the continuation of exploitation and the inequitable distribution of resources. It appears that governments have in fact taken advantage of women's ability to draw on traditional networks of support to introduce policies which have been particularly devastating to women and those for whose care they have been traditionally responsible—children and the elderly.

In Jamaica, for example, women have extended household exchange networks, which increases the amount of goods, services and occasionally cash that flows among relatives, friends, and neighbours. Many women have taken advantage of commissaries at their place of work to purchase scarce items such as dairy goods or baby-care products whether or not they need them themselves in order to exchange them for food, child care or other needed services. Rural and urban kin have linked up, with higglers providing their urban kin with fresh vegetables in return for manufactured goods such as flashlight batteries. A conscious attempt is made to avoid market transactions because of the increasing scarcity of cash.

Survival strategies vary with household composition, and one emerging response to the crisis is to increase household size. Expanding the number of people living in a household potentially increases the number of income earners as well as those available to undertake chores and child care. Dominican sociologist Isis Duarte believes that the incorporation of additional members into the household as a survival strategy may be one explanation for the continued large size of households in the Dominican Republic, which has remained at about 5.3 persons since 1920, despite the sharp decline in fertility levels since the 1960s.[34] Large households generally consist of extended families, among whom 69 per cent have five or more members. Extended families continue to account for approximately 30 per cent of all households, and the percentage is higher in urban than in rural areas, which runs counter to most demographic expectations. The increasingly high cost of housing may be one factor that forces families to double up and results in severe overcrowd-ing among the urban poor.

In a 1981 study in Kingston it was found that there was a greater tendency among female-headed households than among those headed by a stable co-residential couple to incorporate additional kin into the household.[35] These are added for two reasons: they free women from some domestic chores and child care so that they can be full-time workers, and they often contribute to household income through infor-mal-sector activities. Whenever possible, new household members are expected to help with the payment of rent and utilities; this is particu-larly expected of men joining households, whether they are stable part-ners or boyfriends in visiting unions, or fathers of one or more of the woman's children. However, because of the high rate of unemployment among men, particularly in the urban areas, many men are unable to fulfil these traditional financial obligations. In this study, less than a quarter of the women living in visiting unions and none of the single women then living alone with their children received regular support from their boyfriends or the fathers of their children.

While a series of sexual partners may have been a traditional means by which Jamaican women sought financial support, it would seem that the devastating decline in male earning capacity in recent years has made women even more reliant on their own wages and other sources of income. In the study just cited, over 80 per cent of the women who headed households were directly responsible for all major household expenditures; 63 per cent of those in the stable unions also assumed this responsibility. Throughout the English-speaking Caribbean, women express the need to be economically 'independent' as one central to their lives.[36]

In the Dominican Republic, although women have been joining the workforce in increasing numbers, the role of the male breadwinner has remained more intact. The 1981 study of Dominican free-trade zones referred to earlier found that husbands are still considered the principal economic provider in many if not most households, and are responsible for providing such basic items as food and housing. However, the great majority of working women also maintain that their families could not survive without their wages, suggesting that their wages are not just supplementary, but rather, crucial to the household's well-being.[37]

Nonetheless, women's contribution to the household economy is greatest among female heads of household; as mentioned previously, the proportion of such households has been increasing since the 1970s. While the 1981 Census puts the figure at 20.6 per cent, other estimates reach as high as 33.5 per cent.[38] It may be that the increased difficulties men are facing in fulfilling their roles as economic providers are partly responsible for this increase. Although female heads of household have higher rates of labour-force participation than married women, they are a particularly vulnerable group, with lower incomes, higher rates of unemployment and twice as likely to find employment as only occasional labourers as are male heads.[39]

23. GHANA: WOMEN IN THE PUBLIC AND INFORMAL SECTORS UNDER THE ECONOMIC RECOVERY PROGRAMME

TAKYIWAA MANUH

In Ghana, there have been few micro-level analyses of the impacts of the Economic Recovery Programme/Structural Adjustment Programme (ERP/SAP) since it was implemented in 1984; most accounts, notably by the World Bank and the Ghana government, concentrate on macro-level impacts. Additionally, in general, assessment of the impacts on specific groups is constrained by the lack of reliable and timely data and, in particular, by the absence of gender-disaggregated data. This chapter analyses the impacts of the ERP/SAP on women's employment since 1984, with a focus on their employment in both the formal and informal sectors. The ERP/SAP's impact on employment has been disastrous, leading to worries over equity and general welfare considerations. The urban poor, rural dwellers, retrenched persons,[1] the unemployed, women and their children particularly have been identified as vulnerable groups, and through the Programme of Action to Mitigate the Social Costs of Adjustment (PAMSCAD) some poverty-alleviation measures have been initiated. This chapter argues that these measures are inadequate and also ignore the structure of most households in Ghana where there is little pooling of resources or joint decision-making, thus leading to intra-household differences. In this situation, it is women's access to resources or control of an independent income that ensure a certain level of well-being for them and their households.

Female labour-participation rates in Ghana are relatively high. About 90 per cent [of women] are self-employed or unpaid family workers in agriculture, agro-based industries and trade. Women's participation in waged employment increased from 47,000 in 1970 to 207,000 in 1984, compared with 670,000 men. These increases reflect the investments in women's education and their subsequent ability to find jobs in offices and industrial establishments. Most women waged workers are nurses, teachers, secretaries and clerks in lower echelons of the professions, except in nursing which is female-dominated, with both the Chief and Deputy Nursing Officer being women.

Whilst waged employment is not large in absolute terms, its significance lies in the conditions of work for wage-earning employees and their participation in administration and decision-making. Most categories of lower-ranked employees in both public and private sectors are unionized, with women constituting about 25 per cent of members in the 17 unions that comprise the Ghana Trades Union Congress.[2] Few women are, however, found in leadership positions even within the unions they dominate; the women's section within the Ghana Trades Union Congress is only one of five sections under the Organisation Department and faces several constraints.

As a result of union activity, waged employees benefit from minimum conditions such as regular, albeit low, wages,[3] regular hours of work and some degree of social security. Until the advent of the ERP/SAP, most public employees and their dependants enjoyed free health care; women employees are granted a specific period of maternity leave with pay.[4] Most women waged workers must balance domestic and maternal responsibilities with work demands and undergo role strains and conflicts, but waged employment offers a regular and assured means of income in contrast to conditions for the majority of operators in the informal sector.

Thirty-five per cent of all currently married women live in polygynous relationships.[5] Traditionally, there is little pooling of resources between spouses; whilst a man is expected to contribute to the upkeep of his wife or wives and their children, until 1985 when the Intestate Succession Law was passed, wives had no automatic claim on a husband's resources even on his death.[6]

Women are responsible for nearly all domestic tasks, including all child care, washing, cleaning and cooking. They also have major responsibilities for the sustenance and welfare of household members, even when they live with a husband. In addition, about 28 per cent of households in rural areas and 33 per cent in urban areas are headed by women.[7]

Women's right to work, as sanctioned under customary law, is increasingly undermined by the almost exclusive definition of household provisioning and maintenance as a woman's responsibility, particularly among poorer and low middle-income-level households. Thus policy measures such as those embodied in the ERP/SAP which not only reduce women's chances of employment and their ability to retain jobs but also raise the price of social services threaten the welfare of women and of their households.

THE SAP AND WOMEN'S EMPLOYMENT

Under the ERP/SAP policy, measures have been implemented seeking to reduce government expenditure, decrease the state's role in economic activity, increase the competitiveness of the export sector and liberalize trade. Restraints consist of ceilings on credit expansion, budgetary constraints, wage restraints, and exchange-rate adjustments and trade policies.

Agriculture's share of total employment increased by 5 per cent in the three years after the start of the ERP/SAP, while the mining sector also doubled its share of employment. These sectors produce cocoa, timber and minerals, the lynchpin of the ERP's export-oriented bias. In contrast, the share of employment of manufacturing and utilities declined considerably, to almost 50 per cent of its 1970 share. Similarly, government services declined from their 1970 share, although their share remained almost unchanged between 1984 and 1987. As the ERP/SAP progresses, this distribution between sectors will change even further to reflect the policy changes undertaken. Retrenchments in the civil and public services will further reduce government services' share in employment.

Conversely, the revamping of roads and greater availability of spare parts have put more vehicles on the roads, while massive investments in infrastructure, such as the repair and construction of roads, bridges, railways and telecommunications, will further increase the shares in employment of transport and communication.

Unfortunately, women workers cannot hope to benefit from increased employment openings in mining, timber logging, transport or communications, as traditionally these sectors do not employ women. Women are prohibited from working underground in mines; they are employed as clerical staff in transport and communications, but not as drivers, road construction or telecommunications workers. More are likely to become unpaid family workers on cocoa farms in response to producer price increases for export crops.

Retrenchment in the civil and public services and public boards and corporations has so far not affected middle- and high-level recruitments, but the employment freeze is likely to do so in due course. The civil-service redeployment schedules, for example, listed labourers, cleaners, drivers, cooks, porters, sweepers, messengers, security personnel and analogous grades: clerical officers, secretarial personnel, stores officers and analogous grades: and executive officers and analogous grades. The redeployments have also resulted in losses for the Ghana Education Service and Ministry of Health workers; a sizeable proportion of these were of women employed as cooks and caterers in educational institutions and departmental canteens, many of which have closed.

A 1988 survey among some retrenched women previously employed as cleaners in the civil service found that the majority were illiterate.[8] Most were divorced or separated and were heads of households. All said the retrenchment had depressed them and affected their contributions to family welfare and nutrition. Further, the study found that the redeployment exercise was exacerbating unemployment among women, who are already disadvantaged in formal-sector employment.

THE SAP AND WOMEN'S EMPLOYMENT IN THE INFORMAL SECTOR

The informal sector is important for the survival of a large sector of the population, particularly in urban areas, and the 1984 population census showed that about 3.8 million persons worked in agriculture and trade, in addition to 679,000 unpaid family workers. Informal-sector workers engaged in trade, processing, small-scale manufacture and agro-based industries. Women constitute the majority of operators in the sector.

In 1989, the author conducted a survey among 209 market traders in the two largest urban centres in Ghana—Accra and Kumasi—to find out the impacts of the SAP on them.[9] Only those who had traded for more than five years were selected and questioned about what changes had occurred in commodities traded, and in business volumes over time, and about their knowledge of the ERP/SAP and its impact on business, services, consumption and expenditure patterns.

Findings from the survey highlighted major policy measures which have affected traders. These include trade and currency liberalization, which saw the removal of price controls, devaluation of the cedi, and unrestricted flow of imported consumer goods, all of which have led to high prices for goods and services as prices have found their own levels. The promotion of export crops has led to high producer prices for those crops, while food producers for the local market face competition from imported substitutes, and the terms of trade have worsened for small producers. The higher prices for goods and services in the market-place and higher prices for utilities and social services have led to lower consumption levels, at the same time as wage-restraint measures have reduced the overall demand for goods. The rehabilitation of roads and the transport sector has opened up the market, both to goods and new entrants, and allowed a quicker turnaround for traders between markets. But it has also increased competition for older traders from new traders and redeployees who have relocated to the market.

Traders cite lack of credit as a major constraint: few traders have access to institutional sources. The SAP has worsened their situation as the credit squeeze on banks, as part of the financial-sector reforms, has limited access to bank credit for all. Reliance, for informal sources of credit, on relatives who may have benefited from bank credit is therefore more constrained. Meanwhile, traders are not included in any of the schemes for financial assistance such as FUSMED initiated by the World Bank,[10] and the market is increasingly polarizing between large traders with sufficient capital and smaller traders who now have to depend on them.

With reduced profits, traders reduce their own consumption levels as they pay higher charges for medical care, school fees, electricity and water bills and attempt to meet their obligations to their children and other dependants.[11]

Under the SAP, credit has been provided by the World Bank and other donors for urban infrastructural development, and, as has been noted, major rehabilitation of city roads, drainage and construction have been undertaken.[12] While laudable, the rehabilitations have been accompanied by major dislocations for traders who have been forcibly relocated to remote markets by municipal authorities intent on 'beautifying' their city. Traders have had their stalls and kiosks demolished and lost their wares as pavement traders and hawkers have been forcibly removed, thereby depriving poorer traders, especially those who come from rural areas to city markets, of access to the market as open-air traders.[13]

THE SAP AND RURAL WOMEN'S EMPLOYMENT

These effects on women's employment in the informal sector apply in varying degrees to rural informal-sector operators. In addition, some categories of rural women have lost employment opportunities as a result of structural adjustment. These are women who were employed on cocoa, coffee, oil palm, copra and other cash-crop plantations by the Ghana Cocoa Board, the State Farms Corporation and the Food Production Corporation. Most were members of the Ghana Agricultural Workers Union or, in few cases, of the Industrial and Commercial Workers Union and did planting and nursery work.[14] Some were permanent staff, whilst the majority were employed as casual labourers for specific periods. In reality, casual labourers stayed on for longer periods and were converted into permanent staff after some time, and both categories provided significant rural employment for both men and women. In addition, both categories of employees often had access to lineage or rented land and used the proceeds to supplement their income.[15]

Under structural adjustment, many of these jobs have been lost. The GAWU estimates that it lost 14,000 workers in the cocoa sub-sector alone, an additional 10,000–12,000 workers from the Food Production Corporation and 9,000 from the State Farms Corporation; its total membership declined from 150,000 to about 110,000 by 1988.[16]

CONCLUSIONS

Assessment of the impacts of structural adjustment on women's employ-ment in the public and informal sectors has been constrained by the general lack of data and specifically by the lack of sufficiently disaggre-gated data, particularly on the informal sector. In addition, apart from general survey data there is little monitoring on a continuous basis by any agency in Ghana on the specific impact of structural adjustment on women and households. Specific studies on the SAP and employment are needed, and the Trade Union Congress, for example, needs to commission studies on the SAP and public-sector employment as it affects them. The National Council on Women and Development, Ghana's national machinery on women, also needs to collect data, commission studies and monitor the impact of structural adjustment on women if it is to succeed in influencing policy on their behalf.

A number of conclusions can be attempted. First, women have been found to be extremely vulnerable in many of the retrenchment exercises as a result of their lower educational levels and their concentration in many of the sectors targeted for redeployment. For many of them who also happen to be heads of households, the loss of employment affects family welfare in major ways, and many feel stressed and depressed as a result of this. The loss of public-sector employment not only affects women's economic status but also their access to information and to decision-making.

Second, women traders have been affected by policy measures deployed under structural adjustment, and the already-insecure condi-tions for the majority have been worsened by increased competition, higher prices and consequent low purchasing power, given the general level of incomes. Neither have traders been recognized in any scheme of government or donor assistance such as has been attempted for re-trenched persons and some small-scale entrepreneurs under PAMSCAD.

Under PAMSCAD, US$88 million has been made available to provide economic assistance to groups and individuals, and social infrastructure to communities in 22 projects over a three-year period that ended in 1991. There are food-for-work programmes which aim to transfer income to individuals whose wards are in boarding schools. Public works and construction projects initiated under PAMSCAD employ mostly men, and whilst some of the incomes gained will go to women as wives or sisters for food and other domestic expenses, it would be incorrect to regard all this money as family income having regard to household struc-ture in Ghana. There is a credit line for small-scale enterprises under PAMSCAD which targets 40 per cent of total credit to women's activities in cooperatives and groups, but the total credit line is small.

To make more money available for women's activities and in recognition of women's needs for a separate income, a gender-specific project under PAMSCAD has been initiated by the National Council on Women and Development to enhance opportunities for women in development, initially targeted at poorer women in rural communities in three regions in Ghana; it is jointly funded by the Ghana government and the United Nations Development Programme (UNDP), United Nations Population Fund (UNFPA), the United Nations Children's Fund (UNICEF) and the US aid agency USAID. It is expected that by 1993, when the project ends, about 7200 women (an average six persons per household gives a 43,200 catchment group) will have benefited in 36 districts in the three regions. About US$1.8 million has been secured for personnel, costs and activities under the project, consisting of: training programmes for beneficiaries and implementors; the provision of a revolving loan fund to provide repayable credits; the distribution and dissemination of technologies for beneficiaries; and the strengthening of the capacity of local institutions to provide services to women.

A scheme of employment-generation begun since structural adjustment is the Entrepreneurship Development Programme (EDP) financed by the World Bank. Under it, some people have been trained and assisted to set up enterprises. According to returns from the implementors of the programme, the National Board for Small-scale Industries, 18 per cent of the 140 trainees are women, aged from 24 to 45 years. The EDP lists as its target women, science and technology graduates, unemployed youth, unemployed graduates and retired/redeployed public persons. It seeks to orient women away from traditional occupations to new ventures such as castor-oil extraction, flour milling, copra-oil extraction, tie-dye/batik production and marmalade making. A few women have set up their own enterprises with assistance from participating banks. However, the entrepreneur is expected to contribute up to 25 per cent of the costs of the project before loans are granted.

Without a doubt these schemes, which are ad hoc, short-term and reach only a few women, cannot provide an answer to the unemployment and serious problems facing informal-sector workers in Ghana today. It is clear from the situation on the ground that for the majority of retrenched men and women, solutions are still found at the individual level, as households struggle with the daily round of survival.

The lack of an employment focus in the ERP/SAP needs to be tackled as an urgent measure, and policies must be formulated to improve real incomes through a vigorous programme of employment-generation in all sectors, as the International Labour Office/JASPA study found. This would lead to an assessment of the real capacity of the informal sector to meet the employment needs of ever-increasing numbers of women and men, and to questioning of the strategies employed under structural adjustment. This becomes even more crucial when the official figures for unemployment are discounted and the real figures are acknowledged. In these conditions, the ability of men and women to provide for their households becomes ever more difficult, and affects not only nutritional and growth levels of household members and children, but ultimately the growth and development of the economy and the society.

B. State Policy and Women's Health, Sexuality and Reproductive Rights

This section includes readings on the changing policies of governments on family policy, health, reproductive rights and sexuality. Themes include the politics of international population control, sexual servicing of the military and a discussion of women and the AIDS epidemic.

---

24. ABUSES AGAINST WOMEN AND GIRLS UNDER THE ONE-CHILD FAMILY PLAN OF THE PEOPLE'S REPUBLIC OF CHINA

MARLYN DALSIMER AND LAURIE NISONOFF

Beginning in the late 1970s the Chinese government inaugurated new economic and social policies designed to modernize the nation's economy, to increase national production and income, and to raise people's standard of living. These policies loosened the control of centralized, state planning and permitted more free-market activities in both urban enterprises and rural agriculture. Agriculture was transformed into the 'family-responsibility system', in which individual male heads of family contracted with former state collectives for specific plots of land on which families farmed and tried to turn a profit.

At the same time that the state permitted privatization of parts of the Chinese economy, it also began a nation-wide campaign to curtail population growth—a strict policy known as the One-child Family Plan (1CFP). Announced in 1979, the 1CFP introduced a host of rewards and punishments to secure compliance, as well as a timetable of specific quotas and targets for national population reduction. It was a bold, unprecedented mass-mobilization campaign which used the authority of the state to compel the Chinese people drastically to alter their reproductive behaviour.

From the outset it was obvious that, from the point of view of rural peasants, the 1CFP collided with the decollectivization policy in agriculture. Just at the time that rural families were permitted to augment their incomes through private farming and 'sideline' activities (selling agricultural surplus like honey, hogs, eggs, as well as household handicrafts like baskets), they were deprived of their traditional strategy to maximize their labour pool: having many children, and especially sons. 'We cultivate our own land, eat our grain and bring up all our children on our own. We have taken responsibility for the land, and there is no need for you to bother about our child birth' (Croll, 1984: 134).

Because of patrilocal marriage practices, rural Chinese value sons more than daughters. Sons, their wives and children provide the labour for their family and ensure the old-age security of grandparents. In addition, the son's male children continue the patrilineage, the central component of traditional Chinese religion. From the point of view of mothers, anthropologist Margery Wolf has explained that rural daughters-in-law, uprooted at marriage from the kin networks of their natal villages, feel great urgency to produce sons, thereby creating for themselves a new 'uterine family' upon which they can later depend in old age (Wolf, 1972). Many traditional Chinese sayings embody these son-preferences, for example: 'A man will no more support his mother-in-law than a pot will make its own beancurd'. On the futility of investing in daughters, rural peasants say, 'Why weed another man's garden?'.

Both the agricultural and 1CFP policies for rural areas were supposedly 'gender-neutral'—that is, none of them had gender-specific goals or targets. Policies, however, are rarely sex-blind. We show that these policies have had deleterious effects on Chinese women, particularly at the point where the policies collide. While the 1CFP *discouraged* childbearing, the family-responsibility system *encouraged* rural peoples' desires for larger families and especially for sons.

Now that the modernization policies have been in effect for almost twenty years in rural China (where about 70 per cent of the total national population, about 900 million peasants, lives), we can begin to evaluate them. Both policies have carried a price for Chinese women. Although rural families' incomes have increased substantially due to the new family-responsibility system, the reforms have precipitated shifts in labour allocation. Skilled male farmers have found new jobs in town enterprises like transport, construction and commerce. On the other hand, rural women have, in some cases, become 'surplus labour' (unemployed, due to the dismantling of the collectives), their work contributions becoming privatized and 'hidden' within the 'household income', with a concomitant decrease in both their public recognition as workers and their intra-family bargaining power (Dalsimer and Nisonoff, 1987; Aslanbeigui and Summerfield, 1989). The effects of the birth limitation policies are even more serious, because the terrain of struggle of the 1CFP is women's bodies. In this discussion, we examine, in turn, the incidence of coercive reproduction practices; the 'missing girls' of the 1980s; the deterioration of subsidized social services for rural families; and the responses of women to these crises.

Many urban Chinese seem to have accepted the 1CFP, both for positive and negative reasons. The state offered some rewards to one-child families, e.g. day-care and preferential housing placement, measures more available in cities. Also, urban women workers often earn pensions, which make them valuable to their families who are concerned for old-age security (Wolf, 1985: 197). On the negative side, reproductive surveillance of women is very tight in urban workplaces and residential areas (Lavely et al., 1990: 824–5; and Mosher, 1993: 263–85). Family-planning cadres keep close tabs on women's menstrual cycles and the workplace unit constantly exhorts women to wait their turn for planned births, for the good of the whole unit.

In the countryside, however, the 1CFP has not fared as well. Official surveillance is weaker, and the new private economic arrangements have emboldened Chinese peasants to try to take control of their reproductive, as well as productive, activities. Given the patriarchal value placed on sons, it is not surprising that rural Chinese have resisted the 1CFP. By the mid-1980s, many local authorities bowed to the inevitable; the one-child policy unofficially became a two-child policy in some rural areas, especially for families whose first child was a daughter.

Contrary to the notion that people are responding only to positive incentives and to the larger social goals of the 1CFP, many western analysts believe that most birth-control measures in China are involuntary, and therefore coercive. The former senior researcher of the China Branch of the US Census Bureau's Center for International Research, John S. Aird, has identified a host of euphemisms in official documents which essentially instruct family-planning officials to use any means necessary to adhere to the birth quotas. 'Taking remedial measures', for example, means mandatory abortions, and 'technical services' means birth-control surgeries like IUD (inter-uterine device) insertions, abortions and compulsory sterilizations. Even innocuous phrases like 'study classes' and 'heart-to-heart talks' with pregnant women amount to heavy-handed threats that women and their family members will lose jobs, be fined, have farm profits impounded, consumer goods confiscated and even have their electricity and water supplies cut off or their homes blown up. None of the provincial family-planning laws prohibits or penalizes the use of coercive tactics (Aird, 1990: 70–73; *New York Times*, 25 July 1995: 1, 8).

In addition to reproductive coercion of adult women, feminists have expressed concern about the extent of female infanticide and/or the neglect of female children. China has a history of both these practices, involving families of all classes and regions (Lavely, *et al.* 1990: 817). Since the implementation of the 1CFP, Chinese authorities have blamed scattered reports of female infanticide on 'feudal ignorance', rather than on state policies.

Development theorist Amartya Sen has raised the issue of 100 million 'missing women' in the world (Sen, 1990). (The term refers to women who should appear in census tabulations but who have not survived because they did not receive food, health care and social services comparable to men in their respective societies.) Demographer Ansley J. Coale revises Sen's estimate downward to about 60 million missing women, of whom 29 million are Chinese (Coale, 1991: 522). Sen uses China as a special example, in which he notes that the trend towards increased longevity since the 1949 Revolution has been interrupted and even reversed for women since the new state policies came into effect in 1979. He speculates that the causes may be female infanticide, the general crisis in health services and the unfavourable impact of the agricultural-responsibility system on women's involvement in recognized gainful employment and on old-age security. Sen reminds us that 'rapid economic development may go hand in hand with worsening relative mortality of women' (Sen, 1990: 63).

Demographers are currently engaged in an intense controversy about 'missing' Chinese girls. Terence H. Hull of the Department of Demography, Australian National University was disturbed to find statistically significant differences between the normal birth/sex ratio (106 males/100 females), and the results of the 1987 One Percent Survey of Chinese Population. This survey showed 'quite dramatic patterns of high sex ratios [i.e., more male babies than normal] for second and higher-order births'. The sex imbalance in births was particularly significant (over 111/100) in eight rural provinces: Hebei, Jiangsu, Zhejiang, Anhui, Shandong, Henan, Guangxi and Sichuan (Hull, 1990: 65–6). Hull posited a half million missing female births for the year 1987 alone, and suggested that discrimination against female children was the cause. Swedish demographers, Sten Johansson and Ola Nygren, analysed the Fertility Survey of 1988 and found similar patterns; they concluded that the phenomenon of missing girls in China in the 1980s bore a conclusive relationship to the government's population policy (Johansson and Nygren, 1991: 40–41).

Experts have offered several possible explanations for the 'missing girls': sex-selective abortions; informal adoption of girl babies; conceal-ment or non-registration of female births; and female infanticide. Most sources agree that sex-selective abortions were probably not a significant factor in the 1980s because the necessary technology was not yet widely available in rural areas; more recently, however, even small rural outposts are reportedly acquiring ultrasound equipment (Schmetzer, 1993: 1ff.). Hull estimates that sex-selective abortions probably accounted for no more than five per cent of all abortions in the 1980s (Hull, 1990: 75).

Both official and informal adoptions became significant in China, beginning in the 1980s. Johansson and Nygren offered statistics which indicated that half a million children were adopted in 1987. Of these 1987 adoptees, girls accounted for 73 per cent (Johansson and Nygren, 1991: 44–5). The *New York Times* (22 June 1992) reported that foreign couples adopted 13,600 Chinese babies in the previous decade and that the Chinese government was considering liberalizing foreign adoption procedures. Most of the adoptable babies were girls 'who [had] been abandoned by parents who wanted boys'. Yet it appears that many aban-doned girls are languishing in makeshift orphanages in China. 'The Dying Room' documents the warehousing of girls who can not be placed with families. Many are ill and attended by overworked staff and older children. The film reports that as many as one-half of these abandoned babies die (Blewett and Woods, 1995).

Instead of abandonment, some families may conceal girls who are first-borns, so that they can try a second time for a son. Unregistered persons do not qualify for food allotments and for state social services. If adop-tion or registration-avoidance were the main explanations for the missing girls, Chinese officials would probably produce documentation, if only to protect themselves from international criticism, like that which appeared in the *New York Times* of 16 and 17 June 1991, reporting the first results of the 1990 Census in which 'several million little girls' were missing. Because Chinese sources have been unable to produce credible evidence to account for these children, we regretfully conclude that some of them are dead.

We agree with Hull's conclusions that state policy has exacerbated the neglect and abuse of girls:

> If children are being hidden from surveys and registration systems,
> it is likely that they are also being deprived of the various benefits
> of child-care, schooling, and protection from exploitation to which

they are entitled. If they are being illegally aborted, put to death or mistreated so as to cause premature death because of their gender, they represent a class of innocent victims whom the state is committed to protect. (Hull, 1990: 76)

Although the Chinese Constitution guarantees the equality of the sexes, Chinese officials have barely reacted to these abuses. We agree with Hull that 'it is important for the government to develop responses adequate to the challenge revealed in the statistics' (ibid.).

In a carefully researched report issued in 1996, Human Rights Watch/Asia documented a cruel record of deliberate abuse of China's abandoned children in government orphanages, to which Terence Hull tentatively alluded in 1990. With the cooperation of many doctors, lawyers, journalists, child-care workers and officials in China, Human Rights Watch/Asia was able to compile a compelling record of malign neglect, including specific case studies of many infants and children deliberately left to die. Human Rights Watch estimates that 'in China's best-known and most prestigious orphanage, the Shanghai Children's Welfare Institute, total mortality in the late 1980s and early 1990s was probably running as high as 90 per cent'. Even official Chinese statistics reveal 'the annual deaths-to-admissions ratio at 77.6 per cent in 1991, and partial figures indicate an increase in 1992' (Human Rights Watch/Asia, 1996: 2). This disturbing report further asserts that most abandoned children in China are completely hidden from view and never even reach the dubious benefit of arriving at a state-run orphanage. The cause for the surge in abandoned children, according to Human Rights Watch/Asia, is in part 'due to the one-child population-control policy and in part due to policies restricting adoption by Chinese couples who are not childless'. The report asserts that 'the vast majority of children in orphanages are, and consistently have been during the past decade, healthy infant girls, that is, children without serious disabilities who are abandoned because of traditional attitudes that value boys more than girls' (ibid.).

The Chinese government has consistently denied the accuracy of these reports, has accused outsiders of misunderstanding and meddling in its internal affairs, and has defended the high mortality rates on the grounds that state orphanages receive children in such poor condition that they cannot be saved. Human Rights Watch/Asia refutes many of these defences, and puts the responsibility where it belongs: on deliberate government policy.

Sadly, the many negative consequences of the collision between the rural family-responsibility system and the 1CFP could have been anticipated and alleviated by state planners. During our 1981 field research in

China, various officials of the All-China Women's Federation (ACWF) expressed concern about these potential outcomes. Yet, at the same time, the ACWF officials were confident that the 1CFP would bring better maternal and obstetrical care and would provide more benefits for children in nutrition, education and health. They called this 'fewer but better children' approach 'eugenics'. Although the ACWF officials acknowledged that the 1CFP required 'hardships and sacrifices', they believed that mothers and children would ultimately be better off. In 1991, however, the Chinese government announced a more explicit eugenics technique: forced sterilization of mentally handicapped adults. These measures, followed by suggestions in 1994 to broaden the forced sterilization to physically handicapped adults, have encountered criticism from western nations (Sullivan, 1995: 230–33).

Unfortunately, there is little evidence, especially for rural families, that social services have improved over the past few decades. In fact, most analysts link the dismantling of rural agricultural collectives to a deterioration of subsidized health care, old-age pensions and schooling. Barefoot doctors' services have disappeared in many locales; payment-for-services health clinics are more and more common. Rural families no longer contribute to old-age and disability funds which were formerly maintained by some agricultural collectives. Population Council demographer, Susan Greenhalgh, reports that even though the government still offers minimal welfare support (the 'five guarantees') to the destitute elderly, 'the meager level of collective support [has] brought home the fact that any rural resident wishing a decent level of living in old age ha[s] no choice but to have a son' (Greenhalgh, 1990b: 85).

In 1987 we proposed several policy initiatives to forestall the potential negative consequences for women who felt compelled to produce sons. One was that parents of only daughters could be awarded bonuses double or triple those presently offered by the 1CFP to one-child families, to be placed in special savings accounts, earning interest, and paid to the parents for retirement and illness insurance (Dalsimer and Nisonoff, 1987: 599). Hull reports that officials in Wenzhou City, Zhejiang Province attempted to organize such a fund, but it failed, due to 'resistance among parents and to the unwillingness of village governments to contribute to a trust account. Complaints centered on high current costs, uncertainty of the fund's future value in the face of inflation, and the irrelevance of the fund to meeting the emotional needs that can be satisfied only through having sons' (Hull, 1990: 80–81).

The emotional and psychological needs of Chinese peasant families for sons cannot be overestimated. Patriarchal values, in place for centuries, cannot be overturned in two decades. One peasant woman living in the mountains of Sichuan province testified that before 'Heaven' sent her a son (after six daughters, born before the 1CFP began), her neighbour taunted her, calling her a 'barren old hag ...I'd sit home weeping with fury'. She concluded: 'having sons is what women come into the world for. What's the point of it all if you don't have a son? It's what we live for' (Jenner and Davin, 1987: 131).

Given the precarious situation in which Chinese rural women find themselves, how have they responded? We have found no evidence of mothers' complicity with female infanticide, but it has probably occurred. The pressures on mothers to build their own uterine families are considerable. Combined with the exhortations of government officials, of husbands and of in-laws, it is probable that women have sometimes agreed, for example, to the drowning of a girl baby after home delivery. Alternately, a mother might concur, however reluctantly, with a familial decision to forego medical attention for a sick daughter or to place a girl child for adoption.

Yet we also find scattered reports of women's resistance to various official and familial sanctions. Young Chinese students in the US report underground networks of women in the countryside which help pregnant women flee from coercive officialdom. Others have joined a growing 'floating population' of Chinese who evade family-planning cadres; they flee their rural villages and live on the fringes of urban society, without official registration papers and ration coupons for food and other essentials. The Chinese press characterizes them as an 'excess-birth guerrilla corps', numbering as many as 50 million people nationally (Aird, 1990: 73). The New York Times correspondent Patrick Tyler describes 'a human shell game' where families live in 'fetid train-station halls and squalid shantytowns, shifting children among relatives'; and 'others take to boats and get lost in the labyrinth of riverine China' (Tyler, 1995). A few Chinese have successfully sought political asylum while overseas, on the grounds that the 1CFP violates human rights and that they would be subjected to economic and political persecution if they returned to China with an unauthorized second child (Mosher, 1993: 332).

Some women stay at home and fight. The Sichuan peasant woman recalled that when 'they sent people here to work on me ['heart-to-heart talks'] ... a whole crowd of them cadres ... I never said a thing; I just listened ... until they got fed up talking and went away ... In the end I went into hiding ... at my mother's'. Her sister-in-law, who had six daughters and was trying for a son, acted even more boldly: 'When the family-planning people came to question her she didn't go into hiding: she drank pesticide! And she did it twice! That gave them such a fright that they never came back again' (Jenner and Davin, 1987: 131–2).

Another strategy women use is to work especially hard at their household sideline enterprises in order to save money to pay the fine for an unauthorized birth. '… this boy of mine [cost] 1300 [yuan] … I paid cash on the nail. If I hadn't they'd have taken the furniture—and if that wasn't enough to cover the fine, the tiles on the roof, too' (Jenner and Davin, 1987: 131). Family-planning officials at the local level (who are themselves often from peasant backgrounds) sometimes levy fines as substitutes for more coercive 1CFP sanctions, both because they have fewer effective means to control peasants' reproductive behaviour since the decollectivization of agricultural units, and because they are sympathetic to the cultural and economic imperatives of their fellow villagers (Greenhalgh, 1990a: 222–4).

When women are unable to defend themselves against reproductive coercion, they manoeuvre to maximize their limited options. They understand the connections between production, reproduction and family security. One woman, for example, agreed to abort an unauthorized pregnancy, on the condition that village officials guaranteed her a paid job. Another woman threatened to sue for divorce and called on the principle of gender equity ('we are in the new society; men and women are equal', paraphrasing the Constitution) to compel her husband and in-laws to reconcile themselves to her first-born daughter (Dalsimer and Nisonoff, 1987: 595 and 605, n. 44).

Still, despite all their rambunctiousness and manoeuvring, the alternatives for rural Chinese women are few, caught as they are in a web of colliding state policies and familial needs. We find that these policies place women at risk—at birth, in childhood, during their childbearing years and in old age. Rather than offering creative policies that might have enhanced the liberation of women or, at the very least, protected them from predictable negative consequences of the national birth-limitation campaign, state policies have instead reinforced traditional patriarchal values and practices and have abused women.

A Chinese woman, Chi An, analysed the 1CFP from both her perspectives as a family-planning nurse responsible for enforcing the 1CFP and subsequently as a mother who desired a second child and was forced to abort her pregnancy:

> I see now that China's continuing ills … are in large part the direct result of nearly a half century of Party misrule. How convenient for the authorities to have a prestigious foreign theory—overpopulation—that allows them once again to shift the blame onto the Chinese people.
>
> The Party is again making use of this ploy in the one-child campaign, in effect holding women and children responsible for all of China's problems. In the West there is a name for such deceptions: it is called blaming the victim (Mosher, 1993: 334).

Increasing urbanization and rapid economic development have created opportunities for a few, but most, especially rural Chinese women remain at serious risk. Reproductive abuses of women will likely continue, unless and until Chinese officials adopt a sweeping, national affirmative-action policy—in employment, education and political leadership—to raise the value of women to their families and to society. Ultimately, no single economic or demographic change will improve the status of women, in China or anywhere else. Only political will—to make policy as if women mattered—can do that.

25. WOMEN, POPULATION AND THE ENVIRONMENT: WHOSE CONSENSUS? WHOSE EMPOWERMENT?

BETSY HARTMANN

In the corridors of power, the tailors are at work, stitching yet another invisible robe to fool the emperor and the people. Population control is back in vogue—with a vengeance. [In Washington,] The US Agency for International Development's (USAID) new 'Sustainable Development' strategy identified population growth as a key 'strategic threat' which 'consumes all other economic gains, drives environmental damage, exacerbates poverty and impedes democratic governance' (USAID, 1993, 7). In middle-class households across the US, newspapers and junk mail routinely bring alarming messages of imminent environmental and social collapse caused by overpopulation. The only consolation is that one can now recycle the paper these messages are printed on. Barring major catastrophes, the demographic momentum built into present human numbers is inevitable, but it should be a subject of rational discourse, not of official hyperbole and public paranoia.

If globalization and the free market are good, then population growth perforce has to be bad, for there is no way advanced capitalism can deliver all the goods to all the people and 'sustain' both the natural environment and the present grossly inequitable distribution of wealth. The best way to shrink the numbers of the poor (and the labour supply) is to limit their births. Never mind that population-growth rates are coming down in virtually every area of the globe already—they must come down even faster through the aggressive promotion of modern contraception.

While the essential logic of population control is crude, its ideological

packaging is becoming more sophisticated, as witnessed by the appropriation of feminist and environmental concerns. This appropriation has
a positive side: it attests to the power of feminist and environmental
movements, but it is also an important component of a new strategy to
obscure class, gender and racial inequalities in a grand consensus in
which everyone's interests are ostensibly served simultaneously.
'Women, population and the environment' have become formally linked,
a holy trinity in the consensus cosmology.

According to this consensus, the provision of modern contraceptives
will help liberate women and concurrently reduce the birth rate, considerably reducing pressure on the environment and economy, making
everyone on the planet, rich and poor, better off. The United Nations
Fund for Population Activities (UNFPA) has done the most to articulate
this view, particularly at the International Conference for Population and
Development in Cairo, 1994. In the USA, a well-funded and influential
population/environment lobby has developed and the Clinton administration has expounded this perspective.[1]

This consensus poses real problems for feminists who, on the one
hand, want to defend women's right to control their own fertility through
access to safe contraception and abortion, but who, on the other, are critical of population control. They are caught between a rock (the Vatican
and other fundamentalist forces) and a hard place (the office towers of
USAID, the World Bank, UNFPA, etc.). While there is some political room
for manoeuvre, it is a tight squeeze. A key strategic task is to take apart the
consensus and expose its flaws and contradictions.

THE ENVIRONMENTAL EQUATION

Consensus thinking identifies rapid population growth as a major, if not
the main cause of global environmental degradation. It draws heavily on
the work of Stanford biologist Paul Ehrlich and co-author Anne Ehrlich
who have popularized the now famous I=PAT equation: The Impact of
any human group on the environment equals Population size times the
level of Affluence (or average individual resource consumption) times an
index of the environmental disruptiveness of the Technologies which
provide the goods consumed (Ehrlich and Ehrlich, 1990, 58).

Taking the equation at face value, people can and do argue about the
relative weights which should be attached to P, A and T. Even though the
Ehrlichs recognize the environmental destruction caused by affluence
and technology, they return inevitably to population as the main factor.
Critics of course point out that affluence has far more to do with the
depletion of natural resources than has population size. The industrialized nations, with 22 per cent of the world's population, consume 70 per

cent of the world's energy, 75 per cent of its metals, 85 per cent of its wood, and 60 per cent of its food (Vittachi, 1992). The much smaller populations of northern industrialized nations generate almost three-quarters of all carbon-dioxide emissions, which in turn comprise nearly half of the 'man-made' greenhouse gases in the atmosphere (Mazur, 1992). They are also responsible for most of the ozone depletion. Other critics, notably environmentalist Barry Commoner, have argued convincingly that the nature of technology is the decisive factor determining environmental quality (Commoner, 1991). On a global level, then, it does not make sense to blame environmental degradation on population growth.

The main problem with the equation, however, is what it leaves out, namely the question of social, economic and political power, and the systems by which current power relations are enforced. These underlie P, A and T, and the interaction between them.

Take P, for example. The very word 'population' lumps all people together, into a set of statistics to be both feared and acted upon. In her critique of I=PAT, environmentalist H. Patricia Hynes notes how P is gender, race and class-blind, all but ignoring different people's differing impacts on the environment. Moreover, it neglects the crucial factor of human agency by viewing all humans as *takers from* rather than *enhancers of* the natural environment. 'This truncated, culture-bound view of humans in their environment originates from an industrial, urban, consumerist society' (Hynes, 1993, 23).

Rarely is the question asked: why is the population size what it is? Rapid population growth is often a symptom that people's survival is endangered because of high infant mortality and lack of security, and because women in particular lack economic and political power within the family and society at large. P also ignores the issue of population distribution, which arguably has a greater impact on the environment than population size as such. Fifteen million people crowded into a megalopolis as the result of poor economic planning degrade the environment far more than if they were more evenly distributed in villages and towns, with secure access to land or other employment opportunities.

And precisely what is A? Affluence is not simply a matter of *per capita* consumption. Profound systemic inequities underlie consumption patterns; debt repayment and the hegemony of 'free market' economics in the 1980s and 1990s has meant an even greater concentration of wealth in the hands of the rich. Global income disparities have doubled in the last three decades (UNDP, 1993: 11).

In terms of both quantity and quality of consumption, advanced capitalism orchestrates needs carefully through mass advertising, destroying non-commodity-based culture and values. The planet may not have enough resources for everyone to have two cars and three TVs, but surely systems of production and consumption are possible wherein everyone's basic needs are met. Hynes points to the need to differentiate between luxury and survival consumption and technologies (Hynes, 1993, 13).

Regarding T, why is current technology so inappropriate and destructive? Why in so many societies, for example, have public transport systems been sacrificed to the private automobile? Throughout the world industries are allowed to pollute without bearing the cost. Public funds for technological research and development flow to the military, and scarcely trickle down to new environmentally sound initiatives in energy and agriculture. These technological 'choices' all reflect an absence of basic democracy, of popular control over technological development.

Conspicuously absent from the I=PAT equation is the chief enforcer of the status quo, the military. Militaries also happen to be the main environmental criminals on the planet today. The German Research Institute for Peace Policy estimated that one-fifth of all global environmental degradation was due to military and related activities. The Pentagon alone was found to generate more toxic waste than the five largest multinational chemical companies combined (Hynes, 1993, 20; Seager, 1993, Chapter 1).

While macro models such as I=PAT obscure power relations at the global level, the new consensus also masks the precise dynamics of environmental degradation at the local, regional and national levels. Deforestation, in particular, is often attributed to the fertility of the poor: the UNFPA holds population growth responsible for 79 per cent of deforestation in developing countries (UNFPA, 1992a, ii.).

In an extensive study of the social dynamics of deforestation, the UN Research Institute for Social Development (UNRISD), noted that while many observers blame deforestation on forest clearing by poor migrants, they ignore the larger forces attracting or pushing these migrants into forest areas, such as the expansion of large-scale commercial farming, ranching, logging or mining: 'To blame poor migrants for destroying the forest is like blaming poor conscripts for the ravages of war' (Barraclough and Ghimire, 1990, 13). Furthermore, the study found an absence of any close correspondence between deforestation rates and either rates of total or agricultural population growth.

Brazil is a case in point. Starting in the late 1960s, highway construction, largely financed with bilateral and multilateral aid, initiated destruction of the Amazon rain forest and its indigenous inhabitants. Between 1966 and 1975, 11.5 million hectares of forest were cleared—an estimated 60 per cent by highway developers and cattle ranchers, and only 17.6 per cent by peasants (Guppy, 1984). Moreover, the government encouraged peasant colonization of the Amazon in lieu of land reform in other regions.

This is not to deny that the poor are involved in deforestation, though they are clearly not the main culprits. Moreover, it is important to look at the underlying reasons why poor people degrade their environment when they do. In some cases the reason may be the scarcity of fuel wood and the lack of alternative energy forms, in others the need to farm marginal land because the best land is controlled by a powerful few. Population pressure can contribute to the problem, but it is rarely the root cause. Sparse population densities can also contribute to environmental degradation since human labour is required to sustain ecologically sound agricultural techniques. This is a problem noted by Franke (1981) in parts of Africa where large-scale male migration to work in cities and mines created a critical labour shortage in peasant agriculture.

Almost all analysts agree that more case studies are needed in order to understand the precise dynamics of deforestation, and the complex layers of interaction between people and the environment in diverse settings (Barraclough and Ghimire, 1990: DAWN *et al.*, 1991). In much population propaganda, however, the case studies misrepresent reality as much as the statistics.

In UNFPA's *1992 State of World Population*, for example, a case study of 'Population growth and deforestation in Madagascar' blamed the country's serious loss of forest almost entirely on population growth as poor peasants migrated from more crowded areas, cleared forests on the hillsides and cut back on the fallow cycle needed to restore soil fertility. The author, Paul Harrison, visited a village where he interviewed a poor peasant woman who could not afford to leave her land fallow because she had four children to feed. Near the end of the study, Harrison notes in passing that 'her husband died nine months earlier, when the logging lorry he worked on crashed' (UNFPA 1992a, 27). Logging lorry? Up to this point, Harrison has given us the impression that there is no commercial logging in Madagascar, just land-hungry peasants, and he declines to say anything more. Nor does he refer to any national or international economic policies that might affect peasant livelihoods. It is as if the only force impinging on the village is rapid population growth.

Out of the consensus view of the relationship between people and their environment comes the simple-minded emphasis on population control as the solution—not car control, cattle control, corporate control, arms control. The mainstream is obsessed with how population is about to 'overshoot' the natural 'carrying-capacity' of the planet.

Maybe the earth has a *political* carrying-capacity too, which is less about human numbers than human systems of labour and resource exploitation.

MANAGING WOMEN

The new consensus acknowledges the importance of women explicitly in the relationship between population and the environment, which UNFPA expresses in the form of a population, environment and development triangle (Figure 25.1). Note that women are at its very centre. Moreover, the interaction between these four sectors 'creates a powerful synergy that can either enhance or retard the achievement of a more balanced style of development' (UNFPA, 1992b: i).

Figure 25.1: *Population, Environment and Development Triangle*

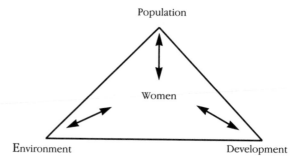

Source: UNFPA, 1992b: 2

What exactly is this powerful synergy? According to UNFPA, the role and status of women affect each point of the triangle and are in turn affected by them. Women influence the environment through their daily tasks of fetching water, collecting wood, etc., and their management of family resources. Women influence population through their reproductive behaviour. They affect development through their economic and political roles in family and society. Then with a sleight of hand, UNFPA tilts the triangle so as to once again over-emphasize population: 'Poverty is an overriding factor which intensifies the positive or negative nature of this web of relationships'.

And what is the main cause of poverty? Population growth, of course. 'In poor countries with high rates of population growth, large increases in human numbers can quickly over-stress natural resources needed for sustained economic development', as well as 'outstrip a society's ability to generate viable employment opportunities and provide needed services'. This, in turn, deepens poverty and offsets 'the benefits of development' (UNFPA, 1992b: 2).

Are the poor really the ones gobbling up resources? The 1993 *Human Development Report* estimated that developing countries spent only one-tenth of their national budgets on human-development priorities. Their military expenditures meanwhile soared from 91 per cent of combined health and education expenditures in 1977 to 169 per cent in 1990. According to the UN, the poorest 20 per cent of the world's population receives only 1.3 per cent of global income (UNDP, 1993: 10, 27, 177). As their numbers mount, no doubt each individual's share of that 1.3 per cent diminishes—but that ignores the other 98.7 per cent of the pie.

From the time of Malthus, it has been politically expedient to blame poverty on population growth, but now, in a new twist, the onus is put on women. According to the UNFPA, improving women's status speeds fertility decline, thus reducing considerably 'the overall negative impact of population on environment and development' (UNFPA, 1992b: 2).

This view of improving women's status as a means to an end—the reduction of population growth and hence poverty and environmental degradation—rather than as laudable in and of itself, objectifies women, targeting their wombs and turning them into the mechanical components of yet another exercise in misconceived social engineering.

The women presented in the triangle are also an undifferentiated mass. There is little recognition, for example, of the profound differences between how a peasant woman relates to the environment, and a city dweller. Moreover, within both these categories there are important class differentiations which affect resource use.

In addition to enabling women to regulate their fertility, the UNFPA believes that the other key way to incorporate them into population, environment and development programmes is 'to improve and enhance women's role as resource managers' (UNFPA, 1992b: 14). For most poor women, it is greater power over resources which is required, not better management expertise alone. Moreover, in many peasant societies, poor women—and men—have long known how to manage environmental resources; it is external interventions in the form of commercial agriculture and logging that have largely undermined more environmentally sound traditional practices as well as appropriated land from the poor.

UNFPA views management as a modern phenomenon, however: 'Women who are able to manage their environment, instead of simply reacting to it, are likely to be better educated (literate) and have the ability to make decisions about the key aspects of their life' (UNFPA, 1992b: 11). Notwithstanding the value of literacy, it is patronizing to assume that illiterate peasant women simply 'react' to their environment. An illiterate peasant woman in Bangladesh, for example, is likely to be a far-better manager of environmental resources than a college-educated professional in New York. The latter probably generates more unrecyclable waste in a week than the former does in her entire life.

EMPOWERING WOMEN THROUGH FAMILY PLANNING

A devil's advocate might argue that, even if it is for the wrong reasons, the attention now being paid to empowering women and giving them contraception is a step forward.

A problem with the consensus view of women's empowerment is that family planning is emphasized above all else, despite the lip service paid to women's need for education, employment, property rights, access to credit, etc. To address women's economic rights adequately would challenge the status quo, and that is to be avoided. Literacy receives slightly more attention, rhetorically at least, because it is considered politically safer and more closely correlated with fertility decline. It is, of course, ironic that the sudden interest in female literacy comes at a time when public education budgets have been slashed for structural adjustment purposes.

A further problem has to do with how population control distorts the delivery of both family-planning and health-care services. Population agencies often argue that they are only trying to fulfil women's 'unmet need' for contraception. It is impossible to separate unmet need for contraception from unmet need for health care. Good quality family services depend on the existence of a functioning health-care system, a fact which many population-control advocates continually try to avoid or deny (Hartmann and Standing, 1989). In fact, in a number of countries, most notably India, Bangladesh and Indonesia, population control has enjoyed a much higher priority than basic health care (Hartmann, 1995; Ravindran, 1993).

In the 1980s the World Bank encouraged governments in Africa to make family planning the 'cornerstone' of health policy (World Bank, 1989); now it may come to dominate the Bank's 'minimal package of essential clinical services' for the poor. The very act of defining such a basic package forces untenable trade-offs—while family planning automatically gets included, for example, treatment for cervical cancer and cataract removal do not (World Bank, 1993: 10).

Population control also skews the kinds of contraceptive technologies that are promoted. The current thrust of control programmes is on the introduction of long-acting, provider-dependent contraceptives, in health systems which are often ill-equipped to distribute them safely or ethically. The hormonal implant Norplant, for example, which is inserted in a woman's arm, is effective for five years and must be removed by trained medical personnel. In population programmes in Indonesia, Bangladesh and Egypt, there are many instances of women being denied access to Norplant removal (Mintzes *et al.*, 1993). A number of new contraceptives in the pipeline—vaccines which immunize women against reproductive hormones and the non-surgical quinacrine steriliza-tion pellet—pose even more serious problems in terms of both health risks and the potential for abuse at the hands of zealous population-control officials (Schrater, 1992; Hartmann, 1995).

In addition to targeting women and minimizing user control, these long-acting technologies, unlike barrier methods, do nothing to protect women from sexually transmitted diseases, notably HIV. They perpetu-ate the notion that contraception is a woman's responsibility, furthering the neglect of male methods such as the condom and vasectomy.

The bottom line of the new consensus is contraception as technical fix, for everything from poverty to women's liberation to environmental degradation to crime. The contraceptive revolution 'is as impressive as the green revolution in agriculture, and perhaps equally important in averting widespread famine in many developing countries', claimed Sheldon Segal of the Population Council and Stephen Sinding of the Rockefeller Foundation (Sinding and Segal, 1991).[2] Peter Adamson of UNICEF went even further: 'Family planning could bring more benefits to more people at less cost than any other single "technology" available to the human race' (Adamson, 1992: 30–31).

Even the demographic transition is being reframed in these terms. A much-publicized article in *Scientific American* asserts that the belief that 'development is the best contraceptive' is passé—instead, 'contracep-tives are the best contraceptive' (Robey *et al.*, 1993: 65). The 'good' news is that the aggressive promotion of modern contraception through family-planning programmes and the mass media can drive down birth rates in poor countries such as Bangladesh, even in the absence of economic development.

While the availability of contraception can assist fertility decline, the kind of simplistic analysis outlined above reduces the complex interac-tion of demographic dynamics into a single family-planning variable. In Bangladesh, for example, observers have noted that more female employment outside the home is one of a number of social changes contributing to the desire for smaller families (Mahmud, 1996). Distress-related reductions in birth rates are also occurring among the urban poor in countries such as Brazil and Mexico, but it is the shrinking of livelihoods—not the expansion of family planning services in them-selves—which is the driving force (Benería, 1992; Mello, 1992).

FROM CHIAPAS TO CAIRO

The new consensus is firmly rooted within the dominant free trade/global-ization economic model. It comes as no surprise, for example, that seven of the major mainstream environmental groups in the US lent their support to the North American Free Trade Agreement (NAFTA). Two of them, the National Wildlife Federation and the National Audubon Society, are key actors in the population-control lobby (*New York Times*, 1993).

The mainstream environmental movement displayed virtual ignorance of how NAFTA is likely to affect the livelihoods of Mexico's poor. Competition from cheap US corn, for example, will probably wipe out Mexico's peasant corn producers, whose fields are also a vital reservoir for the grain's genetic diversity. It took the Zapatista army in Chiapas to remind the environmental mainstream that peasants still exist in Mexico, and that they are not terribly pleased about NAFTA.[3]

In the new consensus thinking, the population dislocations caused by free trade, war and maldevelopment create the need for much stricter immigration controls, not for a closer look at economic and political priorities. Hispanic illegal 'aliens', with their higher birth rates, are blamed for the economic crisis in California; 'guest workers' in Europe are suddenly surplus populations, vulnerable to racist attacks. The liberal gospel of free trade goes hand in hand with a conservative siege mental-ity. As birth rates continue to decline, the population/environment lobby may well shift more and more attention to immigration.

The international women's movement has already found some politi-cal space within the consensus to negotiate for improved access to higher-quality contraceptive, abortion and health services. But the real political space lies outside, in an alliance with progressive development activists, social-justice environmentalists and anti-racist organizers for whom empowerment is more than just a word.

26. AIDS: WOMEN ARE NOT JUST TRANSMITTERS

Claudia Garcia-Moreno

Until recently, AIDS was perceived in the West as a problem affecting mainly homosexual men. The biggest impact of AIDS on women's lives had been until recently as carers for people with HIV disease or AIDS. However, more women are now becoming infected and the number is likely to increase in the next few years—in New York AIDS is already the leading cause of death in women between 25 and 34.[1] In Africa and some parts of Latin America, mainly the Caribbean, HIV has always been transmitted predominantly through heterosexual sex, and in these areas AIDS has affected women and men equally.[2] Yet women have received, until recently, little attention in the AIDS literature and when they are referred to it is usually only in their role as transmitters of the infection. There has been little focus on women as sufferers from AIDS.

PROSTITUTES

Prostitutes especially have been singled out as a high-risk group, and have even been portrayed as being responsible for the spread of the HIV and AIDS epidemic in some places. The word 'prostitute' means different things in different cultures. In some countries prostitutes are an easily identifiable group, whereas in others they are much less visible. Where prostitutes form a definable group they are accessible and easy to study and have become the focus of research in some cities of Africa.[3] They have been found to have a higher rate of HIV infection than the rest of the population.

A common assumption in much of the AIDS literature is that prostitutes are always female. In some countries this is not the case and male prostitutes may be common. Yet women, particularly prostitutes, are frequently referred to as AIDS transmitters. While they may constitute a pool of infection, the role of their clients in transmission is rarely mentioned. Gabriella Leite, a prostitute in Brazil, put it bluntly:

> As for AIDS, official bodies, society, attempt to define it in terms of people: prostitutes, homosexuals, the promiscuous, drug users. The political question is, what about the people who frequent prostitutes? They are not regarded as a high-risk group … Sure AIDS kills, but so do many other things. Prostitutes have always been at risk of diseases and the government and health services have never lifted a finger before.[4]

The concern with prostitutes is as transmitters of AIDS, not as sufferers. This is not new or limited to AIDS. An article from Brazil draws a comparison with what happened previously with syphilis and gonorrhoea.[5] In the 1930s and 1940s a poster aimed at soldiers in World War II portrayed a young woman—underneath the caption reads:

> SHE MAY LOOK CLEAN—BUT … pick-ups, 'good-time' girls, prostitutes … Spread syphilis and gonorrhoea. You can't beat the Axis if you get VD.

This in spite of the fact that female-to-male transmission of gonorrhoea is documented to be around 20–25 per cent after a single exposure, and from male to female 50–80 per cent. The same article points out that although 95 per cent of the AIDS cases in Brazil are male, the official information on prevention portrays the face of a woman with the message, 'You can't see AIDS when you see the face', i.e. she may look beautiful, but ...

The possibility that a prostitute may catch HIV from an infected customer is rarely considered. For example, a study in *The Lancet* on the effectiveness of condom promotion and health education among prostitutes in Kenya concluded.[6]

> We believe that this programme has prevented the transmission of a large number of HIV infections in men ... In view of the sexual activity of these women and their high prevalence of HIV, every day approximately 3750 men are sexually exposed to HIV through contact with them.

The phrasing makes one wonder whether the researchers were equally concerned about the health of the women. In the Philippines 'hospitality girls' have identified this risk for themselves and together demanded testing for the men from the army who are frequent clients.

Men infecting women is never highlighted. However, in fact, the little information that is available on heterosexual transmission seems to suggest that male-to-female transmission is slightly higher than the other way around.[7] Also, in many African countries, men who have acquired the infection in the cities then return to their wives in rural areas and possibly start a new cycle of infection. There are anecdotal reports from some countries where HIV is prevalent in urban areas that some men are now looking for younger women in rural areas for the exchange of sexual favours, thinking that such women are less likely to be infected with HIV.

'Sex tours' for Western businessmen are well-known, particularly in some Asian countries, yet this group is not usually mentioned as a high-risk group. A study of prostitutes in London showed that they were more likely to use condoms with their clients than with their own partners, even though these partners often engaged in high-risk behaviour such as intravenous drug use.[8]

Harsh economic realities push women into prostitution, particularly in developing countries; for poor women on their own in urban areas there may be few choices other than becoming domestic servants or prostitutes. Often, they have been abandoned by a partner and have children to support. Women refugees also frequently end up resorting to prostitution, sometimes illegally, as their only survival strategy. With little education or access to other resources, their opportunities are non-existent, and it is unrealistic to blame prostitutes and single them out for education and other programmes without offering them some kind of economic alternative. While education may help them to protect themselves (though even as prostitutes women are not always in a position to enforce the use of condoms by their clients), for many of these women abandoning prostitution would mean destitution.

Projects which aim to support women in prostitution or women sex workers should not limit themselves to giving health education; condoms need to be made available at an affordable price. General health services, including access to birth control, are also important. It is also essential to explore alternative income-generating activities with these women and to provide the relevant assistance, as well as to explore other social and economic needs they may have.

WOMEN AND AIDS IN AFRICA

The number of women infected with HIV in some African countries is high, particularly in certain urban areas. The female-to-male ratio is approximately one to one i.e. at least 50 per cent, or sometimes slightly more, of those infected are women.[9] The peak incidence of infection for women in Africa is between 20 and 29 years while for men it is between 29 and 39, probably reflecting an earlier start of sexual activity for women. Yet few AIDS-control programmes have considered women's particular needs; neither those of urban women nor of the wives of men returning to the rural areas bringing HIV with them.

AIDS cannot be separated from the extreme poverty, lack of resources and the heavy burden of work of women. For women the possibility of transmission to their babies is a cause for additional concern and when it occurs it adds to the guilt and worry.

Women have traditionally been the carers for children, the sick and the elderly and have already experienced the problem of caring for partners or others with AIDS. Who will take over this role for women when they themselves need to be cared for?

A research project in a capital city of an African country is following a sample of 1500 women (selected from those attending antenatal care in the national hospital) for five years. The study, concerned with more than the research itself, has expanded to provide a valuable educational service, condoms and spermicides, and counselling for the women as well as offering counselling and testing for their partners. Discussions with the women have helped to identify areas where they would like to receive some help. Testing was carried out, with informed consent and appropriate counselling. Approximately 25 per cent of the women were found to be seropositive. Marital conflict arising after disclosure of a positive result and the role of counselling in helping to overcome this have been particularly relevant.

This study exemplifies many of the problems faced by women in relation to HIV infection and AIDS. Many of these women were single and had little in the way of social or economic support. It is a generalized assumption that in Africa the extended family provides support and care for the sick. However, among the group of HIV seropositive women interviewed, 60 per cent of them said they would not be able to rely on husband or family for support.[10] Support from self-help groups, particularly with an income-generation component, was very relevant to these women.

The same study identified the needs of women with AIDS. The provision of child care, food and funeral services were major areas of concern to them. For women who were seropositive but asymptomatic, housing and employment assistance were a higher priority, although another important consideration was concern about preparing for the future in the event of illness or death. It is important to identify priorities and needs with the women themselves and to support projects which allow them to have more control over their situation and improve their economic status whenever possible.

Many of the women experience feelings of terrible isolation after being told they are seropositive; stigmatization is real and many have been abandoned by friends, relatives or lovers; nurses and health workers have been known to refuse care. Hopefully, this rejection will decrease with appropriate information and education. Meanwhile, in the words of 'Rosie' (a pseudonym), a sick woman in Zimbabwe.[11]

> That's the worst part, the loneliness ... I have it (AIDS). I can't change that, but if only I could talk about it openly, and stop hiding it. People think I've got cancer, because that's what I tell them, I can't admit I have AIDS, I would be stoned.

AIDS AND CHILDREN

The majority of women with HIV or AIDS are of childbearing age. HIV can be transmitted from an infected mother to her child, either during pregnancy or at birth. There have been eight reported cases so far where transmission has been possibly related to breast-milk, all of them in special circumstances. (Present evidence is that the benefits of breast-feeding far exceed the potential risks and breast-feeding should continue to be encouraged.)

The risk of a baby being infected is still not known with certainty. Results from different studies vary from less than 10 per cent to 30 per cent, and the risk of transmission appears to be associated with the stage of the disease.[12] The problem is bigger in those places in Africa and the Caribbean where a large number of women may be infected. In the West, women with HIV are advised to avoid pregnancy or to consider termination of pregnancy but for most women in developing countries these are not options. (And in some areas the risk of a baby dying of other diseases in the first year of life is probably higher than that of dying of AIDS.)

The debate on whether women should be offered testing for HIV as part of antenatal care is an ongoing one. In a survey in one African country about half the women said that knowing their HIV status would not affect their decision to become pregnant. In a clinic in London when women were offered a confidential test, 99 per cent of them declined. In some developing countries women have been tested without their knowledge. In the USA some reports suggest that women, mainly from deprived or minority groups, accept testing because they fear they will be denied access to health care if they decline.[13] It is imperative that confidentiality be maintained if one is to encourage those women most in need of counselling and support to come forward. Even though it is now well-recognized that pre- and post-test counselling is an essential part of testing for HIV, in many places it is often lacking. Doctors often have not informed patients of their diagnosis because they lack counselling skills and feel unable to provide the necessary support.

POLICY IMPLICATIONS

The above discussion has relevance to health and health-education policies. Women's needs are different from men's and policy-makers have to take this into consideration.

Women should be offered appropriate information and education so that they can make informed choices. This should take into account their particular social and economic circumstances, as information is not enough if women are not in a position to have control over their own lives and bodies. The messages will be different depending on which women are being addressed. Sex workers, women in stable relationships or adolescent girls about to start sexual activities need to be approached with messages that are relevant to their particular situation. In the case of prostitutes it is important not to make them scapegoats. Health education should be aimed at their clients as well.

Education on prevention of HIV infection/AIDS and other sexually transmitted diseases (STDs) should ideally be in the context of education and information on sexuality. There is a need for sex education which empowers women and encourages them to feel more confident to express their own needs and to negotiate over condom usage with a partner. Education with men on these aspects is necessary as well. Participation of the male sexual partner in an education and testing programme in Rwanda positively affected change to lower-risk sexual behaviour. Access to family-planning services offering appropriate choice and to early treatment of other STDs is also important.

The experiences of women who are beginning to organize themselves and to come up with their own solutions for support, sharing of child care and income-generating activities need to be taken into account. In relation to income-generating activities, particularly for prostitutes, it is important to ensure that activities are genuinely productive. 'Traditional' income-generating projects like jam-making, knitting, weaving, etc., do not usually generate much money and large-group activities are not profitable in most cases. It is difficult to find successful income-generating projects but access to credit through revolving credit schemes could be explored. Access to child care remains an important issue on which self-help groups could, with some external support, organize their own schemes.

There are various groups which are attempting to deal with the problems of women in a different way. Some of these are particularly concerned with helping women sex workers. Empower is one such group in Thailand. It is an association of bar workers set up to help women working in Patpong (a sex centre in Thailand where about 4000 women work). They have staged shows on safer sex aimed not just at sex workers but at their clients and bar and brothel owners. They also have a drop-in centre which gives information on AIDS and other STDs, nutrition, safe drug use and family planning, and they provide education for the women. The main problems they face are discriminatory attitudes towards sex workers who often get beaten up when they insist on the use of condoms. Yet women are still blamed for transmission (the local Thai expression for STDs is 'woman's disease').[14]

Another example of positive activities is those undertaken by Gabriela, a national coalition of Filipino women's groups. This group has been involved in demanding the dismantling of US military bases in the Philippines and the compensation by the US government for 'hospitality women' infected with HIV.[15] It has drop-in centres and provides information and education for sex workers. It has also formed a Task Force on AIDS to do advocacy work and attempt to educate people in the media and general public about the problems of AIDS in particular and the sexually prostituted in general.

In Zimbabwe a group of women have formed the Women's AIDS Support Network. The Network aims to make AIDS a concern for all organizations working with women in the country and to help women gain confidence to fight AIDS in a society where they have little control over the sexual behaviour of men.[16]

C. Women and Ideological Change

This section includes a discussion of the issues for women arising with conflicts and accommodations between feminist movements and national liberation struggles. Our discussion also focuses on the impact of Muslim fundamentalism on women's issues and women's movements because of the widespread shift toward fundamentalism in religious movements and their impacts on women.

---

27. GENDER, NATION AND COLONIALISM: LESSONS FROM THE PHILIPPINES
DELIA D. AGUILAR

Let me begin with a narration of two disparate events, divergently located in time and place, as a way of positioning my argument. The first occurred in the early 1980s at an FFP (Friends of the Filipino People) annual conference where I was expected as a matter of course to speak on 'women's issues'.

At this particular yearly meeting, six Filipino men known to be followers of the NDF[1] came as friendly observers. Because I was aware that feminism was not received favourably by the revolutionary movement at home, I took a theoretical approach, emphasizing the deficiency of the productivist orientation that underpins orthodox Marxism. My presentation was followed by the enthusiastic response of the Filipino women who were there, and by the American women and men, in what became a 'speak-out' on male chauvinism. Conspicuously silent, my Filipino male compatriots were apparently not impressed with my lecture on Marxist feminism. How could a critique of the base/superstructure gulf have been anything short of heretical? Nor were they particularly pleased by the consensus that sexism is a problem that tends to have a life of its own apart from relations of production. The following morning, all six packed their bags and left.

The second case is a more recent one, and the setting was St Scholastica's College in Manila in 1992. There I had the opportunity to facilitate a module in an intercultural women's-studies course with 17 Asian/Pacific women as participants. Thirteen countries were represented, 11 of which belong to the Asian/Pacific region: the Philippines, Nepal, India, Sri Lanka, Malaysia, Myanmar, Indonesia, South Korea and Papua New Guinea, among others. In addition, there was a woman from Zambia, and two white American women.

What figured prominently in the sessions I handled was the manner in which most of the women regarded the Philippines as removed from the rest of the Asian countries. No doubt the presence of the two women from the US, whose participation in the programme was questioned from the very beginning (these two paid for tuition and living arrangements; everyone else was on scholarship), served to exacerbate these tensions. Filipinos suffer from 'a lack of their own culture', according to the half dozen or so voices raised. The symptoms of this deprivation were evidenced as much in the way Filipinas dress and comport themselves (there was a citation of the 'domineering' manner of Filipino women but, curiously enough, vulnerability to 'western' feminism was not openly impugned) as in the world-view inscribed in ubiquitous images projecting the good life broadcast by various media. Uma from Pakistan was especially outspoken in this regard: 'We are proud of our culture. We do not look up to America as our model'.

Two themes arise from the above. One is the progressive movement's refusal or inability to acknowledge the significance of feminist insights in the articulation of transformational politics. It persists in viewing issues surrounding gender as of secondary importance since, after all, these will be solved once large-scale social changes are achieved. Few feminist Filipinas will fail to recognize this as a lingering difficulty despite the fact that the Philippine women's movement is currently considered one of the most vigorous in the developing world (Mitter, 1986: 153; Mirkinson, 1992: 11). Recently, for example, I attended a conference organized for the purpose of 're-examining and reviewing the Philippine progressive vision'. According to some of the women who took part in organizing that meeting, sexism was in evidence in the confinement of 'gender' as a category separate from the other, ostensibly more weighty topics [for discussion]: democracy, power and transformation; the crisis of the left; equity, growth and the environment, to name a few. Clearly much educational work has to be done so that 'progressive' male honchos finally grasp the inseparability of gender from 'real politics'. Feminism has been described as 'the most potentially powerful challenge to the status quo' precisely because it calls for struggle against *all* forms of oppression (Sen and Grown, 1987: 19). If this is so, feminism is profoundly implicated in any discussion on democracy, power and transformation, and certainly in any conversation about the crisis of the left.

Now the second theme: the suggestion that, 'lacking a culture of our own', we are little more than unfortunate clones of the West is one that we cannot take lightly because it not only raises questions about national self-determination but hits at the very core of our sense of ourselves as a people. It is the inextricable intertwining of these two motifs—feminism and the quest for national identity—that constitutes the imperatives for the women's movement in our country at the moment. I will try to explain why I hold this view and why, in spite of the enduring ignorance of many of our male colleagues, I would probably address the subordination of women differently from when I addressed that FFP annual gathering over a decade ago.

Today, nine years after the founding of Gabriela (a national federation of women's organizations, the goals of which include genuine independence and the dismantling of patriarchy)[2] the women's movement has both established its presence and attained an autonomy that is rare in Third World nations. The proliferation of women's organizations in the last few years, including the setting up of women's-studies programmes, has brought to the public consciousness a range of issues heretofore unacknowledged, e.g. domestic violence against women. It can no longer be said that the women's movement simply obeys party dictates, privileging the economic over the cultural or ideological. It is in fact in the realm of culture that women have been most energetic and most passionate. In the publication of books and journals, the staging of plays, music composition, the visual arts, performances on radio and TV—the utilization of women's talent, imagination, creativity and resources has been remarkable and inspiring.

Several factors account for the flourishing of feminism immediately following the Marcos era and thereafter: the 'democratic space' opened up by Aquino's restoration of civil liberties and re-establishment of Congress; the weakening of the left due to both tactical and strategic errors; and changes in the global arena, particularly the collapse of the Soviet Union. All of these helped legitimate the hard, patient, day-to-day work that feminists undertook [in building] an autonomous women's movement. A few years ago debates about the place of feminism in the revolutionary agenda as formulated by the Communist Party of the Philippines were still taking place (Lansang, 1991). Today, with serious divisions wracking the left, there exists the possibility that, released completely from an economist paradigm on the one hand and drawn to the perquisites extended by international feminist networks and foreign funding sources on the other,[3] feminism could make a shift in another direction. That direction could be liberalism, the goal of which would be reform—in laws, courts, education, etc—permitting some women to achieve individual success. A corollary might be a concentrated focus on social and psychological factors, such as ways of being and habits of mind that privilege men, and less attention on discrepancies in the material conditions of daily life.

In the meantime, the urgency as well as the types of problems facing the majority of Filipino women prevent a move like this from taking place suddenly. In so far as the women's movement retains its charge of advocacy for grass-roots women and for those suffering adversity shaped by neocolonialism, feminism in the Philippines will maintain its 'Third World' character. This is evidenced in important feminist work by activists and academics alike which has taken as its subject phenomena such as prostitution and migrant labour, [both] telling symptoms of exploitative North/South relations (Palma Beltran and Javate de Dios, 1992; Miralao, Carlos and Fulleros Santos, 1990). There is little indication that the disintegration of the 'Second World', its absorption into a global capitalist system and the present reshuffling among industrial powers will mean anything other than an intensification of the economic woes of developing countries. Yet how these economic ordeals are handled depends on the initiative of liberation movements whose alternatives have been limited by this historical convergence of diverse economic, cultural and political forces across nation-state boundaries (Petras and Fischer, 1990).

In the post-Marcos years, the declining influence of the left as well as the macho stance of the revolutionary movement at its height have functioned, ironically, to invigorate the feminist enterprise. Up to this point, feminist analysis subscribed wholly to the use of grand narratives indispensable to understanding socio-political and economic arrangements in developing nations, which in the past decade or so have become anathema to intellectuals in the West. Feminist reflection on the tribulations women face has [since] relied on the efforts of political organizers and the empirical findings of activist university researchers. Such a marriage of thought and action, although not always in perfect harmony, informs the work of feminists (Medel-Anonuevo, 1990–91). At the very least, it is the vision of that fusion that has spurred feminist activity [in recent years].

The conditions I have described can best be summed up as fluid and highly volatile, unavoidably situating feminism at a crossroads. So what's in store? In any projections of what could transpire, changes in the world picture have to be factored in, [given] the status of 'peripheral' countries. Without question, the weakening of the progressive movement as a whole can not but have considerable impact on the women's movement in the long term, if not in the near future.

The exact nature of that impact is difficult to predict. At worse, it could spell the erosion of feminist militancy, a watering-down of leftist explications of women's socio-economic troubles, or the ultimate abandonment of a revolutionary platform and a flight into the less-hazardous terrain of cultural struggle and liberal reform. Through conversations during my last visit, I could glean some of this taking effect already. The mushrooming of women's offices, desks and committees, while boding well, could also take an inauspicious turn— the creation of a feminist bureaucracy dependent on dole-outs from foreign sources, for one. Well-supplied offices and high-tech communication systems need not mechanically equate with bureaucratization or a concentration of authority in the hands of a few. Yet already some women speak of a growing gap between feminists and the grass roots, and an imminent 'femocracy' in programmes erected on development assistance from foreign governments (de Vera, 1992: 16). The spirit of activism has been replaced by an officialism presumably made necessary by grant requirements.

As I write, there is talk about grant sources drying up due to the loss of geopolitical interest in the Philippines on the part of donor countries. This development, which could spell the demise of NGOs, may well accelerate a reorganization of the left in the absence of remedial measures to alleviate people's poverty (admittedly, this view is baldly economistic); also to be monitored (in terms of its consequences for the general populace) is President Fidel Ramos' grandiose, will-o'-the-wisp plan to convert the Philippines into an NIC by the year 2000.[4]

What about the feminist frameworks purveyed by the women's movement, particularly in the context of the aggressive stance it has taken in the building of international feminist networks? From what I can gather, the wish to perceive all women as sisters, a tendency that usually accompanies the initial awakening to gender asymmetry, still occupies feminist thinking. In the women's-studies course at St Scholastica's, this push for a universal sisterhood found expression in a number of ways: [e.g.] in the desire to unite all women via the cross-class, cross-cultural experience of rape or battering by men; or in the solidarity-inspired assertion that 'a victory for women anywhere is a victory for us'.

Such essentialist inclinations bear examination because their consequences are contingent on who is making the call for unity; i.e., the belief that there is an immutable essence or unchanging humanity that all women share is always modified by relations of power. In the 1970s and 1980s African-American, Latina and other women of colour fought tenaciously to unmask the white, middle-class woman masquerading as the 'universal woman'. It was this white, middle-class, usually professional woman who, having the authorial voice, could speak of her own experience of subordination and appear as though she were representing womankind.

That universal woman, displaced somewhat in the West, is alive and well in international feminist circles. A friend in Manila [tells of] feminists still called on by foreign visitors to explain how it is that poverty is a feminist issue, and whether Grabriela is an organization of feminists or of nationalist women (i.e. dupes of men)? The wondrous ease with which First World feminists take it upon themselves to dispense advice never fails to astonish. A case in point: one academic blithely offered 'coming-out' workshops for Filipino lesbians, with little regard for cultural practices that unavoidably mediate expressions of sexuality. Speaking out in a public forum, another US women's-studies expert dismissed as 'unproductive' Filipino feminists' ascription of their lowered status to Spanish and US colonization.

We as Filipino feminists need to understand that, while alleging sisterhood in a common oppression, women in a superordinate position can at once claim generic status—i.e. speak on our behalf and/or question our stand—and preserve their superiority. When we, however, subscribe to the idea of a universal sisterhood, the effect is radically different—we erase ourselves from the picture! That is why it is hard to imagine a white woman in the US celebrating a victory of, say, women slum-dwellers in Metro Manila (assuming that she even has access to this sort of news) and identifying with that triumph as if it were her own.

Perhaps I can illustrate this self-obliteration with a more earthy example. In a talk I gave in a graduate women's-studies seminar at the University of the Philippines, I picked out a sexist joke from an essay on male bias in language. It went this way: 'Getting married is like finding a toilet seat still warm—it feels good, but you keep wondering who has been there before'. My point was that this bit of 'humour' was a direct import from a colder climate and had no pertinence whatever to us, in view of our warm weather. I assumed that this was a fairly simple idea, but the responses I got were unusually strange. Someone noted that the majority of us don't even have toilets. Another challenged why I would deny Filipinos the right to development goals, which would include having comfortable flush toilets!

Our colonial mentality makes it almost second nature for us to assume the persona of our colonizer. Consequently, our susceptibility to conceptions of shared sisterhood among all women acts merely to reinforce our neo-colonial standing. It would not hurt us to realize that the very phrase 'as a woman' has been labelled the 'Trojan horse of feminist ethnocentrism' (Spelman, 1988: x). As Maria Lugones contends, in the US racism is the major source of tension where women of colour are concerned; internationally it is cultural imperialism (1991: 19). According to her, they are interactive phenomena but the latter is not as perceptible because it entails no person-to-person mistreatment. This can explain our inability as Filipinos to discern racism in the conduct of those who would uplift and enlighten us (unless residence in the US and elsewhere has educated us).

In the past several years in the West, the notion of a universally shared oppression among women has lost purchase. In fact, essentialism as a theoretical current has been practically demonized [with] exclusionary tendencies now attributed to it. Can we relax, then? Chilla Bulbeck writes: 'Western feminism has become less Eurocentric and, indeed, now discusses the differences among women with a vengeance' (1991: 77–8). It is true that elaborations of 'difference', with their theoretical under-girding derived from post-modernist constructionism, have come to frame feminist discussions. Because social constructionism argues that 'woman' is never a pre-given entity but is created in the social process, it is posed as a corrective to essentialism.

Through the use of post-modernist devices, the concept of 'universal woman' has been deconstructed and denaturalized (Riley, 1988; de Lauretis, 1986, 1–19). Put simply, social constructionism declares that woman is made, not born. This sounds sensible enough, but let's go on. Instead of the essential woman, we are confronted by subjectivities that are fragmentary, multiple, contradictory and in constant flux. To the singular focus on gender has been added a list of other forms of oppression—racism, classism, homophobia, ableism, etc—all of which are mutually determining and none of which supersedes the others in importance. The meaning of 'woman' is now constantly deferred and never fully established since this depends on how gender intersects with multiple other axes at any given moment.

With this new scheme called the 'politics of difference', our attention is turned to the local and specific—the personal, the subjective, the everyday. One might conclude that, at last, the 1960s' challenge to politi-cize the personal has been met and consummated. Maybe so, but Kauffman argues that the present vision informing identity politics devi-ates from that of the 1960s. At that time, consciousness-raising groups became the principal method through which women exchanged personal stories and attempted to arrive at the underlying social forces that would explain what they discovered to be shared everyday realities. Whereas consciousness-raising stressed the social nature of individual experience and was seen as a prelude to political change, today self-transformation is itself political change (1990: 74, 77). It cannot be other-wise since the earmark of current feminist approaches is the rejection of a cosmic view adopted from post-modernism.

What does all this mean for us Filipino women? To be sure, the empha-sis on heterogeneity and pluralism connotes a refreshing acceptance of experiences that are eclipsed by posing women as a unitary group. The problem is that relations of power are hidden by the stringing together of a series of oppressions (Gordon, 1991: 106–7; Carby, 1990: 84–5), mutually defining though these may be, in the end insuring the preservation of things as they are. How [therefore] will such a stance assist us in ridding ourselves of our colonial predisposition toward self-erasure?

If the above is true, then maybe it is not too bad that Filipino feminists have not yet discovered the 'politics of difference'. We're not likely to maintain our innocence, however, for research on Filipino women along these ideological lines is already being conducted. What do these studies look like? I had occasion to read an otherwise interesting dissertation on gender, the military and violence that I believe will soon be published. Among many unusual opportunities the author had access to, one allowed her closely to observe the workings of both the AFP (Armed Forces of the Philippines, the government military) and the NPA (New People's Army, the guerrilla arm of the Communist Party). Using the Foucauldian conception of power as capillary, relational, contradictory and heterogeneous, she wound up claiming parallel power for the NPA and the revolutionary forces, discursively diffusing the violence of the AFP, the vigilantes and other state-backed agencies. She discovered on arrival in the Philippines that all actors were ultimately aligned either for or against the state. Her theoretical perspective, however, compelled her to re-align them to fit a predetermined pattern, namely, to flatten out and reduce all contending forces to the same level. We need to ask, who benefits from this point of view?

In the United States today I am finding that few among my students have any conception of how the world economic system is organized. They know little about the imperial adventures of their country in the recent past and not much more about the reasons for its preoccupations in the present. Sadly, much of current feminist writing can hardly be said to enlighten students in this respect. For instance, the idea that power is diffused, as in Grewal and Kaplan's (1994) notion of 'scattered hegemonies' and their proposal for 'transnational feminist practices' sidestep the predatory nature of a system based on the maximization of profit and its continued reliance on the power of the state. Such formulations often manage to blur the power plays that continually transpire among particular nation-states, in effect projecting the illusion of equal ineffectuality in the face of transnational corporate might.

Lest we dismiss these theoretical innovations as far-fetched, I should mention that at the recent conference I attended, the phrase 'totalizing theory'[5] was bandied about like a bugaboo, as though it had caused the crisis of the left in the Philippines. Surely we need to worry about authoritarianism in our progressive movement, but is it grand narratives that are responsible for this? Without an overarching framework, how can we begin to grasp the shape of capitalism or any other social formation? Not knowing the nature of the social system we live in, how can we begin to work for change? Can we afford a retreat from political struggle, which is what this trend of thought ultimately implies?

Let me sum up. Several factors have contributed to the notable growth of feminism in the Philippines, among which has been the attrition of the progressive movement. Even progressive men in search of democratic alternatives have failed to reckon with feminist interrogations of Marxism, and continue to ghettoize women. This male stubbornness can only aid the [national] women's movement. Yet with active networking in the now worldwide women's movement, an unrehabilitated colonial outlook makes us vulnerable to the influx of ideas (not to say the seductiveness of grant possibilities, travel, hobnobbing with feminist luminaries, and so on) [whose] uncritical acceptance could signify nothing more than a feminist replication of neo-colonialism. Developments in the Philippines as well as in the international arena warrant a feminism that is vehemently anti-colonial and staunchly nationalist. It is time to reinscribe nationalism into the feminist agenda.

28. WOMEN, MARRIAGE AND THE STATE IN IRAN

Haleh Afshar

The Islamic ideology regards women with a mixture of fear and paternalism, and sees them both as the source of all evil and as the most vulnerable members of the household, in need of constant surveillance and protection. The policies of the majority of Muslim states are framed accordingly, often equating women with children and the insane.

Islam, which literally translated means 'total submission', is not merely a belief system, but also a way of life and Muslims are expected to run their lives according to the Koranic injunctions. In many respects the teachings of the Koran are quite specific, for example Muslims cannot disinherit their descendants,[1] and even the exact proportions inherited by the spouse and children are stated in the relevant verse. There are, however, other poetic and ambiguous injunctions in the Koran which are open to different interpretations, and many of the teachings concerning women fall in this latter category.

The Shiia sect of Islam as practised in Iran interposes the

Mojtahedin, religious leaders, between the Koran and the people. The Mojtahedin, being wise and learned men, have the authority to explain the teachings of Islam to the Shiia Muslims. So long as the clergy were in opposition in Iran, their role as intermediaries between the word of God and His followers enabled them both to offer protection to those persecuted by secular law,[2] and to provide a degree of flexibility and bring the religious dicta into line with secular practices. At the same time as there was a tacit political truce between some leading members of the clergy and the state about the Shah's rule, Iranian women were able to use this temporary peace and obtain a degree of religious approval for the slow and difficult progress towards sexual equality. Thus, during the 80 years preceding the Islamic revolution, Iranian women fought for and gained access to education (1910), the abolition of the veil (1936), the vote (1962), a curb on the unequivocal male right of divorce and the right to contest for the custody of children (1973), free abortion on demand (1974) and a ban on polygamy and the right to maintenance after divorce (1976). Although equal opportunities were still a long way away, the women's movement had great expectations of success in the 1970s.

LEGISLATION AND INEQUALITY

The conviction that women are biologically and intellectually unequal has led to new legislation which excludes women from many legal rights, while making them equally subject to the harsh treatment of the current Islamic laws of retribution *qassas*. These laws demand exact retributional justice, taking an eye for an eye and a life for a life, though the latter is more rigorously applied in the case of murdered men than women.

Within months of his takeover in March 1979, Khomeini issued a decree dismissing all women judges and barring female students from attending law schools.[3] Subsequently, he closed the Law Association, *Kanouneh Vokala*, and replaced secular courts by religious ones, often presided over by theological students with one or two years' religious training.[4] The laws now implemented do not admit women's evidence unless it is corroborated by men.

The exclusion of women from the legal and public domain has been justified in the Iranian press through numerous interviews with leading religious figures. The arguments are entirely based on the 'God-given' nature of women. Men have been given a status above women[5] and authority over them[6] by the Koran. The Iranian clergy explain that this superiority is an inherent right of men who are endowed with a 'calm and orderly nature'. Their 'wisdom, judgement, integrity and farsightedness' enables men to 'control and curb the hiatus caused by the unruly passion of women.'[7]

The 'natural' and 'biological' inferiority of women is described as a fundamental law governing all social and political activities. The Majlis (parliament) speaker, Ayatollah Hashemi Rafsanjani, a leading member of the clergy, denounced the West for 'over-reacting' to feminist demands and creating total anomie as a result. In his view western women have been 'forced to abandon their natural talents, as created by God and endorsed by men'. They have been pushed out of their 'natural and humane domestic environment' and 'propelled from school to offices and subjected to the harsh demands of factories and workplaces', 'obliged to adopt shameless and dishonourable roles which go against their gentle and sensitive nature'. The unnatural 'displacement' of women [had], according to Ayatollah Rafsanjani, imposed the double burden of domestic and waged labour on the women, against their own interest. The result has been the failure of many to fulfil their holy duty of motherhood or, in some cases, even to deny this very instinct: 'this has resulted in the birth of an unloved and uncared-for generation which lacks the fundamental basis of mother love and tenderness, and which has become an alienated and disrupted society'.[8]

HEJAB

Iranian women have become the reluctant standard-bearers of the public face of the Islamic regime. The republic's fragile honour can now be threatened by the mere appearance of women. National honour is secured by women covering themselves at all times, except in the privacy of their husband's bedroom. Iranian women have been understandably reluctant to accept this heavy responsibility and made several attempts to prevent the imposition of *hejab*. The first directive requiring women to don the veil was issued in March 1979, less than two months after Khomeini's return. There followed numerous protests and large-scale demonstrations by women, but the regime continued its official and unofficial harrassment of those women who still [refused] its decision to make themselves publicly invisible. Shops, restaurants, cinemas and all public places [were] instructed not to serve women who [were] not wearing the *hejab* and all government offices now have individuals responsible for checking that women are properly covered. The open defiance of *hejab* and appearance in public without it is punishable by 74 lashes,[9] and officials who apprehend such women do not need to take them to court 'since the crime is self-evident, the punishment will be immediate'.[10] The members of the 'Party of God' the Hezbolahis, usually fanatical government supporters, ensure that the regulations are enforced in the street. Women who are considered inadequately covered are attacked by these men with knives or guns and are lucky to survive the experience. The Hezbolahis also indulge in frequent 'spontaneous' demonstrations protesting against the 'shameless nakedness' of women who 'trample on the blood of young men who gave their lives to the revolution and died a martyr's death'.[11]

The Iranian clergy have determined that women must cover everything except for the face and hands. This shrouding of the body is supposed to bestow respect and dignity on women. It is said to denote 'deliverance from the yoke of imperialism' and to represent 'a symbol of liberation, resistance to capitalism, and revolutionary aspirations'.[12] Thus, women who refuse to don the *hejab* and 'flaunt their naked bodies in the streets' are denounced as 'corrupt, seditious, dangerous and destructive of public honour and chastity'.[13] These 'wayward women' are said to be instrumental in the foreign-inspired plot to undermine the revolutionary puritanism. The voice of the clergy calls on the nation to oppose this internal enemy 'with the same vigour as we oppose other terrorists who have sought to sabotage our revolution'.[14]

29. RETURN TO THE VEIL: PERSONAL STRATEGY AND PUBLIC PARTICIPATION IN EGYPT

HOMA HOODFAR

In recent years the western media have revived the image of the veiled and oppressed Muslim woman. Media coverage has reminded us of the orientalists' interpretation of the veil as a symbol of the Muslim woman's subordination and exclusion from all social spheres and even her loss of control over her own life. Colonial powers once used this interpretation either implicitly or explicitly to show the backwardness of Muslim society (Sayigh, 1981; Pastner, 1978). This newly revived image, however, is more startling in that it shows the Muslim woman voluntarily and actively participating in veiling movements and therefore bringing upon herself the evils of oppression and exclusion.

The media show the same Muslim woman, who is supposedly excluded from all social spheres because she is veiled, joining in political demonstrations and liberation movements and daily moving about in the crowded cities of the Middle East. This image has not caused observers to question in any serious way the accuracy of the view that veiling equals oppression and exclusion. Nor has it prompted a re-examination of the social norms and the political and economic forces that influence the persistence of the institution of veiling. As it is no longer possible to portray woman as victim, she too is presented as 'backward' and, at the same time, still wrapped in the exoticism and incomprehensibility of oriental culture. Even less has any attempt been made to differentiate the varieties of veiling movements in the various Muslim societies.

Veiling has existed and continues to exist in a wide variety of economic, political and cultural situations. Although there has been some commonality of themes, it is an institution that has communicated different messages in different societies and during different historical periods. The veil adopted by Iranian women during the anti-Shah movement conveyed to the world a different message (Tabari, 1980; Tabari and Yeganeh, 1982) from the *compulsory* veiling of the Khomeini regime, which represents authority and the attempt to control women by the state (Afshar, 1982). Both cases, however, represent women's active resistance to the imposed gender role envisaged for women by the state. Voluntary veiling among educated working women in Egypt is the outcome of social processes very different from those in Iran. Even within one society or a single cultural entity the veil may be worn for different reasons by different classes or social groups. The presentation of Muslim women as a single social group, together with a unidimensional concept of veiling and seclusion has further served to confuse the issue.

In this chapter the veiling movement among educated Cairene women from a lower income group, most of whom work in government or other public-sector offices and workshops, will be examined. Despite the lack of statistical information, Egyptians and outside observers agree that these women form the most visibly veiled social group in Cairo. It will be argued that veiling in the economic and cultural context of modern Egypt is not an exclusionary measure for this group of women. Rather, it is a means by which they protect the gains and possible opportunities that modernization has brought. Veiling has become an instrument through which women publicly dissociate themselves from some of the culturally disapproved traits and characteristics attributed to the stereotype of the modern woman. At the same time, veiling enables these women to safeguard their traditional rights.

REVEILING

In Egypt's past, as for many other Muslim societies, a manifestation of the increased status of a household was often the total veiling and more restrictive seclusion of women—in emulation of upper-class traditions. However, in more recent years the upper classes have worn a rather modest version of the western type of clothing. Until recently, this practice was closely followed by the middle classes and those inspired by middle-class values. The 1980s, however, witnessed a new phenomenon in that educated and lower-middle-class women returned to the veil.

This modern veil is a style of dress very different in appearance from clothing worn by more traditional *balady* (urban lower classes) or *fela-heen* (peasant) women. The most popular version of the modern veil is an outfit consisting of a long, western-style dress or skirt worn with a kind of turban or a scarf. Whatever is worn on the head covers the hair and sometimes the shoulders as well (Rugh, 1986). This outfit serves to separate the modern educated women from the traditional women whose style of dress carries the implication of 'backwardness' and lack of sophistication.

Reveiling appeared among university students in the early 1970s (Williams, 1979). By the late 1970s, it had become a widespread movement among the lower-middle classes, of which the most visible group were white-collar workers in the public and government sector. By 1985 the majority of younger women in most government offices were veiled (MacLeod, 1987).

This startling picture has evoked a great deal of comment and criticism from both western observers and Egyptians, although little systematic research has been conducted to examine the phenomenon from the perspective of those women who have chosen to veil not merely out of custom. The question is, why should this group of educated and privileged women voluntarily revive the institution from which the preceding generation had struggled to liberate itself? What does the veil do? How does it change the situation to women's advantage? What are the social forces which induce such action? Does the veil offer previously unrecognized privileges to women?

Deprived of the favourable economic situation which had created tremendous possibilities for the acceptance of a new approach to the female role, women have employed veiling as a strategy that enables them to continue to have access to some independent cash income. A review of the circumstances in which some of my informants took up the veil provides some insight on this issue.

Sommayya was in the last year of teacher training when she became engaged to marry, a year after graduation. Once she finished and was going to start her teaching career, her fiancé began to object to her 'working'. His mother and eldest sister came to intervene on his behalf when I was present in her home. A summary of a five-hour visit and discussion will help to demonstrate the way in which these questions are examined by the people involved. They calculated that she and her future household would lose more money than she would bring in if she went out to teach. She would have bus fares to pay and on occasions would eat lunch at work and buy cold drinks for her colleagues. She would also have to spend quite a lot on clothes because it is not acceptable for a teacher to go to work in old or cheap clothes. This would account for virtually all the forty Egyptian pounds per month that she would earn. Furthermore, people would talk, and her reputation might be questioned, because who would know where she really spent her time? In overcrowded buses men who have lost their traditional respect for women might molest her and of course this would hurt her pride and dignity as well as that of her husband and brothers.

When her future mother- and sister-in-law left, Sommayya said that she accepted their logic yet she did not want to give up her future job. She explained to me:

> If I wanted to sit at home I could have been married four years ago and by now have had a complete home and family. I studied hard and my mother suffered to provide the money for my education so that I could 'work'. I cannot imagine staying at home all day. I have gone to school every day since I was 7 years old. I never thought I would live the way my mother did. I can be a good wife and mother and yet have a job where I can have contact with other women like myself. Perhaps one day if I had everything I needed and had children, and my housework demanded I stay at home, I would give up my job. But not now. What if my marriage does not work out? Who knows—my husband might die when I still have young children, like my father did. My mother suffered so much bringing us up after my father died. She did everything she could so that I would not suffer her fate.

I left her then and came again to visit a few weeks later. She was happier and had solved the problem in a way that satisfied both her and her husband. She had gone to the Ministry of Education and demanded her right as a married woman to work near her future home. Her new workplace was a short bus ride away, a distance she could also walk. After discussing the situation with many of her friends and colleagues, she had decided to take up the veil. She had previously declared on many occasions that she would never veil because she did not see it as essential to being a good Muslim. While showing me her new clothes she explained:

> I wear a long skirt and this scarf. First, it is not that bad; it suits me better than many other women because my face is small. Second, if I have only two sets of clothes I can look smart at all times because

nobody expects *muhaggabat* (the veiled ones) to wear new
clothes every day. This will save me a lot of money. It will also
prevent people from talking about me, or questioning my honour
or my husband's. In this way I have solved all the problems, and my
husband's family are very happy that he is marrying a *muhaggaba*.

She continued to explain that none of the women in her fiancé's family
was educated or worked in an office. They had felt a little uncomfortable
before because they thought that educated and 'working' women generally do not attend to their homes well and do not respect their husbands.
Now that they are assured that she is a good Muslim and will respect her
husband, they are at ease with her. She said that her fiancé was
convinced that the problem had been solved and agreed to her going to
work. Of her own accord she had told him that when they had children
she would give up her job and stay at home if they did not need her
income. Apparently he had taken her willingness to accept his reasoning
and compromise as an indication of her being logical and sincere. He did
not continue to insist that she should not work.

She arranged to work two shifts until they were married in order to
buy the items they would need for their future home. She repeated many
times to me: 'A bride with no wealth wins no respect'. After marriage, she
would work only one shift, and so that she could continue to work as
long as she wished, her mother promised to help with child care and
with shopping and obtaining subsidized food. In order to facilitate this,
Sommayya had negotiated and included a condition in the marriage
contract that she should reside not far from her mother.

Clearly, veiling saves a lot on clothing expenditure because *muhaggabat* are no longer compared with women wearing western-style clothing,
who as a rule are expected to have a colourful wardrobe. But the function of veiling is not only an economic one. The veil communicates
loudly and clearly to society at large and to husbands in particular that
the wearer is bound by the Islamic idea of her sex role. A veiled woman
indicates that despite her unconventional economic activity she respects
traditional values and behaviour. By wearing the veil women lessen their
husbands' insecurity; they convey to their husbands that, as wives, they
are not in competition, but rather in harmony and cooperation with
them. Further, wearing the veil puts women in a position to expect and
demand that their husbands honour them and recognize their Islamic
rights. Husbands should not claim their wives' wages and they should
fulfil their duty of providing for the family to the best of their ability.

Soheir lost her father when she was a child and worked as a domestic
help in different households. Finally she managed to get her school
certificate and afterwards she got herself a job as a seamstress. She would

leave work to go to evening school and then return to the shop and work late. She had rented a room in a suburb of Cairo and always took the bus as late as 11 o'clock to go home. She said:

> So often people treated me badly that I would go home at night and cry. One day when I had gone to Sayida Zeinab [a popular shrine in Cairo] to cry and complain to her [the shrine] a woman started talking to me and suggested that I wear the veil. Then people would know that I am a good woman and that my circumstances have forced me to work late at night.

She thought about veiling and discussed it with some of her classmates who thought it was a good idea. So she took up the veil. She said: 'Since then I have had more peace than ever before'. People stopped judging her badly and assumed she must have a legitimate reason for being out late or being out all day. She continued: 'I sometimes miss wearing make-up and making myself beautiful, but there is no way I would give up the veil. When I am married and have a husband, I will put make-up on and let my hair loose for him.'

The women who veil do not necessarily become more religious. My data confirm MacLeod's (1987) findings; none of the women I came to know prayed or read the Koran more after they took up the veil. In fact, few women of the lower-income groups practised their religion strictly. Among the veiled women in my sample, only Sommayya prayed, and she had started to pray five time a day four years before she veiled. For the women who live it, Islam is a way of life, a value system and a recognized set of social behaviours.

There are other social reasons which have encouraged educated and working women to take up the veil. When many of the women marry and set up their own households, they are forced by rising prices to move to cheaper neighbourhoods on the outskirts of the city—much to their distaste (MacLeod, 1986; Hoodfar, 1988a; Shorter, 1989). Living in these neighbourhoods, educated women are more inclined to take up the veil. This is because they are eager to distinguish themselves from the *balady* and *falaheen* women, who are often illiterate and who behave and dress in traditional ways. The educated women thus separate themselves from the other women; yet they are still in good standing as members of the neighbourhood because their behaviour is socially approved. They uphold cohesion of values, but not equality in rank.

D. Women and Socialist Transformations

This section addresses questions about women's issues and socialist processes and transformations in the contemporary period. Are socialist development processes similar or dissimilar to capitalist processes for women? How has the transition from socialism to capitalism affected women?

30. CAPITALISM AND SOCIALISM: SOME FEMINIST QUESTIONS

Lourdes Benería

WHY SOCIALISM ANYWAY?

In this age of continued deregulation and privatization, to raise the issue of socialism seems almost a futile exercise. In the age of post-modernism and deconstruction this exercise seems almost out of fashion, even within progressive circles. Among feminists, there has always been a healthy mistrust of male-defined socialism, which is not to say that feminists have not been interested in progressive social change that might have a lot to do with what we loosely tend to call 'socialism'. Likewise, tired of the effort to deal with the unhappy marriage between Marxism and feminism, some feminists seem to be opting for their separation rather than reconciliation—thereby indirectly raising again the connection between socialism and feminism.[1]

Perhaps the time has come for socialism to be given a different name, or for asking, for the nth time, what we mean by the term. What can we, as feminists, say about it? More specifically, what might feminist socialism mean? Public ownership of the means of production or worker-owned firms? Elimination of hierarchies related to class and gender? Ecologically conscious production and consumption? Full employment? A centrally planned economy or market socialism? Equal share of domestic chores by men and women or collectivization of domestic work? Elimination of racism and homophobia? A moneyless utopia? All of the above? How relevant are these questions and how reconcilable, for example, with feminist utopias like Marge Piercy's *Woman on the Edge of Time*? I do not think that we can give up thinking about these questions if we want feminism to be a source of progressive social change.

More basically still we may want to ask why we need socialism at all. Capitalism has, after all, proved to be a very dynamic system, producing ever larger amounts of goods and services with progressively less amounts of labour. In the industrialized western countries, it has resulted in higher standards of living for the majority. The working class can now afford what would have been classified in the past as luxuries. For many, it has facilitated the acquisition of skills, access to knowledge and professional privileges, and a significant increase in individual freedoms. Why then are we talking about socialism? About feminist socialism? Could we not achieve our goals within the existing capitalist structures?

What follows is not an attempt to answer these questions. It is instead a brief reflection on and a reiteration of some of the most basic criticisms of capitalism and, in particular, a discussion of directions for progressive social change with a feminist perspective. It is done with the conviction that, if feminism is to continue to be a source of inspiration for this change, women need to discuss, as much as ever, the overall economic and social aspects of this transformation.

One of the basic features of capitalism is its foundation on the private ownership and control of the means of production. This implies that social decisions are made on the basis of private (as opposed to social/public) interest. But private and social needs may be convergent or in conflict. For Adam Smith and subsequent advocates of a *laissez-faire* economy, the genius of the market mechanism is that the pursuit of individual self-interest results in the maximization of 'the wealth of nations'. But, as Fritjo Capra has pointed out, the word 'private' comes from the Latin verb *privare*, which means depriving, or taking from communal property.[2] This appropriation by private interests of what were in the past (and could be in the future) communal resources and production is at the heart of why capitalism (and not necessarily the market) produces negative as well as positive results.

Some of the most persuasive arguments for socialism come from the negative results of capitalism: great disparities in the distribution of income and wealth, with corresponding inequalities in control over resources and political power; the appearance and reappearance of poverty in the midst of an ever-increasing capacity to produce goods and services (witness the recent growth in the number of the homeless and beggars in the midst of the extreme affluence and lavishness displayed in the centres of world trade and finance); high levels of unemployment or underemployment with human costs that go far beyond economic survival; the all-encompassing hidden and not-so-hidden injuries of class and their connections with race and gender; the increasing disparities between rich and poor countries and the permanence, and even increase, of hunger and malnutrition despite the existence of food surpluses; the destruction of the environment and the disappearance of natural resources and ecological balances through exploitation for private profit.

Underlying these problems there is the fundamental role played by greed in capitalist institutions and its penetration into the realm of social and individual relations in everyday life. This is not to say that the social experiments of the so-called socialist countries have not created their own set of problems. However, this provides no argument against the need to transcend capitalism and move toward new social experiments that respond more closely to the objectives of a just society in which the gap between our values and real life is minimized.

Women have not played the same role as men in either the positive or negative aspects of capitalist societies. First, they have often been exceptions to the pursuit of individual self-interest by virtue of their *primary* responsibilities in the sphere of the household, where the pressures of the market have penetrated less directly and at a slower pace. Second, given the concentration of resources and power in male hands, men have benefited more than women from the ownership and control of private property and from the benefits derived from capitalism. This is not to say that women have remained outside of the system, but that they have been part of it in different ways.

Similarly, the inequalities generated by capitalism have a specific gender dimension. The feminist literature of the past twenty years has extensively analysed the specific forms that the subordination of women has taken in capitalist societies. To be sure, gender subordination can also be observed in countries that have moved away from capitalist institutions, despite the many achievements registered. As feminists, we want to make note of these achievements while, at the same time, asking critical questions about the reasons behind their limitations.

WHAT DIRECTIONS FOR CHANGE?

The second wave of feminism has generated profound social criticisms, many of which have implications for any discussion of social change. In what follows, I summarize briefly what I think are fundamental aspects in a feminist consideration of alternative societies. My suggestions are not meant to be exhaustive, but simply to contribute some general points to this discussion:

1. The interaction between class and gender in determining women's lives should remain central to our understanding of what sort of changes

we want. Thus, some feminist objectives of eliminating gender asymmetries can be met within the structures of a capitalist society. In the industrialized capitalist world, for example, we have recently witnessed much progress in women's access to traditional male strongholds, such as politics and the corporate world. Yet to the extent that women's position in society is determined by class and economic and social structures, some of the inequalities affecting women require basic changes in these structures and institutions. For example, affirmative action and comparable-worth policies have proved to be important instruments in the pursuit of gender equality in the countries where they have been implemented.[3] Yet the progress made through these policies at some levels is being undermined in the current restructuring of the economy through the creation of new structures of production—such as the low-paid service sector, part-time work and other practices of work flexibilization—that relegate women again to the lower echelons of the labour hierarchy.[4] This is because these policies cannot address the more basic questions of control, exploitation and organization of economic life.

Similarly, the permanence of structures and institutions that benefit from gender inequalities also explains the dangers of a backlash and tendencies toward retrogressive policies that wipe out previous gains—as has happened in the US and other western countries in recent years. In other words, it might be difficult to implement long-lasting changes toward equality between the sexes without structural changes to build a more egalitarian society.

2. The complexity of the interaction between the material and the ideological aspects of women's condition is a second factor to be underlined. Many of the debates on the transition to socialism as well as platforms of left regimes have been dominated by an economistic approach: their emphasis on economics tends to overlook other basic areas of human development and well-being.[5] To the extent that women's condition is affected by economic factors, the debates are relevant for a discussion of women and socialism. But to the extent that the debates neglect ideological dimensions and their interaction with the material,[6] they cannot easily incorporate what Maxine Molyneux has called 'strategic gender interests' or short- and long-term feminist demands.[7] Thus, how gender roles are constructed and reproduced within the family and throughout the educational system, or through the media and other institutions, takes on a special meaning for women (as it does for racial and ethnic groups); not only do they effectively define women socially and politically, they also carry economic significance when translated into, for example, sex-typing of jobs, occupational segregation, lower wages, different promotional ladders and even job accessibility.

On the other hand, emphasis on the ideological only is likely to be ineffective unless it is accompanied by economic change. Campaigns challenging the traditional division of labour within the household are not likely to be very effective unless women have opportunities for employment in the paid labour market. Similarly, an effort to increase women's labour-force participation will be limited by the extent to which child care is available and by the economy's capacity to generate jobs. In Cuba, for example, the government's effort to increase women's labour-force participation seems to have been limited by an insufficient industrial base and its corresponding lack of growth in industrial and service employment.[8] Similarly, campaigns against male violence are likely to be more effective if accompanied by policies that increase women's economic autonomy and self-esteem.

3. A fundamental obstacle to the elimination of gender inequalities has proved to be in the sexual division of labour at the domestic level. The evidence along these lines is overwhelming and cuts across countries and economic systems. In the US, the lack of adequate child-care services for all working women and the limited or non-existent maternity leaves and maternity benefits continue to be a major handicap to the elimination of women's double day, and to their participation in the labour market and in social life under conditions of equality with men.

In countries attempting to build socialist institutions, the commitment to these policies tends to be much greater. However, the evidence shows that the private sphere of the household is at the root of continuing asymmetries between men and women. In some of these countries, an attempt has been made to influence the household sphere through the introduction of family codes, as in the case of Cuba. What we can learn from the Cuban case is that, despite its intrinsic interest and worthy objectives, and despite the debate that the Family Code was subject to, its 'spirit' cannot be imposed solely from the top down. What is also needed is a vigorous questioning at the bottom, fed by women's concerns and channelled through women's own networks and organizations.

4. Feminism has many implications for the question, 'What sort of alternative system?', or 'What form of socialism?' For example, given its emphasis on democratic and bottom-up processes of decision-making, feminism is less compatible with centralized planning and control of the economy than with more decentralized forms that emphasize individual or community control over resources. Thus, social ownership of the means of production does not necessarily imply government control and public enterprise. Other forms of collective ownership that allow control at the community level are likely to be more compatible with feminist processes of participatory decision-making and control. What specific

forms these might take will depend on cultural specificity and traditions and might vary across countries.

Similarly, a preference for collective forms of ownership does not automatically have to exclude private ownership of the means of production, particularly when private accumulation is regulated to prevent the creation of inequalities and the concentration of resources in the hands of a small proportion of the population. For example, retail trade and small business in the service sector do not seem to function efficiently under socialized forms of ownership. Given that resources in the small-business sector are not very concentrated, a system that allows them to organize production privately does not pose a serious threat to socialist principles of equality. Since a characteristic of feminism is its lack of dogmatism with respect to 'solutions', it can opt for what seems more compatible with feminist objectives without having to adapt to a rigid model of social change.

In this sense, feminists should pay attention to the now fashionable debate on 'the global march to free markets', which argues that a new emphasis on the advantages of the invisible hand of the market can be found in both western and centrally planned economies.[9] In both cases, it is argued, the state bureaucracies linked to public ownership and government regulation of the economy create inefficiency and distortions in the price system that slow down growth. Although such arguments need to be heeded, we should keep two points in mind. One is that even in the US we hear many voices pointing to the serious problems created by the new emphasis on the market, deregulation, privatization, and cuts in government services and welfare funds. The new polarization of income and wealth is intensifying social inequalities at a point in history when the tolerance for them has been decreasing. Second, it is not clear whether the new trend toward the use of the market in non-capitalist countries such as those of the former Soviet Union and of China implies a return to capitalism. At the moment, they represent new experiments, the results of which can not yet be fully evaluated.

As feminists, we want to pay attention to these experiments in order to best evaluate how compatible they are with our own objectives and practice. This might lead to contradictory conclusions. Thus, on the one hand, we want to be aware of the dangers of creating male-controlled bureaucracies and institutions insensitive to gender inequalities.[10] On the other, if these bureaucracies are eliminated through the market, we also want to be aware of possible negative consequences. For example, the reprivatization of land in China has eliminated the system of work points. This, together with a feminization of agriculture corresponding to men's tendency to take jobs in the towns, has meant that women's contribution to the household is no longer accounted for socially. The return to the market has, therefore, implied the re-emergence of old male privileges by eliminating mechanisms that decreased gender inequalities.[11] These contradictions, however, can be properly evaluated only at the level of each country's experience.

5. A fundamental aspect in the discussion of any alternative system is how production is organized and controlled and how its surplus is distributed. While this may appear to be a very economistic statement, here I want to emphasize the connections between what Burawoy has called 'the politics of production' and other aspects of everyday life.[12] Thus, hierarchical productive structures—beginning with the differentiation between those who own capital and those who need a wage to survive but including also the multiple dimensions of job differentiation—determine the distribution of income and wealth, shape class differences as well as social and political structures, and therefore have a bearing on individual and household location in society. Where we live and work, whether our children attend school or not and what kind of school, whether we eat at home or can afford to eat out, what we do with our leisure time, who our friends are and where we meet them, are all affected by where we are located within these productive structures.

Control over production and the sharing of the surplus also affect our lives in other ways. Thus, workers' control over production is likely to have an influence on the nature and direction of technological change and on the distribution of the firm's surplus. If women are involved, they are likely to press for day-care facilities and maternity leaves, and to stress policies affecting gender differentiation in the workplace.

Emphasis on the politics of production is also important in terms of evaluating proposals for social change. Maria Mies, for example, has called for a 'consumer liberation movement', to be led by women as primary consumers, that would aim at boycotting certain goods and struggling against business manipulation of consumers, and channel a social awareness about existing commodities in the market.[13] There is of course much ground to argue for actions that would create the true 'consumer's sovereignty' assumed by orthodox economic analysis of the market. Yet it seems naive to expect much from those actions alone. A more effective way to control what is being produced, and how, would be through the exercise of some form of collective control over production and surplus appropriation—hence creating the basis for future decisions on investment and growth. The question is how to do so without creating oppressive bureaucracies of centralized planning. If our objective is to move toward 'an emancipated society in which people make their own history' rather than having history being made 'behind their backs',[14] feminism is likely to emphasize its preference for a fusion of production politics and state politics that work from below. This requires a subtle combination of the need for collective work on the one hand, and respect for the individual and culturally determined social norms on the other.[15]

By way of a conclusion, production under socialism holds the potential to be organized so that it responds to social *need* rather than *profit* and to collective rather than individual planning. Thus, it opens the possibility of addressing those problems of concern to women whose solution may be in conflict with *private* profit-making production. How exactly a socialist collectivity might operate is not easy to establish by way of general principles and needs to be subject to new social experimentation. It is for this reason that socialism represents more a *direction* for change than a set of definitions.

31. DOWNWARDLY MOBILE: WOMEN IN THE DECOLLECTIVIZATION OF EAST EUROPEAN AGRICULTURE
MIEKE MEURS

There is little doubt that the transformations currently taking place in former centrally planned economies (CPEs) will be accompanied by rising inequality. Much of the critical discussion of this issue has focused on the class basis of this increase—inequality emerging between new owners of capital and the rest of the working population (e.g. Ost, 1993). Nonetheless, a growing body of feminist work has emphasized the ways in which rising class inequality in the transition is likely to be accompanied by increased gender inequality (Baer, 1993; Verdery, 1993).

Clearly, state socialism fell far short of creating gender equality. The persistence of occupational segregation and unequal pay is well-documented (Baer, 1993: 32; Meurs, 1993), as is the role of the state in perpetuating an unequal division of labour in the household (Duggan, 1993; Meurs, 1993). Women did, however, enjoy increased access to education, basic medical and child-care services, and guaranteed employment, all of which supported a degree of economic independence and equality.

For some women, state-socialist development policy meant even greater benefits. With rapid industrialization, technological change and the expansion of the service sector, a large number of white-collar jobs was created in areas traditionally dominated by women, such as health care and education, and in completely new areas such as skilled, agricultural jobs, which were not yet gender-defined. In these spheres, women were able to advance quickly to quite highly paid and responsible work.

With the end of the state-socialist experiment, a substantial amount of backlash has occurred against these relative advances by women. In Hungary, for example, political groups exhort men to reclaim their 'natural' role as provider and family authority, while women return to their proper nurturing role (Goven, 1992). This dynamic is accompanied by the withdrawal of social services for women, such as abortion and child care, which made it possible for women to pursue careers alongside men, despite the traditional division of household labour.

The backlash draws on traditional conceptions, unchallenged by state socialism, of the male as the 'main' worker which were reinforced by state policy (Duggan, 1993). New private and state employers participate in enforcing the new norms by discriminating explicitly against women, even in jobs in which women dominated under central planning, such as janitor and medical assistant (Baer, 1993: 43).

Some women are also participating in the backlash—voluntarily withdrawing from the labour force in response to their unhappy experience with the double burden of housework and paid work (Baer, 1993: 40). In Bulgaria, however, a poll showed that only 20 per cent of working women would voluntarily withdraw from the labour force, even if they could afford to do so (Bobeva, 1991: 19).

Important structural factors contribute to rising gender inequality during the transformation, independently of the changing norms. One of the most important is the structure of occupational segregation established under central planning. Those areas offering many of the best jobs to women—health, education and technical services—are precisely those under the greatest pressure from the push to eliminate 'unaffordable' services from the budgets of the state and private employers.[1]

One particular example of this dynamic can be seen in agriculture. I use Bulgarian data to examine the condition of women working in Eastern European collective agriculture and the likely impact of the transformation on these women. Bulgarian agriculture was among the most highly collectivized in Eastern Europe, and the experience of Bulgarian agricultural women is illustrative of those working in East European collective agriculture.[2]

The Bulgarian data indicate that not only are agricultural women becoming unemployed more rapidly than men, but women are also facing the selective elimination of the few skilled, better-paid jobs to which they had access. Combined with weak employment opportunities outside of agriculture, these changes are likely to increase gender inequality.

While inequality by class is also rising, the change in women's employment opportunities is likely to reduce class inequality among women. Unfortunately, there is little chance of this resulting in active resistance on the part of a broad group of rural women, given the history of anti-feminism in Eastern Europe. It does, however, create favourable conditions for an alliance between new private farmers and skilled women agricultural workers. In the final section of the [chapter], I consider the possibility of such an alliance and its potential to promote state policy which would partially combat rising gender inequality among agricultural workers.

THEORETICAL BACKGROUND: GENDER INEQUALITY UNDER PLAN AND MARKET

In a market economy, an individual's access to employment and level of remuneration are theoretically determined by property ownership and skills. Under these conditions, legal, institutional and cultural norms may perpetuate inequality between groups by enforcing inequalities in property and skill acquisition. Even if groups bring relatively equal property and skills to the labour market, however, norms of discrimination in hiring and remuneration will still generate inequalities.

Where legal or cultural norms produce inequalities in labour-market preparation or access by gender, these will, in turn, affect power relations in the home. As women's independent income rises, for example, this is likely to contribute to somewhat greater bargaining power for women in the home (Blumberg, 1988; McCrate, 1987).

Under central planning, the state is expected to intervene to reduce inequality. The most common form of intervention is through state ownership of capital, which limits inequalities resulting from unequal access to property. The state also has central control over education, the media and employment, which can be used to promote equality in skills acquisition and hiring, and to influence social norms. As labour-market options and state policy influence bargaining power within the household (Baer, 1993: 20), the state has the potential to mitigate inequalities both among and within households. In one example, the socialist state altered traditional gender norms in order to decrease the educational gap between rural women and men. In 1934, 57 per cent of rural women were illiterate, compared to 39 per cent of rural men. By 1967, only 6 per cent of rural women were illiterate, compared to 4 per cent of rural men (Statistical Yearbook, 1942: 35).

The state may also choose not to use its control to promote gender equality. Whether institutional power is so used will depend on other goals of the state, as well as the gender interests of the state itself, and on the level of political pressure from other gender-interested groups (Folbre, 1992).

The extent to which state-socialist governments influence both the distribution of skills and social norms plays an important role in the way East European women will experience the transition to a market economy. Where women have continued to face unequal access to skills and property, and norms of discrimination have persisted, the transitions from direct state control to market allocation, and from socialist norms to 'normality', will exacerbate gender inequalities unless countervailing measures are taken.

THE MEANING OF AGRICULTURAL COLLECTIVIZATION FOR BULGARIAN WOMEN

Collectivization and state-socialist development policy did encourage the reduction of gender inequality in a number of ways. By socializing land and actively incorporating women into paid labour, collectivization increased paid employment among women and increased recognition of women's agricultural labour.

In Bulgaria, women played a significant role in agricultural production prior to collectivization. They hoed and weeded certain crops, kept vegetable gardens and small livestock and helped with all crops at harvest time. Although much of this work was done independently of men, in women's mutual-aid groups, men were considered the principal farmers. Women were permitted to market vegetables, butter and eggs, but grain and large-livestock production were men's. Women could, in principle, own and inherit land, but sons generally inherited twice as much as daughters, and daughters often forfeited their claims to their brothers (Sanders, 1937: 54–5).

Collectivization formalized women's employment and thus expanded both their visibility in agricultural production and the share of their work subject to remuneration. According to the official statistics, women in the agricultural labour force increased from 40 per cent of agricultural workers in 1942 to approximately 67 per cent in 1967 (CSO, 1967; Statistical Yearbook, 1942: 37).[3] The collective farms attempted to monitor the labour input of each individual and guaranteed women equal pay for equal work.[4]

In order to encourage women to participate in the labour market, the state extended child care and, in the early 1970s, maternity benefits to farm workers. Women were also encouraged to increase their level of education. In addition to increasing labour-market equality, these developments may have contributed to greater gender equality in the home, as increased income gave women improved bargaining positions within the household.

Substantial gender inequality persisted, however. While the state exercised near-complete control over education and employment, efforts to reduce inequalities in employment opportunities were limited.

As agriculture was mechanized, occupational segregation by gender prevented most women from benefiting from the increasing number of tractors and other machines. Although the vast majority of agricultural workers continued to use only hand tools, as mechanization progressed women found themselves disproportionately represented among this majority of manual labourers—by 1986, an estimated 66 per cent of female agricultural workers as opposed to 35 per cent of male members (Institute of Sociology, 1986).

Very few women gained access to the most mechanized and best-paid jobs. Although women comprised 49 per cent of the agricultural labour force in 1985, they made up only 2–4 per cent of the highest-paying jobs as tractor driver, machinist and combine driver. In the less-mechanized areas of vegetable, fruit and tobacco production, however, women comprised the majority (73–76 per cent) of the workforce. Although no data are available on average wages by gender, an existing breakdown by job category suggests that those for women agricultural workers are well below those for men (see Table 31.1).

Table 31.1: Occupational segregation by gender (blue-collar workers), 1985

	Men	Women	% men	% women	Average pay
Tractor driver/machinist	57,406	1001	0.98	0.02	310 lev.
Combine driver	1995	83	0.96	0.04	488 lev.
Grain worker	33,435	103,428	0.24	0.76	157 lev.
Tobacco worker	32,375	88,337	0.27	0.73	157 lev.
Vegetable/fruit worker	15,237	47,442	0.24	0.76	157 lev.

Sources: CSO, 1987, 1988.

Weak labour-market opportunities limited increases in women's bargaining power in the home, reinforcing the persisting inequality in the distribution of household labour. In rural areas, this labour includes substantial amounts of work in subsistence agriculture on 'self-sufficiency plots', and the processing of production for household consumption. Including labour in growing, canning and curing this production, as well as housework, one study reported that women spent 35.8 hours per week in unpaid labour, compared to 13.9 hours for men (IATUR, 1991).

For some women, however, collective agriculture offered much greater opportunities for improving their position economically and within the household. The creation of large, mechanized units of production generated a substantial number of new technical and administrative jobs (from 21,293 in 1960 to 91,939 in 1985: CSO, 1987). These white-collar jobs were characterized by specialization, and average pay ranged from 18 per cent above that for blue-collar agricultural workers in 1971, to nine per cent above that for blue-collar workers in 1985 (see Table 31.2).

Table 31.2: Occupational segregation by gender (white-collar agricultural workers),* 1985

	Men	Women	% men	% women	Average pay
Management	9611	929	0.91	0.09	380 lev.
Veterinarian	2795	444	0.86	0.14	272 lev.
Head specialist	781	247	0.76	0.24	299 lev.
Engineer	9348	3513	0.73	0.27	249 lev.
Agronomist	6004	2476	0.71	0.29	252 lev.
TOTAL	28,539	7,609	0.79	0.21	291**
Normer	124	428	0.22	0.78	188 lev.
Bookkeeper	10	57	0.15	0.85	207 lev.
Cleaner/doorman	708	4405	0.14	0.86	161 lev.
Cashier	506	3311	0.13	0.87	167 lev.
Secretary	8	663	0.01	0.99	156 lev.
TOTAL	1,356	8,864	0.13	0.87	165**

*Selected occupations **weighted average

Sources: CSO, 1987,1988.

Many of the white-collar jobs were either relatively new and not strongly gender-typed, as in the case of agronomist, or were jobs traditionally considered acceptable for women, as in the case of secretarial work and bookkeeping. As a result, women gained relatively easy access to them. In 1985, women comprised 39 per cent of the white-collar labour force in agriculture, with 11 per cent of all women working in agriculture employed in the better paid white-collar jobs (see Table 31.2).

The new technical and administrative sectors were not immune from occupational segregation, however. Gender breakdowns of white-collar employees reveal that women are weakly represented in certain areas, such as management and veterinarian, where men comprise 91 per cent and 86 per cent of the employees, respectively. In other jobs, women were more heavily concentrated. Bookkeepers and work-point setters, for example, are 85 per cent and 78 per cent female, respectively (see Table 31.2).

Not surprisingly, women are concentrated at the lower end of the pay-scale. In the best paid white-collar jobs of farm management, veterinarian, head specialist, engineer, and agronomist, women comprise approximately 21 per cent of the labour force. In the low-paying jobs of cleaner and doorperson, secretary, basic bookkeeping, normer and cashier women comprise approximately 87 per cent (see Table 31.3).

Table 31.3: *Participation and unemployment of women in agriculture (selected class of work)*

	Share of employees 1985	Share of unemployed 1993
Management	0.09	0.25
Specialist	0.34	0.52
Worker	0.46	0.52

Sources: CSO, 1987; Ministry of Labour, 1993.

Still, women have much greater access to the best white-collar jobs. In farm management, women comprised 18 per cent of the workforce in 1985, well above the 4 to 6 per cent participation women achieved in the best-paid blue-collar work. These jobs provided creative and responsible work for rural women (CSO, 1988).

Interviews conducted in the summer of 1991 also suggest that women with responsible positions in farm management participated to a relatively limited extent in food production for home use (Field Notes, 1991). While still doing most of the housework, these women thus achieved somewhat greater equality in the distribution of household labour.

DECOLLECTIVIZATION AND WOMEN

Under the current Land Law, collective farm holdings will be returned to their pre-collectivization owners, resulting in a radical change in the structure of Bulgarian farms. Prior to collectivization, land was held in small units. In 1934, for example, each farm held an average of 17 units, each averaging 0.4hectares (ha) (CDIA, 1938/39: 165/1/82: 4) for a total of under 7ha per holding. There were few large units: only 11 per cent of the holdings were larger than 10ha, and only 1.5 per cent larger than 20ha (Statistical Yearbook, 1939). Under the decollectivization law, the old units will be further divided among the many children and grandchildren of the original owners.

Fragmented holdings resembling those of 1934 are unlikely to result.

Some parcels will be grouped into larger holdings, as urban heirs choose not to return to farming and instead lease the land to family members or other villagers. In other places, people's inability to afford new, small-scale machinery is encouraging the formation of cooperatives, in which contiguous, individually-owned parcels [of land] can be cultivated collectively using the available machinery.

These new, multi-owner farming units are unlikely to replicate the scale and complexity of the old collective farms, however. In many places, large-scale production cooperatives are being explicitly discouraged by local political forces. Perhaps more importantly, demand for agricultural goods is weak, as a result of the widespread economic recession in the old Soviet trading block and the general saturation of global agricultural markets. In this context, private investors hesitate to lay out the working capital needed to run a large-scale agricultural enterprise.

The emerging productive structure of private, small-scale, often family-based units will have a significant impact on the working conditions of both women and men. Decollectivization will mean the loss of significant social-welfare benefits associated with state employment, such as pensions, paid vacation and subsidized canteens. For women, this will also mean the loss of maternity leave.

As paid labour is replaced by work within the structure of the patriarchal family, many women will also lose in terms of recognition and direct remuneration for their work. In China, the centrally planned economy which has progressed furthest in decollectivizing agricultural production, researchers have noted that in family production, where labour input is measured informally, women are again 'seen as "just helping"' (Davin, 1988: 97).

In Bulgaria, women's customary rights to own land, organize informal women's work groups and earn income from garden plots may limit the degree of their subordination in the family farm. Even in the most inegalitarian households, Bulgarian men may feel that, as one husband in a Chinese family complained, 'Now that [my wife] handles everything inside and outside the house, I've been reduced to her farmhand' (Xiao Ming, 1983, in Davin 1988: 97).[5] Women in such households may actually have greater access to independent income with decollectivization, as they specialize in lucrative vegetables and small-livestock production.

Interviews in Bulgaria during the summer of 1993, however, suggest that this is unlikely to be the dominant dynamic. In three villages in different regions, we found no new, independent women farmers, although women were often reported to be 'helping' their husbands. As to who makes household decisions about farming, new farmers most often responded: 'The man, of course' (Field Notes, 1993). With the reduction in direct remuneration from paid employment, women are also likely to lose bargaining power within the household.

Substantial additional blows to agricultural workers will also result from the elimination of skilled technical and administrative jobs which will accompany the breakup of the large-scale production units. As with cuts in state employment in general, cuts in these jobs will hurt agricultural workers of both genders, and, because men still control the majority of the best white-collar jobs, a greater absolute number of men may be affected than women. Nonetheless, the loss of these jobs will be particularly damaging to women for two reasons.

First, women are likely to suffer disproportionately because of the particular structures of occupational segregation. Men, with their skills as drivers and mechanics for agricultural machines, have had some excellent blue-collar job options, and they appear likely to retain them despite the restructuring. As tractors make their way into the private sector, for example, their drivers often accompany them as contract employees. These drivers are indispensable, because they know the secrets of making the out-dated machines work, especially in the absence of spare parts.

Due to the persistence of traditional perceptions of what constitutes 'appropriate' work for women, women are much more likely to obtain technical education in the areas of secretarial work, bookkeeping or agronomy (see Nickle, 1993 for a discussion of this dynamic in the former German Democratic Republic). These skills are less often employed by the new private farmers. Farming households themselves have few bookkeeping skills, and many of those interviewed during 1993 kept only the most rudimentary accounts of their operations (Field Notes, 1993). Although they are experimenting with many new crops and inputs, farming households also do without technical advice. Many of the skills which women agricultural workers have to offer would thus increase the efficiency of the new farming units. Unfortunately, these services are unavailable to most farming households under the current conditions.

Second, the loss of white-collar agricultural jobs will affect women disproportionately because of the persistence of cultural norms which consider men to be the main breadwinners and women to be secondary workers. Skilled women are being displaced much more rapidly than men; although women comprised 9 per cent of management and 34 per cent of specialists in 1985 (the most-recent available data), as of 30 April 1993 they comprised 25 per cent and 52 per cent of unemployed managers and specialists respectively (see Table 31.3).

There are few options available to these women which will allow them to preserve the gains they have made in income and status. Much of the rural industry built by the state-socialist government has collapsed in the face of new policies and market forces, and national labour markets must contend with more than 120,000 unemployed specialists and more than 50,000 unemployed persons with university educations (Ministry of Labour, 1993).

Independent private farming, perhaps the obvious option for those women with technical agricultural skills, will be difficult for them to develop. Skilled women agricultural workers have less background in private farming. Whereas 61 per cent of women working in unskilled agricultural jobs earned income from private production in 1986, only 33 per cent of skilled women workers earned such income (Town and Village, 1986). This difference is not surprising: as full-time, salaried employees, these white-collar workers had less time to devote to household production than blue-collar workers, whose work varied more on a daily basis.

A second complicating factor in white-collar women's entrance into private farming has to do with access to property. Land will be returned to families in the village where the owner lived at the time of collectivization. Skilled white-collar workers, who have trained in a central city, are now much more likely than their blue-collar counterparts to live far from the village of their parents and grandparents. Farming their own land will mean moving to a distant village where they may have few of the social contacts necessary to begin independent farming. Renting land is an option, but relatively few households currently rent out land, and those that do prefer to rent to family members (Field Notes, 1993).

CONCLUSION

As we have seen, the state-socialist government fell far short of eliminating gender inequality in the workplace or the home. Nonetheless, collective farming did increase the visibility of women's work in agriculture and their access to income generated by their work. In addition, it created a number of white-collar jobs which provided better-paid, higher-status work to some women than was available in blue-collar employment.

With decollectivization and the transition to a market economy, many of these gains are likely to be lost. Women find themselves disadvantaged in their access to property, as persisting inequalities in gender relations within households contribute to unequal control over redistributed farm property. Further, the structure of occupational segregation under central planning has left women with skills which are much more difficult to transfer to private-sector agriculture.

Both mid-career women and men are being marginalized from the labour force in Eastern Europe to such an extent that this group is being dubbed the 'lost generation' (Baer, 1993). But with social norms justifying disproportionately higher rates of dismissal for women, the loss of access to the better jobs is likely to become more than a generational problem. Once the presence of women in skilled agricultural work has been sufficiently reduced, the way is opened for these positions to become 'men's jobs'.

The level of gender inequality will be strongly affected by this truncating of women's income-earning opportunities, while the degree of inequality among women will be reduced. Because women are being systematically excluded from the new upper class of 'bizness*men*', as they are being called, inequalities among women, defined by their own income, are likely to decrease, while at the same time differences among household incomes will increase, i.e. in class terms women will differ but in gender terms they will homogenize. This compression of women's incomes and choices appears unlikely to generate a united political force for protecting women's gains. The long history of anti-feminist rhetoric in Eastern Europe, combined with the current backlash, makes it difficult for women to understand themselves as a social group with particular interests and rights.

Income differentials among agricultural households are also increasing, however, and this creates the possibility of another type of political alliance which could help to preserve some of women's gains. Many of the less-skilled farming households could benefit greatly from the skills which the specialists have to offer. An alliance between the weaker, agricultural households and skilled agricultural workers, around the concrete goal of protecting agricultural extension services, is possible.

Poorly developed markets, uncertainty and financial constraints in the farming sector make it unlikely that extension services will emerge from market stimuli alone. Government support will be needed to coordinate and subsidize these services and to assure that equal-opportunity practices protect women's access to the jobs in this sector.

In the current ideological context, neither role for the state is unproblematic. The state, however, has a unique opportunity. Patterns of household organization and farming are in process of radical transformation, and state policy can have a particularly strong influence in either reinforcing or eroding patriarchal norms of prerogative and control.

The economic and social benefits of such a policy are clear. Promoting agricultural extension work with equal-employment opportunities for the many available women technicians would limit government expenditure compared to the alternatives of retraining workers and creating employment in new branches. At the same time, it would contribute to economic recovery by encouraging a more productive use of women's labour and of other agricultural resources.

The policy would offer clear political benefits to reform-governments.

Significant anti-privatization sentiment has currently stalled reform in the countryside. Potential private farmers resist privatization due to uncertainty regarding their ability to farm successfully. Agricultural technicians and administrators resist because of the threat privatization poses to their livelihood. Women technicians are an important part of this alliance.

The offer to protect a share of skilled agricultural jobs through the creation of an extension service could bring sections of both groups into line behind reform. Such an extension service could also be designed to offer explicit assistance to unskilled farm women, in order to raise their access to independent income.

Whether the state can play this role remains an open question. Although there are clear economic and political reasons to protect the gains of white-collar agricultural women, the gender interests and urban bias of the male-dominated state have prevented serious consideration of these issues to date. Any change in state policy will likely depend on the strength of the emerging alliance—on the ability of skilled agricultural workers and new farms to unite across the lines of both class and gender.

NOTES TO PART 4

CHAPTER 22

1.   Omar Davies and Patricia Anderson, 'The Impact of the Recession and Adjustment Policies on Poor Urban Women in Jamaica'. Paper prepared for UNICEF (Kingston: University of the West Indies, 1987), p. 1.

2.   Ibid., p.5; see also Miguel Ceara, *Situación Socioeconómica Actual y Su Repercusión en la Situación de la Madre y el Niño* (Santo Domingo: INTEC and UNICEF, 1987)

3.   Inter-American Development Bank, *Economic and Social Progress in Latin America, 1989 Report* (Washington, DC: IDB, 1989), Table B-1. This comparison is based in 1988 dollars.

4.   To combat growing malnutrition, the government of Edward Seaga instituted a Food Aid Program for primary-school children, nursing mothers and the indigent. Although half the total population of Jamaica qualifies for this programme (about one million people), in the first six months of the programme it was reaching only 20 per cent of the targeted population. See Derrick Boyd, 'The Impact of Adjustment Policies on Vulnerable Groups: The Case of Jamaica, 1973–1985', in Giovanni Cornia, R. Jolly and F. Stewart (eds) *Adjustment with a Human Face*, Vol II. (New York: Clarendon Press/UNICEF, 1988), p.141.

5.   Giovanni Cornia and Francis Stewart, 'Country Experiences with Adjustment', in Cornia, Jolly and Stewart (eds), *Adjustment with a Human Face*, Vol. 1, p. 115.

6.   Joan French, 'The CBI and Jamaica: Objectives and Impact', Report prepared for the Development Group for Alternative Policies (Washington), 1987, pp. 50–51.

7. World Bank, *The World Development Report*, 1982 and 1989 edns, (Washington, DC: World Bank, 1982 and 1989), Table 32.
8. Ceara, *Situación Socioeconómica*, pp. 55, 28.
9. The World Bank, *World Development Report* 1989, Table 32.
10. Ceara, *Situación Socioeconómica*, p. 29.
11. Nelson Ramírez, Isis Duarte and Carmen Gómez, *Poblacíon y Salud en República Dominicana* (Santo Domingo: Instituto de Estudios de Poblacíon y Desarrollo, Boletín 16, 1986), p. 12.
12. Quoted in Whiteford, 'Sugar and Survival', p. 15.
13. Linda Whiteford 'Sugar and Survival: The Economic Crisis and Health in the Dominican Republic, draft, University of South Florida, 1988, p. 23.
14. Ibid., p. 16.
15. Duarte, 'Crisis, Familia y Participación', p. 12.
16. Davies and Anderson, 'The Impact of the Recession', p. 37.
17. The Reagan administration gave garment producers located in the Caribbean increased access to the US market in 1986, giving CBI-designated countries expanded quotas for garments assembled from US-formed, made and cut cloth; see discussion in Chapter 6.
18. French, 'The CBI and Jamaica', pp. 31–2.
19. Ibid., pp. 33–4.
20. Alfonso Abreu, Manuel Cocco, Carlos Despradel, Eduardo García Michel, and Arturo Peguero, *Las Zonas Francas Industriales en la República Dominicana: El Exito de una Politica Económica* (Santo Domingo: Centro Internacional para el Desarrollo Económico, 1989), pp. 63–7, 141.
21. Susan Joekes, *Employment in Industrial Free Zones in the Dominican Republic: A Report with Recommendations for Improved Worker Services* (Washington, DC: International Center for Research on Women, for USAID/Dominican Republic, 1987), p. 55.
22. Other sources show Dominican wages being slightly higher than in Haiti for that same year; see Abreu *et al.*, *Las Zonas Francas*, p. 130.
23. The 1981 study of women in the free-trade zones of the Dominican Republic was conducted by CIPAF (Centro de Investigación para la Acción Femenina), a feminist research centre directed by Magaly Pineda. Two members of the CIPAF research team, Quintina Reyes and Milagros Ricourt, along with Lorraine Catanzaro, wrote MA theses at the University of Florida using this data. See Quintina Reyes, 'Comparative Study of Dominican Women Workers in Domestic and Free Trade Zone Industries', MA thesis, Centre for Latin American Studies, University of Florida, 1987; Milagros Ricourt, 'Free Trade Zones, Development, and Female Labor in the Dominican Republic', MA thesis, Centre for Latin American Studies, University of Florida, 1986; and Lorraine Catanzaro, 'Women, Work, and Consciousness: Export Processing in the Dominican Republic', MA thesis, Centre for Latin American Studies, University of Florida, 1986.
24. Joekes, *Employment in Industrial Free Zones*, p. 59.
25. Mones and Grant, 'Agricultural Development', pp. 43–5. Also see Francis Pou, *et al.*, *La Mujer Rural Dominicana* (Santo Domingo: CIPAF, 1987). This study, based on the first national sample survey of rural women, found that the percentage of rural women listed as economically active in the 1981 Census was grossly underestimated because of the failure to include all of the ways in which women contribute economically to the household.

26. Patricia Anderson and Derek Gordon, 'Economic Change and Labour Market Mobility in Jamaica, 1979–1984'. Paper presented to the First Conference of Caribbean Economists, Kingston, Jamaica, 1987.

27. See Economic Commission for Latin America and the Caribbean (ECLAC), *Women in the Inter-Island Trade in Agricultural Produce in the Eastern Caribbean* (Trinidad: ECLAC, 1988), and the papers presented at the ECLAC Advisory Group Meeting on Women Traders in the Caribbean, Grenada, 9–11 May 1988, particularly: Alicia Taylor, 'Women Traders in Jamaica: The Informal Commercial Importers', Monique Lagro, 'Women Traders in St Vincent and the Grenadines'; and Daphne Phillips, 'Women Traders in Trinidad and Tobago'.

28. ECLA, *Women in the Inter-Island Trade*.

29. The dimensions of the Caribbean higgling trade are not to be under-rated. A recent study found that approximately 1200 to 1500 Haitians (the majority of whom are women) regularly travel to Puerto Rico, purchasing approximately $13 million worth of goods annually, which are then resold in Haiti. See Paul Latortue and Luis Luna Rosado, 'Los Comerciantes Ambulantes Haitianos en Puerto Rico', Centro de Investigaciones Comerciales, University of Puerto Rico, mimeo (1985).

30. PREALC, 'Empleo y Politica Económica de Corto Plazo', memorandum prepared for ONAPLAN, Santo Domingo, 1983, pp. 8, 15.

31. Baez, *La Subordinación de la Mujer*, p. 50.

32. Helen Safa, 'Urbanization, the Informal Economy and State Policy in Latin America', in Michael P. Smith and Joseph Feagin (eds) *The Capitalist City* (New York: Basil Blackwell, 1987).

33. Among East Indians, their physical and social isolation from the wider society of Trinidad and Guyana allowed them to retain much of their traditional culture and religion. However, family structures such as visiting unions and common-law marriage are now becoming a part of their marital pattern as among Afro-Caribbeans.

34. Duarte, 'Crisis, Familia, y Participación', p. 17.

35. See Bolles, 'Kitchens Hit By Priorities', p. 156.

36. Christine Barrow, 'Finding the Support: Strategies for Survival', *Social and Economic Studies*, 35, No. 2 (June 1986).

37. See Catanzaro, 'Women, Work and Consciousness'.

38. Baez argues that the percentage of female-headed households is underestimated because it relies on the opinion of the informant surveyed (*La Subordinación de la Mujer*, p. 31). The higher figure is obtained, utilizing a method suggested by the United Nations, which measures the percentage of households where there are women with younger children and no adult men. If we assume that headship connotes family authority and responsibility, it could be argued that many women and men are sharing this responsibility. However, census data do not capture these changing patterns of family authority and responsibility, and we have followed the conventional usage of 'male head of household', which was used in most studies we consulted. See Helen Safa, 'Women and Industrialization in the Caribbean', in Jane Parpart and Sharon Stichter (eds) *Women, Employment and the Family in the International Division of Labor* (New York: Macmillan, forthcoming).

39. Carmen Julia Gómez and Maria Gator, 'La Mujer Jefe de Hogar y la Vivienda', *Población y Desarrollo*, No. 19, (1987), p. 13.

CHAPTER 23

1. Redeployment, the official term used in Ghana, connotes relocation of workers from one sector to another, but in practice this rarely takes place. Instead the worker becomes unemployed.
2. Interviews by the author with TUC officials for a study 'Women in Trade Unions in Ghana and the Structural Adjustment Programme', in *The African Crisis and Women's Vision of a Way Out*, AAWORD, Dakar, nd.
3. The index of real wages (1970 = 100) was 32.1 in 1987 and 30.7 in 1987 (Ghana Statistical Service, *Ghana Living Standards Survey*, Accra, 1989), but rural wages were lower.
4. The Labour Decree 1967 provides for three months' maternity leave with pay for formal-sector employees, half before and half after the birth of a child; two half-hour periods for breast-feeding infants up to the age of 9 months are also provided. Although no conditions are attached to these benefits, in practice non-public-sector employers will grant full maternity benefits only to women who have worked for specified minimum periods.
5. Ghana Statistical Service, *Ghana Demographic and Health Survey*, 1989.
6. PNDC Law 111.
7. *Ghana Demographic and Health Survey*.
8. UNDP, 'The Place and Role of Women in Development in Ghana', 1988, Project GH, OPE/88 prepared by E. Ardayfio-Schandorf.
9. Gracia Clark and Takyiwaa Manuh, 'Women Traders in Ghana and the Structural Adjustment Programme', in Christina Gladwin (ed.) *Structural Adjustment and African Women Farmers*, University of Florida Press, Gainsville, 1990.
10. The announcement of the scheme in the Ghanaian newspapers specifically excluded traders. See Clark and Manuh for a discussion of the issues.
11. From Clark's survey, in Clark and Manuh.
12. These are the Urban 1 and 2 programmes in the major cities, financed by the World Bank.
13. Space allocation in city markets is the responsibility of municipal authorities and is often surrounded by a lot of controversy as it becomes yet another instance where power is exercised by powerful local interests over relatively powerless groups and individuals.
14. While GAWU links agricultural workers together in predominantly state farms and plantations, and pre-harvest workers in the cocoa sub-sector employed by the Cocoa Board and its subsidiaries, the ICU deals with post-harvest workers in the cocoa industry.
15. The ILO/JASPA report noted that many retrenched persons had relocated to agriculture, but agricultural extension officers interviewed in Barekese doubted this and suggested that many of those classified as relocating to agriculture had always farmed, but perhaps less intensively. In other words, there were conceptual problems in occupational classification and persons were listed as being in one occupation when they were actually involved in a number of activities simultaneously.
16. Report of the Chairman to the GAWU Congress, October 1987 (unpublished).

CHAPTER 25

1. Parts of this chapter are drawn from my longer paper, 'Old Maps and New Terrain: The Politics of Women, Population and the Environment in the

1990s', presented to the Fifth International Interdisciplinary Congress on Women, San Jose, Costa Rica, 23 February 1993; this paper contains an analysis of how the population/environment lobby formed and how it operates in practice.

2. The 'green revolution' refers to the introduction of highly fertilizer-responsive varieties of wheat and rice into Asia and Latin America, which has led to large increases in agricultural production. There are, however, many environmental and distributional problems associated with green-revolution technology.

3. In 1994, the Zapatista army led a rebellion of poor, indigenous peasants in the southern Mexican state of Chiapas. They demanded redistribution of wealth and democratization, and declared NAFTA an enemy of indigenous people.

CHAPTER 26

1. Women and AIDS Resource Network (WARN) *Women and AIDS: The Silent Epidemic*, WARN, New York, June 1988.
2. J. Mann, 'Global AIDS: Epidemiology, Impact, Projections and the Global Strategy', paper presented at the World Summit of Ministers of Health on Programmes for AIDS Prevention, WHO, London, 26–8 January, 1988.
3. E.N. Ngugi and R.A. Plummer *et al.* 'Prevention of Transmission of HIV in Africa: Effectiveness of Condom Promotion and Health Education Among Prostitutes', *The Lancet*, October: 887–90 1988.
4. J. McGrath, 'No Human Rights—Brazil', Interview with Gabriella, a prostitute, in Rio de Janiero, May 1988 in Tina Wallace and Candida March (eds) *Changing Perceptions*, Oxfam, Oxford.
5. S. Ramos, 'Um Rostro de mulher', magazine article.
6. E. N. Ngugi, 'Prevention of Transmission'.
7. (Abstract) (1988/9), 'Heterosexual Transmission of HIV', *The AIDS Letter*, No.10, Royal Society of Medicine, December/January, p.4.
8. S. Day, H. Ward and J.R. Harris (1988) 'Prostitute Women and Public Health', *British Medical Journal* 297: 1585.
9. J. Mann, 'Global AIDS'.
10. P. Keogh, S. Allen, and R.N. Almeda Calle, 'Study of Needs of HIV-seropositive women in Rwanda'. Study completed in August 1988, report in progress.
11. P. Thornycroft, 'Dying in Silence', *Parade*, Zimbabwe, December 1988.
12. Editorial 'Vertical Transmission of HIV', *The Lancet* 2: 1057–8, 1989.
13. J. Mariam and M. Radlett 'Women Face New Dilemmas', *AIDS Watch 5*, IPPF. 'Empowering Bar Workers in Bangkok', *Community Development Journal* 24 (30): 202, 1989.
14. Women and AIDS Action 'Women, HIV and AIDS', AHRTAG, Issue 9, December 1989.
15. M. Tan, A. de Leon, B. Stoltzfus and C. O'Donnel (1989) 'AIDS as a Political Issue: Working with the Sexually Prostituted in the Philippines', *Community Development Journal* 24 (30): 202, pp. 186–93.
16. Women and AIDS Action, 'Women, HIV and AIDS', AHRTAG, Issue 9, December, 1989.

CHAPTER 27

1. National Democratic Front, a united front composed of various organizations opposed to the Marcos dictatorship.
2. In reply to my query in Manila several months ago about the status of

Gabriela, a friend confirmed that while still significant, the federation is not as central to the movement as it used to be since many groups functioning outside its purview now exist.

3. In recent years, money previously given to the government has been channelled to non-governmental organizations (NGOs), a notable number of which have a women-in-development focus or a mandate toward 'gender sensitivity', (de Vera, 1992: 16; St Hilaire, 1992). For discussions of the implications of this trend, see Constantino-David (1990) and Council for People's Development (1991).

4. A 'newly industrializing country' in the manner of Taiwan, South Korea and Singapore.

5. Also sometimes referred to as a 'grand narrative', a totalizing theory is one that seeks to explain discrete or seemingly unrelated social phenomena as components of an integrated whole.

CHAPTER 28

1. The Holy Koran, Ayeh 4 Surah 2.
2. L.P. Elwell-Sutton, 'The Iranian Revolution', *The International Journal*, Vol. XXXIV, No. 3 (1979), pp. 392–4.
3. A further decree on this subject was ratified by the cabinet on 5 October 1979.
4. For further details see H. Afshar's, 'The Iranian Theocracy', in H. Afshar (ed.), *Iran, A Revolution in Turmoil* (London: Macmillan, 1985), pp. 220–44.
5. The Koran, 2/228
6. Ibid., 4/34
7. Hojatoleslam A.A. Akhtari, *Akhlaqeh Hamsardari Eslami* (ethics of Islamic marriage) serialized in *Zaneh Rouz*, 28 July 1984.
8. Address to women members of the Islamic party reported in *Kayhan*, 26 July 1984.
9. *Qanouneh Taazirat* (Secular code concerning matters not specifically stated in the Koran, which are subject to the decision of the judge, *Hakemeh Shahr*) 29 June 1983, note to article 102. Article 101 of the same act apportions 99 lashes for people of the opposite sex who are not related by marriage, including daughters and fathers and brothers and sisters, seen kissing in public.
10. Ayatollah Moussavi Bojnourdi, interviewed by *Zaneh Rouz*, 18 August 1984.
11. *Kayhan*, 26 July 1984
12. *Kayhan*, 23 July 1984
13. *Kayhan*, 14 March 1983
14. *Zaneh Rouz*, 18 August 1984

CHAPTER 30

1. See, for example, Michèle Barrett's Introduction to the 1988 edn of her book *Women's Oppression Today* (London: Verso, 1980).
2. Frijto Capra. *Turning Point* (New York: Simon and Schuster, 1982).
3. Brigid O'Farrell and Sharon Harlan, 'Job Integration Strategies: Today's Programs and Tomorrow's Needs', in Barbara Reskin (ed.) *Sex Segregation in the Workplace* (Washington, DC: National Academy Press, 1984); and Hartmann, Heidi (ed.) *Comparable Worth: New Directions for Research* (Washington, DC: National Academy Press, 1985).
4. Barry Bluestone and Sarah Kuhn, 'Economic Restructuring and the Female Labour Market: The Impact of Industrial Change on Women'. in Benería, L.

and C. Stimpson, *Women, Households and the Economy* (New Brunswick, NJ: Rutgers University Press, 1988).

5. There are of course exceptions and interesting efforts to include a wider range of topics. See, for example, Richard Fagen, Carmen Diana Deere and José Luis Coraggin, (eds). *Transition and Development: Problems of Third World Socialism* (New York: Monthly Review Press, 1987).

6. See Barrett, *Women's Oppression Today* and L. Benería and M. Roldán, *The Crossroads of Class and Gender* (Chicago: University of Chicago Press, 1987).

7. Maxine Molyneux, 'Mobilization Without Emancipation? Women's Interests, State, and Revolution', in Fagen *et al.* (eds). *Transition and Development*. pp. 280–302.

8. Margaret E. Leahy, *Development Strategies and the Status of Women: A Comparative Study of the United States, Mexico, the Soviet Union, and Cuba* (Boulder: Lynne Riener, 1986).

9. Steve Greenhouse. 'The Global March to Free Markets', *New York Times*, 19 July, 1987.

10. Christine White, 'Socialist Transformation of Agriculture and Gender Relations', in John Taylor and Andrew Turton (eds), *Sociology of Developing Societies—South East Asia* (London and New York: Macmillan and Monthly Review Press, 1988).

11. Phyllis Andors, personal communication.

12. Michael Burawoy, *The Politics of Production* (London: Verso, 1985).

13. Maria Mies, *Patriarchy and Accumulation on a World Scale* (London: Zed Books, 1986).

14. Burawoy, *Politics and Production,* p. 157.

15. Many differences exist, for example, among countries of different cultural norms and traditions. Thus the emphasis on the individual by feminists in western countries tends to be culturally biased and without meaning in societies where the collective, be it the household or a larger social group, is more prevailing. The search for the right combination between the collective and the individual is therefore likely to be influenced by these factors.

CHAPTER 31

1. See Bergmann (1993) for a discussion of the use of the term 'affordability' in political discussions over benefit reduction and restructuring in the United States economy.

2. There are, of course, significant differences in the collectivization experiences of Eastern European countries. With respect to women's participation in agriculture, however, the similarities among those Eastern European countries with collectivized agriculture (Romania, Bulgaria, Hungary, and Czechoslovakia) are significant.

3. Collective farms controlled approximately 87 per cent of farm land. Women comprised 47 per cent of the labour force on state farms, which farmed approximately eight per cent of agricultural land (Dobrin, 1973).

4. Pay was first calculated according to the work day, and later according to task, but no distinction was made between the value of men's and women's working days.

5. Note the persistence of the double burden.

REFERENCES TO PART 4

CHAPTER 23

Anyemedu, K., (n.d.) 'Economic Policies of the PNDC', in E. Gyimah-Boadi (ed.) *Ghana under PNDC rule*. Codesria Book Services, Dakar.

Clark, G. and Manuh, T. (1991). 'Women Traders in Ghana and the Structural Adjustment Programme', in C. Gladwin (ed.) *Structural Adjustment and Africa—Women Farmers*, University of Florida Press.

Elson, D. (1989) 'The Impact of Structural Adjustment on Women', in B. Onimode (ed.) *The IMF, the World Bank and the Africa Debt Problem: Social and Economic Consequences*, London: Zed Press.

Ghana Statistical Service 1970; 1984 Population Census of Ghana; Accra, Ghana Demographic and Health Survey 1989; Ghana Living Standards Survey, Accra, 1988; and 1989 Quarterly Digest of Statistics.

Green, R.H. (1987) 'Stabilisation and Adjustment Policies and Programmes' Country Case Study Ghana', Lyndhurst, NJ: Wider Publications.

ILO (1989) *From Redeployment to Sustained Employment Generation: Challenges for Ghana's Programme of Economic Recovery and Development*, Addis Ababa: Jobs and Skills Programme for Africa.

Manuh, T. (forthcoming) 'Women in Trade Unions in Ghana and SAP' in, *The Africa Crisis and Women's Vision of a Way Out*, Dakar: AAWORD.

Manuh, T. (in preparation) 'Gender and Access to Land in Ghana'.

Public Sector Management Group (1988) 'Manpower Development Study, Toronto, Canada, cited in ILO/JASP.

The Economist Intelligence Unit (1989) 'Ghana Country Profile 1989–90', London: EIU.

UNDP (1988) 'The Place and Role of Women in Development in Ghana', Project No. GH. OPE/88 prepared by E. Ardayfio-Schandorf.

World Bank (1989) 'Ghana Structural Adjustment for Growth', Washington DC: World Bank.

CHAPTER 24

Aird, John S. (1990) *Slaughter of the Innocents: Coercive Birth Control in China*, Washington, DC: AEI Press.

Aslanbeigui, Nahid and Summerfield, Gale (1989) 'Impact of the Responsibility System on Women in Rural China: An Application of Sen's Theory of Entitlements', *World Development* 17 (3): 343–50.

Blewett, Kate and Brian Woods (1995) 'The Dying Room', a documentary film, CBS *Eye-to-Eye*, 17 August.

Coale, Ansley J. (1991) Excess Female Mortality and the Balance of the Sexes in the Population: An Estimate of the Number of "Missing Females"', *Population and Development Review* 17 (3): 517–23, September.

Croll, Elizabeth (1984) 'The Single-child Family: The First Five Years', in Neville Maxwell and Bruce McFarlane (eds), *China's Changed Road to Development*, Oxford, England: Pergamon Press.

——(1994) *From Heaven to Earth: Images and Experiences of Development in China*, London and New York: Routledge.

Dalsimer, Marlyn and Laurie Nisonoff (1987) 'The Implications of the new Agricultural and One-child Family Policies for Rural Chinese Women', *Feminist Studies* 13 (3): 583–607, Fall.

Greenhalgh, Susan (1990a) 'The Evolution of the One-child Policy in Shaanxi 1979–88', *The China Quarterly* 122: 191–229, June.

——(1990b) 'Socialism and Fertility in China', *Annals of the American Academy of Political and Social Science* 510: 73–86, July.

Hull, Terence H. (1990) 'Recent Trends in Sex Ratios at Birth in China', *Population and Development Review* 16 (1): 63–83, March.

Human Rights Watch/Asia (1996) *Death by Default: A Policy of Fatal Neglect in China's State Orphanages*, New York: Human Rights Watch.

Jenner, W.J.F. and Delia Davin (eds) (1987) *Chinese Lives: An Oral History of Contemporary China*, New York: Pantheon.

Johansson, Sten and Ola Nygren (1991) 'The Missing Girls of China: A New Demographic Account', *Population and Development Review* 17 (1): 35–51, March.

Lavely, William, James Lee and Wang Feng (1990) 'Chinese Demography: The State of the Field,' *The Journal of Asian Studies* 49(4): 807–34, November.

Mosher, Steven W. (1993) *A Mother's Ordeal: One Woman's Fight Against China's One-child Policy*, New York: Harcourt, Brace & Company.

Sen, Amartya (1990) 'More Than 100 Million Women Are Missing', *New York Review of Books*, 20 December: 61–6.

Schmetzer, Uli (1993) 'In Controlling China's Population, Girls "Disappear",' *Chicago Tribune*, 27 April: 1, 14.

Sullivan, Lawrence R. (ed.) (1995) *China Since Tiananmen: Political, Economic and Social Conflicts*, Armonk, NY: M.E. Sharpe.

Tyler, Patrick E. (1995) 'Birth Control in China: Coercion and Evasion', *New York Times*, 25 July: 1, 8.

——(1996) 'China's Orphanages, a War of Perception', *New York Times*, 21 January: H 31.

Wolf, Margery (1972) *Women and Family in Rural Taiwan*, Stanford: Stanford University Press.

——(1985) *Revolution Postponed: Women in Contemporary China*, Stanford: Stanford University Press.

CHAPTER 25

Adamson, Peter (1992) 'The Power of Planning Births, *People and the Planet*, 1(1): 30–31.

Barraclough, Solon and Ghimire, Krishna (1990) 'The Social Dynamics of Deforestation in Developing Countries: Principal Issues and Research Priorities, Discussion Paper 16, UNRISD, Geneva, pp. 1–40.

Benería, Lourdes (1992) 'The Mexican Debt Crisis: Restructuring the Household and Economy', in *Uneuqal Burden: Economic Crises, Persistent Poverty, and Women's Work* (eds) Benería, Lourdes and Shelley Feldman, Boulder, CO. Westview Press.

Commoner, Barry (1991) 'Rapid Population Growth and Environmental Stress', *International Journal of Health Services* 21(2): 199–227.

Development Alternatives with Women for a New Era (DAWN) *et al.* (1991) 'Recasting the Population-Environment Debate: A Proposal for a Research Program.'

Ehrlich, Paul R. and Anne H. Ehrlich, (1990) *The Population Explosion*, New York: Simon & Schuster.

Franke, Richard W. (1981) 'Mode of Production and Population Patterns: Policy Implications for West African Development, *International Journal of Health Services* 11(3).

Guppy, Nicholas (1984) *'Tropical Deforestation: A Global View'*, Foreign Affairs 62(4): 930–65.

Hartmann, Betsy (1995) *Reproductive Rights and Wrongs: The Global Politics of Population Control*, Boston: South End Press.

Hartmann, Betsy, and Hilary Standing (1989) *The Poverty of Population Control: Family Planning and Health Policy in Bangladesh*, London: Bangladesh International Action Group.

Hynes, H. Patricia (1993) *Taking Population Out of the Equation: Reformulating I=PAT*, Amherst, MA: Institute on Women and Technology.

Mahumud, Sineen (1996) 'The Latent Demand Hypothesis and Reproductive Change in Bangladesh: A Comment', Dhaka: Bangladesh Institute for Development Studies.

Mazur, Laurie Ann (1992) *Population and the Environment: A Grantmaker's Guide*, New York: Environmental Grantmakers Association.

Mello, Fátima Vianna (1992) 'Sustainable Development For and By Whom? *Contrato (Brazil Network)* 5(1).

Mintzes, Barbara, Anita Hardon and Jannemieke Hanhart (eds) (1993) *Norplant: Under Her Skin*, Amsterdam: Women's Health Action Foundation.

New York Times (1993) 'Environmental Stand on Pact', 5 May.

Ravindran, T.K. Sundari (1993) 'Women and the Politics of Population and Development in India', *Reproductive Health Matters*, 1 (May): 26–38.

Richter, Judith (1996) *Vaccine Against Pregnancy: Miracle or Menace?* London, Zed Books.

Sadik, Nafis, (1990) 'The Role of the United Nations—From Conflict to Consensus', in Geoffrey Roberts (ed.), *Population Policy: Contemporary Issues*, New York: Praeger.

Schrater, Angeline F. (1992) 'Contraceptive Vaccines: Promises and Problems', in Helen Holmes (ed.), *Issues in Reproductive Technology I: An Anthology*, New York: Garland Publishers.

Seager, Joni (1993) *Earth Follies: Coming to Feminist Terms with the Global Environmental Crisis*, New York: Routledge.

Sinding, Stephen W. and Sheldon L. Segal (1991) 'Birth-rate News', *New York Times*, 19 February.

United Nations Development Program (UNDP) (1993) *Human Development Report 1993*, New York: Oxford University Press.

UNFPA (1992a) *State of World Population 1992*, Oxford: Nuffield Press, pp. i–37.

——(1992b) *Women, Population and the Environment*, New York: UNFPA.

USAID (1993) USAID Strategy Papers, LPA Revision 5 October, Washington, DC.

Vittachi, Anuradha (ed.) (1992) 'Sex, Lies and Global Survival', *New Internationalist*. (235):19.

World Bank (1989) *Sub-Saharan Africa: From Crisis to Sustainable Growth*, Washington, DC: World Bank.

World Bank (1993) *World Development Report 1993: Investing in Health*, New York: Oxford University Press.

CHAPTER 27

Bulbeck, Chilla (1991) 'First and Third World Feminisms', *Asian Studies Review*: 77–91, July.

Carby, Hazel V. (1990) 'The Politics of Difference', *Ms*: 84–5, September-October.

Constantino-David, Karina (1990) 'The Limits and Possibilities of Philippine NGOs in Development', Paper delivered at UP Round Table Discussion on NGOs and People's Participation, 9 March.

Council for People's Development (1991) 'Some Perspectives on NGO Work', Manila: Research, Databank and Publication Department.

de Lauretis, Teresa (1986) 'Issues, Terms, Contents'. in de Lauretis, Teresa (ed.) *Feminist Studies/Critical Studies*, Indiana: Indiana University Press, pp. 1–19.

de Vera, Adora Faye (1992) 'The Women's Movement in the 90s: Problems and Promises', *Laya*: 6–16, March.

Gordon, Linda (1991) 'On "Difference",' *Genders*: 91–111, Spring.

Grewal, Inderpal and Caren Kaplan (eds) (1994) 'Introduction: Transnational Feminist Practices and Questions of Postmodernity', *Scattered Hegemonies: Postmodernity and Transnational Feminist Practices*, Minneapolis, MN: University of Minnesota Press, pp. 1–33.

Kauffman, L.A. (1990) 'The Anti-politics of Identity', *Socialist Review*: 67–80, January–March.

Lansang, Sunny (1991) 'Gender Issues in Revolutionary Praxis', *Debate*: 41–52, September.

Lugones, Maria (1991) 'On the Logic of Pluralist Feminism', in Claudia Card (ed.) *Feminist Ethics*, Lawrence, Kansas: University of Kansas Press, 35–44.

Medel-Anonuevo, Carolyn (1990–91) 'Possibilities of Theorizing in the Women's Movement: The Philippine Experience', *Review of Women's Studies*: 50–56.

Miralao, Virginia, A., Celia O. Carlos, Carlos Fulleros Santos, (1990) *Women Entertainers in Angeles and Olongapo: A Survey Report*, Manila: WEDPRO and KALAYAAN.

Mirkinson, Judith (1992) 'A Feminist Guide to the Galaxy', *Breakthrough*: 9–14, Summer.

Mitter, Swasti (1986) *Common Fate, Common Bond: Women in the Global Economy*, London: Pluto Press.

Palma-Beltran, Ruby and Aurora Javate de Dios (eds) (1992) *Filipino Women Overseas Contract Workers … At What Cost?* Quezon City: Women in Development Foundation.

Petras, James and Mike Fischer (1990) 'The Third World's Uncertain Future: From Malta to Panama', *Against the Current*: 42–5, July-August.

Riley, Denise (1988) *Am I That Name?* Minneapolis, MN: University of Minnesota Press.

Sen, Gita and Caren Grown (1987) *Development, Crises and Alternative Visions: Third World Women's Perspectives*, New York: Monthly Review Press.

Spelman, Elizabeth V. (1988) *Inessential Woman: Problems of Exclusion in Feminist Thought*, Boston, MA: Beacon Press.

St Hilaire, Collete (1992) 'Canadian Aid, Women and Development', *Philippines Development Briefing*, London: Catholic Institute for International Relations, December.

CHAPTER 29

Abdel-Fadil, M. (1980) *The Political Economy of Nasserism: A Study in Employment and Income Distribution Policies in Urban Egypt 1952–1972*, Cambridge, MA: Cambridge University Press.

Afshar, H. (1982) 'Khomeini's Teachings and their Implications for Women', *Feminist Review* 12.

el-Guindi, F. (1981) 'Veiling *Infitah*, with Muslim Ethic: Egypt's Contemporary Islamic Movement', *Social Problems* 28 (4): 456–87.

Hoodfar, H. (1988a) *Survival Strategies in Low-income Neighbourhoods of Cairo, Egypt*, PhD thesis in Anthropology, University of Kent at Canterbury.

——(1988b) 'Patterns of Household Budgeting and the Management of Financial Affairs in a Lower-income Neighbourhood in Cairo', in D.H. Dwyer and J. Bruce (eds) *A Home Divided: Women and Income in the Third World*, Standford, CA: Standford University Press.

Keddie, N. and L. Beck (1978) 'Introduction', in Keddie and Beck (eds) *Women in the Muslim World*, Cambridge, MA: Harvard University Press.

MacLeod, A. (1987) *Accommodating Protest: Working Women and the New Veiling in Cairo*, PhD thesis in Political Science, Yale University.

——(1986) 'Hegemony and Women Working and Re-veiling in Cairo, Egypt', Paper presented at the North East Political Science Association Annual Meeting, 15 November, mimeo.

el-Messiri, S. (1978) 'Self-images of Traditional Urban Women in Cairo', in L. Beck and N. Keddie (eds) *Women in the Muslim World*, Cambridge, MA: Harvard University Press.

Nashat, G. (1982) 'Women in Pre-revolutionary Iran: A Historical Overview', in G. Nashat (ed.) *Women and revolution in Iran*, Boulder, CO: Westview Press.

Pastner, C.M. (1978) 'Englishmen in Arabia: Encounters with Middle Eastern Women', *Signs* 4(2): 309–23.

Philipp, T. (1978) 'Feminism and Nationalist Politics in Egypt', in L.Beck and N. Keddie (eds) *Women in the Muslim World*, Cambridge, MA: Harvard University Press.

Rugh, A. (1986) *Reveal and Conceal: Dress in Contemporary Egypt*, Syracuse, NY: Syracuse University Press.

Safiah, K. Mohsen (1985) 'New Images, Old Reflections: Working Middle-class Women in Egypt', in E. Warnock-Fernea (ed.) *Women and the Family in the Middle East: New Voices of Change*, Austin, Texas: University of Texas Press.

Sayigh R. (1981) 'Roles and Functions of Arab Women: A Reappraisal', *Arab Studies Quarterly* 3(3): 258–74.

Scott, A.M. (1984) Industrialization, Gender Segregation and Stratification Theory', Paper presented to the ESRC Gender and Stratification Conference, University of East Anglia, July, mimeo.

Shaarawi, H. (1986) *Harem Years: Memories of an Egyptian Feminist 1874–1924*, translated and introduced by M. Badran, London: Virago.

Shorter, F.C. (1989) 'Cairo's Leap Forward: People, Households and Dwelling Space', *Cairo Papers in Social Science*, Vol. 12, monograph 1, Spring.

Singerman, D. (1990) 'Politics at the Household Level in a Popular Quarter of Cairo', *Journal of South Asian and Middle Eastern Studies* 13 (4).

Sullivan, E.L. (1981) 'Women and Work in Egypt', *Cairo Papers in Social Science* 4(4): 5–29.

Tabari, A. (1980) 'The Enigma of Veiled Iranian Women', *Feminist Review* 5.

Tabari, A. and Yeganeh, N. (eds) (1982) *In the Shadow of Islam: Women's Movement in Iran*, London: Zed Press.

Tucker, J.E. (1985) *Women in Nineteenth-century Egypt*, Cambridge: Cambridge University Press.

Williams, J.A. (1979) 'A Return to Veil in Egypt', *Middle East Review* 11(3): 49–54.

Warnock-Fernea, E. and B. Grattan Bezirgan (eds) (1977) *Middle Eastern Muslim Women Speak*, Austin, Texas: University of Texas Press.

Yeganeh, N. and N.R. Keddie (1986) 'Sexuality and Shi'i Social Protest in Iran', in J.R.I. Cole and N.R. Keddie (eds) *Shi'ism and Social Protest*, New Haven: Yale University Press.

CHAPTER 31

Baer, Ursula (1993) 'The Transformation of Gender Relations in the Transition from State Socialism to Capitalism', Paper presented at the workshop 'The Political Economy of Family Policy and Gender Relations in Germany before and after Unification', American Institute for Contemporary German Studies, Washington, DC, August.

Bergmann, Barbara (1993) 'Economic Issues in Child-care Policy', Paper presented at the International Conference on Childcare Health, Atlanta, Georgia, June.

Blumberg, Rae (1988) 'Income under Female versus Male control, *Journal of Family Issues* 9(1):51–84.

Bobeva, Daniela (1991) 'Iron Ladies', *The Insider* 1(6):4.

CDIA (Central State Historical Archive) (1938/39) Sofia: Government of Bulgaria.

CSO (State Statistical Office) (1967) *Statistical Yearbook of the People's Republic of Bulgaria*, Sofia: State Statistical Office.

——(1987) *Labour Income of Workers and Employees*, Sofia: State Statistical Office.

——(1988) *Demographic and Social-Economic Characteristics of the Economically Active Population*, Vol. II, Sofia: State Statistical Office.

Davin, Delia (1988) 'The Implications of Contract Agriculture for the Employment and Status of Chinese Peasant Women', in S. Feuchtwang *et al* (eds), *Transforming China's Economy in the 1980s*, Vol. I, pp. 137–146. Boulder, CO: Westview Press.

Dobrin, Bogdoslav (1973) *Bulgarian Economic Development Since World War II*, New York: Praeger.

Duggan, Lynn (1993) 'Production and Reproduction: Family Policy and Gender Inequality in East and West Germany', Ph.D. dissertation, University of Massachusetts, Amherst, Department of Economics.

Field Notes (1991) Notes from interviews of agricultural producers and local land reform officials.

——(1993) Notes from interviews of agricultural producers and local land reform officials.

Folbre, Nancy (1992) *Who Pays for the Kids? Gender and the Structures of Constraint*, New York: Routledge.

Goven, Joanna (1992) 'Sexual Politics in Hungary: Autonomy and Anti-Feminism', in *Sexual Politics and the Public Sphere: Women in Eastern Europe after the Transition*, New York: Routledge.

IATUR (International Association for Time-use Research) (1991) *Time-use Studies World Wide*, Sofia: Socioconsult Ltd.

Institute of Sociology (1967) Bound tables from 1966, Town and Village Survey, Sofia: Institute of Sociology

——(1986) Bound tables from 1985, Town and Village Survey, Sofia: Institute of Sociology.

McCrate, Elaine (1987) 'Trade, Merger and Employment: Economic Theory on Marriage', *Review of Radical Political Economy* 19(1):73–89.

Meurs, Mieke (1994) 'From Hoes to Hoes: State Policy, Agricultural Mechanization and Women's Work Under Central Planning', *Review of Radical Political Economics* 26(4), December.

Nickle, Hildegard Maria (1993) 'Women in the German Democratic Republic and in the new Federal States: Looking Forward and Backward (Five Theses), in *Gender Politics and Post-Communism*, New York: Routledge.

Ost, David (1993) 'Labour, Class and Democracy', Working Paper, New York: Hobard and William Smith Colleges.

Sanders, Irwin, (1937) *Balkan Village*, New Haven: Yale University Press.

Statistical Yearbook (1939) *Statistical Yearbook of the Royal Kingdom of Bulgaria*, Sofia: General Direction of Statistics.

——(1942) *Statistical Yearbook of the Royal Kingdom of Bulgaria*, Sofia: General Direction of Statistics.

Verdery, Katherine (1993) *From Parent-state to Family Patriarch: Gender and Nation in contemporary Europe.*

Xiao, Ming (1983) 'What the Responsibility System Brings', *Women of China*, November.

Part 5
Women Organizing Themselves for Change

INTRODUCTION TO PART 5
NAN WIEGERSMA

Part 5 of this reader explores the dynamics of and interconnections between diverse women's organizations ranging from local-neighbourhood mutual-support groups to international agencies and conferences. Women are increasingly forming groups in their communities for mutual aid and support around issues such as health and education as well as organizing in their workplaces over labour issues. They have formed a variety of multi-faceted and single-issue cooperatives, associations and unions to help with their complex household, community and work responsibilities.

Throughout this book we have seen the ways in which women's lives have been affected by political-economic development and structural change in the many less developed areas of Africa, Asia, Eastern Europe and Latin America. Part 5 is devoted to envisioning a place for women in the processes of international transformation by looking at organizations, change and strategic planning. Any forward-looking focus is necessarily concerned both with women's struggles and the planning which is generated when women organize politically. We can view the direction of change of the international women's movement by looking at women's grassroots organizing strategies, their impact on public policy and the 'gender planning' which results from organizational pressures.

GENDER PLANNING

The progressive public and private agencies which have been faced with this pressure for change from women's organizations have tried hard to improve women's access to resources and control over their lives. As a result, the emergent international women's movement has inextricably been interconnected with the gender effects of development programmes or projects as part of the planning agendas of governments, international agencies and non-governmental organizations (NGOs).

In most cultures women have organized themselves traditionally around basic needs in their communities and neighbourhoods, a fact recognized and underlined by Caroline Moser (1992) who describes women's triple working roles in the workplace, the home and in the neighbourhood. But women's organizing has over the past two decades grown far beyond their immediate localities to embrace regional, national and international interest groups.

The United Nations International Women's Decade(s) Conferences (Mexico City, 1975; Nairobi, 1985; and Beijing, 1995) and other supranational agencies and meetings have fuelled women's-group networking and have helped to produce a truly worldwide movement. This international women's movement has, in turn, influenced local and regional organizations in progressive ways (affecting the planning process as described by Young, Chapter 32). A new level of women's organizing increasingly addresses issues of family and community welfare in a way which also leads to improvements in women's status and the rights of women.

Reading

Many of the attempts of the past quarter century to equalize women's access to the benefits of development have been problematic for reasons expressed in our first reading. Kate Young (Chapter 32) explains briefly the process of gender and development planning by describing the conflicts and continuities between welfarism on the one hand and the strategic interests of women in development planning on the other. The welfare (basic-needs) approach to women's project planning, as differentiated from a strategic approach to gender planning, has often led to merely short-term gains, a perspective which has often further compartmentalized and segregated women's interests and/or women themselves. Young sees hope for progress through a process of identifying clearly what women's needs are in the immediate future. The next step is to distinguish which societal changes will lead, in the long run, to more equal access to resources for women and the empowering benefits of sustainable human development. Maxine Molyneaux (1985) originally developed a planning methodology which separated practical gender needs from the more transformational strategic gender concerns. Young develops these ideas by generating three analytical categories for planners: (1) practical needs, (2) strategic interests and (3) empowerment.

NON-GOVERNMENTAL ORGANIZATIONS

In the past two decades privately organized, non-governmental organizations (NGOs) have increased in importance among development agencies. Government support services have been on the decline in most countries during this period and groups of women have tried to compensate by organizing their own institutions, for example, for access to credit (women's banks) and to health care (women's health clinics). International development aid NGOs have also increased in importance along with the currently changing interests of national and international government agencies as the latter restructure and decrease their public roles, frequently passing their responsibilities on to the private sphere.

Women's NGOs are an immense category, including everything from lending/borrowing and merchandise-trading cooperatives to international networks for reproductive rights. Most local groups involve informal cooperation around work and family issues and more formal women's support systems around shelter, food, employment and health matters. Some highly innovative models for support institutions, which generate income as well as political clout, have arisen in South Asia (the Self-Employed Women's

Association and the Grameen Bank). These are being replicated in other regions.

Some of the policy focus of governments and international organizations toward working with NGOs is related to the cutbacks in official government assistance but, as Moser (1993) shows, another factor is the greater effectiveness of smaller and more manageable groups in meeting their development goals. Development NGOs distribute monies increasingly from private sources. Nonetheless, both Moser and Young (Chapter 32) warn us that assumptions about greater effectiveness and recipient participation with NGOs, than with official development agencies, is not always the case.

Many unique groups have formed in less-developed countries around divergent women's issues, from civil liberties (Mothers of the Disappeared in several Latin American countries) to women producers' and traders' credit needs (the Grameen Bank in Bangladesh). In an attempt to categorize the vast field of women's NGOs an assessment tool has been developed by Moser (1993), based on criteria developed by Development Alternatives with Women for New Era (Sen and Grown, 1987). For those interested in further reading, these resources give an appreciation of the breadth and scope of the international women's NGO movement and an assessment tool for particular groups. Some NGOs described elsewhere in this volume include women's marketing societies (Chapter 21) and the reproductive rights networks (Chapter 25).

Women's interests span the household, workplace and community; women's issues are, therefore, public issues. In the arena of electoral politics, too, women have been instigators of change in the post-Cold War era. That women's groups have challenged the legitimacy of ruling political groups is strikingly demonstrated in the film 'Mothers of Plaza de Mayo' (1986) and by Jane Jaquette (1989). With multi-party politics replacing single-party systems in Africa and Latin America, more space has opened up for women in the political arena, where they are increasing their levels of participation in elective politics (Buckley, 1995).

At a global level, international women's conferences convened under UN auspices provide touchstones for women's organizations and their organizers. They have helped women to proceed with assessment, learning and networking around gender and development issues, as well as with planning ahead for future strategies. A host of other local, national and international bodies and meetings also serve to knit together women's concerns and interests. As women and gender issues continue to arise in the process of political-economic and social transformations, innovative and dynamic associations led by southern women (loosely organized under the umbrella of UN agencies and conferences) will continue to be at the centre of the growth and advancement of our international women's movement.

Readings

Chapter 33, an excerpt from Ida Susser's work on women as political actors in a Puerto Rican community group, shows the continuing focus of women's interests in the health and welfare of their families and their communities.

Moser's point, mentioned earlier, about women's special role in community organizing is illustrated in this reading. In this particular case, women's activism comes from their role as guardians of health for their families and their communities. The organization and continuity of leadership is through the women's extended kin networks.

Chapter 34 describes the actions of Korean women in trying to better their situation as workers, even in the export processing zones, where considerable constraints on organizing exist. In the 1970s and 1980s, women workers joined in the countrywide organizing of a labour movement, which pressured employers for more pay and better working conditions. Women's intense radicalism in this movement belies assumptions about women as compliant workers.

In their communities and workplaces, in the public sphere and in the private, women are active participants in the transformation of their world. Whether the struggle is over family health or a reasonable wage, women see and feel increasingly the force of their numbers in organizing for change. Chapter 35 concerns a union of Indian women who have organized as self-employed workers and formed a network to support women's interests through cooperatives and services. It highlights the multiple needs of women and the many services that an effective women's organization can deliver.

FURTHER READING

Berger, Iris (1990) 'Gender, Race, and Political Empowerment: South African Canning Workers, 1940–1960', *Gender and Society*, Vol. 4, No. 3, September.

Bhatt, Ela (1989) 'Toward Empowerment', *World Development*, Vol. 17, No.7.

Bookman, Ann (1988) 'Unionization in an Electronics Factory', pp.159–79 in Ann Bookman and Sandra Morgan (eds), *Women and the Politics of Empowerment*, Philadelphia: Temple University Press.

Bose, Christine Acosta-Belen (1995) *Women in the Latin American Development Process*, Philadelphia: Temple University Press.

Buckley, Stephen (1995) 'African Women Maker Power Moves', *Washington Post*, 28 February.

Bystydzienski, Jill M. (ed.) (1992) *Women Transforming Politics,* Bloomington and Indianapolis: Indiana University Press.

Elson, Diane (1992) 'From Social Strategies to Transformation Strategies', in Benería Lourdes, and Sandra Feldman (eds) *Unequal Burden: Economic Crisis, Persistent Poverty and Women's Work*, Boulder, CO: Westview Press.

Everett, J. and Savara, M. (1983) 'Bank Loans to the Poor in Bombay: Do Women Benefit?', in Gelpi, Hartsock, Novak, Strober (eds) *Women and Poverty*, Chicago: University of Chicago Press.

Gibbons, David (1994) *The Grameen Reader: Training Materials for the International Replication of the Grameen Bank Financial System for Reduction of Rural Poverty*, Penang, Malaysia: Universiti Sains Malaysia.

Jaquette, Jane S. (1989) *The Women's Movement in Latin America: Feminism and The Transition to Democracy*, New York: Monthly Review Press.

Johnson, Patricia Lyons (ed.) (1992) *Balancing Acts: Women and the Process of Social Change*, Boulder, CO: Westview Press.

Kim, Seung-kyung (1992) 'Women Workers and the Labor Movement in South

Korea', in Rothstein, Frances Abrahamer and Michael L. Blim (eds) (1992).

Molyneaux, Maxine (1985) 'Mobilization without Emancipation? Women's Interests, State and Revolution in Nicaragua' *Feminist Studies*, Vol. 11, No. 2.

Moser, Caroline (1992) 'Adjustment from Below: Low-income Women, Time and the Triple Role in Quayaqquil, Equador', in Afshar, H. and C. Dennis (eds) *Women and Adjustment in the Third World*, Macmillan, London.

Moser, Caroline (1993) *Gender Planning and Development*, London and New York: Routledge.

Rose, Kalima (1992) *Where Women Are Leaders: The Sewa Movement in India*, London and New Jersey: Zed Books.

Nash, J. (1988) 'The Mobilization of Women in the Bolivian Debt Crisis', in B. Gutek, L. Larwood and Ann Stromberg (eds) *Women and Work 3*, Beverly Hills: Sage.

Nash, June and Safa, Helen (1986) *Women and Change in Latin America*, South Hadley, MA: Bergin and Garvey (publisher currently in New York).

O'Barr, J. (1984) 'African Women in Politics', in M.J. Hay and S. Stichter (eds), *African Women South of the Sahara*, Longman.

Obbo, Christine (1980) *African Women; Their Struggle for Economic Independence*, London: Zed Books.

Pietilä, Hilkka and Jeanne Vickers (1990) *Making Women Matter: The Role of the United Nations*, London and New Jersey: Zed Books.

Rose, Kalima (1992) *Where Women are Leaders: The SEWA Movement in India*, London and New Jersey: Zed Books.

Rothstein, Frances Abrahamer and Blim, Michael L. (eds) (1992) *Anthropology and the Global Factory: Studies of the New Industrialisation in the Late Twentieth Century*, New York: Bergin and Garrey.

Safa, Helen Icken (1990) 'Women's Social Movements in Latin America', *Gender and Society* 4 (3) September.

Sen, Gita and Grown, Caren (1987) *Development, Crises and Alternative Visions: Third World Women's Perspectives*, New York: Monthly Review Press.

Susser, Ida (1992) 'Women as Political Actors in Rural Puerto Rico: Continuity and Change', Rothstein, Frances Abrahamer and Michael L. Blim (eds) (1992).

Young, Kate (1993) *Planning Development with Women*, London and New York: Routledge.

Women Organizing Themselves for Change

Women in their personal lives and women in the public sphere, e.g. as members of collectives, trade unions and political parties, are organizing for change. Women's struggles, and their personal and public strategies to change their roles in social development are discussed in this concluding section.

32. PLANNING FROM A GENDER PERSPECTIVE: MAKING A WORLD OF DIFFERENCE

KATE YOUNG

Involving women at all levels of development thinking, planning and implementation will make a world of difference not merely to women but to the capacity of society to envisage and carry out planned social change which will permit humankind to live in harmony with nature and itself. To bring women to centre stage, however, will require profound changes in the way that societies conceive of relations between the genders and the dismantling of centuries-old structures of thought and practice. Such changes will take time, but as has become increasingly clear over the past decades women are a tremendous social resource which no society can afford any longer to undervalue or underuse. But women will no longer accept being treated as workhorses for development strategies planned by others; they require to be treated as partners. Planners have a great responsibility: both to listen to women and to build their vision into planning strategies.

In one sense, planning is a technical exercise; it is also always more than this. Policymakers set the general parameters but planners' own perspectives will inevitably influence the degree of fervour with which they follow policymakers' desires. Many a politician's ardour for change has been cooled by the ways in which planners and other bureaucrats drag their feet, or cannot find solutions for certain problems (see Pareja, 1988 for a good example of bureaucratic resistance). Planners are in fact front-line agents of state intervention in the economy and as such are not merely technical experts but also political actors.

The choices they make are in most cases profoundly political because they bear within them the potential for a particular type of society and of social relationships; they are born of collective value judgements which derive from social consensus or a given ideology (Comeliau, 1986). As part of the administrative apparatus of government, planners have not only to meet the short-term goals imposed on them by governments which may change (and often with them the economic, social and political complexion of the society which is envisaged), but also to work within the constraints imposed by planning decisions made in the past and by the structure of the national economy, itself embedded in a global economic system. Their room for manoeuvre may be extremely limited.

PRACTICAL NEEDS AND STRATEGIC INTERESTS

An interesting example of where policymakers have specifically tried to address themselves to these issues is provided by socialist societies because women's emancipation forms part of the socialist programme. A good number of studies conclude, however, that this commitment is rarely successfully implemented (see e.g. Scott, 1974: Markus, 1976; Stacey, 1983). Maxine Molyneux (1985) looks at the question of what a revolutionary government perceives as women's interests. She suggests that these centre on easing women's delivery of traditional benefits to children and family through a wide range of heterogeneous interventions, while drawing them into the labour force and giving them the right to political participation.

Molyneux suggests the need to distinguish between two sets of interests: those arising from the fact that women are allocated certain roles by the sexual division of labour, and those from the fact that women as a social category have unequal access to resources and power. The former can be either short- or long-term and derive from the various responsibilities of women for the care and education of children, the elderly and the sick, household maintenance (family well-being), and servicing kin and neighbourhood (community well-being). Women's unequal access to resources results from their exclusion from the arenas of political and economic power, their inequality within the family and the society, and their lack of control over their lives. In both cases women's actual location in the social structure has important implications for the degree of manoeuvre individual women have.

Molyneux has called these practical gender interests and strategic gender interests. I have found it more useful to talk about practical needs and strategic interests, because a distinction is needed between mundane wants or lacks, and conscious imagining of collective requirements usually involving some degree of change in the existing order of things. The former I call needs, despite the fact that in Molyneux's terms they can (and often do) motivate women to collective action (bread riots are perhaps the classic case); I term the latter strategic interests (see Young, 1987 and 1988).[1]

The identification of practical needs produces a great many similarities across cultures: an adequate food supply, convenient access to safe water, a steady source of income, ready availability of reliable and safe contraception, access to education, training and credit, and so on. In the final analysis, no one can do without food, water, shelter, clothing (the International Labour Organisation's (ILO) basic needs). However, this should not obscure the fact that different practical needs may be prioritized at any one time, nor the likelihood that there will be disagreements about what is a need and what a luxury. Even the obvious starting-point of food as a practical need soon runs into exceptions and difficulties: there may be occasions when an apparent 'luxury' is subjectively more of a need to the person concerned than physical sustenance. Equally, the indicators by which people judge their own well-being are not necessarily the same as those of an outside observer. Rural householders in Rajasthan, for example, put self-respect and independence on as high a level as the possession of assets to provide security against unexpected contingencies.

Strategic gender interests come into focus when women's position in society is questioned. According to Molyneux, a theoretical analysis of the processes of women's subordination gives rise to strategic moral and ethical objectives which are in the interests of all women. Such objectives constitute a 'vision' of the future in which inequalities between men and women are no longer found. This implies that inequalities are neither genetically determined nor sacrosanct and impossible to change.

Although in the abstract the concept of strategic interests may seem reasonably straightforward, there is considerable uncertainty and debate about what actual strategic interests are. As yet, our understanding of what constitutes the bedrock of inequality between men and women is still culture-, class- and race-specific. Despite the differences, feminists maintain that women should and can unite around a number of issues arising from their subordination as a gender so as to find ways of transforming the situation. The issues most commonly identified are: male control of women's labour; women's restricted access to valued social and economic resources and political power, and as a result a very unequal distribution of resources between the genders: male violence; and control of sexuality.

Given that the identification of common strategic interests is full of difficulties, and involves a conscious effort of understanding and commitment to change, women's activists emphasize the need for consciousness-raising and collective empowerment. Once specific categories of women collectively come to understand better the mechanisms and processes of subordination, they are able to identify appropriate strategies for change, which may include forming alliances with a very broad range of other women. Strategies must involve both changing a variety of practices and the way we think about gender and gender relations. Merely changing activities—for example, changing the sexual division of labour, promoted by some as a strategic gender interest—brings little change for women if what women do is still undervalued. In countries such as Britain and the former USSR women have entered all male professions only to see the profession both feminized and devalued within a short time.[2] The pervasive ideology of male superiority has to be changed too, both as an aspect of women's own world-view and that of society at large. This may involve women in long-term changes in the ways they socialize their own children and grandchildren.

What Molyneux's schema implies is a range of potentially common objectives for women which are related to their relative standing to men, their capacity for autonomy and social agency, and a great diversity of more specific concerns which arise from the daily processes of gaining a livelihood. The latter do not challenge the prevailing forms of gender subordination; the former must.

The means of needs identification for development practitioners based on Molyneux's pioneering work is now widely used (see Moser, 1989; Wallace and March, 1991). There is, however, the danger that the usefulness of the distinction between practical needs and strategic interests as a tool of analysis and reflection will be nullified by being used in a mechanical, non-dynamic way: as a blueprint. As such women's practical needs can be listed almost a priori (credit, training, water, etc.) and, particularly in contexts where men are being introduced to WID issues, can be argued to be no more than a women-focused set of basic needs. The question of strategic interests can then be set aside as feminist concerns, i.e. irrelevancies to planners and development practitioners.

TRANSFORMATORY POTENTIAL

Yet this either/or categorization is unhelpful; it neither allows recognition of the potential dynamism of a given situation, nor of the ways in which very practical needs of women are closely enmeshed with their need for structural change. For example, in some cases what would in the blueprint mode be argued to be a strategic interest—the need to end all forms of violence against women, by government, non-government and community means—may in fact be a practical need. If women cannot work outside the home or the village without fear of being physically abused, how can they as mothers ensure family welfare; indeed how can their economic contribution be realized either at the family or the community level? In trying to ensure that the analytical tool of needs and interest is used in a dynamic way, a third concept may be useful— that of transformatory potential (Young, 1987, 1988).

The idea here is to allow the interrogation of practical needs (by women themselves) to see how they can become or be transformed into strategic concerns. In other words have they the capacity or potential for questioning, undermining or transforming gender relations and the structures of subordination?

A rather simple-minded example of how meeting a practical need can have transformatory potential is that of the need for a cash income. This need can be met in a range of ways: by providing piece-work to women isolated within the home; by setting up a small collectivity of some kind which enables women to meet together within a work context which is not highly structured; or by providing factory employment. In the first case, women are left as isolated as before, and the home-based work may merely add to their burden of work. In the third case, the need to fulfil production norms, to complete a fixed and rigid working day within a context in which men are likely to be in positions of power and authority over the women, is unlikely to add to women's sense of self-worth and agency. Forming a locally-based collectivity—a production group, a coop-erative—can provide the conditions for a more empowering experience.[3]

However, provision should be made for space for discussion and exchange of experiences, and an examination of the roots of women's poverty and powerlessness. While this can be empowering in the radical sense of that term, the outcome cannot be predicted just because women are brought together. The stifling of disagreement and the pressure to conform because of an assumed commonality of womanhood can be an entirely un-empowering experience. With forms of organization which do enable the women to gain a greater sense of self-worth, agency and common purpose, and the recognition of difference, then women may use this as a springboard to other activities which have a more clearly directed objective of collective empowerment. This in turn may lead to the formation of alliances with other collectivities of women, or of men and women who are desirous of bringing about structural change.

Another example might be that of lessening rural women's work burden by bringing a mechanical grinding mill to the village. By ensuring that the mill is owned by women as a collective enterprise and that all members learn to run, maintain and service the mill, women will have been helped to own a vital community resource. This should both increase individual women's feeling of self-worth and also bring women collectively greater social recognition. If a proportion of the income from the mill could be set aside for a community project the women would gain influence and greater decision-making power within the community. This might be further parlayed into getting agreement that women take part in critical decision-making arenas at the local level. From there wider opportunities may well become available.

The crucial element in transformatory thinking is the need to transform women's position in such a way that the advance will be sustained. Equally important, women should feel that they have been the agents of the transformation, that they have won this new space for action themselves. It is also important that they realize that each step taken in the direction of gaining greater control over their lives will throw up other needs, other contradictions to be resolved in turn.

In the end the aim should be to set in motion a process which is doubly transformatory: women being transformed into conscious social agents, and practical needs into strategic interests. Of vital importance here is the provision of information. Many studies have shown that giving examples of how other women live, how they have struggled to overcome subordinating and oppressive structures, has sparked off discussion of alternatives which are feasible and culturally appropriate. Women's lack of access to information about their own societies and to the debate about political and economics matters is often a key element in their hesitancy about change.

The assumption behind transformatory potential is that the process of women working together and solving problems on a trial-and-error basis, of learning by doing and also of learning to identify allies and forging alliances when needed, will lead to empowerment, both collective and individual. Experience has also shown that women involved in what have been called welfare-oriented schemes (providing better nutrition for their children, community-improvement projects, etc.) have often, through their collective experience of struggle, become active in questioning their social position and organizing to bring an end to discriminatory practices (see Guzman, 1991).

EMPOWERMENT

The language of 'empowerment' gained prominence in the closing years of the UN's Third Development Decade. The Washington-based Association for Women in Development had 'empowerment' for the theme of its 1989 conference. The World Bank and most aid agencies also claim to wish to empower women. Feminist groups speak of the need for empowerment. But to what are they referring? Are we all talking about the same thing?

Empowerment was originally a demand made by activist feminist groups. In an obvious sense, empowerment is about people taking control over their own lives: gaining the ability to do things, to set their own agendas, to change events in a way previously lacking. This may include affecting the way other people act and consciously or unconsciously forcing changes in their behaviour. But for feminists, empowerment is more than this: it involves the radical alteration of the processes and structures which reproduce women's subordinate position as a gender. In other words, strategies for empowerment cannot be taken out of the historical context that created lack of power in the first place, nor can they be viewed in isolation from present processes. Feminist theoreticians and activists, while accepting and even emphasizing diversity, maintain that women share a common experience of oppression and subordination, whatever the differences in the forms that these take.

Such a view of empowerment implies collective not individual empowerment. 'Women become empowered through collective reflection and decision-making. The parameters of empowerment are: building a positive self-image and self-confidence; developing the ability to think critically; building up group cohesion and fostering decision-making and action' (Programme of Action of the Government of India National Policy on Education, 1986.). In other words empowerment includes both individual change and collective action. What is meant is enabling women collectively to take control of their own lives to set their own agendas, to organize to help each other and make demands on the state for support and on society itself for change. With the collective empowerment of women the direction and processes of development would be shifted to respond to women's needs and their vision. Collective empowerment would, of course, bring with it individual empowerment but not merely for individual advancement. This understanding of women's empowerment is a good deal more radical than the more common approach—i.e. that of economic empowerment or getting women in the cash economy generally through self-employment or income-generation.

It also implies some degree of conflict: empowerment is not just about women acquiring something, but about those holding power relinquishing it. We have argued that relations between men and women are characterized both by conflict and by cooperation. Just as women must organize together to gain the sense of self-worth and understanding of the wider context of their lives that empower and make long-term cooperation possible, so must men undergo a process of reflection and transformation which makes it possible for them to recognize the ways in which their power is a double-edged sword, that it structures their relations with other men in competition and conflict, and makes cooperation and building on advances highly problematic.

COLLECTIVE EMPOWERMENT AS A PLANNING GOAL
It is now being recognized in development circles that economic growth

and social betterment are best achieved when the mass of the population is informed about and involved in development aims and plans, and sees itself as a direct beneficiary of the expanded resources growth should bring. One of the ways to achieve this is structuring the decision-making process in such a way as to ensure widespread consultation at all levels of society about development goals, the processes by which those goals are to be reached and the resources needed to achieve them.

Rather than the 'there is no alternative' single way forward, a range of ways in which goals and targets could be met as well a range of time-frames in which to meet them can be put forward for discussion. Other ways include consultation with groups representing capital, labour and the informal sector; the producers of labour working closely with grass-roots NGOs, especially those involved in development work and educa-tion; giving information through the press; having party branches discuss party policy; holding referenda. It can, however, fairly be said that despite these attempts, there are no instances in which economic macro-level policy-making has been restructured so as to include ideas or demands from the grassroots—when this does occur it is around social-policy planning and programming. As yet there are virtually no mechanisms available for communities which have devised policy to have such policies discussed within a wider social framework, nor for them to be incorporated into national planning systems.

The options mentioned above are only available where a variety of institutions of civil society—a free press, a clear and unmuzzled judiciary, a wide range of pressure groups and voluntary organizations—already exists. Where they do not, a strong argument can be made for encourag-ing the development of such institutions. Government works best when it is responsive and accountable to the bulk of the population; interest groups as well as private voluntary organization (PVOs) or non-govern-mental organizations (NGOs) can play an important role as promoters of the interests and liberties of the citizenry. But in many cases NGOs provide a power base for people from the same social stratum as is in government, whether as politicians, planners or civil servants (see Clarke, 1991). Without the empowerment of their own members, and democratic working practices, such groups are unlikely to act as watch-dogs on behalf of the people. Groups which are truly representative of the grassroots and the poor are rare, but their expansion should be encouraged in all ways possible. Their empowerment can be seen as a potential planning goal.

We have alluded to the importance of ensuring that NGOs experiment with a range of organizational forms and practices so as to give their members, as well as the people they serve, the possibility of their own empowerment, i.e. collective reflection and decision-making, developing the capacity for critical thought and undertaking collective action toward a goal which is of benefit to all. That many NGOs parallel and replicate top-down ways of organization is not often recognized. The absence of comparative research into a variety of organizational forms in terms of their effectiveness both in service delivery and strengthening of grass-roots capacity makes it difficult to draw firm conclusions. Certainly many of the most vibrant development NGOs and women's organizations have experimented with quite flattened power and authority structures, and a range of mechanisms to ensure frequent consultation with the member-ship. The toll on staff time is, however, great (see Ford Smith, 1990), and informal hierarchies and power dynamics which reproduce inequality lead actively to dis-empowerment. Fear of this can in turn lead to a tendency to go for the lowest common denominator in order to get something achieved.

33. WOMEN AS POLITICAL ACTORS IN RURAL PUERTO RICO: CONTINUITY AND CHANGE

Ida Susser

THE EXPORTATION OF INDUSTRY TO PUERTO RICO

Two petrochemical plants were established in the Yabucoa valley in 1969–70. Each hired between 600 and 1000 workers (fluctuating over time), most of whom were men. Women worked as secretaries, for which positions, bilingual skills were preferred.

In the decades following the establishment of the two petrochemical plants, health problems were documented among workers and residents, specifically in relation to the pollution caused by one plant, Union Carbide Grafito, Inc. The overall process through which community residents and workers endeavoured to make the company accountable are documented in an earlier publication (Susser, 1985). Here, I shall focus on the significance of women's participation and their changing roles over time.[1]

KIN CONNECTIONS AND POLITICAL ACTION

The significance of women in political action as consolidators of kin networks can be seen in the fact that the first leader of the social movement opposed to Union Carbide Grafito was linked by marriage to the second leader (his daughter-in-law and the second leader's wife were sisters). In fact, three of the major actors in forming and maintaining the protest movement against the company were related through their wives, who were all sisters. Although the sisters' husbands were of different political persuasions (an *independista*, a socialist and a more conventional democrat), all these men took leading roles in the development of the local protest movement.

In maintaining strong kinship alliances and reinforcing new local ties, the women also assumed the more expected tasks of providing large, filling and acceptable meals for numerous people at short notice and for as little cost as possible. Women were well acquainted with the organization skills involved in mobilizing large groups of people. They could easily adapt these experiences to the task of working to achieve more ostensibly political goals, such as attending demonstrations in San Juan (a 40-mile drive from the *barrio*).

WOMEN'S CONCERN WITH HEALTH

As diagnosticians and healers, women play a central role within the community and within the home. Women keep track of the family's health history and accumulate knowledge, particularly about health problems of children. Women in charge of households kept a store of antibiotics and other prescription medicines which had been prescribed for the ailments of various children over a number of years. When asked, they could identify which bottle or pill had been used for which child when and could suggest what other purposes they might use it for.

ENVIRONMENTAL AND OCCUPATIONAL HEALTH ISSUES

Concerns with occupational health and safety concentrate on conditions in the workplace and the hazards of production. In this instance, the workplace was largely manned by men; however, more than the workplace may be implicated in the hazards of production. Because of the proximity of Union Carbide Grafito to Barrio Ingenio, the population was exposed to some of the same hazards as were the men working in the plant. The gaseous, carbonaceous and petrochemical by-products that afflicted workers were the same agents that appeared to be causing high rates of health disorders within the *barrio* (see Susser, 1985).

The connections between plant and community problems was made apparent by the fact that protest was triggered not when the workers themselves became ill but when their wives and children living in the nearby *barrio* became affected. In the case of men who were active in organizing the community and leading the protest, their own accounts and those of their wives testify that it was the health problems of the family that alerted men to the prevailing conditions and prompted them to action. In one of these cases, the man concerned was an actual employee of the plant, and in the other, an independent craftsman. In both cases, however, it was the wives who pinpointed what they believed to be the cause of new health problems, and in both cases it was the fact that wives functioned as monitors of family health that prompted action.

WOMEN AS PARTICIPANTS IN THE PROTEST MOVEMENT

For the most part, in the first decade of protest (from 1975 to 1985), leadership and the political agenda was set by the men of the *barrio*, and women took less obvious supportive roles. Throughout these years, all members of the community's leadership committees were men. Important battles were fought. The Junta Calidad Ambiental (JCA, the Environmental Quality Board) was forced to recognize the pollution problems, and in 1982 fined Union Carbide US $550,000. In response to the rulings of the JCA, the plant began a new building programme to reduce pollution from the incinerators. The union was organized and managed to enlist help from both the National Institute of Occupational Safety and Health (NIOSH) and the Occupational Safety and Health Administration (OSHA). Both NIOSH and OSHA produced reports citing the plant for pollution, some of which was found to be carcinogenic (NIOSH, 1984). However, by the time the reports were printed, the union had been destroyed by the lay-offs, for over six months, of more than 500 workers. During this same period, a lawsuit was brought by the residents of Barrio Ingenio against the company, citing health complaints of community inhabitants resulting from plant pollution.

The lawsuit was drawn out, as cases tend to be when corporations work for delay. The delays, lack of success and unreliability of the lawyers led villagers to mistrust and undermine their own leadership. As a result of the failures of legal recourse, the protest leader came under attack, and he and his committee abandoned their cause. It was after these setbacks that women emerged in leadership roles.

WOMEN AS COMMUNITY LEADERS

The first woman to take action was in her mid-thirties, about 20 years younger than her predecessor and a decade younger than his wife. Mercedes had four children; two were living with her in the *barrio* and the two others were with relatives in the United States. Mercedes herself had just returned from the US and was bilingual in contrast to either of the previous leaders. On discovering that the lawsuit had foundered through the neglect of the community's lawyers, Mercedes and her newly formed committee, which was made up of both men and women, sought out a new lawyer who was willing to fight their cause. Ironically, considering the lack of political critique among committee leaders, the lawyer they found was a well-known figure in the Puerto Rican socialist party. After two years of energetic pursuit of the lawsuit, Mercedes went back to the US, leaving the community once more to conduct their legal affairs without leaders.

In 1990, when I returned to Yabucoa once more, the lawsuit was still pending. The lawyer whom Mercedes and her committee had enlisted was still working on the case in an effort to re-open the issues. The leadership that emerged at this time reflected the long history of the movement. The committee was now being led by Theresa, a bilingual mother of two young sons who had worked as a secretary at the plant and was the daughter of one of the men who founded the first Ingenio committee. She was living with her husband, and both he and her parents supported her leadership role. They drove together with other Ingenio residents to San Juan to discuss the progress of the suit with their lawyer. In August 1990, the lawyer informed them that there was still some possibility that they might win the case, although they would have to wait for the decision of the Supreme Court judge. The decision would be made on the basis of written materials collected over 10 years by the company and the community, and required extensive work. The current leadership was not planning to move and was prepared to wait.

In conclusion, Union Carbide Grafito, Inc., spent 20 years in the Yabucoa valley generating profits for the US corporation. During this time, it consumed much of the water-table and expelled pitch and polluting gases into the atmosphere. For example, it was possible to identify new leaves on plants around Barrio Ingenio in 1990 because they were not covered with the sticky black dust of leaves lower down the bushes, as by 1990 the corporation had removed most of its operation from the valley. However, the health problems of the population, the unused physical plant and the waste precipitated by the chemical processes remained. Throughout the two decades, residents and workers struggled to cope with or prevent the deterioration of their environment and health. Some major changes, such as improved incineration at the plant, were won; and major defeats, such as the destruction of the union and the laying off of hundreds of workers with plant seniority, occurred.

Women were central to all phases of the negotiations between plant managers, workers and community residents. However, as problems became less dramatic and as failures loomed larger, it was the women who continued to press for reparations and held tenaciously to the original goals of the movement.

34. WOMEN WORKERS AND THE LABOUR MOVEMENT IN SOUTH KOREA
Seung-kyung Kim

South Korea is known for its spectacular economic growth, but as recently as the 1950s it was one of the poorest countries in the world. Since then, it has made great progress in industrialization, although it remains heavily dependent on foreign capital, technology and trade. A crucial factor for Korean economic development has been its well-disciplined, hard-working labour force. Korea's development strategy would not have succeeded without its workers' high level of productivity and their acceptance of low wages and long working hours.

Korea's export-orientated industrialization concentrated on light, labour-intensive industries, where cheap, unskilled labour was required (for example, textiles, rubber footwear and electronics), and it absorbed massive numbers of women workers because young women were the least expensive labour force available. Newspapers and television often referred to these women as the backbone of Korean economic development. Despite the praise lavished on them, their hard work did not translate into higher wages or improved working conditions. During the 1980s, workers became more conscious of the gap between their own experiences and the 'economic miracle', and became increasingly distrustful of such government slogans as 'Development first, distribution later'.

The extent of women workers' involvement in the labour movement is illuminating because it contradicts the commonly held notion that women workers are docile and subservient (a major reason why multinational corporations hire women workers).

WOMEN WORKERS AND THE LABOUR MOVEMENT

The 1970s saw a sharp increase in the number of female workers employed in the manufacturing sector (Kim, 1986:32). Between 1966 and 1978, female participation grew from 33.6 per cent to 46.1 per cent (Choi, 1983: 82). Female workers' experience was even harsher than that of male workers since they had to work longer hours at lower wages. As in other parts of the world, female labour is treated as providing supplementary income and is concentrated in unskilled, simple, repetitive jobs, which are the lowest paid. According to the statistics provided by the South Korean Labor Ministry for 1985, female workers work an average of 238.1 hours per month and 40.5 hours overtime while male workers in the manufacturing sector work an average 234.9 hours per month and 38 hours overtime.

During the 1970s the labour movement was not led by the formal national labour organization but was spontaneous and unorganized. Women workers sustained the Korean labour movement during the 1970s and became increasingly important after 1975. In-ryong Sin contended that from 1975 to 1980 only the women workers' movement was significant, and that during the repressive period immediately following the *coup d'état* in 1980, women's labour movements were the only ones that existed (1985: 51).

THE LABOUR UPRISING, JULY–AUGUST 1987

The nation-wide uprising began on 5 July, in Ul-san at a subsidiary of the Hyun-dae company. The workers organized a democratic labour union, which sparked similar movements in other Hyun-dae subsidiaries. By August the struggle had spread around the country to workers in other large conglomerates, eventually workers in small- and medium-sized companies became involved. Between June and September there were over 3000 labour disputes reported nation-wide (*Kyoungbyang Daily News*, 14 September 1987). According to Ministry of Labor statistics, disputes occurred at a rate averaging 44 cases a day. The events of 1987 are characterized as the first mass labour struggle to occur in Korean history.

THE LABOUR UPRISING IN THE MASAN AREA

Early in August the movement reached Chang-won, a heavy industrial estate that employs mostly male workers. Workers started strikes, demanding democratic unions and wage increases. This uprising provided inspiration for female workers in nearby Masan, where unions were banned. By September, more than half the companies operating in the Masan Free Export Zone (MAFEZ) (41 out of 73) had experienced sit-ins. The four main demands of the workers were wage and bonus increases, better treatment, improved working conditions and seniority allowances.

Most strikes in Masan were unorganized and were motivated by the need for higher wages. Management accepted the inevitability of increasing wages and bonuses, and went along with this and the other basic demands of the workers. Allowing permanent labour unions to organize was another matter. After the initial disputes had been settled, management was able to persuade many workers to withdraw from the unions. Most workers were not aware of their importance. For workers, paying union dues, even though they were low, seemed like one more burden.

The 1987 experience taught workers a valuable lesson about how to organize themselves to fight against management. When they faced another labour struggle in March 1988, the women workers of Masan were able to organize more quickly and effectively. Union activities led to significantly higher factory wages, from US$4 a day in 1987 to US$7 a day in 1988. Workers' consciousness has also increased greatly in the past few years. Higher wages and increased union activities of women workers, however, have made the Masan Free Export Zone less attractive to its foreign investors.

THE CONTINUATION OF THE STRUGGLE

The conflicting aims of multinational corporations and Korean workers are illustrated by the events leading up to the departure of the T.C. Electronics Company from the Zone. T.C., the largest US based company in Masan, was established in 1972, and was wholly owned by the Tandy Corporation. Its main products were stereo components, telephones and computer components.

During 1988, workers seeking to unionize the company clashed with anti-union supervisors controlled by management at the T.C. Electronics factory. Several union women required hospitalization, but the labour union survived the confrontation. By mid-1988, about half the women workers had joined the union. The management was disturbed by these developments and began to talk about closing down. The chairman of the Tandy Corporation in the US threatened to move some production lines out of Korea because of the 'general level of cultural change and political uncertainty' (quoted in the *New York Times*, 26 August 1988). However, he stated that the company did not plan to pull out of Korea.

Management warned workers that orders from the parent company were decreasing. They instituted a hiring freeze in Masan and tried to move machines to subcontracting factories outside the zone. Union members threw themselves in front of the movers in an effort to stop the removal of the machines from the factory. In February 1989, management sued the union for its role in blocking the removal of equipment, and for obstructing daily procedures on the shop floor.

Both sides hardened their positions during these confrontations. Management accused the union members of slowing down productivity so that they could not rely on their workers to produce goods in time to meet shipping deadlines. The union accused management of hiring thugs to disrupt the operations of the factory so that T.C. Electronics could use 'declining productivity' as an excuse to close. T.C. Electronics described the confrontations at the factory as being between men and women workers, and unrelated to management policies.

In April 1989, the workers' worst fear came to pass. Tandy Corporation declared that it was closing its factory in Masan and dismissed its entire staff. It paid the wages for April and the minimum legal severance payment (two months wages) to workers, following legal requirements.

The core membership of the union refused to accept the plant closing and occupied the factory building, demanding that the company re-open the plant. When they were ignored by Tandy, about 20 workers went to T.C.'s research institute in Seoul. They found the company president in the institute and took him hostage, holding him for four days before he escaped. Their demand for direct negotiations with the parent company in the US indicated that they still felt that the problems that had occurred in the Masan factory were due to local mismanagement rather than being intrinsic to the structural problems of export processing zones. They felt that if head office understood their desperation, it would be sympathetic and re-open the factory. However, the union's kidnapping of the president of its Korean subsidiary did not convince Tandy to negotiate, but rather confirmed it in its decision to close the factory.

CONCLUSION

Women workers in MAFEZ are part of the Korean labour movement but as part of the new international division of labour, they are part of a global movement as well. From an international perspective, the closing of the T.C. Electronics factory may be a labour victory after all, since it radicalized workers and contributed to the development of a working-class leadership. The lives of many women were drastically changed by the 1987 uprising.

Workers in both developed and developing countries need to organize internationally to prevent multinational corporations from continually moving their operations to cheaper and more oppressed labour markets. 'In order for those alliances to be effective, workers must extend their organizations to overseas branches to overcome the competitive downgrading of the wage scale worldwide' (Nash, nd: 25). Unions from the developed and the developing countries must get together if they want to check the power of multinational corporations. Multinational unions are needed to deal with multinational corporations.

35. SEWA: WOMEN IN MOVEMENT
KALIMA ROSE

Based in Ahmedabad, the largest city of India's western state of Gujarat, and working under a name which translates as 'service', the Self-Employed Women's Association (SEWA) successfully integrates a complex myriad of lives, occupations and issues into one union. Under SEWA, women have forged a new model of what a trade union can be— a Third World model, which defies conventional conceptions about who unions organize and what they do for their members. Most unions in the world organize workers in one kind of industry, who share one fixed workplace and concern themselves only with problems which revolve around the work issues of their members. Some unions do take up issues related to women workers, or include a women's wing in the larger body of the union, but there are few unions in the world which are devoted entirely to a female membership, as is SEWA. SEWA organizes women who work in their homes, in the streets of cities, in the fields and villages of rural India, with no fixed employer, carving their small niches in the economy, day by day, with only their wits to guide them against incredible odds of vulnerability, invisibility and poverty.

These are the common denominators around which SEWA has gathered 30,000 members into its fold since its inception in 1972: they are women, they are 'self-employed' and they are poor. From these common bases, diverse individuality in trades, religious and ethnic backgrounds, and living environments are brought together. Where these women are individually extremely vulnerable to the forces of their day-to-day poverty which are compounded by financial exploitation, physical abuse and general social harassment, they have found that collectively they are able to struggle against these odds to effect change in their lives and work. SEWA's choice of the term 'self-employed' to define this large sector of workers was consciously made to give positive status to people who are often described negatively as informal, unorganized, marginal or peripheral. How can the self-employed workers who make up 55 per cent of Ahmedabad's workforce and 50 per cent of Calcutta's and Bombay's workforces be considered marginal? How could the majority of rural women who are engaged in the food production of the country be considered peripheral? According to SEWA estimates, women account for at least 60 per cent of the self-employed population. Only 6 per cent of India's census-recognized female workforce is in regular employment; 94 per cent of working women are self-employed.

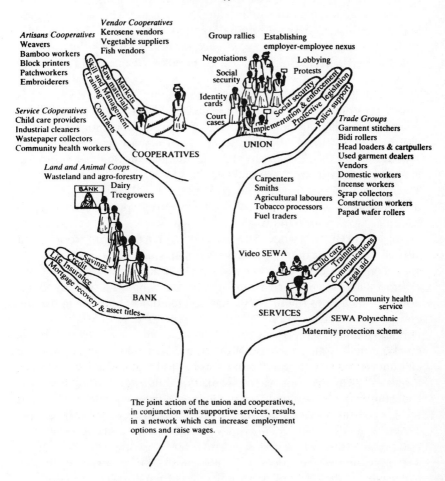

The SEWA Tree
A Women's Support Network

Artisans Cooperatives — *Vendor Cooperatives*
Weavers — Kerosene vendors
Bamboo workers — Vegetable suppliers
Block printers — Fish vendors
Patchworkers
Embroiderers

Group rallies — Establishing employer-employee nexus
Negotiations — Lobbying
Social security — Protests
Identity cards
Court cases

Service Cooperatives
Child care providers
Industrial cleaners
Wastepaper collectors
Community health workers

Skill and Training — Raw materials — Markets — Management — Contracts

Social security — Implementation & enforcement — Protective legislation — Policy support

COOPERATIVES   UNION

Trade Groups
Garment stitchers
Bidi rollers
Head loaders & cartpullers
Used garment dealers
Vendors
Domestic workers
Incense workers
Scrap collectors
Construction workers
Papad wafer rollers

Land and Animal Coops
Wasteland and agro-forestry
Dairy
Treegrowers

BANK

Carpenters
Smiths
Agricultural labourers
Tobacco processors
Fuel traders

Savings — Credit — Life Insurance — Mortgage recovery & asset titles

BANK

Video SEWA

Child care — Training — Communications — Legal aid

SERVICES

Community health service
SEWA Polytechnic
Maternity protection scheme

The joint action of the union and cooperatives,
in conjunction with supportive services, results
in a network which can increase employment
options and raise wages.

Self-employed is a broad term covering all the workers who are not in a formal employer-employee relationship. It means women who work at home—weavers, potters, garment and quilt stitchers, patchworkers, embroiderers, bidi rollers, incense-stick makers, milk producers, spinners, basket and broom weavers, metalworkers, carpenters, shoemakers, painters, sculptors and toymakers. It includes women who sell or trade their services or labour—agricultural workers, headloaders, hand-cart pullers, waste-paper collectors, acrobats, cleaners and construction workers—and the multitude of hawkers and vendors who carry out trade in the streets and markets from their baskets or cartloads of wares. Both traditional and modern occupations come under SEWA's definition of self-employed, from the bartering of goods to capitalistic piece-rate work.

Women all over India are struggling for survival in a world where the physical resources they have traditionally depended upon for survival are degraded and diminishing in the face of intense population and industrial pressure. Though they are all economically active, they have not acquired the skills necessary to make an adequate living in an industrializing economy, nor are there sufficient jobs for all those in need of them. The hillsides and plains where severe erosion, floods and drought follow deforestation mirror the faces of families whose deprivation and degradation are written into them.

Not only in Gujarat, where SEWA's work has become firmly rooted, but also all over the country, where its work has begun to make inroads, some common pictures of how women are dealing with their problems emerge. First, women are better fighters than men of the day-to-day poverty which faces them. They exercise incredible ingenuity in making ends meet. It is common for men to remain unemployed for long periods of time when no 'job' can be found. Women, on the other hand, combine many jobs and occupations simultaneously, bringing in small amounts of cash, trading for foodgrains or clothing, exchanging services for access to a small hut, vending small quantities of consumer goods, collecting wood or fruits or recyclable waste from common lands, and using what specialized skills they possess to earn wages. They endow society with their labour, providing cheap services, strong backs and traditional skills. Wherever they are given the opportunity, women contribute modernized ideas and skills as well. They request very little in exchange for their labour, consuming small fractions of the country's resources in relation to what they produce.

Second, besides being able to piece together the family income out of ingenuity and necessity, women spend almost all of their earnings on the family. Whatever little they do earn, they spend on food, clothing and their meagre shelter. SEWA women confirm this fact, but countless other women all over India have also attested that if they earn, for example, Rs8 a day, they spend all of it on food for the family, whereas their husbands contribute a much smaller part of their earnings to the household—if there is a husband, and if he has earnings. Up to 30 per cent of poor families are supported solely by women who are self-employed.

The third quality that has emerged is women's concern about the future. They want their children's lives to be better than their own, and make repeated sacrifices in order to ensure this. Not only do they work 12 to 20 hour days to try and effect this change, they also reveal an exceptional ecological consciousness. While their menfolk often opt for cash income from wood crops, women organizing across the country insist on protecting trees, or planting trees which will provide fuel and fodder and be a long-term resource. They increasingly understand the effects of deforestation, droughts, soil erosion and saline encroachment on both the land and their families' lives as they lose the local resources that they depend upon.

Because of their ability to be flexible, to combine domestic work and income-earning activities, and to shift occupational skills as the season or market demands; because they do not need to fit the terms of formal jobs in order to be economically active; and because they have needs which are not fulfilled by the formal sector of society, self-employed women require a different kind of union than the traditional unions can meet. Out of their intense needs for fair credit, maternity protection, fair wages for whatever work they are engaged in, skills training, year-round work and legal help when they are exploited or abused, SEWA came into being.

The organization began on a small scale. When women who pull freight on carts and headload textiles between markets saw what advantages the textile unions were gaining for their members, they approached the Textile Labour Association (TLA), India's largest union of textile workers. They were directed to Ela Bhatt, a lawyer who was then heading the TLA's Women's Wing. They asked her, 'What about us? Can't we get any of these benefits?' At that time, Bhatt had been dealing with labour issues for 14 years through jobs with the TLA and the Labour Ministry of the Gujarat government. Though dealing with organized labour, she was constantly exposed to the realities of the poor working class and the numerous problems of the unorganized workers of India. When these self-employed women first approached her, she was ready to hear their questions. She responded with an idea she had been formulating for many years: 'You need to organize yourselves if you want to get some of these benefits'.

About two dozen women came together and pooled a few *paise* and took some decisions to demand that their wages be regularized. Soon used-clothes and vegetable vendors wanted to join them for protection from police brutality and extortion. Then home-bound women in the Muslim community who stitch textile waste into garments and quilt covers requested some support. Agricultural workers came to these meetings to discuss how they could get the minimum wage they were due under law. Carpenters and metal-smithing women came seeking access to small loans for working capital. The exploitation bidi workers and incense-stick makers faced brought them into the fold of the union. Women who had migrated to the city for textile-mill jobs but had faced retrenchment and were reduced to picking recyclable waste from the city's garbage dumps had several ideas of how to alter their circum- stances, and came to the union for services and support. Weavers, basket- makers and block printers, all facing displacement of their skills or loss of raw materials or markets, came seeking help to hold on to the only occu- pations they knew. Women who had been victimized for asking for legal wages in the tobacco-processing plants came seeking legal assistance.

In this way SEWA grew, organically, slowly absorbing more and more trades, rooting itself in the reality of poor working women. Each of these trades is usually associated with one or two particular communities, which makes for an unusually varied and vibrant coalition in the organi- zation. The spirit and diversity of SEWA would presently be difficult to come by anywhere else, though this is what its members are working on promoting across India. Tribal, Hindu, Harijan, migrant and Muslim women; tattooed Vaghari women, women in *purdah*; sinewed, muscular smiths; sun-darkened cart-pullers and agricultural labourers; young nimble girl bidi rollers with their mothers and grandmothers, progres- sively more thin and bent from years of sitting over their rolling work; street-wise and bawdy vendors alongside women emerging timidly from home-bound communities; all in different dress; speaking different languages and dialects; practising different trades—all are coming together to generate strength. It is an amazing convergence to witness.

SEWA Executive Committee

NOTES TO PART 5

CHAPTER 32

1. The discussion of needs is not furthered by the confusion in much of the literature as to what a need is; much the same is true of interests. One useful treatment is provided by Connell (1987) who notes that: 'an interest is defined by the possibility of advantage and disadvantage in some collective practice' (p.137). See his discussion on the articulation of interests, pp. 262–5.
2. The classic example in Britiain is the shift from male clerks to female secretaries; in the former USSR as more women got into the medical profession as general practitioners, so men moved into higher status specialism. For the example of the banking profession in Australia see Game and Pringle, 1984.
3. I am assuming that the co-operative/collective is making something for which there is a market, and that the women are not involved in a soul-destroying treadmill of low productivity: low reward work which undermines rather than empowers.

CHAPTER 33

1. The activities of women were studied using participant observation and ethnographic-fieldwork methods. John Kreniske and I spent four months in Yabucoa in 1982; stayed for three months in 1983; and returned for shorter periods in 1985, 1987, 1988 and 1990. On these occasions, we interviewed and talked informally with *barrio* residents, Carbide workers, Carbide management and state regulators and politicians. In 1982 and 1983 we conducted a systematic self-report survey of health in the *barrio*. We lived with two different families and sat for many hours in different kitchens and front patios observing interactions and talking with *barrio* residents. The interview survey (which could take, depending on the friendliness of the person, between one hour and an entire afternoon) allowed us to visit over 90 households and observe interactions among people in daily life. The data presented here are based on observations over a period of eight years in which we revisited the households of community leaders and other residents many times. The main locale of the study was Barrio Ingenio, a village of about 350 households in the municipality of Yabucoa, situated 500 yards from the Union Carbide Grafito plant.

REFERENCES TO PART 5

CHAPTER 32

Comeliau, C. (1986) *Questions aux Planificateurs,* DEV/EPD/44, Paris: UNESCO.

Connell, R.W. (1987) *Gender and Power*, Oxford: Polity Press and Basil Blackwell.

Ford Smith, H. (1989) *Ring Ding in a Tight Corner*, Women's Programme, ICAE, Toronto.

Game, A. and R. Pringle (1984) *Gender at Work*, London: Pluto Press.

Gugman, V. (1991) 'Desde les proyectos de desarrollo a la sociedad', in V. Gugman, P. Portocarrera and V. Vargas (eds), *Geneva en el desarrollo*, Lima: Ediciones Entre Mujeres.

Markus, M. (1976) 'Women and Work, Emancipation at a Dead End', in A.

Hegedus *et al.* (eds), *The Humanisation of Socialism*, London: Allison and Busby.

Molyneux, M. (1985) 'Mobilization without Emancipation? Women's Interests, State and Revolution in Nicaragua', *Feminist Studies* 11; 227–54, Summer, also in Fagan, R. *et al.* (eds) (1986) *Transition and Development: Problems of Third World Socialism*, New York: Monthly Review Press, pp. 280–302.

Moser, C. (1989) 'Gender Planning in the Third World', in *World Development* 17 (11).

Pareja, F. (1987, 1988) 'Problems That Concern Women', in K. Young (ed.) (1988).

Scott, H. (1974) *Does Socialism Liberate Women?* Boston: Beacon Press.

Stacey, J. (1983) *Patriarchy and Socialist Revolution in China*, Berkeley, CA: University of California Press.

Wallace, T. and C. March (eds) (1991) *Changing Perspectives*, Oxford: Oxfam.

Young, K. (1987) 'Further Thoughts on Women's Needs', in *Planning for Women at the National, Regional and Local Level*, UNESCO and republished in revised form in 1988.

—(1988) 'Reflections on Meeting Women's Needs', in K. Young (ed.), *Women and Economic Development: Local, Regional and National Planning Strategies*, UNESCO, Berg Publishers/Paris, Oxford.

CHAPTER 33

Baver, S. (1979) 'Policy Making for Industrialization in Puerto Rico, 1947–76'. PhD dissertation, Columbia University.

Garcia, N. (1978) 'Puerto Rico Siglo XX: Lo Historico y lo natural en la ideologia colonialista', *Pensamiento Critico* (8): 1–28, September.

Susser, I. (1985) 'Union Carbide and the Community Surrounding It: The Case of a Community in Puerto Rico', *International Journal of Health Services* 15, No. 4: 108–17.

CHAPTER 34

Choi, Jang-jip (1983) 'Interest Conflict and Political Control of South Korea: A Study of the Labor Unions in Manufacturing Industries, 1961–1980', PhD. dissertation. University of Chicago.

Kim, Kum-su (1986) *Hanguk Nodong Munje ui Sanghwang Gwa Insik* (The circumstances and interpretation of the Korean labour problem), Seoul: Pulbit.

Nash, June 'Segmentation of the Work Process in the International Division of Labour', manuscript. (nd).

Sin, In-ryong (1985) *Women, Labor and Law* (Yosong, Nodong, Beob), Seoul: Pulbit.

INDEX

Dominica, 180
Dominican Republic, 267–76
dowry, 90
Duarte, Isis, 275
Dwyer, D., 106

Eastern Europe: 'lost generation', 342;
    anti-feminism, 335, 343
ecofeminism, 24–5, 68–72
ecology: consciousness, women, 385;
    crises, 63–6
Ehrenreich, Barbara, 180
Ehrlich, Anne, 294
Ehrlich, Paul, 294
electronics industry, 193–4, 200–1,
    204, 212, 274
Ellis, F., 131
Elson, Diane, 26, 179, 181
employment insecurity, 200
'empowerment', 26, 36, 38, 371–3
endogamy, 89–90
Engels, Friedrich, 21, 49–50, 198
Enloe, Cynthia, 180, 260
Entrepreneurship Development
    Programme, Ghana, 283
environment: degradation, 73–4, 295,
    299; destruction, 71, 294;
    protection, 58–62
Environmental Summit, 1992, 3
environmentalism, patriarchal, 67
'equity' approach, 52
Escobar, Arturo, 26, 28
essentialism, 56, 71–2, 312, 314
Ethiopia, 78
ethnocentricism, 6; feminist, 313
exploitation, patriarchal, 223
exports: -led development, 177–9, 378;
    manufacture, 219, 222–3, 225, 272;
    processing, 269–70, 273; processing
    zones (EPZs), 22, 179, 258, 364, 381

family: cultural differences, 127;
    structure, 107
family-planning, 286; aggressive, 300
Fanon, Frantz, 195–6
female: -intensive industries, 227;
    labour, Java, 120–5; -headed
    households, 107, 155–61, 204, 259,
    276–7, 280; sexuality control,
    142–9,
'feminine principle', 64–5, 67, 73

feminism, western discourse, 79–83
'feminist environmentalism', 73–5
Fernández-Kelly, María Patricia, 179,
    181, 203
Folbre, Nancy, 104, 129, 131
food, subsidy reductions, 267
Foucault, Michel, 315
Frank, Andre Gunder, 218
Franke, Richard W., 297
free market model, 4; fetishization,
    331–2
free trade zones (FTZs), 179–80, 184,
    192, 271–3, 276
Fuentes, Annette, 180
fundamentalism, protestant, 261;
    religious, 257

Gabriela group, Philippines, 308, 310,
    313
Gallin, Rita, 107
Gambia, 87
garment industry, 178, 183, 201, 204,
    206, 214, 270–4
gender: role construction, 329; -
    ascriptive relations, 195–8
Gender and Development (GAD),
    17–19, 23–4, 28, 51–3, 60
gender subordination, recomposition,
    199–200
General Agreement on Tariffs and
    Trade (GATT), 4
German Research Insitute for Peace
    Policy, 296
Ghana, 259; Trades Union Congress,
    277–8
Giddens, Anthony, 120, 130
Global Assembly Line, The, 180
global-energy planning, 54
Grameen Bank, 363
greed, capitalist, 129, 328
Green Movement, western, 71
Green-revolution, technology, 57
Greenhalgh, Susan, 126–7, 290
Greenham Common, 71
Grewal, Inderpal, 315
grinding mills, co-operative, 370
Grown, Caren, 26, 28, 104
'guest workers', 217
Gupta, A., 131

Haiti, 269, 271, 273